Jeff Rostocil

LIES OF OUR FATHERS

LIES OF OUR FATHERS

JEFF ROSTOCIL

Copyright © 2021 by Jeff Rostocil. All Rights Reserved.

No part of this publication may be reproduced, distributed, or transmitted in any form or by any means, including photocopying, recording, or other electronic or mechanical methods, or by any information storage and retrieval system without the prior written permission of the publisher, except in the case of very brief quotations embodied in critical reviews and certain other noncommercial uses permitted by copyright law.

Unless otherwise noted, all Scripture quotations taken from the *New King James Version.* Copyright © 1979, 1980, 1982 and 1999 published by Thomas Nelson, Inc.

Cover design by Mario Ay

ISBN: 978-1-7377004-0-1

SQI Books
8109 Carlisle Way
Vallejo, CA 94591 USA

Dedication

David was known for being a man after God's own heart. But how did he express his passion? What kept it burning so fervently? Psalm 119 is the smoking gun. In the longest chapter of the Bible, we discover a man after God's instruction.

In every stanza of Psalm 119, David sings the praises of God's laws. His heart burns as he writes, *"Oh, how I love your Torah! I meditate on it all day long"* (Ps.119:97). He boasts, *"Your commands make me wiser than my enemies, for they are ever with me"* (Ps.119:98). He laments, *"Rivers of water run down from my eyes, because men do not keep your Torah"* (Ps.119:136).

David loved the Torah. Without question his affection for Scripture was extreme. Throughout his journal he praises God's law and embraces it as the beautiful, eternal, poetic Word of God. Statutes, judgments, precepts, laws, ordinances, commandments, testimonies, revelation – all are God's ways. The king of Israel found great delight in wholeheartedly keeping them as a heartfelt expression of His affection for the Holy One.

Yeshua of Nazareth, the Root of Jesse, the Son of David, the King of kings, the Living Word of God shares a similar zeal for Scripture. Jesus loves the Torah. This book is dedicated to him and to all who carry his passion for truth. I pray it makes you wiser than your enemies. Most of all, I pray it glorifies our Father in heaven.

Contents

Preface
Introduction
Chapter 1 – Unindoctrinated
Chapter 2 – Luther Was Wrong
Chapter 3 – Lies Of Our Fathers
Section I: Words Of Jesus
Chapter 4 – John 8
Chapter 5 – Matthew 5:17a
Chapter 6 – Matthew 5:17b
Chapter 7 – James 2:8, Romans 13:8-10, Galatians 5:14
Chapter 8 – Galatians 6:2, Matthew 22:37-40, Luke 10:25-28
Chapter 9 – Threefold Division Of The Law
Chapter 10 – Spirit Of The Law
Chapter 11 – Matthew 11:11-14, Luke 16:14-17
Section II: Diet & Gentiles
Chapter 12 – Mark 7:1-16
Chapter 13 – Mark 7:17-23
Chapter 14 – Acts 10
Chapter 15 – Acts 11
Chapter 16 – Jews & Gentiles
Chapter 17 – Acts 15:1-11
Chapter 18 – Acts 15:12-31
Chapter 19 – Romans 14, 1 Corinthians 8
Section III: Animal Sacrifices
Chapter 20 – Acts 21:15-26
Chapter 21 – Acts 21:27-28
Section IV: Paul & His Epistles
Chapter 22 – Paul's Life & Doctrine
Chapter 23 – Paul's Letter To The Galatians
Chapter 24 – Galatians 1
Chapter 25 – Galatians 2:1-3
Chapter 26 – Galatians 2:4-5
Chapter 27 – Galatians 2:11-15
Chapter 28 – Galatians 2:16, Part I
Chapter 29 – Galatians 2:16, Part II

Chapter 30 – Galatians 2:17-21
Chapter 31 – Galatians 3:1-5
Chapter 32 – Galatians 3:6-14
Chapter 33 – Galatians 3:19-22
Chapter 34 – Galatians 3:23-29
Chapter 35 – Galatians 4
Chapter 36 – Galatians 5
Chapter 37 – Galatians 6
Chapter 38 – Paul's Letter To The Romans
Chapter 39 – Romans 1-2
Chapter 40 – Romans 3
Chapter 41 – Romans 4
Chapter 42 – Romans 6
Chapter 43 – Romans 7:1-13
Chapter 44 – Romans 7:14-25
Chapter 45 – Romans 10:4
Chapter 46 – Philippians 3:2-9
Chapter 47 – Colossians 2:11-14
Chapter 48 – 1 & 2 Timothy
Chapter 49 – Timothy's Circumcision
Chapter 50 – 2 Corinthians 3:5-11
Chapter 51 – 2 Thessalonians 2:7-8

Section V: Sabbath & The Feasts

Chapter 52 – 1 Corinthians 5
Chapter 53 – Galatians 4:10-11
Chapter 54 – Colossians 2:16-23

Section VI: New Covenant

Chapter 55 – Galatians 3:15-22
Chapter 56 – Galatians 4:21-31
Chapter 57 – 2 Corinthians 3:12-18
Chapter 58 – Hebrews 8

Section VII: Book Of Hebrews

Chapter 59 – Introduction To Hebrews
Chapter 60 – Hebrews 1-6
Chapter 61 – Hebrews 7:1-11
Chapter 62 – Hebrews 7:12-28
Chapter 63 – Hebrews 9:1-12
Chapter 64 – Hebrews 9:13-28
Chapter 65 – Hebrews 10-11

Chapter 66 – Hebrews 12-13
Section VIII: Book Of James
Chapter 67 – James 1
Chapter 68 – James 2-4
Section IX: Writings Of John
Chapter 69 – The Letters Of John
Chapter 70 – Conclusion
What Now?
Literature Consulted
About The Author

Preface

When I was first introduced to the idea of Gentiles pursuing the Torah, I was patently resistant. A friend and respected leader handed me an audio version of D. Thomas Lancaster's book *Restoration: Returning the Torah of God to the Disciples of Jesus*. Our home fellowship listened to it together. Over the ensuing months the topics of Jews, Gentiles, grace and the law stirred up many questions, some healthy debates and more than a few concerns. Though not really my cup of tea at the time, the topic made for spirited discussion.

It was 2008. I was an ordained minister and at this point had been in full-time ministry for almost fifteen years. I was no stranger to unorthodox doctrines. I gave my life to Christ at the age of five. Being an avid reader with a modest library, I had an adequate understanding of most Biblical perspectives. I grew up attending Sunday school, youth camps, Bible classes and graduated high school with a Christian school education. After earning a business degree from San Jose State University and serving as a campus missionary for six years, my wife and I had an established ministry traveling as itinerant evangelists. We led outreach teams overseas, speaking in churches and conferences. I had completed five years of theological training in earning my master's degree and credentials. That year I finished my first book, *Unshakable*.

Having the opportunity to be in churches internationally and across the nation, I was all too aware of the warts of the evangelical church. I sat down with countless pastors who shared grievous stories of embezzlement, lawsuits, adultery, heresy, greed, church splits and board-driven power plays. I also observed some behind-the-scenes behavior that was more than a little disturbing. It became painfully obvious that something was fundamentally wrong with the western church.

I knew our programmed system of worship was broken and in need of change, but reformation in this manner and of this magnitude was not in my wheelhouse. I thought our ills could be cured with an old fashioned revival of repentance and power. A movement that called for a return to our Jewish roots was a deeper cut than I anticipated and reached further back than I was willing to venture. Needless to say, the church reinventing herself in light of the Torah seemed counter-productive, in my opinion.

My greatest conflict came in reconciling this new teaching with my theological understanding of Scripture. What about the book of Galatians? Romans? Hebrews? Doesn't Paul argue that Christians are not obligated to obey the law? Didn't Jesus fulfill the Torah and set aside the ceremonial commands? Wasn't Peter's vision about dietary liberty? Aren't all foods clean? What about the decision of the Jerusalem council and the woman caught in adultery? Didn't the apostles consider Sunday the new Sabbath? The opinion that Jews could observe Sabbath, the feasts and a Biblical diet was acceptable, but it went against all that was ingrained in me when that expectation included Gentile Christians.

However, because the material came from a respected source, I determined to be a Berean in the matter. I expected it would take only about one pass through the New Testament to reaffirm my position regarding the law and arm me with fresh material useful for dismantling this new brand of legalism. The first place I turned was the book of Galatians. Thus began the eye-opening adventure that continues to this day.

Over the course of six months many of my fiercest criticisms were met with surprising answers. It would revolutionize the way I approach Scripture and propel me into new ways of expressing my faith in Christ. It is safe to say that I experienced a rending of the garment moment. That twelve-year season of study has resulted in this book. I now invite you into my journey.

I am well aware of the challenges of tackling such a topic. This book was as difficult for me to write as it may be for some to read. I am prepared for the likelihood my conclusions will be perceived as controversial, provocative and dangerous. There are those who might label me legalistic, destructive or even a heretic. This is not because I have forsaken Scripture or written from an inflammatory tone. It is because, for many, theology is quite personal, and doctrinal positions too easily become irrationally politicized. We tend to cling to them like children clinging to security blankets. When called into question the dissenting voice often gets marginalized and vilified.

But while sacred cows are not easily toppled, they do make the best steaks. For this reason, I have sought to focus on the text and allow Scripture to interpret itself.

You will notice the verses emphasized are New Testament heavy and almost exclusively deal with the law. This is purposeful so that what Jesus and the apostles believed and taught concerning the Law of Moses can be clearly inspected. Early on it became clear to me that the "theological science" regarding the Christian's obligation to the Torah is not yet settled. Our relationship with the law is not as easily defined as I once assumed.

This book addresses the most formidable arguments I once held pertaining to the law and the New Testament. In my estimation, the principal question boils down to: What should be our attitude toward the Law of Moses, and what place should the Torah hold in the Christian community?

I hope to answer this by taking an honest, in-depth look at the most misunderstood and misinterpreted passages of the New Testament traditionally thought to abolish the Law of Moses. The purpose of Biblical hermeneutics is to determine the original intent of the passage and draw conclusions based on sound exegesis. Setting aside common assumptions and textual misconceptions, I aim to examine each passage according to its historical and hermeneutical context so as to present a simple, rational, contextualized interpretation.

My objective in writing this book is five-fold: (1) To identify the most common misconceptions we hold concerning the Law of Moses, (2) To determine the role of the law in the writings and practice of the apostles, (3) To demonstrate that certain neglected aspects of the Torah deserve a larger place of influence in our current Christian economy, (4) To provide a rational explanation and doctrinal legitimacy to Gentiles pursuing the whole counsel of Scripture, and (5) To call God's children to a fresh appreciation for God's commands.

For this reason, I wish to draw attention to the verses that have traditionally led us toward a negative view of the law. When lifted from their context, these verses can appear to repudiate the Torah. But when placed within their proper context and within the larger construct of Scripture, a different mosaic emerges - one that sheds a positive light on the Torah. In highlighting verses customarily deemed to be at odds with the law, centuries of theological misconceptions concerning the Torah come to light that demand our attention.

My desire is that the body of Christ would be reunited and reinvigorated with the Bible as a whole. The Torah is the dictionary of the Bible. We cannot properly understand the rest of Scripture without it. Just as the Bible is the foundation for the Christian faith, so the Torah is the foundation for the Bible.

I adamantly oppose a return to rabbinic Judaism or Gentiles seeking Jewish status to merit salvation. Paul and the apostles stood up to this notion, and so should we. But by restoring the relevancy of the Old Testament to New Testament believers, I do hope to establish common ground between believing Jews and believing Gentiles to help map out a path toward unity.

I reject the notion that the New Testament stands in opposition to the Old Testament or that the God of the Old is somehow different from the God of the New. Our Heavenly Father is not dispensationally moody! He never changes nor does his standard of righteousness change – a standard that is established in the Torah, the Prophets, the Gospels and revealed in His Son.

Six months after diving into the book of Galatians with fresh eyes, it became clear to me that Jesus and the apostles not only sought to wholeheartedly obey all of God's commands but also encouraged Torah obedience within their teachings. This book is my humble appeal for the church to reconsider her position regarding the writings of Moses and reassess how they should be properly applied to the life of a new covenant believer.

There is an iron wedge that has been driven between the law and the gospel. This book seeks to remove it.

My prayer is that you can approach this material as a Berean and withhold judgment until you have carefully weighed all that is being presented. Wisdom reminds us to first consider a matter before critiquing it. Solomon writes, "If one gives an answer before he hears, it is his folly and shame" (Prov. 18:13, ESV). If the Christian community seeks to have a meaningful and constructive conversation around the topics of law and grace, we must resist succumbing to condemnation before investigation.

This project was no small task for me. Torah's place in my life and in the body of Christ has profound implications that greatly affect our worship. For this reason, I consider this topic to be of supreme importance. This book is not designed to be an exhaustive study on the subject. I do hope, however, that my contribution adds to the dialogue and helps toward clarifying (what I believe is) one of the most deep-seeded misunderstandings of the New Testament.

This book was not written on a three-week sabbatical retreat to a mountain cabin for the purpose of fast-tracking it onto bookshelves. It has been over a decade in the making. These thoughts have been forged in the fires of prayerful study and birthed in the trenches of everyday living. The conclusions drawn here have been time tested, carefully scrutinized and born of academic research. My wife and I have been *working* this out and *walking* this out with a community of believers for close to 15 years. Only now do I feel the maturity to write on this subject.

INTRODUCTION

For the purposes of this book, I use the words *Torah* and *Law* (or law) synonymously. The writers of the Septuagint chose to translate *Torah* using the Greek word *nomos*, which means *law*. Subsequent manuscripts of the New Testament followed suit. Unfortunately, *Law* is a weak rendering for the word *Torah*. Torah has a much fuller meaning than just legal regulations. While it does include the whole of God's law, it entails more than just laws.

Torah means *teaching, guidance* or *instruction*. Torah is God's instruction for living and a guide to navigating a life of faith. Unfortunately, Law and Torah are not synonymous. Only because it obliges obedience and punishes disobedience does Torah take on the sense of law.

Because of our English translations, we are most familiar with the word *law*. Accordingly, I use it interchangeably with *Torah*. However, I want you to be comfortable with the word *Torah*, so I have opted to use it as much as possible.

In general, when I use the word *Torah*, I am referring to the first five books of the Bible, also called the Pentateuch. In truth, the Torah is not limited to strictly the writings of Moses. Since Torah is God's instruction, in this sense, all of God's word is His Torah. A narrow definition refines the Torah to the five books of Moses, more precisely the Ten Commandments. A broader definition includes the Prophets, the Writings, the New Testament and to many Jews, the Talmud and Midrash.

I am aware that the word *Torah* carries with it a negative connotation and has become a polarizing term in some Christian circles. We have unfairly classified it as a Jewish expression and have almost exclusively associated it with the old covenant. This is unfortunate. I do not want you to be alarmed or intimidated by the word *Torah*. It is a beautiful Hebrew word much like *hallelujah* and *amen*. Adding it to our faith vocabulary would serve us well.

I have also opted to employ the terms *Hebrew Scriptures* and *Apostolic Scriptures* when referencing the Old and New Testaments. Of all the man-given titles, I have found Hebrew Scriptures (Old Testament) and Apostolic Scriptures (New Testament) to be more accurate descriptors of the content presented. In using them I am not seeking to redefine the Bible or suggesting a revision to the canon beyond what is generally accepted. I am merely choosing terms I find less confusing and do not contribute toward further misperception.

Additionally, the terms *Jew* and *Israelite* are used interchangeably throughout the book. I do recognize there is a distinction, but that distinction is not directly pertinent to our study. For the sake of simplicity, Jew and Israelite are both used in reference to the children of Abraham through Isaac and Jacob.

As with all Biblical interpretation, it is important to remember that we are dealing with an ancient translated document. It is no small task to ascertain the correct interpretation of a passage when factoring in language, age, and culture. A certain amount of understanding will always slip through the proverbial cracks.

Most English readers, for example, are unaware that James of the New Testament (*Yakov*) shares the same Hebrew name with Jacob of the Old (*Yakov*); or that *Yeshua* (or *Yehoshua*) is the Hebrew name of both Jesus and Joshua. The fact that these names are identical gets lost in translation.

I would be in favor of keeping proper nouns in the Bible un-transliterated. Using names and places as they appear in their original language would be a welcomed step toward clearing up simple translation confusions. This is one of the reasons why I use the name *Jesus* and *Yeshua* interchangeably throughout this book.

I do not see a difference between the person of Jesus and the person of Yeshua. He is the same Lord and Savior his followers have known for 2,000 years. Neither do I adhere to the claim that Jesus is the name of a pagan god and that any work done in that name is false.

INTRODUCTION

I like to think of Yeshua as the given name of our Messiah and Jesus as his translated nickname. In using Yeshua I am merely seeking to call him by His Hebrew name, the name that his parents, siblings and disciples knew Him as.

I heartily acknowledge that many of these thoughts are not original. I am grateful for the numerous voices, past and present, that have spoken on these topics. I have drawn from a wide range of books, scholars, articles, essays, papers, podcasts, lexicons, dictionaries, encyclopedias, historical documents and Biblical commentaries. Where possible, I cite my sources and seek to give proper credit. You will find each chapter footnoted. Please refer to the appendix for a more exhaustive list of literature consulted.

While some of this material may seem new, it is not new at all. In fact, it is well established. Many have walked this path before us. The fact that it seems new only serves to prove how far removed we are from our heritage and how significantly we've strayed from our origins.

UNINDOCTRINATED

Truth #1: *We have inherited lies.*

There is a story about an Indonesian boy who washed up on a remote island after his canoe was thrown off course and destroyed in a typhoon. A skilled hunter and savvy fisherman, the boy was able to survive on the small but fertile island. He remained stranded and isolated the majority of his adult life until discovered by a team of Dutch engineers surveying the area. Through a concerted effort they brought him back to civilization after having no contact with the outside world for close to 60 years.

One of the few items the man possessed was a Bible written in his own dialect that he recovered from an old shipwreck on the island's eastern shore. With no other reading material, the man read the Bible cover to cover well over 500 times during his 59 years in isolation. In the process he had memorized large portions of Scripture. He sincerely believed every word he read and was determined to walk according to the ways of God as outlined in the book, even if he died alone and undiscovered.

Upon his re-entry to society and introduction to Christianity, the man was perplexed by what he observed from the "people of the book." Too often their deeds did not match their creeds. They brought idols into their homes and into their places of worship. There was hypocrisy, gossip and rumors of compromise. Their leaders elevated the writings of the apostles above the writings of the prophets and held animosity toward the Hebrew race. They neglected God's appointed times, practiced strange customs, ate prohibited meat and abandoned the Sabbath.

After much disappointment, the man came to the realization that some rituals and practices of "civilized" believers were not based on God's word but on contemporary culture and manufactured doctrines. These man-made doctrines had been handed down for generations and perpetuated for centuries to the extent that modern Christianity was unrecognizable to him. The example of these Christians clashed with how he envisioned the disciples of Jesus should resemble.

The man was ultimately reunited with his family and ended up living another 35 years. He settled in Papua New Guinea and spent the rest of his life seeking to "un-indoctrinate" others through his writings and lectures.

This man's story is profound, and he is not wrong in his assessment of the church at large. We have strayed from God's instructions. We've practiced strange customs and idolatry. We've taught lawlessness and elevated the traditions of man above the commandments of God. The Christian church has been influenced by synthetic principles and reformed doctrines to our own detriment, particularly as it relates to Jews, grace and the law.

I would not characterize today's church as blindly indoctrinated or brazenly lawless. Many sincere believers seek to honor God's Word, and in so doing keep much of the Bible. I would like to think that most still consider the Ten Commandments a good baseline for Christian morality. Even if we fall short, in theory, Christians ascribe to being faithful, merciful, honest, loving, just and peaceable – all major themes of the Torah.

But there is a small list of commandments that have been discounted and largely ignored. They have been deemed obsolete. They're often branded only for Jews and are commonly rejected by the Gentile church. Theology lies at the root of the problem. It is these doctrines and this theology that this book addresses.

Jeremiah spoke of a time when,

> "Gentiles shall come to You from the ends of the earth, and say, 'Surely our fathers have inherited lies.'" - Jeremiah 16:19b

You and I have inherited lies from our spiritual fathers. We have been taught:

- The Law of Moses has passed away and is obsolete.

- Jesus fulfilled the law for us; therefore, we don't need to obey it.

- The new covenant frees Christians from Old Testament commands.

- The Torah was crucified on the cross.

- Obeying the commandments is the works of the law.

- *Under the law* means being under the obligation to obey the Torah.

- Gentile Christians need only to obey the moral laws of the Bible.

But I say: Surely our fathers have inherited lies.

For every lie, there are a million truths. Here are 70 truths concerning the Law and the new covenant that I've discovered on my journey.

2

LUTHER WAS WRONG

Truth #2: *The Reformation is not over.*

When Martin Luther nailed his 95 Theses on the door at Wittenberg, no one could have imagined the ripple effects it would create. Luther became the catalyst for the Protestant Reformation and would eventually rise to become one of the fathers of modern Christianity. Much of Protestant Christian doctrine concerning law and grace is based on the teachings of Martin Luther. His life and doctrine have guided our theology, worship and polity. It is not a stretch to say there may not be another church leader in the last five hundred years who has influenced western Christianity more than Martin Luther.

But Martin Luther was wrong…though not about everything.

He was right to nail his grievances to the chapel door. He was right to call out the abuses of the papacy. He was right to oppose indulgences. He was right to denounce sacerdotalism (the belief that Catholic priests are mediators between God and man) and antinomianism (the view that there is no law Christians must obey). He was right to champion salvation by grace through faith. He was right to identify the Bible as the primary source of divine knowledge. He was right to translate the Bible into German. He was right to call people to repentance.

But the relatively small amount he was wrong about has greatly affected you, me and the entire world.

What was Martin Luther wrong about?

(1) *Luther was wrong about Paul.*

Martin Luther wrote, "The epistles of St. Paul and St. Peter far surpass the other three gospels, Matthew, Mark and Luke."[1]

Luther found a kindred spirit in the apostles, particularly Paul. He shared Paul's passion for the gospel and identified with the struggles of the apostle.[2] Luther seemed to see himself in Paul and Paul in himself.

Elevating the doctrines of the apostles above the works of Christ, however, was a colossal mistake. In his zeal for apostolic theology, Luther inexplicably, and I have little doubt, unintentionally belittled the example of Christ. His misstep was interpreting the Gospels through the writings of Paul instead of interpreting Paul's epistles through the Messiah.

This may be nitpicky, but we make this same error today. We still tend to interpret Paul's theology in isolation from the teachings of Christ. Perhaps this is one reason why scholars have had such difficulty reconciling Paul's letters with the rest of Scripture. While Paul's epistles do comprise the majority of the Apostolic Scriptures, we should not assume that the pen of the apostle carries more weight than the voice of the Master. We would be wise to weigh the doctrines of the apostles and the teachings of the church in light of the words of Christ, not the other way around.

(2) *Luther incorrectly presumed that the legalism of his time was the same legalism of the first century.*

In Luther's day, the Roman Catholic Church was apostate. The Pope sought political power. Priests sold indulgences. Penance was required of the penitent, and a person's place in purgatory could be purchased for a price.

---

[1] Hans J. Hillerbrand, *The Protestant Reformation*, (New York: Harper Torchbooks, 1968), 42

[2] Charles J. Ritchey, "Luther and Paul," *The Journal of Religion*, vol. 50, No. 4, 1917 [Online]. Available: www.jstor.org/stable/3135831

The reformers fought against the doctrinal abuses of the Roman Church. They campaigned for *sola Scriptura*, calling for a return to the Bible as the supreme authority on spiritual matters. In many ways reformed theology is an attempt to return to Biblical Christianity. For this we are truly grateful.

This scenario, however, does not accurately depict Paul and the Jews. Whereas Luther wrangled with a works-based religion that predicated justification, Paul clashed with status-based policies that accompanied justification. Luther stood up to conventional legalism. Paul stood up to covenantal nomism (the belief that one must be Jewish and keep the Torah in order to be in God's covenant). Luther took issue with performance-oriented righteousness. Paul took issue with ethno-centric righteousness. Unlike the priests and cardinals of the sixteenth century, rabbis of the first century did not commonly teach salvation through self-righteous deeds.

Martin Luther imagined first-century Judaism was just like sixteenth-century Catholicism – self-righteous and legalistic. In his war with hypocritical corruption, Luther supposed the apostles combated a common legalism in their time. He was mistaken. The type and manner of religious pressure the apostles faced was separate and distinct from Luther. While there are some similarities, first-century Israel was dissimilar to sixteenth-century Europe. The problems in Luther's day were not the same challenges the apostles faced.[3]

This matters because this presumption shaped Luther's view of Paul's doctrine and in turn has shaped Protestant orthodoxy. Much of what is taught today about Paul and his doctrine is filtered through the pen of Martin Luther, the father of the Reformation, and John Calvin, the father of Reformed theology. Reformed theology, derived from the Reformation, is the predominant school of thought in Christian academia today. It accounts for much of how we teach and understand the Apostolic Scriptures, particularly Paul's letters.

---

[3] E.P. Sanders, *Paul and Palestinian Judaism*, (Minneapolis: Fortress Press, 1977), 49

Unfortunately, Luther's supposition influenced the way he approached Paul's writings, making Luther's interpretation of Galatians and Romans anachronistic. Martin Luther was neither privy to the trove of knowledge scholars possess today about first-century Palestinian Judaism, nor had access to the Dead Sea Scrolls. One can only wonder how his position might have changed if he had the privilege of modern scholarship.

Martin Luther was a beacon of light in a time of considerable darkness. His radical reforms paved the way for dissenting voices within Christianity to have a place to speak. The accomplishments of Martin Luther are well documented and still enjoyed today. Like all of us, however, Luther was not without his shortcomings, and his doctrinal positions are not infallible.

(3) *Luther was wrong about Jews. Dead wrong.*

It is not a stretch to say that Martin Luther was an anti-Semite.

In the beginning of his ministry, Martin Luther displayed a genuine care for the Jewish community. He was sympathetic to their skepticism of the Catholic Church and was hopeful Jews would embrace his reforms. When that didn't happen to his liking, he grew frustrated with Jewish leaders and a deep-seeded resentment developed.

In 1537, he successfully campaigned the removal of all Jews from Saxony[4] and later had them expelled from Brandenburg and Silesia.[5] He characterized Jews as "given to babbling and lying" and began using incendiary language in his descriptions of them.[6]

In 1543, Luther published a scathing 65,000-word treatise entitled, *On the Jews and Their Lies*. Luther wrote:

---

[4] Marianne Dacy, "Anti-Judaism in the New Testament and Christian Theology," *International Council of Christians and Jews*, 2013
[5] Martin Brecht, *Martin Luther*, Vol. 3, (Minneapolis: Fortress, 1985-1993), 336
[6] Martin Luther, *Against the Sabbatarians*, 1538, Public domain

"What then shall we Christians do with this damned, rejected race of Jews? We must prayerfully and reverentially practice a merciful severity. They are surely being punished a thousand times more than we might wish them.

First, their synagogues should be set on fire, and whatever does not burn up should be covered or spread over with dirt so that no one may ever be able to see a cinder or stone of it. And this ought to be done for the honor of God and of Christianity in order that God may see that we are Christians, and that we have not wittingly tolerated or approved of such public lying, cursing and blaspheming of His Son and His Christians.

Secondly, their homes should likewise be broken down and destroyed. For they perpetrate the same things there that they do in their synagogues. For this reason they ought to be put under one roof or in a stable, like gypsies, in order that they may realize that they are not masters in our land, as they boast, but miserable captives, as they complain incessantly before God with bitter wailing.

Thirdly, they should be deprived of their prayer-books and Talmuds in which such idolatry, lies, cursing, and blasphemy are taught.

Fourthly, their rabbis must be forbidden under threat of death to teach any more.

Fifthly, passport and traveling privileges should be absolutely forbidden to the Jews. For they have no business in the rural districts since they are not nobles, nor officials, nor merchants, nor the like. Let them stay at home. If you princes and nobles do not close the road legally to such exploiters, then some troop ought to ride against them, for they will learn from this pamphlet what the Jews are and how to handle them and that they ought not to be protected. You cannot protect them, unless in the eyes of God you want to share all their abomination.

To sum up, dear princes and nobles who have Jews in your domains, if this advice of mine does not suit you, then find a better one so that you and we may all be free of this insufferable devilish burden – the Jews. Such a desperate, thoroughly evil, poisonous, and devilish lot are these Jews, who for these fourteen hundred years have been and still are our plague, our pestilence, and our misfortune. They deny all of this. However, it all coincides with the judgment of Christ, which declares that they are venomous, bitter, vindictive, tricky serpents, assassins, and children of the devil, who sting and work harm stealthily wherever they cannot do it openly. For this reason, I would like to see them where there are no Christians. The Turks and other heathen do not tolerate what we Christians endure from these venomous serpents and young devils. Next to the devil, a Christian has no more bitter and galling foe than a Jew. There is no other to whom we accord as many benefactions and from whom we suffer as much as we do from these base children of the devil, this brood of vipers."[7]

In this same treatise, Luther called Jews a "whoring people full of the devil's feces in which they wallow like swine."[8] He described the synagogue as "an evil slut" and "their boast of lineage, circumcision and the law must be accounted as filth."[9]

Later that year Luther distributed a pamphlet depicting Jews as "the devil's children, damned to hell," adding, "Perhaps, one of the merciful saints among us Christians, may think I am behaving too crude and disdainfully against the poor, miserable Jews in that I deal with them so sarcastically and insulting. But, good God, I am much too mild in insulting such devils."[10]

In one of his final sermons in 1546, Luther categorized Jews as "our public enemy."[11] He died four days later.

Without knowing who made these statements, one might attribute these words to a Nazi leader rather than a man of God. Dreadfully, and maybe unsurprisingly, it was only a few hundred years later that prominent leaders of the Third Reich cited Martin Luther as justification for exterminating Jews. Some of the S.S. guards were

---

[7] Martin H. Bertram, *Luther's Works,* Vol. 47, (Philadelphia: Fortress, 1971) Excerpts from Martin Luther's *On The Jews and Their Lies*
[8] Ibid
[9] Ibid
[10] Martin Luther, *Of The Unknowable Name and The Generations of Christ,* 1543, Public domain
[11] Martin Luther, *Warning Against the Jews*, 1546, Public domain

trained in German seminaries under the teachings of Luther and were taught that God rejected the Jewish people. This provided some with the theological license to eradicate the "accursed people."

One example of this is found at the end of World War II. The Allies captured German propagandist Julius Streicher, publisher of the anti-Semitic newspaper *Der Stürmer*. At the Nuremberg trials of 1946, Streicher said in his defense,

> "I did not intend to agitate or inflame but to enlighten. Antisemitic publications have existed in Germany for centuries…Dr. Martin Luther writes that Jews are a serpent's brood and one should burn down their synagogues and destroy them. Dr. Martin Luther would very probably sit in my place in the defendants' dock today, if this book had been taken into consideration by the Prosecution."[12]

William Shirer writes,

> "It is difficult to understand the behavior of most German Protestants in the first Nazi years unless one is aware of two things: their history and the influence of Martin Luther. The great founder of Protestantism was both a passionate anti-Semite and a ferocious believer in absolute obedience to political authority. He wanted Germany rid of the Jews. Luther's advice was literally followed four centuries later by Hitler, Goering and Himmler."[13]

We cannot blame Luther for Hitler and the Holocaust. Adolf Hitler was demonized and deceived. His unspeakable atrocities against the Jewish people were of his own volition. Luther called for a *merciful severity*. Hitler imposed a *merciless brutality*.

Adolf Hitler was wrong.

---

[12] Bernard Howard, "Luther's Jewish Problem" [Online]. Available: https://www.thegospelcoalition.org/article/luthers-jewish-problem

[13] William Shirer, *The Rise And Fall of the Third Reich*, (New York: Simon & Schuster, 1990), 236

We can't say with any certainty that Hitler used Martin Luther's words as a pretense for wickedness. It does appear, however, that some Nazis exploited Martin Luther's teachings to silence the German pulpits.

To be fair, Martin Luther said some friendlier things about Jewish people. He encouraged his followers to "not seek vengeance" against the Jews[14] and to "receive them cordially. If some of them should prove stiff-necked, what of it? After all, we ourselves are not all good Christians either."[15] Luther added, "Show them Christian love and pray for them that they may be converted to receive the Lord, whom they should properly honor more than we...If the Jews would be converted and stop their blaspheming and whatever else they have done to us, then we will gladly forgive them."[16]

Some insist that Martin Luther was not an Anti-Semite; that his position regarding Jews was based solely on religion, not race. This may be. But Luther's words speak for themselves. His spiteful rhetoric against Jews is repulsive and cannot be glossed over. Nazis used his words to incite violence, and Luther's doctrine did nothing to prevent the rise of Hitler and his army of Brownshirts. While he may not have killed Jews physically, Luther vilified them with his words.

The Protestant Reformation is not Martin Luther's only legacy. His acrimony for Jews affected his doctrine and in turn has infected ours as well. His writings have prejudiced modern theology. They have inculcated our doctrine with anti-Semitism, antinomianism, dispensationalism, replacement theology and the threefold division of the Torah.

Furthermore, Luther's assumptions about Paul and the law have opened the door to a Pauline-elevated gospel based on a miscalculation of first-century tension. Although he publically

---

[14] Luther, *On The Jews and Their Lies*
[15] Walter Brandt, *Luther's Works,* (Minneapolis: Fortress, 1957), 200-201, 299. Translation of Martin Luther's *That Jesus Christ was Born a Jew*
[16] Luther, *Warning Against the Jews*

opposed antinomianism, Luther's anti-Semitic statements did nothing to quell these erroneous beliefs and only served to propagate them. His words must bear at least some responsibility for the inaccuracies of reformed theology and for the atrocities done in the spirit of his doctrine.

Conclusion

In all this I do believe it is possible to honor Martin Luther's life without celebrating his hatred. He was both a liberator and an oppressor, a hero to some, a villain to others. The man deserves credit. His defiance started something that has not yet been completed, as he helped set into motion a reformation that has yet to cease.

This reformation has not run its course. The Bridegroom is not done perfecting His bride. What started 500 years ago lives on. What Luther refused to reform is now being embraced.

From protest to pro-Torah, from reformation to the restoration of all things (Acts 3:21), where Luther's reforms stopped short we must press forward. You and I are living in strategic times. God is reshaping the theological landscape of the church. The Holy Spirit is still reforming God's people. He has invited us to rediscover the ancient paths of our forefathers and recalibrate our walk to the original expression of faith that Jesus exemplified and desires for us to enjoy.

3
LIES OF OUR FATHERS

Truth #3: *Our doctrine has been corrupted.*

Martin Luther might be the most chronicled, but he was not the first church father to promulgate Christian anti-Semitism. Sadly, Luther was largely passing along what had been openly taught in the church for centuries.

The Epistle of Barnabas is thought to have been penned as early as the last decade of the first century. Not actually written by Barnabas, this letter casts a negative light on Jews, Judaism and the Torah.[1] By the turn of the century, Ignatius, the first Gentile bishop of Antioch, sought to distance early followers from Jewish associations. He articulated a more "overt and unequivocal negative tone toward the beliefs and traditions of the founding fathers."[2] This set the stage for one of the earliest and most prolific Christian writers of the early church to emerge.

Born in 100 A.D., Justin Martyr was a philosopher from the ancient Samarian city of Shechem (Roman city of Neapolis). An uncircumcised pagan who came to Christ as an adult, Martyr targeted Gentile audiences with his teachings, writing several treatises in defense of Christianity.[3] He spent many years teaching in Rome at his own school of philosophy. Under the reign of Marcus Aurelius, he was arrested by the Roman prefect Junius Rusticus and given a sham trial. When Justin refused to recant his faith, he was

---

[1] J.B. Lightfoot, *The Epistle of Barnabas* [Online]. Available: http://www.earlychristianwritings.com/text/barnabas-lightfoot.html; Daniel Juster, *Jewish Roots,* (Shippensburg: Destiny Image, 2013), 188-189
[2] A.M. Bibliowicz, *Jews and Gentiles in the Early Jesus Movement,* (London: Palgrave Macmillan, 2013), 167
[3] L.W. Barnard, *Justin Martyr, His Life and Thought,* (UK: Cambridge University Press, 2008)

beheaded at the age of 65 with a number of his pupils. He was later given the surname "Martyr" as a badge of honor.[4]

Unfortunately, Justin Martyr despised Jews. He denounced them for having crucified Christ and was gleeful when reflecting on the destruction of Jerusalem. In a pseudo-debate with a Jew named Trypho, Martyr gloats,

> "We, too, would observe your circumcision of the flesh, your Sabbath days, and in a word, all your festivals, if we were not aware of the reason why they were imposed upon you, namely, because of your sins and the hardness of heart.
>
> The custom of circumcising the flesh, handed down from Abraham, was given to you as a distinguishing mark, to set you off from other nations and from us Christians. The purpose of this was that you and only you might suffer the afflictions that are not justly yours; that only your land be desolated, and your cities ruined by fire; that the fruits of your land be eaten by strangers before your eyes; that not one of you be permitted to enter your city of Jerusalem. Your circumcision of the flesh is the only mark by which you can certainly be distinguished from other men…as I stated before it was by reason your sins and the sins of your fathers that, among other precepts, God imposed upon you the observation of the Sabbath as a mark."[5]

Justin Martyr's anti-Semitic rhetoric greatly influenced his theology and overall interpretation of Scripture. He argued vehemently against Jews and repudiated the Torah. He was one of the first to teach replacement theology, which contends that God has rejected the Jewish people, abolished His covenant with Israel and transferred the promises of Israel to the Gentile church. He believed that the Gentile church replaces the Jews as the new spiritual Israel.

Not long after Justin Martyr's death, Origen of Alexandria was born to Christian parents. As a boy, he was a prodigious student of the

---

[4] W.A. Shotwell, *The Biblical Exegesis of Justin Martyr*, (London: SPCK, 1965); Jules Lebreton, "St. Justin Martyr," *The Catholic Encyclopedia,* Vol. 8, (New York: Robert Appleton Co., 1910)
[5] Justin Martyr, *Dialogue with Trypho*, 155-170 A.D., Public domain

Bible and would become one of the most brilliant Christian scholars of the third century. His father and mentor, Leonidas, was beheaded for his faith when Origen was still a teenager. This had a profound impact on Origen's commitment to Christ.[6] In his piety, Origen is said to have slept on the floor, walked without shoes, eaten meager meals and fasted twice a week. He even notoriously castrated himself for the sake of Christ.[7]

His greatest work, *De Principiis*, is credited as being the first systematic exposition of Christian theology ever written. Origen was so prolific that a wealthy convert funded and supplied him with seven secretaries just to assist him in the task of writing.[8]

Unfortunately, Origen propagated the same anti-Semitic pomposity of Justin Martyr, helping to advance replacement theology into the third century. He writes:

> "We may thus assert in utter confidence that the Jews will not return to their earlier situation, for they have committed the most abominable of crimes, in forming this conspiracy against the Savior of the human race…hence the city where Jesus suffered was necessarily destroyed, the Jewish nation was driven from its country, and another people was called by God to the blessed election."[9]

In the fourth century, Bishop Ambrose of Milan argued that crimes against Jews were not the same as crimes against other people groups. Because Jews rejected Jesus as Messiah, burning a synagogue was justified and should not be considered a sin.[10]

In the fifth century, John Chrysostom, the golden-mouthed bishop of Constantinople, raised the vitriol to another level. He railed against

---

[6] Mark Edwards, "Origen," *The Stanford Encyclopedia of Philosophy* [Online]. Available: https://plato.stanford.edu/archives/sum2018/entries/origen/
[7] Henry Chadwick, *Origen: Contra Celsum*, (UK: Cambridge University Press, 1980); "Origen," *Christianity Today*, August 2008
[8] Ibid
[9] Léon Poliakov, "Anti-Semitism and Early Christianity," *The History of Anti-Semitism*, (Pennsylvania: UP Press, 2003), 23
[10] Juster, 189

all things Jewish, writing eight sermons against the Jews.[11] Of the synagogue, he thundered:

> "The synagogue is worse than a brothel...it is the den of scoundrels and the repair of wild beasts...the temple of demons devoted to idolatrous cults...the refuge of brigands and debauchees, and the cavern of devils. It is a criminal assembly of Jews...a place of meeting for the assassins of Christ...a house worse than a drinking shop...a den of thieves, a house of ill fame, a dwelling of iniquity, the refuge of devils, a gulf and an abyss of perdition...I would say the same things about their souls...As for me, I hate the synagogue...I hate the Jews for the same reason."[12]

Church councils such as the Council of Alvira (fourth century), the Council of Antioch (fourth century) and the second Council of Nicea (eighth century) condemned Hebrew practices for all Jewish believers. Evidently, there was no room for Jewish identity within the body of believers.[13]

In the twelfth century, Peter the Venerable resurrected the same anti-Semitic disdain of the early church fathers, preaching:

> "Yes, you Jews. I say, do I address you; you, who till this very day, deny the Son of God. How long, poor wretches, will ye not believe the truth? Truly I doubt whether a Jew can be really human...I lead out for its den a monstrous animal, and show it as a laughing stock in the amphitheater of the world, in the sight of all the people, I bring thee forward, thou Jew, thou brute beast, in the sight of all men."[14]

John Calvin was a French contemporary of Martin Luther. He was only eight years old when Luther's Ninety-Five Theses hit the printing presses. He rose to prominence as a theologian in the second

---

[11] Ibid

[12] John Chrysostom, 344-407 A.D. Quote taken from Malcolm Hay, *The Roots of Christian Anti-Semitism,* (San Francisco: Anti Defamation League of B'nai, 1984), 28

[13] Juster, 191

[14] Peter the Venerable. Quote taken from Hay, *The Roots of Christian Anti-Semitism,* 30

wave of the Reformation. The father of Calvinism, John Calvin is credited with being the man who codified the Reformation. Unsurprisingly, he had an opinion on Jews as well.

> "Their rotten and unbending stiffneckedness deserves that they be oppressed unendingly and without measure or end and that they die in their misery without the pity of anyone."[15]

Conclusion

Christian anti-Semitism has plagued the church since the first century. Instead of showing appreciation to the people, the land and the Scriptures from which we derive our faith, these renowned men, revered as church fathers, spewed contempt for Jews and spread animus across Europe and the Middle East. They chose to disregard the critical role Jews and the Torah play in end time events and the new covenant.

How can we say we honor the Scriptures yet despise the people who preserved the Scriptures for us? How can we worship the King of the Jews while still harboring hatred for Jewish people? From the Crusades to the Inquisition to the Holocaust, our track record is more than spotty, to say the least.

The fallout has been our loss. We have inherited their bigotry, their blindness and their boasting. The bias of our fathers has corrupted our theology, prejudiced our doctrine and shaped the culture of the church.

Still today, Christian academia throws shade at Jews and the Torah. Our doctrinal positions about the law have been largely unchanged and unchallenged for centuries. We fall into the same traps and perpetuate the same fables of our fathers. Anti-Semitism, antinomianism, dispensationalism and replacement theology are

---

[15] Gerhard Falk, *The Jew in Christian Theology*, (Jefferson: McFarland and Company, 1931). Excerpt from John Calvin's, "Ad Quaelstiones et Objecta Juaei Responsio"

deeply entrenched in the western church, further widening the gap between Jews and Gentiles in Christ.

But we are not Martin Luther's church. We are the body of Christ. We cannot allow the lies of our fathers to misrepresent the love of our Father.

SECTION I

WORDS OF JESUS

JOHN 8

Truth #4 - *Jesus used the Torah to liberate the woman caught in adultery.*

In John Chapter 8, scribes and Pharisees bring a woman to Jesus, saying "Teacher, this woman was caught in the very act of adultery. Now the Law of Moses commands that she be stoned. But what do you say" (John 8:4-5)?

It was a trick question, nevertheless an important question. It's a question we must answer. Was Jesus going to uphold the Law of Moses?

The fact that the law condemned her to death could not be denied. Leviticus 20 and Deuteronomy 22 charge that both the adulterer and the adulteress were to be brought to the gate of the city and stoned so that "you put away the evil from among you" (Deut. 22:24).

But where was the adulterer? It goes without saying that adultery is a sin involving a willing accomplice. Why were these Pharisees so eager to get Yeshua to condemn this woman when her companion, perhaps even seducer, was not being held accountable? They were demanding the unscrupulous enforcement of one commandment while turning a blind eye toward another. Disregarding certain portions of Scripture inconvenient to their agenda was not uncommon for these men.

The scribes and Pharisees had Jesus trapped. No matter how he responded they would have grounds to form an accusation against Him. If He said, "Come on boys. Have a little heart and forgive her," they could argue, "This man is not the Messiah. He sanctions adultery and instructs others to break the Law of Moses."

They would be right. According to Deuteronomy 18, the promised Prophet would uphold all of God's commandments. If he presumed to speak against the Torah, against the Lord or in another name, he should be considered a false prophet. For Yeshua to be a prophet, let alone the sinless Messiah, he could not be sinning by breaking God's commands and encouraging others to as well.[1]

If Jesus answered, "Stone her," they could bring charges against Him before the Roman government, for Rome had stripped the Jewish courts of capital punishment. Under Roman rule, the Sanhedrin lost its authority to invoke the death penalty,[2] though this didn't always succeed in preventing death threats and stonings.[3] This is why Jesus was not executed at the hands of the Jews when standing trial before Caiaphas. They had to try him before Pilate in a Roman court to secure a death sentence.[4] If Jesus had sanctioned the woman's execution, they could have had him arrested, accusing him of being an enemy of Rome and rebelling against Caesar.

Obviously, this come-to-Jesus meeting was not under the purest of motives. These men didn't want to preserve the integrity of Scripture. They weren't concerned for this woman, the community or the families affected by this immorality. Nor were they seeking counsel from the wise Teacher. Their motive was jealousy, not justice. They called Him *Rabbi* to his face but *Deceiver* behind his

---

[1] To say that Jesus broke God's commands essentially concludes that Jesus was (a) a sinner, and (b) not the Messiah. Cf. Ezek. 37:24. Heb. 4:15, 9:28

[2] D. Thomas Lancaster, *Restoration* (Littleton; FFOZ, 2005), Chapter 4; Shira Schoenberg, "Ancient Jewish History: The Sanhedrin," [Online]. Available: www.jewishvirtuallibrary.org/the-sanhedrin

[3] John 10, Acts 7. The Torah does not support mob justice or vigilantism. For someone to be executed for breaking the Torah, it required a ruling body such as the Sanhedrin to declare a sentence. An individual could not simply take the law into their own hands and kill the perpetrator. Additionally, capital punishment was rarely, if ever, applied. Stonings were so uncommon that Rabbi Elazar Ben Azariah remarked that a Sanhedrin should be considered destructive if it were to execute someone once every seventy years (*Mishnah Makkot* 1:10). This is why Jesus was not executed at the hands of the Jews when standing trial before Caiaphas. He had to be tried before Pilate in a Roman court to secure a death sentence.

[4] John 18:31

back.[5] It was all a ploy, a preconceived, well-thought-out, carefully conspired setup. This adulteress provided the perfect ruse, and provision had most likely already been arranged for the guilty man to escape punishment.

John reveals their true intentions, explaining,

> *"They were trying to trap Him into saying something they could use against Him." - John 8:6a, NLT*

Had Yeshua contradicted Moses they could pronounce him a false prophet. Had he condemned the woman they could accuse him of usurping civil authority. They had effectively backed the Teacher from Galilee into a no-win corner. But the One who knows the hearts of all men was fully aware of their Machiavellian ways.

Yeshua bent down and wrote with his finger on the ground. As they continued to press him, he stood up and said,

"He who is without sin among you, let him throw the first stone."

One by one the woman's accusers walked away until Jesus was left alone with the woman.

He asked, *"Woman, where are those accusers of yours? Has no one condemned you?"*

"No one, Lord," she replied.

Jesus answered, *"Neither do I condemn you; go and sin no more"* (John 8:6-11).

Without even saying a word the Advocate turned the attention away from the woman's immorality to the accusers' hypocrisy. In doing so, he withdrew the witnesses. According to the Torah, a crime punishable by death must have the testimony of two or three witnesses.

---

[5] John 7:47

> *"Whoever is deserving of death shall be put to death on the testimony of two or three witnesses; he shall not be put to death on the testimony of one witness." - Deuteronomy 17:6*

What a brilliant response. By law, she could not be indicted on the testimony of one man.

In a stroke of genius, Jesus upheld God's law without incriminating himself. He neither throws a stone of accusation at the woman nor compromises the law. Instead, he skillfully and masterfully disqualified all the witnesses. With no eyewitnesses, there could be no trial, and with no one left to accuse her she stood only before the Nazarene. Remarkably, Yeshua worked within the parameters of the Torah to save the woman.

This is a far cry from the notion that Jesus trumped the law with one stroke of His Messianic veto pen or that he used His Son of God credentials to mercy-up Moses. He did nothing of the sort. Instead, he showed compassion to the woman through the boundaries already established in the Torah.

Go & Sin No More

Just so there was no mistaking his stance on adultery, Jesus sends the woman away with the charge to *"Go and sin no more"* (v.11). Reminiscent of the warning given to the paralytic at the pool of Bethesda, with this one statement Yeshua neither bends the law nor endorses lawlessness. Instead, he sets her on a path toward righteousness.

This begs the question: Where could she find this path, and how was she to know what was sinful? The Torah, of course. Going forward, the Good Shepherd expected her to know, honor and live by God's commands as outlined in the Law of Moses.

Jesus did <u>not</u> say to her, "I have come to supersede the Law of Moses," or "I do not condemn you, because the Torah is growing obsolete," or "Moses condemns you, but I forgive you. Go and live lawlessly." He neither declared that the law was coming to an end, nor sought to divorce her from its reach. Instead, Yeshua upheld the Torah and established it as the only standard by which we all must live and be measured by.

In his *Annotated Reference Bible*, Finis Dake noted that some early believers were hesitant to read this story in public.

> "Early Christians thought Jesus was not condemning adultery here, but the idea was that He was not a magistrate and since no man of her accusers stayed to condemn, He was not going to pass sentence on the woman, taking it upon Himself to execute the law of Moses. Jesus did not say He did not condemn adultery as a sin. He simply forgave the woman as He had done others who were sinful (Mt. 9:1-8, Lk. 7:37-50)."[6]

Dake is right. Jesus was not a magistrate, and he did not sanction adultery. Instead, as the Son of God, he carefully and precisely executed the whole Law of Moses. By execution, I do not mean termination. I mean that Christ implemented and carried out the full application of God's law perfectly.

Yeshua is a builder of His Father's work, not a destroyer. God's Word of Life is not in the business of divorcing us from the life of God's word. That role is reserved for the thief who comes to steal, kill and destroy. The Son of Heaven preserves, perfects and completes all things that come from heaven, including the Torah.

Go and sin no more was not a get-out-of-jail-free card for the woman. It was a charge for her to change her loose regard for God's ways. The woman lived as a lawbreaker, and it was her breaking of God's commands that got her into this sinful mess to begin with. It would be a slap in the face to the Lawgiver if she were to get up, shake off the dust and continue to disregard the Torah as she once did. Continuing to break God's laws after we have been shown mercy is a violation of the spirit of grace.

---

[6] Finis Dake, *Dake's Annotated Reference Bible* (Lawrenceville: Dake Bible Sales, 1961), John 8:11, 103

Go and sin no more communicates to us that when we are raised with Christ and delivered from our sin, our relationship with the law changes. Before Christ, it condemned us. In Christ, it consecrates us. Where it once revealed our sin, it now illuminates our path out of sin and leads us to a Savior.

When we meet Jesus, we come into the good graces of the Torah. His instructions no longer guilt us but guide us as we follow our Guide. When we bow at the feet of Jesus, like this woman, the law ceases to throw rocks at us but emerges as a solid foundation upon which we can rely. Through Christ, the grace of God and the Holy Spirit empower us to walk in a righteousness revealed in the Scriptures. God's law no longer brings upon us a curse but a blessing. It no longer is our demise. It is our delight.

Matthew Henry writes,

> "The law is the Christian's rule of duty, and he delights therein. If a man, pretending to be Christ's disciple, encourages himself in any allowed disobedience to the holy law of God, or teaches others to do the same, whatever his station or reputation among men may be, he can be no true disciple."[7]

Ask most Christians today to describe the laws of the Torah and delight may not be high on the list. *Harsh* or perhaps *condemning* would probably be more popular. *Old, outdated, irrelevant* and *legalistic* would likely be on that list. Is this how Jesus characterized the Law and the Prophets? Was this the attitude of the apostles? Modern sentiment depicts God's instructions as archaic, demanding and something that should be relegated to antiquity, but is this Heaven's commentary? It is in our best interests to find out how Jesus and his earliest followers lived, believed and taught.

God's word, whether new or old, written or spoken, should be music to our ears, not drudgery to our souls. The Torah is God's word. It is truth that never changes and wisdom that never expires. It is bursting

---

[7] Matthew Henry, *Concise Commentary on the Bible* (Nashville: Thomas Nelson, 2003), Matt. 5:17-20

with compassion. The Bible characterizes the Torah as a gift from God that should be cherished and enjoyed.

Since God is love, there is love in everything he does. There is love in his laws just as there is love in his grace. There is love in his judgments just as there is love in his mercy. There is love in reconciliation just as there will be love on the Day of Reckoning. Whether in destruction or redemption, there is found loving kindness sewn into the fabric of every act of God, including his commandments. If I cannot find delight in God's word, the problem is not with God's word. The problem is with my heart.

Finger of God

John does not elaborate what Jesus wrote on the ground that day, and we are only left to speculate. Using the dusty stones as a chalkboard, the Messiah bent down, used his finger as a stylus and one by one excused the crowd. What we do know, however, is that this was not the first time Heaven bent down to earth and wrote on stone with a finger.

Two thousand years prior, on a mountain in the Sinai desert, Heaven showed up and showed off in an awesome display of glory. The mountain trembled in a cloud of glowing radiance. A mixed multitude stood at the foot of the elevation, heard the thunder of God's audible voice and witnessed the fire of His presence. It was terrifying. It was magnificent. It was unprecedented. Never before had the God of heaven personally and so profoundly revealed himself to millions of people at one time.

Jewish tradition holds that the Most High spoke in seventy languages at once to all who were present.[8] Why seventy? There are seventy (or seventy-two) grandsons of Noah listed in Genesis 10. Some Babylonian Hebrew scholars concluded that seventy nations were scattered throughout the earth after the flood.[9] Perhaps the

---

[8] See Rashi's commentary on Deut. 27:8
[9] Kaufmann Kohler and Issac Broydé, *Jewish Encyclopedia,* Nations and Languages, "The Seventy" [Online]. Available: www.jewishencyclopedia

number seventy is attached to this story to illustrate that God summoned all the nations to his holy mountain and proclaimed His word to every people group on earth. By speaking in seventy languages simultaneously, each family coming out of Egypt could hear the word of God in their native tongue. Whether this tradition is fact or legend is speculative, but it is certainly not beyond God's scope of ability.

Given that the Feast of Pentecost is the traditional anniversary of the giving of the Torah, the similarities of what happened on that mountain and what happened in the upper room are fascinating. Wind. Fire. Tongues. All these elements are found in both Acts 2 and the Hebrew telling of the Sinai encounter. Just as God's Spirit was given at Pentecost, so it was at Sinai. Just as three thousand died at the hands of their Hebrew brothers at Sinai,[10] three thousand were saved at the preaching of Peter at Pentecost.[11]

After forty days and nights, Scripture records that the Ten Commandments were written with "the finger of God" (Ex. 31:18, Deut. 9:10). This means that the same finger that wrote the Ten Commandments was the same finger two millennia later that wrote on the ground and dismissed the adulteress' accusers.[12] We can take comfort in knowing that the finger of the law is also the finger of mercy. If the law that points out our sin also points to a sinless Savior, then written into every corner of the law is the love of God.

I have come to view the Ten Commandments, together with all of the Torah, not just as a collection of prohibitions, stories and inspired principles. I see them as God's hand-written love letter birthed in the fire of His glorious presence and written to all of creation. They are an oath of his covenant with humanity; his pledge of commitment to all who call upon His name. Perhaps God carved

---

com/acticles/11382-nations-and-languages-the-seventy
[10] Ex. 32:28
[11] Acts 2:41
[12] Asher Intrader, *Who Ate Lunch With Abraham* (Frederick, MD: Revive Israel Media, 2011), 37

the Ten Words onto stone tablets to assure us that his faithful promises are as strong and permanent as stone.

Torah & the Gospel

How is it that we have misunderstood the story of the woman caught in adultery for so long? One reason is that we've inherited a predetermined, theological narrative that insists Jesus came to free us from any obligation to the law. This premise has colored the way we interpret the Bible. The result is a scholarly discounting of the Torah that leaves us ill-equipped to understand certain portions of Scripture. This story is just one example of how we have drawn inaccurate conclusions based on a misreading of the passage.

A deeper dive into this passage, however, changes the entire meaning of the story, underscoring why our approach to the Torah is so important. Without a proper understanding we are ultimately left with a skewed perception of the Bible and a perverted image of our Lord. When carefully read, however, this story beautifully illustrates what Jesus came to accomplish.

You and I are the woman caught in adultery. We are guilty of sin and stand before our Maker condemned. Satan is the stone-holding prosecuting attorney accusing us before the court of heaven. When faced with the reality of our sin, the Prince of life was moved with compassion. In our defense, Yeshua didn't answer our accusers with arguments but with action. He stooped down from heaven, carried the sin of the world and bore our punishment. By dying on a cross, the Son of Man put to death our sin nature and took upon Himself the curse of the law, for "Cursed is everyone who hangs on a tree" (Deut. 21:23). In dismissing our accusers, our condemnation was averted, setting us free from the penalty for our sins. This is the redemptive work of Christ.

This story illustrates that Jesus did not discount the law but obeyed it in order to set us free from the penalty of violating it. In His mercy, the Lamb of God died for us so that we could escape the consequences of our rebellion, as Paul writes, "He made Him who knew no sin to be sin for us, that we might become the righteousness of God in Him" (2 Cor. 5:21). The good news is that when we die with him, we also live with him. The law is no longer our condemner, for "there is therefore now no condemnation to those who are in Christ Jesus" (Rom. 8:1).

Like the woman caught in adultery, keeping the Torah is our joyful response to the merciful work of Christ. We do not obey God's commands in order to be forgiven. We obey God *because* we have been forgiven. Our faithfulness to him is the result of our salvation, not the cause of it.

No one should ever feel the need to follow God's commandments in an attempt to earn his favor. We already have been given the favor of God through Jesus Christ. We now keep his commands because we humbly seek to please the One we owe our freedom to.

Conclusion

This story beautifully depicts a Savior brimming with compassion while still upholding the authority of God's Law. Jesus didn't abolish the letter of the law in favor of the spirit of the law. Instead, he brought the law and the Spirit together, exemplifying both the letter and the spirit of the Torah. By honoring the law and operating within its boundaries, he extended mercy to the woman, a mercy now extended to you and me.

We, like Israel at Sinai, have escaped from Egypt, passed through the waters of baptism and come to the mountain of God. And like this woman, we are commissioned to *go and sin no more*. Our Master places before us the Torah as a lighted pathway that pleases the Father's heart. Pursuing Torah is not a backwards slide into legalism. It is a loving act of appreciation for his kindness. It demonstrates our heartfelt gratitude for his mercy.

There is nothing in this story to support the view that Jesus ignored the stipulations of the law for the purpose of releasing the woman, or that he disregarded the Torah in favor of a new order of grace. The Messiah neither broke the law nor gave the woman license to keep on sinning. He simply forgave her and graciously instructed her to pursue God's standard of righteousness going forward.

We can be comforted knowing that our Savior forgives sinners and bids us all to come follow him. When we do, he is faithful to show us his Father's ways and empower us to walk in them just as he did.

MATTHEW 5:17A

Truth #5 – *Jesus endorsed the Law of Moses in His Sermon on the Mount.*

Yeshua's first recorded teaching about the Torah is found in the Sermon on the Mount. Matthew 5 lays the foundation for the rest of the sermon and provides insight into how the Sermon on the Mount should be understood. Here, we find Jesus' most definitive theological position regarding the law.

> *"Do not think that I came to destroy the Law or the Prophets. I did not come to destroy but to fulfill. For assuredly, I say to you, till heaven and earth pass away, one jot or one tittle will by no means pass from the law till all is fulfilled. Whoever therefore breaks one of the least of these commandments, and teaches men so, shall be called least in the kingdom of heaven; but whoever does and teaches them, he shall be called great in the kingdom of heaven."* – Matthew 5:17-19

Jesus is using a teaching method known as a *midrash* in the Sermon on the Mount. Typical of first-century teachers, he elaborates on a host of topics such as anger, murder, lust, adultery, retaliation, generosity, prayer, fasting, money, worry and judgment. Yeshua breaches the topic of the Torah in verse 17 with the declaration that He did not come to destroy the Law and the Prophets. *Do not think* (v.17) was a challenge to all who sought to discredit His ministry. He was boldly calling out those who were spreading rumors about Him and questioning His doctrine.

To clear up any confusion, Yeshua categorically sets the record straight. His position regarding the Law of Moses was fixed. He even repeats Himself for further clarity.

> *"Do not for a moment suppose that I have come to abrogate the Law or the Prophets: I have not come to abrogate them but to give them their completion." - v. 17, Weymouth New Testament*

The Greek word used for destroy is *kataluo*.[1] Weymouth translates it *abrogate*. It can also be translated:

Abolish
Demolish
Annul
Dissolve
Discard
Disunite
Throw down[2]

These words accurately depict what the Messiah did <u>not</u> do to God's law. He did not abolish, demolish, annul, dissolve, discard, disunite or throw down the Law of Moses. It seems as though Yeshua wanted His audience to know from the beginning that any doctrine suggesting that He sought to discard any portion of God's Torah is being put on notice.

Furthermore, He divulges that not one iota will cease from the Torah.

> *"For assuredly, I say to you, till heaven and earth pass away, one jot or one tittle will by no means pass from the law till all is fulfilled." - v.18*

The *jot* is the smallest letter in the Hebrew alphabet. According to Jewish tradition, it is irremovable. A *tittle* is a small hook or accent

---

[1] James Strong, *Strong's Exhaustive Concordance of the Bible* (Peabody: Hendrickson Publishers, 2009), #G2647 καταλύω
[2] Joannes Louw, *Greek-English Lexicon of the New Testament* (Minneapolis: Fortress, 1988), *Kaluo;* W.E. Vine, *Vine's Expository Dictionary of the New Testament* (Nashville: Thomas Nelson, 1996), "destroy;" Joseph Thayer, *Thayer's Greek-English Lexicon of the New Testament* (Peabody: Hendrickson, 1996), Matt. 5:17

point used by grammarians to denote one word from another. Of them, Marvin Vincent writes:

> "If all men in the world gathered to abolish the least letter in the law, they would not succeed. The guilt of changing those little hooks which distinguish between certain Hebrew letters is declared to be so great that, if such a thing were done, the world would be destroyed."[3]

It seems that the whole world is less reliable and more volatile than one small tick of the Torah. According to Yeshua, the commandments given to Moses will not cease but will last until the end of the age. As long as heaven and earth remain, God's spiritual laws will remain.

If Jesus meant to usurp the authority of the Torah and introduce his disciples to a post-Torah era, this would've been a prime opportunity for Him to state that certain portions of the Bible would become irrelevant upon His death and resurrection. He did not. He would not. His words stand on their own merit. In his kingdom the Torah is present and here to stay.

Heart of the Matter

A careful reading of the Sermon on the Mount reveals that Yeshua raises, not lowers, the standard of behavior beyond what is written in the Torah. When teaching about murder, for example, He quotes Exodus 20:13, using the Torah as a baseline for His teaching. He is not contradicting the sixth commandment. He is affirming, confirming and expounding upon it. His sermon digs deep into the heart of the matter, identifying anger as the root cause of murder. He neither nullifies nor modifies the commandment. He simply reveals the core of the commandment.

Likewise, Yeshua upholds the commandment to not commit adultery, pinpointing lust as the gateway drug to immorality. Far before an illicit act is ever committed, adultery is hatched in the eyes

---

[3] Marvin Vincent, *Vincent's Word Studies* (Peabody: Hendrickson, 1985), Matt. 5:18

of the heart. By declaring that murder and adultery are broader than the act itself, Yeshua strengthens the Torah's reach, not weakens it. This provides further evidence that Jesus had no intention of abolishing the Torah.

Yeshua was Heaven's messenger who delivered the Torah to Moses on the mountain. Why would He want to compromise the very Torah He had a hand in writing? Since the Torah is the foundation upon which the Messiah builds His words, we should interpret the Sermon on the Mount in light of the Torah, not in opposition to it.

Conclusion

Some suggest that Jesus cancelled the Torah and replaced it with the Sermon on the Mount. This is simply not true. There is no anti-Torah sentiment here, and there is no clear evidence that the doctrine of Christ is not Torah inclusive. If we take Yeshua at His word, we shouldn't even entertain the thought that He came to abolish the Torah.

Still today, Yeshua's words speak to those who think He came to destroy the Torah. Those who stray from God's commands, using His life and words as an excuse, have been put on notice. Heaven's Prophet speaks prophetically to those throughout church history that might draw such a conclusion.

By His own pronouncement, Jesus informs His audience that He has no intention of superseding God's law. He didn't come to change the law. He came to change their understanding of it.

Jesus loves the Torah. He taught it, spoke it, memorized it, prayed it and lived it. The Son of David is the very essence of the Scriptures – the Living Torah, the "Word made flesh" (John 1:14), the eternal "Word of God" (John 1:1, Rev. 19:13). In the Gospels, Yeshua never said or did anything to undermine what is written in the Torah of Moses.

Jesus makes it abundantly clear in this passage and from the onset of his ministry. He was for Torah, not against it. He came to fulfill it, not destroy it.

MATTHEW 5:17B

Truth #6 - *The fulfillment of Christ does not bring an end to the Law.*

The fact that Jesus came to preserve the Torah is plain enough, but what does it mean that He came to "fulfill the law" (v.17)?

> *"Do not think that I came to destroy the Law or the Prophets. I did not come to destroy but to fulfill (plēroō)." - Matthew 5:17*

Plēroō, the Greek word used here for fulfill, means to *accomplish, complete* or *bring to pass.*[1] It carries the connotation of *ratification, consummation* or *obedience.*[2]

Contrary to what we have been taught, *fulfill* does not suggest the cancellation of something as if one were to bring it to an end. *Plēroō* is better understood to mean verification, ratification, consummation, perfection or bringing into full effect.[3] In this sense, Jesus *filled up* and *filled full* the law.

I like how James Hastings puts it.

> "The Old Testament leads us up to Christ, and Christ takes it and puts it back into our hands as a completed whole. He bids us study it as 'fulfilled in him,' and 'put ourselves to school with every part of it.' The old lesson-book is not to be thrown away or kept as an archeological curiosity; it is to be re-studied in this fresh light of further knowledge."[4]

---

[1] *Strong's* #G4137 πληρόω; Woodhouse, *English-Greek Dictionary,* 348; *Thayer's,* Matt. 5:17
[2] Larry Pierce, *The Outline Of Biblical Usage,* Matt. 5:17 [Online]. Available: www.blueletterbible.com
[3] Louw, *Greek-English Lexicon of the New Testament, Plēroō; Vine's,* "fulfill"
[4] James Hastings, *Great Texts of the Bible,* Matt. 5:17

It is beneficial to note that Matthew is writing to a Jewish audience and that the phrase *fulfill the law* is a Hebrew idiom. David Bivin points out that *fulfill the law* is an idiomatic expression that means *to sustain the Torah through proper interpretation.*[5] A teacher is said to have fulfilled the Torah when correctly interpreting and applying the text. In bringing out its truest and fullest meaning, the instruction can then be properly walked out as God intends. Conversely, Bivin also identifies *abolish the law* as a Hebrew expression that means to *nullify or misapply the Torah through misinterpretation.*

Bivin's explanation is not foreign to scholarship. Many scholars today translate *kataluo* and *plēroō* using the Hebrew words *levattel* (to cancel) and *lekayem* (to uphold).[6] In reference to the Torah, these antonyms form a figure of speech that mean, respectively, *to break or disregard* and *to observe or treat with importance.*[7] Since Yeshua likely spoke to His audience in Hebrew and Matthew likely penned his gospel in Hebrew, finding a Hebrew equivalent for these terms can be useful in gaining a proper understanding.

Clearly, the Messiah neither nullified nor misapplied the Torah. Through proper interpretation, application and demonstration, the Son of God reassures His Hebrew-speaking audience that He came to observe, uphold and treat with importance the commandments of His Father. The rabbis feared an untrained Galilean might possibly misapply the Torah and inadvertently misrepresent portions of Scripture. Perhaps this is one reason the Pharisees opposed Yeshua. But this is exactly what Jesus assured them He came not to do.

---

[5] David Bivin, *New Light On The Difficult Word Of Jesus* (En Gedi: Lois Tverberg & Bruce Okkema, 2005), 94

[6] Franz Delitzsch, *The Delitzsch Hebrew Gospels* (USA: Vine of David, 2011), xx-xxi; *Sefer Seder Olam Rabbah Vezuta Umegillat Ta'anit,* appendix; *The Bible Society in Israel* modern Hebrew translation, Matt. 5:17; See also the translation produced by the *London Society for Promoting Christianity among the Jews*, a group of evangelical Anglicans in the 1800's of whom William Wilberforce was a member.

[7] Examples in rabbinic literature include *Shevu'ot* 3:6, *Avot* 4:9, *t. Sanhedrin* 14:13, *j. Kiddushin* 61c

Abolish Not

There is the opinion that the law ended and became obsolete at the fulfillment of Christ. It maintains that the Torah has run its course, and Jesus intended for it to be discontinued altogether.

One commentary sums up this position:

> "[Jesus] replies that he has not come to destroy it, but to fulfill. He does not say that he has come to perpetuate it…He was the end of the law."[8]

This viewpoint presumes that Jesus never meant to perpetuate the Torah. Instead, He intended to bring it to an end.

Though I once held this position, I can't get behind this notion anymore. Here's why.

If the Torah were indeed obsolete, wouldn't all the commandments be obsolete? The commandment to worship the Lord your God, the commandment to have no other gods, the commandment to love the Lord with all your heart, the prohibitions of murder, adultery and theft – all these would cease to have meaning or relevancy.

If the Torah had ended, the God of Abraham, Isaac and Jacob would be foreign to us. There would be no document in place that defines sin, condemns sinners and points us to a sinless Messiah. What standard would the wicked be judged by? The concept of redemption through innocent blood would be meaningless. The context for Jesus as the Lamb of God would be lost. There would be no prophecies to point us to a Redeemer, and any reference to the Old Testament found in the New Testament would be negated.

I have found that a better approach is to consider that the teachings of Christ don't cancel God's commandments but properly interpret

---

[8] B.W. Johnson, *People's New Testament*, Matt. 5:17 [Online]. Available: www.biblestudytools.com

them. From this perspective, they don't supplant them. They supplement them.

To insist that Jesus fulfilled the Torah to the point of terminating it requires that we take on the position that He came to destroy the law, thus invalidating His own words. This is self-contradictory. It can't be both ways. Either He put an end to it or He didn't. Either He ended all of it or He ended none of it.

Dake wanders down this path.

> "Every jot and tittle of the whole law or contract at Sinai was fulfilled, ended and abolished and done away by Him when He made the new covenant."[9]

Dake gets out over his skis a bit here. His position equates the old covenant with the Torah, treating them as synonymous. This is clumsy. There is a marked difference between the old covenant and the law. The old covenant is not the Torah. The old covenant was Israel's pledge to obey all that is written in the Torah.

As well, the Bible clearly states that the Torah plays a significant role in both the old and the new covenants. We find no change to the Torah in the new covenant. The change is to where the Torah is written.

> *"I will put my Torah in their inward parts, and write it in their hearts." - Jeremiah 31:33*

The law doesn't change in the new covenant. It is our hearts that change. It can only be that since the Torah is in us, it is still alive and active.

To ignore the inscription of the Torah upon our hearts is to ignore one of the chief assignments of the Holy Spirit within us. Denying the Torah denies our hearts. If the Torah is truly abolished and dead,

---

[9] Dake, Matt. 5:17, 4

as this interpretation maintains, then God intentionally wrote something dead and obsolete upon our hearts.

Macdonald explains the antinomian position further, writing:

> "There is an end, then, to the obligation to offer animal sacrifices, to perform Levitical lustrations, to observe the ceremonial Sabbaths, to submit to circumcision. Jesus did not formally abolish these, but left them to dissolve of themselves. The synagogue became gradually converted into the Christian church. The Sabbath of the seventh day became merged in that of the first. Gentiles coming into the Church led to altered views respecting circumcision, meats and purifications. Secondary things are regulated by great principles."[10]

An end to Sabbaths, the ceasing of circumcision, the dissolving of meat restrictions – this is exactly what Jesus explicitly proclaimed He came not to do. While this position rightly admits that Jesus didn't personally abolish these, it advocates that He left them to dissolve through Christian osmosis. Oh boy! If we applied this to everything Christians have neglected, the whole Bible would be obsolete. We'd no longer have a verse to stand on.

Sabbath, circumcision, tassels, dietary guidelines and Biblical holy days may not be common in today's church, but this does not suggest they are abolished or phased out. Our inattention to certain commandments is not sufficient evidence to prove that Christ Himself wished they be eliminated. While certain prohibitions such as tattoos and fornication may be commonly practiced among those claiming Christianity, it does not make them more or less Biblically sanctioned.

Priestly Instructions

I find it misleading to lump animal sacrifices and Levitical lustrations into the same consequence as circumcision, Sabbath and meat regulations. The temple was destroyed in 70 A.D. The function

---

[10] H.D.M. Spence and Joseph Exell, *The Pulpit Commentary*, Book 33, Vol. 1 (New York: Funk & Wagnalls, 1945), 214

of the priest is non-operational. The instructions regarding ceremonial cleanliness and temple activity do not have an application when the temple (or tabernacle) is non-functional.

Most scholars refuse to call our attention to the fact that the laws pertaining to the priest and temple are not observed today for a completely different reason than some of the others. Instructions for the tabernacle are not observed today, because there is no standing temple and no temple context for them to be applied.

This, however, is not the case for those commandments we have theologically discounted. Sabbath, Biblical holy days and dietary guidelines do not require a fully functioning temple to be observed. All too often they are neglected due to doctrine and preference. They have been conveniently labeled Jewish and/or too outdated for modern Gentile Christian expression.

MacDonald's commentary suggests that it is the will of God that the Torah be replaced by Gentile influences – that the church replaces the synagogue, that the seventh day merges with the first, that unclean meats are added to God's dietary menu, and that principles replace commandments. It considers these laws to be "secondary things" replaced by "great principles."

Whether purposely or not, this view subtly chips away at the Word of God. Nowhere does the Bible advocate replacing Sabbath with Sunday church-going. Neither does the Christian church eradicate the Jewish synagogue.

One commentary deduces that Jesus came to "turn rules into principles."[11] This idea should alarm us. Yeshua did not reduce the Scriptures to just good suggestions and nice principles. This approach to the text takes the fear of God out of the word of God. Violating a commandment sounds serious, but violating a principle – eh, that's not so bad.

---

[11] Charles Ellicott, *Ellicott's Bible Commentary for English Readers* (Harrington: Delmarva Publications, 2015), Matt. 5:17

Replacing God's word with self-help principles should give us pause, because it was the practice of the Pharisees to supplant the word of God with religious values. In my opinion, any interpretation that presumes Jesus turned God's laws into mere principles is a doctrine more in line with the enemies of the gospel than with the true gospel.

This selection insists that Gentile influence gradually "altered" and perverted the purity of God's Word. This I can agree with. However, it's unfair to hold Jesus directly, or in this case, indirectly responsible for this.

Our ambivalence to certain portions of Scripture is not of His doing. We can only hold ourselves accountable for turning our backs on God's word and for the many evils done at the hands of Christians. We alone are responsible for the anti-Semitic and antinomian doctrines of the church. I cannot get away with blaming Jesus for my neglect of even the least of God's commands, and it would be scandalous to say that my inattention to them is the will of Jesus.

Yeshua did not leave Sabbath, circumcision and other commandments to "dissolve of themselves." Since *dissolve* is a synonym for *kataluo* (destroy), this position stands in direct defiance to Christ's own declaration that He came not to destroy the Torah. Whether abolished or left to dissolve, the result is still the replacement and destruction of God's truth, and it unfairly makes Jesus the culprit.

Rewriting History

There are teachers today who take it upon themselves to rewrite the Bible through addition and subtraction. In doing so, they invalidate established truths that stand in the way of pet doctrines. This is sticky. If one portion of Scripture can be discounted or discarded, it is only a matter of time before all of it will be rejected. This path has proven to be a treacherous one.

One position takes this to a radical extreme, contending that translators misunderstood Jesus and mistranslated Matthew 5:17.

Instead of it reading that He came to fulfill and not destroy the Torah, they believe Yeshua meant to say that He fulfilled the law by denying it.

That's what one writer relays, stating that Jesus was merely catering to His Jewish audience and being sympathetic toward Orthodox Judaism. He sees no reason for Yeshua to state that He came to fulfill the law.[12] This writer believes this passage is only included here because Palestinian Jewish Christians were being sensitive to Jewish attitudes toward the Torah.[13]

Another man, a Talmudic scholar named Shabbetai Zvi of Smyrna, was thought to be the messiah and king of Israel by many sophisticated rabbis of the seventeenth century. He even assembled military adherents from Palestine, the Near East and parts of Europe.[14] Zvi openly renounced the Ten Commandments and declared that those who forsook God's laws were "blessed." He taught that, "Denying the law is fulfilling the law."[15] It is not surprising that Shabbetai Zvi was revealed to be a false messiah in 1666 when he chose to convert to Islam to avoid martyrdom.

Marcion of Sinope, the Christian heretic and Gnostic whose disdain for Torah and the Torah-Giver is well documented, took it a drastic step further. He taught that the entire Old Testament and many sections of the New Testament should be removed altogether. He believed that early Judaizers of the apostolic age altered Jesus' words. He advocated that Matthew 5:17 should be re-written as, "Think ye that I came to fulfill the Law or the Prophets? I came not to fulfill, but to destroy."[16]

Marcion's extreme take represents the baseless antinomian bias in a nutshell, and in a nutshell is probably where it belongs since it's

---

[12] T.W. Manson, *The Sayings of Jesus* (Grand Rapids: Eeardmans, 1979), 153
[13] Colin Brown, *The New International Dictionary of New Testament Theology*, Vol. 3 (Grand Rapids: Regency Reference Library, 1967), 181
[14] *Jewish Virtual Library* [Online]. Available: www.jewishvirtuallibrary.org/shabbetai-zvi
[15] Risto Santala, *Paul* (Finland: Bible and Gospel Service, 1995), 134
[16] Ellicott, Matt. 5:17

nuts. It's an oxymoron, because only an ox or a moron could come to this conclusion. Even staunch antinomians find it hard to take Marcion's assertion seriously.

There is simply no credible evidence to support any of the claims of these men, yet strangely enough popular theology in practice essentially sides itself with them. The conclusion that Jesus destroyed the Torah through fulfillment is the outgrowth of a doctrine that tolerates and legitimizes the rewriting of Scripture.

Conclusion

Jesus did not come to destroy the Torah. Man has taken up that task. We've turned commandments into principles and precepts into policies. Instead of allowing the words of Christ to confront our preconceptions, we are guilty of allowing preconceived conclusions about the Torah to prompt the way we read the words of Christ. We cleverly push aside the written law thinking we're obeying the spirit of the law, but in actuality we may be breaking both. When we choose the traditional interpretation over the written command, we run the risk of rejecting the plain teachings of our Master.

Some teach that Jesus fulfilled the Torah and effectively brought it to an end; that Christ fulfilled the law as if one were fulfilling a duty. Once His duty was complete, the need for further fulfillment ended.

But Yeshua didn't fulfill the law in order to destroy it. He fulfilled the law to accomplish it, to make it fully alive and fully functional. Jesus makes the Torah complete, not obsolete.

Yeshua states in no uncertain terms that He did not come to destroy the Torah. He is for the Torah, not against it. He came to obey it, not destroy it. This cannot be edited out of the text. The rationale that Jesus brought an end to the law, thereby rendering it obsolete is simply contrary to how Matthew 5 reads. Yet traditionally our doctrine insists on the contrary.

The Son of God is the consummation of God's revealed word. He is the cornerstone of the kingdom and the target of the Torah. Our

Redeemer is the crowning work of God's redemptive plan on earth. Like a judge upholding a legal document, He ratified, perfected and obeyed the Torah to its fullest extent. He effectively signed, sealed and delivered God's Torah to us.

Unlike some of the teachers of His day, Yeshua did not abolish or nullify the Torah through misinterpretation. Instead, He came to uphold the Torah and demonstrate for us how to walk it out.

JAMES 2:8, ROMANS 13:8-10, GALATIANS 5:14

Truth #7 – *We are to fulfill the Law just as Jesus did.*

There is an argument that maintains that since righteousness comes by faith in Christ, we no longer need to follow Torah commands. Through the life, death and resurrection of Yeshua, the Torah has been righteously satisfied and completely done away with. This position explains that because Jesus fulfilled the law, we don't have to. The Messiah fulfilled the law for us; therefore, we don't have to keep it.

Many hold to this opinion, as I once did. But there are some inconsistencies with this viewpoint.

For one, this opinion implies that the law could, at one time, save us and once served as a redemptive placeholder until the coming of the Messiah. It reasons that upon His arrival, Torah keeping was done away with. But in taking this position, one must concede there are (or were) two contrasting paths to salvation: (1) The old path of Torah keeping, and (2) the new path of faith in Christ. The strength of this argument is lost in this assumption.

Nowhere does the Bible teach duplicitous salvation. There have never been two separate paths to eternal life, but only one – by faith. Abraham "believed in the Lord, and He accounted it to him for righteousness" (Gen. 15:6). "The just shall live by his faith" (Hab. 2:4). "Without faith, it is impossible to please Him" (Heb. 11:6). The "By faith" statements of Hebrews 11 establish that even for the saints of old, faith is the path of the righteous and the only way to receive God's grace.

Salvation was never designed to come through Torah observance, because (1) the Torah is not the means by which we attain redemption, and (2) it requires no faith to observe the Torah. Anyone can obey or attempt to obey the law, regardless of faith. But only by faith can a person follow Christ. This lends to the notion that Torah keeping and faith in Christ are not actions opposed to one another.

Additionally, this position does little to distinguish between imputed righteousness (right standing) and moral righteousness (right behavior). Faith in Christ gives us right standing with God, but it does not guarantee that our subsequent conduct will be ethically or morally right. We have been made righteous in God's sight, but righteous behavior is our duty, not His. It is now our responsibility to act righteously. Our actions do not become automatically pure in God's eyes just because we profess Christ.

For example, according to the law, ex-convicts have legally served their time for their wrongdoing. They are no longer subject to additional punishment for their crimes. The law has been satisfied. Upon their release from prison, however, it is their responsibility to leave behind their criminal past and choose to be law-abiding citizens. Though they are released from any further penalty, they must continue in that freedom in order to remain guiltless.

In the same way, Yeshua opened prison doors for us, but it is our responsibility to leave our past and walk out of that prison. The cross gives us right standing with the Judge and releases us from His judgment. It does not release us from our personal responsibility to be law-abiding citizens of God's kingdom.

In this way, a person's righteousness is proven not in their rebellion but in their commitment to demonstrating God's righteousness through upright conduct. This is sanctification. As it has been said, who we are is God's gift to us, but who we make ourselves to be is our gift to Him.

JAMES 2:8, ROMANS 13:8-10, GALATIANS 5:14

Fulfilling the Law

The opinion that Jesus fulfilled the Torah so we don't have to falls short when we consider that the verb *fulfill (plēroō)* means *to bring into realization through proper behavior*. As stated in the previous chapter, it does not imply expiration or termination.

To rightly understand how Jesus fulfilled the law, we must take into account the other uses of the word *plēroō* in Scripture. We run across the phrase *fulfilling the law* elsewhere in the Apostolic Scriptures. James writes,

> "If you really *fulfill (teleo)* the royal law according to the Scripture, 'You shall love your neighbor as yourself,' you do well." – James 2:8

James quotes Leviticus 19:18, "You shall love your neighbor as yourself," to convey that loving our neighbor fulfills the law. He uses the synonym *teleo* for 'fulfill.'

Why would James encourage the law to be fulfilled if, as some teach, the law had already been fulfilled and done away with? There would be no law left to fulfill. Fulfilling it would be counterproductive to the work of Christ.

If the Torah was nullified at the coming of Christ, then the instruction to love our neighbor as ourselves would also be nullified. According to this logic, we would be under no obligation to love our neighbors anymore. In light of this verse, this position is perplexing, especially since it contradicts the clear directive of Yeshua.

Furthermore, the very next verse after the instruction to love our neighbor reads:

> "You shall keep my statutes." – Leviticus 19:19

In keeping with the context of Leviticus 19, the same chapter that instructs us to love our neighbor also instructs us to keep God's statutes (Lev. 19:19), honor the Sabbath (Lev. 19:3) and refrain from tattooing our bodies (Lev. 19:28). If given more parchment to write,

James might have cited all of Leviticus 19 for context, but the context is well noted. The strength of James' teaching is supported by a detailed chapter of the Torah rich with God's commands.

Why is it that we quickly accept one small part of Leviticus 19 but reject the rest? How can we maintain that loving our neighbor is binding but tattoos, Sabbath and others are not? If we are truly intent on fulfilling the law as James instructs, it would be wise to seek to obey all of God's commandments as a practical and positive step toward loving God and our neighbor.

One might counter, "We only need to love God and love our neighbor. This is what Jesus taught." True, but this is not *only* what Yeshua taught. In addition to loving God and our neighbor, Jesus instructs us to keep even the least of God's commands, assuring that those who teach and obey the Torah will be called "great" in his kingdom.

> *"Whoever therefore breaks one the least of these commandments, and teaches men so, shall be called least in the kingdom of heaven; but whoever does and teaches them, he shall be called great in the kingdom of heaven." – Matthew 5:19*

If breaking one of the least of God's commands makes a person least in God's kingdom, we can safely conclude that the King of the kingdom demonstrated godliness by honoring even the least of God's commandments Himself. If He truly is the greatest in this kingdom, would the King place a higher standard for His citizens than He has for Himself? Of course not. Since He obeyed even the least of the commandments, it is not beneath us to do likewise.

You and I are not too big for small matters, even the most trivial commandments of the Bible. Our Lord has given us a divine invitation to find greatness in his kingdom. Attention given to even the smallest of God's commands is what He calls kingdom behavior. It is in our best interest to be like Him in all things, even those things that seem insignificant.

JAMES 2:8, ROMANS 13:8-10, GALATIANS 5:14

Life-giving Instructions

In the story of the rich young ruler, Yeshua is asked what must be done to inherit eternal life. He responds, *"If you want to enter into life, keep the commandments."*

"Which ones?" asks the rich young ruler.

"'You shall not murder.' 'You shall not commit adultery.' 'You shall not steal.' 'You shall not bear false witness.' 'Honor your father and your mother,' and 'You shall love your neighbor as yourself'" (Matthew 19:17-19).

Jesus explains to this young man that the path to eternal life involves keeping God's commands, in which Jesus includes *loving our neighbor* in His list of life-giving instructions. Why? Because loving our neighbor has no context outside of the rest of God's commands. God's commandments are how we love God and love others. Loving God and loving our neighbor is not to the exclusion of the other commandments. They are the grand summation of them.

Our understanding of what it means to keep God's commandments needs to be interpreted in light of love. We demonstrate our love for our neighbor by following God's commandments. When we follow his commands, we are loving our neighbor. Loving others and keeping the commandments are intentionally and eternally intertwined. They don't compete with one another. They complement each other. The Golden rule to treat others the way we wish to be treated (Matt. 7:12) is simply Yeshua's paraphrase of Leviticus 19:18.

Love is the best motivation for obedience. Loving God and loving others doesn't replace God's commands. They are the natural result of honoring them. This is what it means to fulfill the law.

One may ask, "But how is it loving to be obligated to obey God's commandments?" Think of it like this:

A man has two children. To the first, he gives a detailed list of expected behavior. Work hard. Be generous. Don't steal. Respect others. Be honest and kind. To the other, however, he gives no guidance or expectations whatsoever. He merely leaves him to his own devices. Consequently, this child grows up to be self-absorbed, disrespectful and angry.

The question is: Which child did the father love more?

Neglect is not love. Guidance is. A father disciplines the children he loves, *because* he loves them. His instructions are for our benefit. When we ignore them, it hurts us, and it pains God to see us hurt. When we remove all boundaries, we remove love.

God's love is instructional, not passive. There is love in his laws, just as there is love in his grace. Our Father's instructions for living and loving are not a burden – they are a glorious blessing. Our Maker has deliberately communicated to us his will, not wanting and not willing to leave us ignorant of his ways of life. This is true love!

Paul weighs in on this topic, writing to the Romans,

> "He who loves his fellowman has *fulfilled (plēroō) the law*. The commandments, 'Do not commit adultery,' 'Do not murder,' 'Do not steal,' Do not covet,' and whatever other commandment there may be are summed up in this one rule: 'Love your neighbor as yourself.' Love does no harm to its neighbor. Therefore love is the *fulfillment (plērōma) of the law*." – Romans 13:8-10

And to the Galatians,

> "For the whole *law is fulfilled (plēroō)* in one word, 'You shall love your neighbor as yourself.'" – Galatians 5:14 NASB

Like James, Paul cites Leviticus 19 to support his teaching and encourages Christians to *plēroō* (fulfill) God's instructions just as Yeshua did. Clearly to Paul, fulfilling the law does not mean to bring to an end. Otherwise, why would he encourage believers to fulfill the law? It can only mean to rightly put into practice what the Torah requires, just as Jesus taught.

Nowhere in the Apostolic Scriptures does the word "fulfill" take on the connotation of death through fulfillment. When Yeshua spoke of fulfilling the law, it was not only in reference to His prophetic satisfaction of the law but also to His example of honoring it.

Some suppose Paul is introducing a new commandment here and replacing the entire Torah with one single command. This is incoherent, since loving our neighbor is not a new commandment but is lifted directly from Leviticus 19. The commandment had already been in writing for centuries at this point. Paul is simply aggregating the Torah into its simplest form. Loving our neighbor isn't a replacement for God's commands. It is the basic sum total of God's commandments.

Repealing the Law

The most glaring inconsistency of the antinomian viewpoint is that it modifies the text ever so slightly to say that Jesus fulfilled the law *for us*. By adding this clause, it makes it seem as though we need not fulfill the law ourselves. But Jesus did not say He fulfilled the law in our stead. He merely states that He came to fulfill the Torah. As it turns out, we are also called to fulfill the Torah just as Yeshua did, as the apostles instruct.

By adding to the text and altering the definition of the word *fulfill*, antinomian interpretation negates the primary and produces a forced outcome. The result is a reverse interpretation that repeals the Torah. Instead of reading Matthew 5:17 for what it is (that Jesus obeyed Torah and didn't abolish it), it gets twisted into *Jesus obeyed the Torah for us, so we don't have to. Therefore, it is now abolished for us*. This kind of circular reasoning is dishonest with the text.

Conclusion

We are grateful that the blood of Yeshua frees us from the curse of unrighteousness, but it does not guarantee the blessings of a righteous life. In His perfection, our Savior obeyed the law, and in His obedience, He perfected us. Our imputed perfection, however, cannot emancipate us from an obligation to his commands.

The apostles encouraged us to fulfill the law, because it very much is still alive and relevant. When have we ever been given the permission to break God's laws?

We are now given the privilege to be like our Master in all things – to walk as He walks, live as He lives, heal as He heals, honor what He honors, and fulfill the Torah as He does. As long as the kingdom of heaven is solvent, the Torah will remain relevant.

Galatians 6:2, Matthew 22:37-40, Luke 10:25-28

Truth #8 – *Loving God and loving others are commandments found in the Torah.*

Another popular opinion holds that Jesus superseded the Law of Moses and gave us a new law – the law of Christ. Whereas the Law of Moses is old, Christ is new. This new law of Jesus uproots and replaces the Torah.

I understand why this position is taken. Yeshua is the manifested Word of God, the living, breathing Torah. Without a doubt the Torah is fully completed and rightly interpreted through His life and teachings. Jesus embodies the law, perfects it and gives it its fullest meaning. But to argue that the Sermon on the Mount or any other teaching replaces the Torah and renders it useless is inconsistent.

If true, Yeshua would have spoken disparagingly of the Torah instead of quoting it authoritatively. Instead of considering those great who practice the least of the commands, He should be rebuking them. Instead of condemning as workers of Torahlessness those who shun the will of God, He should be praising them. If the Sermon on the Mount was meant to supersede the Torah, Yeshua would not have said, "I have not come to abolish the Law and the Prophets," but rather, "I have come to replace them."

The Messiah makes no such claim in His Sermon or anywhere else in the Gospels. There is no indication whatsoever that He sought to undermine the Torah. On the contrary, He defended its authority. He praised those who practiced the least of God's commandments and identified Torah keepers as those who do the will of His Father.

The concept that Jesus introduced an overruling higher law comes from one verse found in Galatians. It reads:

> *"Bear one another's burdens and so fulfill the law of Christ." – Galatians 6:2*

There is no other verse in the Bible that specifically mentions the law of Christ. There are, however, several that mention a new commandment.

> *"A new commandment I give to you, that you love one another." – John 13:34*

> *"Brethren, I write no new commandment to you, but an old commandment which you have had from the beginning. The old commandment is the word which you heard from the beginning." – 1 John 2:7*

> *"And now I plead with you, lady, not as though I wrote a new commandment to you, but that which we have had from the beginning: that we love one another." – 2 John 1:5*

It seems obvious to me that this new commandment of Christ is not really new but merely God's law summed up as love. It includes bearing one another's burdens and loving one another. What the apostles are getting at is that loving one another is the basic message of Yeshua. This is what is meant by the *law of Christ*. The law of Christ is the new commandment.

Love & the Law

When approached with the question of which was the greatest commandment, Jesus answered,

> *"'Love the Lord your God with all your heart and with all your soul and with all your mind.' This is the first and greatest commandment. And the second is like it: 'Love your neighbor as yourself.' All the Law and the Prophets hang on these two commandments." - Matthew 22:37-40*

In a similar exchange, a lawyer stood up to test Jesus, saying,

"Teacher, what shall I do to inherit eternal life?"

Yeshua replied, *"What is written in the Torah? What is your reading of it?"*

The lawyer answered, *"'You shall love the Lord your God with all your heart, with all your soul, with all your strength, and with all your mind,' and 'your neighbor as yourself.'"*

Jesus said, *"You have answered rightly; do this and you will live."* - Luke 10:25-28

There is a lot of talk about love in Christian circles and rightfully so. Love is a central theme of both the Torah and the Apostolic Scriptures. But what does it mean to love? Ask ten people and you may get fifteen different answers, ranging anywhere from being nice to warm feelings to a wanton act.

While it may be impossible to overemphasize love, it is possible to under-define it. When we fail to properly define love, we end up watering it down and forcing it into abstract corners. Without a working definition, love becomes reduced to mere concepts, ideas and generalities instead of actual, concrete behavior. Without a Biblical understanding of what it means to love, we run the risk of being influenced by the world's skewed and perverted notion of love.

Jesus concentrated the Torah into two simple instructions: love God and love your neighbor. In saying this, Yeshua is neither replacing Scripture nor discounting the Ten Commandments. He is merely summing them up and breaking them down into their most basic values. Loving God and others is the whole of the Bible and the universal will of God for every person's life. This is the Torah of Christ.

But what does it mean to love God? Is it faithfully attending church, waving a hankie in worship or street witnessing? Is it attending

Christian conferences, going on a mission trip or listening to worship music? These may be evidence that someone loves God, but in and of themselves they are not love for God.

John weighs in.

> *"For this is the love of God, that we keep His commandments. And His commandments are not burdensome." – 1 John 5:3*

And,

> *"This is love, that we walk according to His commandments. This is the commandment, that as you have heard from the beginning, you should walk in it." - 2 John 1:6*

Jesus was not the first to link loving God and others together. Loving God and keeping his commandments is a recurrent theme that appears multiple times together throughout Scripture.

Exodus 20:5-6
For I, the LORD your God, am a jealous God, visiting the iniquity of the fathers on the children to the third and fourth generations of those who hate Me, but showing mercy to thousands, to those who <u>love Me and keep My commandments</u>.

Deuteronomy 7:9
"Therefore know that the LORD your God, He is God, the faithful God who keeps covenant and mercy for a thousand generations with those who <u>love Him and keep His commandments</u>."

Deuteronomy 10:12-13
And now, Israel, what does the LORD your God require of you, but to fear the LORD your God, to walk in all His ways and to <u>love Him</u>, to serve the LORD your God with all your heart and with all your soul, <u>and to keep the commandments of the LORD and His statutes</u> which I command you today for your good?

Deuteronomy 11:1
Therefore you shall <u>love the LORD your God, and keep His charge, His statutes, His judgments, and His commandments always</u>.

Deuteronomy 11:13-14
And it shall be that if you earnestly <u>obey My commandments</u> which I command you today, to <u>love the LORD your God</u> and serve Him with all your heart and with all your soul, then I will give you the rain for your land in its season, the early rain and the latter rain, that you may gather in your grain, your new wine, and your oil.

Deuteronomy 13:4
You shall walk after the LORD your God and <u>fear Him, and keep His commandments</u> and obey His voice, and you shall serve Him and hold fast to Him.

Deuteronomy 30:16
<u>Love the LORD your God, walk in His ways, and keep His commandments, His statutes, and His judgments</u>, that you may live and multiply; and the LORD your God will bless you in the land which you go to possess.

Deuteronomy 30:19-20
I call heaven and earth as witnesses today against you, that I have set before you life and death, blessing and cursing; therefore choose life, that both you and your descendants may live; that you <u>may love the LORD your God, that you may obey His voice</u>, and that you may cling to Him, for He is your life and the length of your days; and that you may dwell in the land which the LORD swore to your fathers, to Abraham, Isaac, and Jacob, to give them.

Joshua 22:5-6
"But take careful heed to do the commandment and the law which Moses the servant of the LORD commanded you, to <u>love the LORD your God, to walk in all His ways, to keep His commandments</u>, to hold fast to Him, and to serve Him with all your heart and with all your soul." So Joshua blessed them and sent them away, and they went to their tents.

Nehemiah 1:5
And I said: 'I pray, LORD God of heaven, O great and awesome God, You who keep Your covenant and mercy with those who <u>love You and observe Your commandments</u>."

Daniel 9:4
I prayed to the LORD my God, and made confession, and said, 'O Lord, great and awesome God, who keeps His covenant and mercy with those who <u>love Him, and with those who keep His commandments</u>.

John 14:15, 21
If you <u>love Me, keep My commandments</u>. He who has My commandments and keeps them, it is he who loves Me. And he who loves Me will be loved by My Father, and I will love him and manifest Myself to him.

John 15:9-10
As the Father loved Me, I also have loved you; abide in My love. <u>If you keep My commandments, you will abide in My love</u>, just as I have kept My Father's commandments and abide in His love.

1 John 2:3-6
And we can be sure that we know him if we obey his commandments. If someone claims, "I know God," but doesn't obey God's commandments, that person is a liar and is not living in the truth. But <u>those who obey God's word truly show how completely they love him</u>. That is how we know we are living in him. Those who say they live in God should love their lives as Jesus did. (NLT)

1 John 5:2-3
By this we know that we love the children of God, when we love God and obey his commandments. <u>For this is the love of God, that we keep his commandments</u>. And his commandments are not burdensome. (ESV)

2 John 5-6
And now I plead with you, lady, not as though I wrote a new commandment to you, but that which we have had from the

beginning: that we love one another. <u>This is love, that we walk according to His commandments</u>. This is the commandment, that as you have heard from the beginning, you should walk in it.

Loving God and obeying his commands are not opposites after all. They are actions that complement one another and are intertwined throughout Scripture. Perhaps this is to show that attention given to God's instructions best communicates our love for Him.

When we honor our father and mother, we show love to God and our parents.[1] When we remember the Sabbath, we express our love for God and the work He has given us to do.[2] When we are faithful in our marriage, we are loving our spouse and loving the One before whom we made our marriage vows.[3] When we refuse to take a bird from its mother's nest, we are respecting our Creator and His creation.[4] Love is built into all of God's instructions, however small and insignificant they may seem. In this way, the Torah helps us to love God.

Love is too important to be left to vague interpretations, nebulous acts or personal discretion. God knows this. Love must be able to be defined and recognized, or how else would we know how to love each other? This is why He gave us his commandments. A loving Father does not want us left in the dark on how he wants us to live and how to practically love those around us.

We need both love and the law. Love fulfills the law. The law fulfills love. Law tells us what to do. Love gives us the motivation to do it.

Conclusion

God's word is our instructions for righteous living. Through it we learn that sorcery is an abomination and that mercy is a virtue. It

---

[1] Ex. 20:12
[2] Ex. 20:8-11
[3] Ex. 20:14
[4] Deut. 22:6-7

teaches that covetousness is sinful and honoring our parents honors God. It is the Torah that rescues our faith from conceptual principles and relative truth. It is the Torah that shows us how to practically love God and love people.

Jesus and the apostles identify love as the grand summation of the Torah – the supreme interpretation of all of the Scriptures. When we obey Torah, we are loving our Father in Heaven. When we love God, we are living out the Torah through loving our neighbor. The Torah is written proof that the Heavenly Father loves all His children.

Do not think for one second that God is limiting you or restricting you by giving you directives. He is protecting you. He is communicating how to love others and how He wants to be loved. God's commandments are the "how-tos" of life, a concrete example of love.

> *"Let us not love in word or tongue, but in deed and in truth." – 1 John 3:18*

Whether we do it cheerfully or begrudgingly, there is a blessing found in keeping God's commands. The greatest blessing, however, is found when we do it in heartfelt devotion. We should not view obedience as something servile. It is, in the words of S. D. Gordon, "Intelligent loyalty to God, because it aims to learn his will and then to do it."[5]

If I were to say that it's just too hard to obey all of God's commandments, I would be admitting that my love for God is too small. Obedience to God only becomes burdensome when our heart is not in it. When love is the motivation, it is not an unrealistic goal to seek to live in obedience to all that God asks of us.

Those who preach that Christians don't need to obey God's laws are absolutely right. We don't have to obey. We get to. God doesn't need our devotion. He deserves it. It's not legalism. It's called love!

---

[5] S.D. Gordon, *Quiet Talks on Power* (Shippensburg: Destiny Image, 2003), 152

THREEFOLD DIVISION OF THE LAW

Truth #9 – *The threefold division of the Law is not a Biblical doctrine.*

Dividing the Torah into two or three parts has been widely practiced by scholars for centuries. Although not specifically outlined in Scripture, this doctrine espouses that the Torah consists of three classifications of laws: *moral, ceremonial* and *judicial.*

Moral laws are those precepts governing individual duty and personal ethics such as lying, stealing, murder and the like. They typically include loving God, loving our neighbor and following the Ten Commandments. *Ceremonial laws* are described as religious rites and modes of worship consisting of things such as offerings, sacrifices, temple requirements, food laws, festivals and ritual cleanliness. *Judicial laws* are civil statutes for the nation of Israel.

Those who hold to this doctrine maintain that (a) *moral laws* are eternally binding and irrevocable, (b) *ceremonial laws* can be changed upon circumstance, and (c) *judicial laws* are only applicable to Jews and the nation of Israel. Some even insist that only those moral commandments that are reiterated in the New Testament are binding for Christians.

You will find that this threefold division of the Torah is a popular way of grouping and categorizing the law. It dominates the interpretation of Yeshua's words in Matthew 5 among modern commentaries.

One commentary sums up the doctrine, stating that Jesus came to fulfill the moral laws but not the ceremonial laws.

> "The law of God is perfect, the ceremonial law was imperfect. The moral law being perfect, the impress of the Divine image, it cannot be done away."[1]

Another adds,

> "The words seem at first to imply that even the ceremonial law was to be binding in its full extent upon Christ's disciples. The usage of the time, however, confined the word to the moral laws of God."[2]

Another writes,

> "He came to abrogate and repeal it, blotting out and nailing to his cross the hand-writing of ordinances."[3]

A good many scholars conclude that what Jesus meant to say is that he came to uphold the moral laws but destroy ceremonial laws. Even John Wesley committed to this idea, implying that Jesus came only to fulfill moral laws.[4]

This viewpoint is sometimes presented in an attempt to try to explain why we no longer observe animal sacrifices, offerings and washings. What's the danger in this?

If in saying that the so-called ceremonial laws are imperfect we mean that the laws pertaining to priests and the temple would not have an application after the destruction of the temple, there is no alarm in this. Jesus is our Great High Priest. Our body is his temple. However, the cause for concern is when an interpretation calls for the discarding of Scripture, even if it is believed to be of God's doing.

---

[1] W. Kemp, *The Biblical Illustrator* (Electronic Database by Biblesoft, 2003), Matt. 5:17
[2] Ellicott, Matt. 5:19
[3] Joseph Benson, *Commentary on the Old and New Testaments* [Online]. Available: www.biblehub.com, Matt. 5:17
[4] John Wesley, *Wesley's Notes on the Bible* [Online]. Available: www.biblestudytools.com, Matt. 5:17

God is not at odds with himself. Can one part of God's word be perfect and another imperfect? Can one be eternal and another temporary? Hopefully we can agree that God is not double-minded.

David writes,

> "The entirety of your word is truth, and every one of your righteous judgments endures forever." - Psalm 119:160

And,

> "The Torah of the Lord is perfect." - Psalm 19:7

God's word is eternal and flawless.[5] It is not like the tax code – it does not change. If one part is unreliable, then all is unreliable. If one part can be superseded, then all can be superseded. The Torah is either all true or untrue. If we insist that God's judgments are irrelevant and obsolete, then so must the Lawgiver himself.

In considering the doctrine of the threefold division of the Torah, a few red flags stick out to me.

(1) *Biblical Silence.* The Bible is completely silent when it comes to this doctrine. The classification of moral, ceremonial and judicial laws is not specifically outlined or mentioned in Scripture.

The two or threefold division of the law is a way in which scholars seek to digest the Torah, understand our obligation to it and explain why certain laws are seemingly irrelevant. There is nothing disturbing about this in my opinion. Cataloguing and labeling parts of Scripture can be useful and helpful. Not every teaching has to be expounded upon in the Bible in order to be factual. The fact that certain groupings are not specifically outlined in the Bible does not make them automatically false.

They should not, however, be taught as if they are Scripturally true. Often this concept is. The idea of a threefold division of the Torah is

---

[5] Prov. 30:5, Ps. 100:5, 117:2, 146:6, 119:116

a doctrine of man through and through. It shouldn't carry the same weight as clear Biblical doctrines.

(2) *Singularity.* There are multiple places in the Bible where all the commandments of God are referred to as one singular instruction. They are referenced as *the commandment* by Moses (Deut. 6:1), Joshua (Josh. 22:5), David (Ps. 19:8) and the Torah-Giver Himself (Ex. 24:12). Paul echoes this same sentiment in Romans.

> *"I was alive once without the law, but when the commandment came, sin revived and I died. And the commandment, which was to bring life, I found to bring death. For sin, taking occasion by the commandment, deceived me, and by it killed me." – Romans 7:9-11*

Separating the Torah into categories and sections is not how the writers of Scripture chose to characterize the law. This communicates to us that the commandments of the Torah are to be understood as a unified whole, not as a divided revelation.

(3) *Subjective Morality.* Because there are no Biblical parameters for these groupings, any person can lump whatever commandment they like into whatever pile is most convenient to their liking. For example, if I like lobster, I can consider the Bible's dietary laws to be ceremonial and non-binding. If I loathe the Sabbath, I can simply label it a Jewish law that is not applicable to me. If I want to write-off Biblical holy days, I can regard them as the feasts of Israel and make them judicial. If I want to excuse idolatry and covetousness, I just yank them from a moral classification and tag them as ceremonial. It's a clever and convenient way of getting around moral absolutes. One man's moral law is another man's ceremonial. Who's to judge?

By pitting so-called ceremonial laws against moral laws, a person (or organization) is allowed to pick and choose which laws they accept or reject through re-grouping. If something is commonly accepted as good or is obviously sinful, it goes into the moral/immoral classification. But if something seems outdated or is culturally archaic, it gets the ceremonial/judicial tag and can be rendered obsolete.

What's the criterion for a law being moral, judicial or ceremonial? Who gets to determine it? By what standard is this determination made? Can a law change its classification? Are these lines movable based on cultural standards or popular opinions? Can a statute be moral for one culture and ceremonial for another? Can a command be moral for one age and judicial for another? Can a law be moral, ceremonial and/or judicial at the same time? Since Scripture is silent on this topic, who's the final authority?

By moving certain commandments in and out of the moral column, a person can theologically justify immoral behavior by discounting certain precepts. The result is a subjective morality that makes God's truth relative and a matter of personal interpretation. It is a shrewd way of getting around what Jesus and the Torah actually teach. A study of church history shows these lines have moved from culture to culture, from one generation to another to our detriment.

(4) *Post-Dated Interpretation.* Suppose I claimed to excavate a hand-written letter from Socrates that read: "I found the answer to life's deepest question by googling it." For obvious reasons this letter would be a fraud. No one on the planet would or should believe me.

Or suppose I resurrected a sermon of John the Baptist instructing his audience to turn to Colossians chapter 3? Epic fail. Not only had Paul's letter not yet been written in John's time but also dividing the New Testament into chapter and verse did not first occur until the thirteenth century.[6]

In the same way, the teaching of the threefold division of the Torah came well after the time of Christ and the completion of the canon. How could Jesus be referencing a concept that had not yet been taught or even conceived?

One might suppose that perhaps Jesus was alluding to a doctrine that was not yet revealed. This may be, but this approach to Scripture is

---

[6] Stephen Langton, cardinal and archbishop of Canterbury, is credited with dividing the Bible into the chapter arrangements used today.

anachronistic. You should be leery of post-dated Biblical interpretations. They hold the door open for anyone to dream up any sort of doctrine and justify it by attaching it to an un-contextualized Bible verse. This approach to Scripture has produced the most damaging and reckless doctrines among us.

The truth is that Jesus makes no mention of moral, ceremonial or judicial classifications anywhere in the Gospels. He could not be discounting ceremonial and judicial laws in Matthew 5, because these categories are not found in the Torah, the Prophets or anywhere in Scripture. They had not yet even been conceived.

(5) *Doctrinal Inconsistency*. This doctrine maintains that Jesus taught and practiced only the moral laws, because unenlightened Jews were incapable of separating the moral from the ceremonial. The question I have is: Who is the final authority on what is ceremonial and what is moral? The Bible? The church? The Holy Spirit?

The Bible is silent on this teaching, and there is no consensus about what the Holy Spirit is saying. Any conclusion regarding Torah classification is speculative at best. The only way to reconcile a difference of opinion when it comes to church doctrines and the voice of the Holy Spirit is to allow Scripture to be our final arbiter. In this case, the threefold doctrine is inconsistent with its own doctrine concerning Scripture.

Take Sabbath, for example. The commandment to honor the Sabbath is one of the Ten Commandments. According to the tenants of this doctrine, the Ten Commandments are moral laws – irrevocable, immutable and eternally binding. This means that the seventh-day Sabbath is an absolute, permanent moral law according to their definition. If they were consistent, those who hold to the threefold division of the law should be the strictest Sabbath keepers among us. Since they believe the so-called moral laws are eternally binding, they should be the strongest advocates for honoring a seventh day Sabbath. They should cheer the Jewish community for holding to a strict definition of *Shabbat* and encourage Protestants and Catholics to follow suit.

It comes as no surprise that most don't. Why not?

Herein lies the contradiction. While classifying the Sabbath as an irrevocable moral law, in practice it is treated as a ceremonial or judicial law. This position obviously allows for exceptions to its own rule. I have no problem with this, but if it is acceptable to break the rule, it is safe to conclude that the rule is not divine. It must be man-made.

It doesn't take long to realize that neatly configuring the Torah into rigid categories is an impossible task, making the conclusions drawn from this doctrine largely presumptuous. Moreover, this view is inconsistent with the practice of Yeshua, as Jesus didn't treat the Torah in such ways. He followed all of his Fathers instructions, including those deemed ceremonial and judicial. He wore tassels (*tzitzit*) and observed the feasts. He followed the dietary laws and honored the seventh-day Sabbath. The apostles and Paul followed suit.

Does this make Sabbath moral or ceremonial? Are Biblical holidays ceremonial or judicial? If we follow the conventional thinking, no one knows, and everyone's opinion is right. Since Yeshua is our ultimate example, it would solve a lot of our doctrinal disputes if we just sought to do and live as he did.

Whether moral, ceremonial or judicial, the conclusion of the matter is that all of God's word is moral, even the commandments governing the body, the temple, the calendar and the nation of Israel. We have the tendency to infuse genetically modified teachings within our interpretation of the Bible and, in this case, the Sermon on the Mount. But just as there is no mention of Torah replacement in Matthew 5, there is no mention of a threefold division of the Torah anywhere else in Scripture.

(6) *Prophetic Application.* If the civil and ceremonial laws truly expired, we should <u>not</u> find them referenced in unfulfilled prophecies. In other words, they wouldn't pop up in any future events spoken of in the Bible. Do they?

Isaiah,

> *"'For as the new heavens and the new earth which I will make shall remain before Me,' says the LORD, 'So shall your descendants and your name remain. And it shall come to pass that from one New Moon to another, and from one Sabbath to another, all flesh shall come to worship before Me,' says the LORD." – Isaiah 66:22-23*

Ezekiel,

> *"David My servant shall be king over them, and they shall all have one shepherd; they shall also walk in My judgments and observe My statutes, and do them." – Ezekiel 37:24*

Zechariah,

> *"Then it will come about that any who are left of all the nations that went against Jerusalem will go up from year to year to worship the King, the LORD of hosts, and to celebrate the Feast of Booths...Every cooking pot in Jerusalem and in Judah will be holy to the LORD of hosts; and all who sacrifice will come and take of them and boil in them." – Zechariah 14:16, 21 NASB*

John,

> *"Blessed are those who do His commandments, that they may have the right to the tree of life, and may enter through the gates into the city." – Revelation 22:14*

In these prophecies we find our future spiritual descendants offering burnt offerings, honoring dietary boundaries, keeping God's commandments, and celebrating Sabbath and the Feast of Tabernacles. This is problematic for those who classify these observances as ceremonial and/or civil laws.

The counter argument is that these laws will be reinstated in the millennial age. Unfortunately, however, this negates the finished work of Christ. If Jesus truly abolished these laws, they cannot be reinstated, for his work on the cross is complete.

We can conclude that, under their own definition, Sabbath and the feasts cannot be ceremonial or judicial. They are and will be viable and relevant. According to this classification, they must be considered and treated as moral laws for us, especially since there is still yet a future application of them.

(7) *Questionable Origins.* The idea of a divided Torah is not a new one. John Calvin and his successors allude to a division of the law.[7] It is referenced in various church creeds and confessions of the sixteenth and seventeenth centuries.[8] Thomas Aquinas and his predecessor John of La Rochelle spoke of a division in their writings,[9] as well as Augustine.[10] It can even be traced as far back as Tertullian, Origen, Clement of Alexandria and Justin Martyr.[11] In fact, this doctrine is so well regarded in traditional orthodoxy that it has become one of the foundational pillars of reformed theology.

In an article published by *Reformation Today* entitled, "The Threefold Division Of The Law," Jonathan Bayes claims to have identified a second century Gnostic named Ptolemaeus as the originator of this doctrine.[12] In this article, he quotes Johannes

---

[7] John Calvin, *Institutes of the Christian Religion,* 2.7 (Philadelphia: Presbyterian Board of Publication, 1813), 408-430; Francis Turretin, *Institutes of Elenctic Theology* (Phillipsburg: P&R Publishing, 1997), Topic 11

[8] *Belgic Confession,* Article 25, 156 C.E.; Church Of England, *The Thirty-Nine Articles,* Article 7, 1563 C.E.; *Westminster Confession of Faith,* 1646 C.E.; *London Baptist Confession,* 1677 C.E.

[9] Thomas Aquinas, *Summa Theologiae* (Cincinnati: Benzinger Bros, 1947), Vol. 1, Questions 99-105, 1381-1474; John of La Rochelle, *Tractatus de Divisione Potentiarum Animae,* 1233, Public domain

[10] Augustine, *On the Spirit and the Letter,* 412 AD [Online]. Available: www.newadvent.org/fathers/1502.htm; Augustine's Reply to Faustus the Manichaean *Contra Faustum,* Book VI [Online]. Available: http://www.documentacatholicaomnia.eu/03d/0354-0430,_Augustinus,_Contra_Faustum_Manichaeum_%5BSchaff%5D_EN.pdf

[11] O.M.T. O'Donovan, *Towards An Interpretation Of Biblical Ethics,* (Tyndale Bulletin 27, 1976), 59; Christopher Wright, *Walking in the Ways of the Lord* (Downers Grove: InterVarsity, 1995), 93; Philip Ross, *From the Finger of God* (Scotland: Christian Focus Pub, 2010), 20-25

[12] Jonathan Bayes, "The Threefold Division of the Law," *Reformation Today,* Issue 177

Quasten who is explaining Ptolemaeus' original thoughts. Speaking of the Torah, Ptolemaeus is said to have written:

> "The first section contains the pure law, untainted by evil, in other words the ten commandments. This is the section of the Mosaic law which Jesus came to fulfill rather than suspend. The second section is the law adulterated with injustice, namely that of retaliation, which was suspended by the Saviour. The third is the ceremonial law which the Saviour spiritualized."

There are some reservations about the credibility of this article, but I only mention it since it's in circulation.

For argument's sake, let's suppose that Bayes is onto something. Let's assume that his findings are accurate, and that Ptolemaeus was a second century Gnostic who initially classified the Ten Commandments as pure laws and considered the rest of the Torah "suspended", "spiritualized" and "adulterated with injustice." Should we be in agreement with a purported heretic who embraced Gnostic beliefs? Is it wise to be obligated to accept an extra-Biblical teaching from heretical writings and allow it to shape the way we interpret the words of Christ? On what basis do our commentaries lean toward this position? Would the apostles approve of this teaching? According to Bayes and Quasten, we are adhering to a transforming, foundational doctrine that originated from a known enemy of the gospel.

I do not take issue with Bayes or with this Ptolemaeus gentleman, if he even existed. To me, the origin of this doctrine is not the most disturbing part. If the truth is true, the source shouldn't matter. It is still true.

What concerns me is that many proponents of this doctrine are eager to discard Gnostic doctrines as heretical but unwilling to denounce this doctrine upon discovering that it may have been born of Gnostic thought. We should not be forced to judge the merits of a hypothesis that is completely foreign to Scripture.

In this same article, Bayes quotes John Metcalfe, who writes,

"What! Rend asunder the one law of God into three mutilated parts, inventing the names moral, judicial, and ceremonial, just so that you can discard two and retain one? It is *the law*, integrally, the whole of it, all that Moses commanded, and none of it can be separated from any other part of it."[13]

This might be the best quote of the whole article. Even though Bayes is admittedly an advocate for the threefold division of the law, in acknowledging that the origins of this doctrine might have originated from the pen of a heretic, he undermines the very doctrine he purports.

Conclusion

For all of these reasons, the doctrine of the threefold division of the law lacks viable credibility. In claiming that Jesus is speaking about *these laws* but not *those laws,* it creates a moral free-for-all, inviting a private interpretation into the text. For those who wish to explain away some of the more convicting words of Christ, it gives them an escape hatch, even when there is no Scriptural basis for such a distinction.

This position might be better stated: *Jesus came not to destroy but to divide*, because it separates truth into ambiguous sections and discards any part deemed ceremonial or judicial. In slicing, dicing and isolating those parts unwanted, we run the risk of discarding something quite valuable. When we go down this road, Biblical commands become easier to divide, conquer and discount, ultimately compromising the authority of Scripture.

One rendering for the word destroy in Matthew 5:17 is *disunite,* which is something this doctrine seems to accomplish. This is precisely what Christ pronounced he came *not* to do.

In all this, the threefold division of the Torah loses much of its luster. In my opinion, it is unbiblical, indefinable, divisive,

---

[13] Bayes quoting John Metcalfe, *Deliverance From The Law: The Westminster Confession Exploded*, 5,8

presumptuous and inconceivable. For these reasons, I find no textual support for it.

Spirit Of The Law

Truth #10 – *Pursuing the Torah is not contrary to the will of God.*

There is yet another interpretation of Matthew 5:17 that states Jesus fulfilled the Torah spiritually, rescuing it from outward observation. It holds that the spirit of the law is imprisoned in the letter of the law and that Jesus came to set it free. It teaches that the principle of a commandment carries more weight than the commandment itself. When we understand the spirit of the law, we are then released from obeying the letter of the law. No longer are we obligated to obey the Torah *physically,* because Jesus fulfilled it *spiritually.*

This conclusion sounds reasonable in theory. But when we sink our teeth into it, we come to the realization that identifying the spirit of the law is an inexact science. Determining why God gave a certain injunction is often quite subjective. To make this claim, it requires a certain amount of assumption, presumption and extra-Biblical revelation. To presume to know why God gave a command is anyone's guess. Anyone who does runs the risk of misinterpreting the will of God.

For example, I have heard many theories over the years as to why God gave dietary restrictions – Jewish ignorance, unsanitary food preparations, unsatisfactory ancient refrigeration methods, to name a few. But an explanation as to why certain animals are not to be consumed is not specifically given in Scripture. We could speculate, but we are merely given a list of inedible flesh.

Theologians have developed complicated doctrines that assign reasons as to why particular commands are given. When they think that those reasons are no longer relevant, it is argued that the commandment should be discounted altogether.

The problem with this is that any attempt on our part to determine their purpose is speculation. We don't know the reasons why God has instructed us about certain things. To assume to understand why God has given us certain laws quite often leads to disregarding them when the purpose, in our minds, is no longer valid.

Spirit of the Law

I have found that the major drawback to this interpretation of Matthew 5 is that it over-spiritualizes the text while under-cutting our obligation to it. By generalizing the definitions of *spiritual* and *spirit of the law,* it makes the Torah subject to private interpretation, reducing it to principled suggestions and insubstantial behavior. This school of thought permits a person to be more committed to a hidden principle found within the commandment than the actual commandment itself. The result is always some form of conceptual compliance that falls short of simple obedience.

Let's use the Sabbath again as an example. You've heard it taught that there is no need to observe the physical seventh-day Sabbath as long as you honor the principle of rest? This argument follows that if a person goes to church and takes a nap on Sunday, is mindful to have some downtime during the week and/or lives from a place of restful peace, they are obeying the spirit of the command. This seems acceptable until you realize this is not at all what Scripture instructs.

> *"The seventh day is the Sabbath of the Lord. In it you shall do no work." - Exodus 20:10*

The Sabbath is not a principle. It is a day. It is not Sunday or any day of our choosing but the seventh day of the week. If the Sabbath were merely a general principle of rest, wouldn't God state it as such? Is he incapable of making himself clear? If God's word doesn't say what it means and mean what it says, then it really doesn't say or mean anything to anyone.

What if we interpreted other parts of the Bible using this method? Take water baptism, for example. One could say, "The letter says to be immersed in water, but the spirit of the command is to be cleansed from sin. Can physical water really take away sin? A spiritual bath seems more in line with the spirit of this command. Besides, metaphorical immersion is more convenient. We don't have to go through the trouble of finding a stream or wasting water by filling up a large baptismal. We could be economical with our time while being environmentally friendly." Water baptism would then be reduced to a mental exercise or a figurative experience instead of a simple, physical, spiritual act of discipleship.

Or what if we spiritualized communion? We could come together eating imaginary bread and passing around pretend wine. Wouldn't that be jolly? Think of all the hassle and money we could save on stale grape juice and melt-in-your-mouth crackers!

This is silly, which is my point. Communion is not ethereal. Water baptism is not an abstract feeling, and Sabbath is not a general principle of rest. They are spiritual in their physical observation. They do not become more spiritual by ceasing to physically observe them.

While they do have deeper spiritual connections, we must be careful not to divorce the spiritual from the physical, for they are artfully interwoven. We deceive ourselves if we think we can spiritually obey God's commands while physically breaking them. The spiritual benefit can only be gained by exercising them.

One reformed scholar encapsulates this position.

> "Christianity is the spirituality of the Mosaism liberated from the chrysalis of formal commands, and set free to show itself as the beautiful winged thing that it is. God's new is always his glorified old."[1]

Another writes,

---

[1] Spence and Exell, *Pulpit Commentary*, Book 33, Vol. I, 224

> "Christ certainly did come to destroy the law and the prophets — the outside of them. He knew perfectly well, if He had foresight, that they would be, as they have largely been, swept away; but He said, 'That which these externalities include — the kernel, the heart — I came to fulfill.'"[2]

Yet another,

> "The law was essentially spiritual; but on account of the hardness of the Jewish heart, it was fenced in under the Old Testament by outward ordinances, which, for the time, prevented the full manifestation of its depth. Hence, in order to 'fulfill it,' Christ broke through the barriers, and thus unfolded its true glory; while the Pharisees contravened the spirit of the law by the observance of its letter, which in reality destroyed, instead of fulfilling it."[3]

If outward ordinances are the oral laws and spiritless rule keeping practiced by the Pharisees that destroy the true glory of the Torah, I concur. But if this opinion is suggesting that it is the outward observance of God's commands that is responsible for destroying the Torah, this is certainly a strange take.

Here the villains are externalities, formal commands and outward expressions of the Torah when the real enemy should be lawless, loveless *dis*obedience. The attempt is commendable, but the revile is misdirected.

Obedience to God is never contrary to the will of God. A believer's heartfelt, outward response to God's word is not in opposition to the spirit of the law. It is the spirit of the law! In determining the heart of a commandment, we must resist internalizing it to death. It is written to govern our outward behavior.

---

[2] H.W. Beecher, *The Biblical Illustrator* (Electronic Database: Biblesoft, 2002), Matt. 5:17

[3] Otto Von Gerlach, quoted by Johann Peter Lange, *Lange's Commentary on the Holy Scripture*, Vol. 6 (Grand Rapids: Zondervan, 1960), Matt. 5:17

No doubt Jesus foresaw the sweeping away of useless customs, but the sweeping away of God-given commandments must grieve his heart. Perhaps this is why he emphasized that he came not to abolish the Torah and the Prophets. This is His reminder that if any of God's commands have been swept away or destroyed, we cannot assume it is of Christ's doing.

Conclusion

We can all agree that Jesus kept the Torah internally and externally, but how is it being like Christ to only keep the Torah internally? If so, no Christian's actions would ever resemble Christ.

In an attempt to determine the heart of the commandment, this interpretation kills the text through over-spiritualization. It removes the actual practice of the commandment. It assumes to know the spirit behind the command and replaces it with a principle. Thus, it eliminates any usefulness of the precept. The unintended consequence is the discouragement of simple obedience to the Scriptures.

But the spirit of the commandment is heartfelt obedience through the empowering Spirit of God. To conclude that we no longer need to put into practice any commandment once we gain some sort of insider knowledge as to why God gave the command is a foolish presumption. This was the error of the Gnostics.

Jesus honored the Sabbath. He obeyed the dietary laws. He wore tassels and observed Passover. Does your theology permit you to walk as Jesus walked and live as Jesus lived?

MATTHEW 11:11-14, LUKE 16:14-17

Truth #11: *Jesus and John are a continuation of the Law and the Prophets.*

In Matthew 11, Jesus is lauding the imprisoned John the Baptist, speaking of his prophetic place in history. Yeshua proclaims,

> *"Assuredly, I say to you, among those born of women there is not one risen greater than John the Baptist; but he who is least in the kingdom of heaven is greater than he. And from the days of John the Baptist until (heos) now the kingdom of heaven suffers violence, and the violent take it by force. <u>For all the prophets and the law prophesied until (heos) John</u>. And if you are willing to receive it, he is Elijah who is to come." - Matthew 11:11-14*

A similar statement is found in Luke 16. After hearing the parable of the unjust steward, the Pharisees ridicule Yeshua. He responds,

> *"You are those who justify yourselves before men, but God knows your hearts. For what is highly esteemed among men is an abomination in the sight of God. <u>The law and the prophets were until (heōs) John</u>. Since that time the kingdom of God has been preached, and everyone is pressing into it. And it is easier for heaven and earth to pass away than for one tittle of the law to fail." - Luke 16:14-17*

The Greek word *heōs* is translated *until* in both of these passages.[1] There's little discrepancy that *heōs* means *till* or *until now* and is properly translated.[2] Etymologically, however, *heōs* supports those things that come before it. It more accurately marks a point in time, identifying those things that have previously come.

---

[1] *Strong's* #G2193 ἕως
[2] Louw, *Greek-English Lexicon, heos*; *Thayer's*, "until"

A conclusion is drawn that the law and the Prophets were binding until the arrival of John. At which point the age of the kingdom arrived, replacing the authority of the Torah. Is it true that the Law of Moses ended with John the Baptist?

I understand why this position is taken, but let's consider a few things.

After stating that "The law and the prophets were until John," (v.16) Jesus affirms the permanency of the Torah.

> *"And it is easier for heaven and earth to pass away than for one tittle of the law to fail." - Luke 16:17*

If Yeshua meant that the Hebrew Scriptures ended with John, he contradicted himself in his next breath. Only by isolating verse 16 from verse 17 can the above conclusion be drawn. According to Jesus, even the smallest hook in the Hebrew alphabet is more eternal than heaven and earth.

Notice that *were* has been added to verse 16 in translation. It is common for translators to insert a supplemental word in English to assist with the flow of a sentence. This is helpful to readers. King James placed inserted words in italics to indicate that these words do not appear in the original manuscript. In this case, *were* provides a necessary verb in the English rendering.

Without the addition, however, it reads:

> *"The law and the prophets until John." – Luke 16:16*

Other renderings of Matthew 11:13 support this reading.

> *"For the prophets and the law have prophesied unto John." (DBY)*

> *"For before John came, all the prophets and the law of Moses looked forward to this present time." (NLT)*

> *"For the prophets and the law prophesied with a view to the time of John." (NMB)*

Read this way, Yeshua's words become less an action against the Torah and more a declaration of endorsement. Instead of belittling the Hebrew Scriptures, Yeshua is elevating John and the preaching of the kingdom to a prophetic, Scriptural level. Essentially, the prophets looked forward to John and prophesied the coming of the kingdom. In this way, the message of repentance is to be seen as an extension and fulfillment of what had already been established in the Hebrew Scriptures.

We find something similar in John 1:17.

> *"For the law was given through Moses, but grace and truth came through Jesus Christ."*

But is also added by translators. This addition leads to the impression that John is making a statement of contrast. Without the *but* addition, however, we can understand it as a statement of distinction. Moses gave the Torah. Yeshua brought grace and truth. Whereas Moses codified the Law, Jesus provided grace and truth to lawbreakers through his atonement and outlined the consequences of breaking God's law.

Noted scholar David Stern writes,

> "Up to the time of Yochanan the Immerser there were the *Torah* and the Prophets giving their prophetic and predictive witness to the coming of the Kingdom of God. The verse does not mean that the authority of the *Torah* and the Prophets came to an end when Yochanan appeared (an error even the notable Hebrew Christian thinker David Baron made). But since then, in addition to their witness (v. 31, Yn 5:46, Ro 3:21), the Good News of the Kingdom of God, which is now 'near,' has been proclaimed directly, first from

Yochanan (Mt 3:1-2) and now by Yeshua (Mt 4:17, Mk 1:15), with the result that everyone is pushing to get in."[3]

According to Stern, the authority of the Hebrew Scriptures did not conclude with John. Instead, Yeshua and John are now members of that group and openly proclaimed what had been spoken of long ago. The unfolding revelation of the kingdom of God started in the Torah, continued through the Prophets and culminated with Christ.

Up until John, the law and the prophets were the only reliable source of God's revelation prophesying the coming of the Messiah King. In proclaiming the kingdom of God, John did not take away from but added to the testimony of the Hebrew Scriptures.

John the Baptist was like a sprinter handing off a baton. He ran ahead of Yeshua and prepared the way for his kingdom to reign. But John was neither the leader nor the anchor of this race. The role of the other runners cannot be diminished. Just as Jesus does not silence the voice of John, John does not silence the voice of the Torah and the Prophets. Each has a place in bringing about the revelation of God and bearing witness to the King.

Yeshua's point is that the prophecies that had been recorded concerning the coming of the Anointed One were taking place right before their eyes. They were living in prophetic times. The Torah was established in Moses' generation. The Prophets came after, and with the preaching of John and Jesus the gospel of the kingdom was advancing.

Peter echoes this sentiment.

> "All the prophets who have spoken, from Samuel and his successors onward, also announced these days." - Acts 3:24

If the Torah had indeed failed with John the Baptist, John himself would have certainly proclaimed and practiced this fundamental

---

[3] David Stern, *Jewish New Testament Commentary*, (Clarksville: Jewish New Testament Publications, 1979), 134

doctrine. But there is no Biblical indication of this. Instead, we read of John defending the standards of the Torah at the cost of imprisonment and martyrdom.[4]

If John had ended the law and Prophets, what Scriptures would be left for Jesus to fulfill? The prophecies proving Jesus is the Messiah would have expired before His ministry ever began!

This school of thought stands in contradiction to the notion that Jesus ended the law through fulfillment. Who is responsible for ending it – Jesus or John? And when exactly did it cease?

Bradford Scott writes,

> "Until the time of *Yochanan*, the word of *'Elohiym* was taught when they gathered together every Sabbath. However, with the scattering of His people throughout the nations, the word of *'Elohiym* was now going to be preached by the subsequent disciples of *Yeshua'* to the four corners of the earth. It is not the words of YHVH that have changed, but rather the method by which His Word was to be taught to the scattered tribes of Israel."[5]

According to Scott, the method by which the gospel would spread changed, not the message itself. From this point on, the gospel of the kingdom would advance beyond Israel to the ends of the earth.

Conclusion

Yeshua states that both the law and the prophets prophesy, which is to say that the Torah, the Prophets and John all prepared the way of the Lord. They all point us toward a fuller revelation of God's redemptive plan. This plan culminates in the life and resurrection of Jesus Christ. Just as John was a prophetic sign of the Messiah, so now are we.

---

[4] Matt. 14:3-12
[5] Brad Scott, *A Concordance Of Law in the New Covenant Scriptures* (Vernal: The WildBranch Ministry, 2019), 23

You and I have now been handed the baton. We anchor the race that John the Baptist ran and that Yeshua won. We are the last and the least in the kingdom. We are the eleventh hour workers. We are commissioned to take hold of the kingdom and proclaim the gospel to those pressing into it.

Section II

Diet & Gentiles

MARK 7:1-16

Truth #12 – *The Pharisees disputed with Jesus about bread, not unclean meat.*

A cursory reading of Mark 7 might lead to the impression that Jesus cancelled the dietary restrictions of Leviticus 11 and Deuteronomy 14. In fact you'd be hard-pressed to find a commentary that doesn't draw such a conclusion. But did Jesus intend to eliminate all food guidelines and Biblical meat distinctions here? Let's examine.

> *"Then the Pharisees and some of the scribes came together to Him, having come from Jerusalem. Now when they saw some of His disciples eat bread with defiled, that is, with unwashed hands, they found fault. For the Pharisees and all the Jews do not eat unless they wash their hands in a special way, holding the tradition of the elders. When they come from the marketplace, they do not eat unless they wash. And there are many other things which they have received and hold, like the washing of cups, pitchers, copper vessels, and couches. Then the Pharisees and scribes asked Him, 'Why do your disciples not walk according to the tradition of the elders, but eat bread with unwashed hands?'"* – Mark 7:1-5

The scribes and Pharisees observed that some of Yeshua's disciples were not washing their hands before eating bread, and this bothered them. Why did it matter? It was a tradition of the elders to wash hands and utensils in a ceremonial manner before eating. Some sages taught that while in the marketplace one might touch unclean things. Therefore, lifting hands in prayer and washing up to the wrist before eating was necessary to remove any impurity.

Ritual purity was important to Judean Pharisees and to those living in close proximity to the Temple. Some presumed that if a person were to eat perfectly acceptable food with unwashed hands it could render them and the food ceremonially unclean, preventing them from serving or worshipping in the temple. This practice of ritual washing, perhaps connected to the *n'tilat yadayim* prayer, is an oral tradition that is still observed in Orthodox Judaism today.[1]

Washing hands and utensils before a meal might not be a bad idea, but sanitation was not what the Pharisees had in mind. This custom was practiced for religious purposes, not hygienic. These Pharisees were concerned that a person might be participating in idolatry if they ate food that had been spiritually contaminated or had come into contact with an idol. As a remedy, they taught that a person must wash their hands in a specific ceremonial manner to ensure that the perfectly acceptable food their hands touched (in this case, bread) remained spiritually undefiled and fit for consumption.

Though not a Biblical commandment, some rabbis taught this hand-cleansing practice as if it were a law and regarded eating with unwashed hands as grounds for excommunication.[2] In fact, it was so firmly entrenched in their doctrine that one rabbi even likened eating food with defiled hands to entertaining a prostitute.[3]

I once observed a man practicing something similar a few years ago while in Jerusalem. He poured running water over each hand several times while reciting a blessing before entering the Wailing Wall area. In Yeshua's time the Jews had even developed a special two-handed bowl for the express purpose of pouring clean water over each hand individually. Similar cups made of silver are sometimes used today.

In this incident, the Pharisees were not accusing the disciples of eating forbidden meats. They were inquiring as to why the disciples didn't stick to the hand-washing tradition. To relate it to our culture, one might understand it as the disciples didn't pause to say grace before their meal. This observation caused the Pharisees to question what Yeshua was teaching his disciples.

---

[1] Stern, *Jewish New Testament Commentary*, 92
[2] Ronald Eisenberg, *What the Rabbis Said* (Pittsburgh: Praeger, 2010), 76
[3] *Gemara*, Naschim, Sotah 4b

Mark 7:1-16

Command over Tradition

Notice that it was not all of his disciples who didn't wash and not even Yeshua Himself. Yet Jesus was quick to rush to their defense.

> *"He said to them, 'Well did Isaiah prophesy of you hypocrites, as it is written: "This people honors Me with their lips, but their heart is far from Me. And in vain they worship Me, teaching as doctrines the commandments of men." For laying aside the commandment of God, you hold the tradition of men-- the washing of pitchers and cups, and many other such things you do.'"* - Mark 7:6-8

This is similar to the Pharisee's criticism of the disciples plucking the heads of grain as they walked through the grain fields on Sabbath.[4] In both cases, Yeshua defends the actions of his disciples. They were eating bread. They were not dishonoring the Torah's dietary standards just as they were not breaking the Sabbath by plucking the grain. It was the customs of the Pharisees that were being disregarded, and this offended the Pharisees.

Yeshua's criticism of the scribes and Pharisees is noteworthy. He characterizes them as (1) hypocrites, (2) who honor God with words but dishonor Him with their hearts, and (3) teach the traditions of man as if they were the commandments of God. The Pharisees were not overly zealous, legalistic lovers of the law as they are so often mischaracterized today. The popular line that they were strict adherents to the letter of the law but violators of the spirit of the law doesn't fit here or with other gospel accounts.

The Pharisees sought to proselytize their interpretation of the law, a version that added various external rites and rituals to the Torah. In most cases, these additions bore more weight than the written Torah itself, essentially altering the revelation of God.

Daniel Boyarin writes,

---

[4] Matt. 12:1-8, Mark 2:23-28, Luke 6:1-5

> "The Pharisees were a kind of reform movement within the Jewish people that was centered on Jerusalem and Judea. The Pharisees sought to convert other Jews to their way of thinking about God and the Torah, a way of thinking that incorporated seeming changes in the written Torah's practices that were mandated by what the Pharisees called 'the tradition of the Elders.'"[5]

These traditions are generally referred to as oral laws.

The Pharisees wanted to be perceived as strict in their adherence to God, but they did *not* strictly follow God's commandments. According to Jesus, they gave equal authority to the temporal traditions of man as to the eternal commandments of God. They were hypocritical Torah breakers who taught one thing but did another. This is Yeshua's consistent criticism of the Pharisees throughout the Gospels.

This is evident in Matthew 23:23 when Jesus says,

> *"Woe to you, scribes and Pharisees, hypocrites! For you pay tithe of mint and anise and cumin, and have neglected the weightier matters of the law: justice and mercy and faith. These you ought to have done, without leaving the others undone." – Matthew 23:23*

Yeshua didn't scold the Pharisees for their scrupulous calculation of the tithe, as they even tithed on volunteer plants that sprang up from the ground. He actually pays them a compliment for giving careful attention to the smaller matter of tithing. It was their blatant disregard for the weightier matters of the Torah that warranted a rebuke and made their behavior hypocritical.

Jesus faults the Pharisees for "laying aside the commandment of God" and "rejecting" God's law. They were guilty of disregarding God's commands for the sake of their customs.

Yeshua's issue was not with their precise observance of Torah. It was the exact opposite. These men had drifted so far into unbiblical

---

[5] Boyarin, *The Jewish Gospels* (New York: The New Press, 2012), Ch. 3

practices that they had taken on a yoke of rabbinic customs that no man could bear. In the process, they had overlooked the clear commandments of Scripture. They were breaking both the letter *and* the spirit of the law. They preferred their self-made laws to God-given law. In short, they had chosen tradition over Torah.

One school of thought on this passage maintains, "Christ asserts that *Levitical* uncleanness, such as eating with unwashed hands, is of small importance compared with *moral* uncleanness."[6] If *Levitical* implies man-made rules imposed by some Levite priests, I could agree with this assessment. But if Levitical infers laws governing cleanliness as outlined in the book of Leviticus, this viewpoint falls flat since there is nothing Biblical about what the Pharisees were advocating. There is no commandment in the book of Leviticus or anywhere else that requires one to wash their hands before eating bread.

The widely held belief that spiritually defiled hands could defile food is plainly absent from Scripture. The Pharisees had drifted off into self-made rules and were blindly following oral precepts to the neglect of Biblical mandates. It is possible that we have incorrectly identified the players here. The clash here is not between the Levitical and the moral. It's between tradition and command.

Tradition vs. Traditionalism

Tradition is not inherently bad. Jesus was not opposed to tradition, as he himself lived with tradition. The issue was *their* tradition, for their tradition had devolved into traditionalism. Jaroslav Pelikan writes, "Tradition is the living faith of those now dead; traditionalism is the dead faith of those now living."[7]

According to Jesus, tradition crosses the line when it contradicts Scripture and negates clear Biblical obligations. These men treated

---

[6] Archibald Thomas Robertson quoting Dr. Martin Vincent, *Word Pictures in the New Testament*, Vol. I (Grand Rapids: Baker Books, 1930), 324

[7] Jaroslav Pelikan, *The Vindication of Tradition* (New Haven: Yale University Press, 1984), 84

their tradition like it was the written word of God, and it was their blind loyalty to these traditions that prevented them from obeying God. This angered Yeshua.

As the spiritual leaders of Israel, it was the responsibility of the scribes and spiritual leaders to teach the people the oracles of God. Since no commoner possessed a copy of the Scriptures, the people relied on rabbis and teachers for their knowledge of God's word. By not making a distinction between a man-made doctrine and a God-given commandment, they were guilty of adding to Scripture and misrepresenting God.

Equating tradition to Torah is not just irresponsible; it is spiritually negligent. Yeshua didn't fault them for having traditions. He faults them for not making a clear distinction between their traditions and God's word. He scolds them for choosing tradition over command.

According to Jesus, eating perfectly acceptable food with unceremonious hands does not defile a man. While washing up before you eat may indeed be a smart idea, it is certainly neither a Biblical mandate, nor should it be taught as if it were.

Jesus continues,

> *"All too well you reject the commandment of God, that you may keep your tradition. For Moses said, 'Honor your father and your mother'; and, 'He who curses father or mother, let him be put to death.' But you say, 'If a man says to his father or mother, "Whatever profit you might have received from me is Corban"--' (that is, a gift to God), then you no longer let him do anything for his father or his mother, making the word of God of no effect through your tradition which you have handed down. And many such things you do." - Mark 7:9-13*

Again, Yeshua criticizes the Pharisees for "rejecting the commandment of God" and "making the word of God of no effect." It is for the purity of the Torah that Jesus quarrels with them. Jesus was defending the Torah, not slamming it. The scribes and Pharisees were polluting the ways of God. This was something that Jesus sought to remedy.

Notice that Yeshua quotes Moses and the law authoritatively. Clearly he considers the Torah the source of God's truth and the measure by which the will of God is ascertained. Any disagreement regarding the Torah was not in *whether* to observe it but in *how best* to observe it.

How ironic that some twist this portion of Scripture to claim that Jesus was disparaging Moses and seeking to undo the laws of Torah. If this were the case, his argument from Torah would be illogical and lose credibility. Would Jesus cite the Torah as an authority only to argue that the Torah should not be authoritative? That would be equivalent to a Supreme Court justice decreeing the Constitution to be unconstitutional! Yeshua is not contending *against* the Torah but fighting for it to be rightly understood, properly interpreted and cheerfully put into practice.

Yeshua then uses this confrontation as a teaching moment.

> *"When He had called all the multitude to Himself, He said to them, "Hear Me, everyone, and understand: There is nothing that enters a man from outside which can defile him; but the things which come out of him, those are the things that defile a man. If anyone has ears to hear, let him hear." - Mark 7:14-16*

Using the confrontation over the hand-washing ritual as a springboard, the Master now addresses heart issues. He broadens the conversation from man's rules to matters of the heart. His point is that the purity of one's soul is of greater importance than ritual purity, for evil spreads by what touches the heart, not by what touches the hand.

Conclusion

It is important to note that this passage has still neither addressed nor introduced the topic of clean and unclean meats, which is the focus of the Torah's dietary laws. In fact there is not one mention of animal meat anywhere in this story. To bring Leviticus 11 and Deuteronomy 14 into the picture is to go beyond the context and has the appearance of attempting to advance a predetermined narrative through the text.

MARK 7:17-23

Truth #13 – *Jesus did not declare all animals clean.*

How is it that some drag Leviticus 11 into the Mark 7 narrative and teach that Jesus abrogated God's dietary directives? The confusion comes in the following verses.

> *"When He had entered a house away from the crowd, His disciples asked Him concerning the parable. So He said to them, "Are you thus without understanding also? Do you not perceive that whatever enters a man from outside cannot defile him, because it does not enter his heart but his stomach, and is eliminated, thus purifying all foods?" And He said, "What comes out of a man, that defiles a man. For from within, out of the heart of men, proceed evil thoughts, adulteries, fornications, murders, thefts, covetousness, wickedness, deceit, lewdness, an evil eye, blasphemy, pride, foolishness. All these evil things come from within and defile a man." - Mark 7:17-23*

This section needs closer consideration, particularly verse 19. The problem lies with how various translators have handled it.[1] Before examining the Greek, we can gain a better understanding first by comparing various English translations.

Literal English translations such as the Authorized, BRG and King James versions translate verse 19:

> *"Because it entereth not into his heart, but into the belly, and goeth out into the draught, <u>purging all meats</u>."*

The phrase in question is: *purging all meats*. Wycliffe and Darby render it as King James does: *purging all meats*. Young has it

---

[1] Mark 7:19 - ὅτι οὐκ εἰσπορεύεται αὐτοῦ εἰς τὴν καρδίαν ἀλλ᾽ εἰς τὴν κοιλίαν καὶ εἰς τὸν ἀφεδρῶνα ἐκπορεύεται καθαρίζον πάντα τὰ βρώματα

purifying all the meats. The 1599 Geneva Bible is *purging of all meats* and the New King James *purifying all food.*

We can tentatively ascertain from these early English translations that Jesus is offering a basic lesson in food digestion. Food enters the stomach, is processed and eliminated from the body. This makes contextual sense in light of the story. The process of digestion, as dirty as it might seem, actually cleanses the body and purges it from pollutants. When Jesus states that food enters the "stomach, and is eliminated, thus purifying all foods," he is referencing the body's gastrointestinal processes.

His point is that even bread considered ritually unclean by the Pharisee's standards could not defile the body since the digestive system effectively purges the food from the body. In this way spiritual defilement comes not from the stomach but from the heart. He wants all his disciples, you and I included, to be less concerned about what passes through our hands into our stomachs than about what passes through our minds into our hearts. This is the context of Yeshua's words as it reads in English. This interpretation also coincides with Matthew's parallel rendering.

> *"Do you not understand that whatever enters the mouth goes into the stomach and is eliminated." - Matthew 15:17*

Some scholars opt to translate the phrase *purging all foods* a bit differently. Here are some examples:

RSV, ESV, NASB: "(This he declared all foods clean.)"
NIV: "(In saying this, Jesus declared all foods clean.)"
NET: "(This means all foods are clean.)"
CJB: "(Thus he declared all foods ritually clean.)"
NOG: "(By saying this, Yeshua declared all food acceptable.)"
WE: "By saying this, Jesus meant that food does not make a person dirty."
TLB: "(By saying this he showed that every kind of food is kosher.)"
NLT: "(By saying this, he declared that every kind of food is acceptable in God's eyes.)"

CEB: "By saying this, Jesus declared that no food could contaminate a person in God's sight."
NCV: "(When Jesus said this, he meant that no longer was any food unclean for people to eat.)"
The Message: "(That took care of dietary quibbling; Jesus was saying that *all* foods are fit to eat.)"
The Amplified Version: "Thus He was making *and* declaring all foods [ceremonially] clean [that is, abolishing the ceremonial distinctions of the Levitical Law]."

Translators that stray from the literal translations do so for good reason. There is a textual variant in this sentence that makes it a bit more difficult to translate. Based on sentence structure, some have concluded that the opening participle of this phrase attaches itself to Jesus, making him the subject of the masculine participle. In layman's terms, it gives the appearance that it is Jesus who is doing the purifying, not the stomach. Origen takes this position.[2]

This leads some translators to conclude that Mark is interjecting his own editorial comment into the story just as he did in verses 3-4. This is not uncommon for Mark, which clarifies why some translators use parentheses around this phrase. This approach renders Mark's editorial as:

(He is purifying all foods.)

In order to arrive at this translation, however, the scholar must ignore the contents of the story and stray from the obvious context of the passage. This interpretation also chooses not to factor in the parallel account of Matthew and how Levi characterizes the words of Yeshua.

You should be aware that there is a credible alternative translation of the Greek. It is not uncommon for a nominative masculine participle to be used when its antecedent is not mentioned. Using this

---

[2] Origen, *Commentary on Matthew*, Book XI, Section 12, 578-580 [Online]. Available: http://www.documentacatholicaomnia.eu/03d/0185-0254,_Origenes,_Commentarium_in_evangelium_Matthaei_[Schaff]_EN.pdf

approach, it is not inferior to view that it is the body's process of elimination that is doing the purging here, not Jesus. This approach to the sentence is just as acceptable in the Greek. It is also a perfect match when it comes to context.[3]

Translators that take the phrase *purging all foods* and loosely translate it as *thus he declared all foods clean* have to add the word *declared* to the text for context. This word is not found in the original manuscripts. Generally, this is not a problem. Sometimes a translator needs to inject a word or two to help us understand the meaning of the text. As long as they let the reader know, it can be beneficial.

Scholars also use parentheses and/or italics to show that these particular words are added in as a gloss, or in this case, not the original words of Christ. You should be aware that, in light of the context, the phrase *thus he declared all foods clean* is a flimsy interpretation of the phrase *purging all foods*.

As students of the word, our challenge is to not interject our personal bias into the text. Like anyone else, however, even scholars are not immune to doctrinal preferences. There are some translations of the Bible that make you wonder if they intentionally lay down their translator's pen in exchange for a commentator's hat.

In this passage, how one approaches the text alters the meaning of Jesus' words more than slightly. Instead of an analogy about the call of nature, some translations imply it to be a blanket argument for the cancellation of all Biblical dietary guidelines. Somehow the conversation about food digestion and a clean heart takes an immediate left turn into contradicting and invalidating an established Biblical truth. This is no small matter.

To what can we liken it? Imagine you and I are standing in your backyard having a conversation about landscaping when I make an offhand remark about how my toddler is forced to drop off my polar

---

[3] Tim Hegg, *Ten Persistent Questions* (Tacoma: TorahResource, 2009), 17-23

bear wife at her ballet class due to those greedy Wall Street investors. You might give me a bewildered look of *"Huh?"* Exactly! In light of the clear context already of Mark 7 and Matthew's parallel account, the conclusion that Jesus is addressing and including unclean meats into this particular teaching should elicit such a response from everyone who reads this story responsibly.

The mainline interpretation that Jesus is cancelling God's dietary guidelines is not even in the vicinity of the actual contextual meaning of the passage. There is very little to base this conclusion on. It is an illogical interpretation that is grounded in neither context nor common sense. When we examine the subject matter, it is obvious that this story is about tradition, bread and the heart – not Torah, meat and dietary restrictions.

I am not pointing a finger at any translator here. Bible translation is incredibly difficult work and not always absolute. Various translations take diverse approaches and draw from different manuscripts. I have great respect for those who have dedicated their lives to bringing the Scriptures to life. We are all indebted to their insightful work.

Historically speaking, however, Christian academia has lined up in opposition to the Torah. Scholars and those of us who teach can sometimes fall prey to the same vices we resist. We too easily disseminate the traditional doctrines that have been handed down to us, unknowingly contributing to the problem and further muddying the waters. I have little doubt the motive is pure, but sometimes the data is incomplete. For the most part, our posture has not helped in pointing out and clearing up antinomian and anti-Semitic sentiment within Biblical scholarship.

Scripted

An example of this is that it is widely believed that Mark received much of his eyewitness accounts from Peter and recorded them in his gospel.[4] One position argues that Mark added his own words to this particular text. It supposes that because the *purging all foods* phrase does not appear in Matthew's parallel account, Jesus must not have uttered it. It assumes that Mark inserted these words at a later time. Robertson explains:

> "The words do not come from Jesus, but are added by Mark. Peter reports this item to Mark, probably with vivid recollection of his own experience on the housetop of Joppa when in the vision Peter declined three times the Lord's invitation to kill and eat unclean animals."[5]

This idea purports that Peter convinced Mark to add these words to the story in light of his vision at Joppa. Of course there is no way to corroborate this. As evidence to support an abolished-dietary hypothesis from the text, Peter's recollection of his vision about the sheet is cited. Fresh off his rooftop vision in Joppa, it is imagined that Peter must have been eager to assert his newfound dietary liberty. Therefore, he rushed to find Mark and scripted him to add this phrase to Yeshua's words for context.

I find this perspective speculative on a few levels. Allow me to point out a couple major concerns.

(1) The idea that Mark interjected commentary at various points in his gospel is factual. But the assertion that Peter scripted Mark to color the passage in a certain light on account of his vision of the sheet is a bold assumption. How does anyone know this happened? Even if we had in our possession the original handwritten manuscript of Mark's gospel, there is no way to corroborate this.

For the sake of argument, let's suppose this did happen. Suppose Mark did add these words as proof that Jesus cancelled the dietary laws. We are now faced with a whole new set of red flags that undermine the credibility of Mark's gospel.

---

[4] This was the position of Eusebius who quoted Papias of Hierapolis and the elders of the first century. Tradition holds that Mark served as Peter's interpreter in foreign nations.

[5] Robertson, *Word Pictures in the New Testament*, Vol. I, 324

Was this Peter's original account of the story, or did he add these words in light of his vision? Did he suddenly remember what Jesus intended to say years later? Is Peter's stated interpretation of the vision in Acts 10 accurate? If these words didn't come from the lips of Yeshua, should we trust them? Should they be added to the text as if Jesus meant to say them? Why didn't Jesus feel the need to say these words Himself? Is Jesus incapable of making himself clear? What if our assumption about Peter relaying his account to Mark is mistaken? Whose words bear more weight - Mark, Peter or Jesus?

It opens up a whole new and hairy can of worms. Considering the implications of such a monumental position, it is surprising this proposition is given a pass and goes relatively unchallenged by modern academia.

(2) This idea that Mark added these words seeks to interpret one portion of Scripture using the mishandling of another, in this case, Peter's vision of the sheet. Unfortunately, a predetermined theological orientation contributes to a presumed conclusion.

This interpretation supposes Peter was given extra-Biblical dietary liberty and must have added his own words to the text accordingly. But in actuality it is this interpretation that adds to the words of Christ by insisting that *purging all foods* does not come from the lips of Christ but from an insertion of Mark.

When we examine Peter's vision in the next chapter, you will see how this is a common but hasty miscue. Peter was *never* under the impression he had been given authorization to indulge in unclean meats, nor does the text suggest it. Peter's vision is without question about Gentiles and the gospel.

The logic about Peter's vision is flawed and is based on a faulty interpretation that consequently skews what Jesus is communicating. When we start with a wrong premise, we get a wrong outcome. When one interpretation is misunderstood and unsupported, then so is the structure that leans upon it. This is a slippery slope.

The supposition that Peter inserted these words into Mark's gospel in light of his vision has been repeated so many times that it has become a generally accepted matter of fact among scholars. Somehow a teaching about a clean heart gets convoluted into Mark adding words to Yeshua via Peter to emphasize a vision that is plainly misinterpreted. It leaves us with an all-too convenient doctrinal excuse for dishonoring God's dietary standard.

Another common misinterpretation of this passage maintains that Jesus was:

> "Abolishing the ceremonial distinctions of the Levitical law...Peter never forgot the 'What God hath cleansed, that call thou not common.'"[6]

About the disciples, it speculates:

> "They had been trained in Judaism, in which the distinction between clean and unclean is ingrained, and could not understand a statement abrogating this."[7]

Adding,

> "Jesus here is a critic of Moses as well as the scribes, and introduces a religious revolution."[8]

It is reasoned that the twelve disciples were so indoctrinated by what was considered clean and unclean, they are to be blamed for not being able to comprehend a statement that disavowed these distinctions. In other words, the disciples were so steeped in Judaism that they were blind to the truth of what Yeshua was presenting.

---

[6] Kenneth Wuest, *Word Studies In The Greek New Testament*, Volume I (Grand Rapids: Eerdmans, 1973), 149

[7] Ezra Gould, *A Critical and Exegetical Commentary on the Gospel according to St. Mark* (Edinburgh: T&T Clark, 1896), 131

[8] Wuest, *Word Studies,* citing *Expositor's Bible Commentary*, 149

Ironically, I wonder if this same accusation could be said of us. Are we so steeped in Torah abolitionism and ingrained with the idea that we are liberated from keeping God's commands that we can't accurately recognize a statement where Jesus is clearly not disavowing the law? Are we so manipulated by Christian anti-Semitism that we characterize the disciples as being blind for honoring Scripture? Have we been programmed to misinterpret the teachings of Christ?

This theory arrives at the radical and, in my opinion, unsupported conclusion that Jesus was being critical of Moses, repealing the laws of Torah and launching a dietary revolution. This whole theory is based on a poorly translated phrase that they don't even believe Jesus said because it's not found in Matthew's version of the story. Much ink has been spilled and libraries have been filled with these kinds of unchallenged assumptions, and you should be aware of it.

Purging All Foods

How did we make such a drastic leap from a fence law about defiled hands to Jesus wiping away all God-given meat classifications? In order to answer this, we must turn to the Greek and further break down the phrase: *PURGING ALL FOODS*.

(1) PURGING: *Katharizo* – This Greek word is translated *cleansing, purging* and *purifying*.[9] Its root is *clean* or *pure*[10] and is where we derive the English word cauterize.

When used in a spiritual context, *katharizo* can be a pronouncement of clean in the Levitical sense. When used in a moral context, it refers to consecration and freedom from guilt, defilement or wickedness. When used in a physical context, *katharizo* is physical cleansing from dirt, stains and disease.[11] *Katharizo* is found 39 times in the Apostolic Writings describing things like cleansing from filth

---

[9] *Strong's* #G2511 καθαρίζω; S.C. Woodhouse, *English-Greek Dictionary* (London: Routledge & Kegan Paul, 1972), 658
[10] Newman, *Greek-English Dictionary of the New Testament*, "Purging"
[11] *Thayer's, katharizo*

(Matt. 23:25, Luke 11:39), cleansing from leprosy (Matt. 8:2,3, 10:8), freedom from the pollution of sin (Acts 15:9, 2 Cor. 7:1, Titus 2:14, Heb. 9:14, James 4:8, 1 John 1:7-9) and legal purification (Heb. 9:22-23).[12]

Because the word *katharizo* is used, it is understandable why some translators might assume Yeshua is addressing food laws here. If Jesus were teaching on Leviticus 11 or having a discussion about unclean meats, one could be justified in making this assumption if the context permitted. However, the context does not permit. The conversation has nothing to do with Levitical laws or kosher meat requirements. The analogy is digestion. The food in question is bread and the teaching is about the heart.

In making His point, Yeshua contrasts that which occurs in the bathroom to that which occurs in the heart. To bring Leviticus 11 or Deuteronomy 14 into the picture is a dereliction of the context and violates the rules for sound Biblical exegesis. This word is accurately translated as *purifying, expelling* or *purging*.

(2) All: *Pas* – The word is rightly translated *all*.[13] However, *pas* must also be interpreted in light of its context. The stated context is bread and food, not all things someone might possibly endeavor to consume.

We would be taking Jesus out of context to assume that by his statement, "There is nothing that enters a man from outside which can defile him" (Mark 7:15), he means nothing at all from our environment. Certainly there are things we can ingest that can defile and harm us, such as cocaine and plutonium. His nothing is in the context of food. It does not imply *anything* and *everything* that can possibly be shoved into the human mouth.

---

[12] William Barclay, *New Testament Words* (Philadelphia: The Westminster Press, 1974), 124; Spiros Zodhaites, *The Complete Word Study New Testament* (Grand Rapids: Eerdmans, 1973), 911-912

[13] *Strong's* #G3956 πᾶς; Louw, *Greek-English Lexicon, pas*

Additionally, we must take into consideration how food was defined by first-century Israel. An argument can be made that Jesus could never be referring to unclean meats in this statement simply because unclean meats were never considered food to him or to his audience. From a Hebraic perspective, food meant only those things God permitted to be eaten. It would not include that which was Biblically unfit for consumption.

For example, it would be unheard of to find rocks or manure on the menu of any five-star restaurant in America, simply because they are not classified as food items in our culture. In the same way, bottom-feeders, birds of carrion and swine would unquestionably be absent from the menus of local Jewish eateries and from the meat department of any first-century Hebrew market. They were considered inedible animals.

Yeshua's definition of food would only include those things considered food and deemed fit to eat by his Father. Any description of the animals of Leviticus 11 would not be accompanied with the words *edible* or *food*. So, just as battery acid and poison ivy is not considered food in our culture, neither was dead vermin to them.

Context is as critical to Biblical interpretation as it is to daily life. Words only have meaning within a context. If you ordered a pizza with everything on it, you wouldn't expect it to come topped with relish, caramel or sprinkles. While these may be toppings, these are toppings of a different kind. What is more, you'd be troubled to open the box and find your pie garnished with lice, cement and rat poison! Your *everything* would be understood in the context of available pizza toppings, not anything or any kind of topping imaginable.

Context is king. The common practice of cherry-picking verses regardless of context has led to many strange and erroneous doctrinal conclusions within Christendom. This verse is no exception. This kind of distorted deduction of Bible study leads to an interpretation that is contrived and swindled.

The *conned text*, as I call it, is a version of the Bible that is read out of context and leads to conclusions contrary to what is written. This manner of Biblical interpretation is greasy. When we remove the text from its context, we are left with only a con. Chuck Missler once quipped, "If you torture the text long enough, it will eventually confess to anything." It's only by knowing and grasping the *proper* context that one can avoid being duped by the *conned* text.

David Stern writes,

> "Yeshua did not, as many suppose, abrogate the laws of kashrut and thus declare ham kosher! Since the beginning of the chapter the subject has been ritual purity as taught by the Oral Torah in relation to n'tilat-yadayim and not kashrut at all! There is not the slightest hint anywhere that foods in this verse can be anything other than what the Bible allows Jews to eat, in other words, kosher foods."[14]

(3) FOOD: *Brōma* – *Brōma* is the Greek word for food.[15] King James employed the archaic term "meats" to describe *brōma*. However, this word is universally considered food and is rendered food in almost every modern translation. *Brōma* can be a reference to meat in general but not exclusively, as it includes fish, fruit and vegetables.[16] It comes from the root word *to eat*.[17] *Brōma* is used 17 times in the Apostolic Writings, referring to food that is eaten.

Because *brōma* is translated "meat" in some older translations, there is some reason as to why translators jump to the conclusion that Jesus was breaching the topic of meat consumption. However, like *katharizo*, this conclusion is based on archaic translations and un-contextualized readings of the passage. This word should be properly translated *food*.

Putting this all together gives us the clearest meaning of Mark 7:19. Jesus is rejecting the Pharisaical tradition of the elders. Food eaten

---

[14] Stern, *Jewish New Testament Commentary*, 93
[15] *Strong's* #G1033 βρῶμα
[16] Louw, *Greek-English Lexicon, brōma;* Albert Barnes, *Barnes Notes* (Glasgow: Blackie & Son, 1884-1885), 1 Tim. 4:5
[17] Brown, *The New International Dictionary of New Testament,* Vol. 2, 268

and touched with dirty hands cannot spiritually defile a man, because,

> *"it doesn't go into his heart but into his stomach, and then into the sewer, thereby expelling [katharizo] all [pas] foods [brōma]." (ISV)*

This rendering hits the mark when considering manuscript, language, context and Matthew's parallel.[18] Unfortunately, modern paraphrases such as The Amplified, The Message and The Living Bible misrepresent the words of Jesus and add to the false notion that He is addressing animal meat matters.

For the sake of argument, let's assume that Yeshua's statement was an intentional albeit obscure bombshelling of all dietary directives. Wouldn't Mark recount an immediate, explosive reaction coming from the camp of the Pharisees as he does in other accounts? Wouldn't these words have vehemently been used against Yeshua as evidence when standing trial before Caiaphas?

This surely would have been the smoking gun that Yeshua's enemies were so frantically seeking. It would have proved, once and for all, that Jesus was not the Messiah, but instead was a law-breaking imposter who taught others to forsake God's Word. They would have needed no further evidence to render a guilty verdict.

Furthermore, if Jesus were actually relaxing God's dietary guidelines here, wouldn't we observe the disciples at some point operating in this newfound liberty just as they exercised their freedom to forgo the hand-washing ceremony? In the next few chapters of Mark we should find them standing in line next to Yeshua at the local Greek eatery ordering frog legs and fried crab cakes smothered in snail sauce. This, of course, never happens.

The fact is that it was a full decade after Yeshua's resurrection that Peter was given the vision of the sheet. Defending himself before

---

[18] Franz Delitzsch supports this rendering, translating verse 19 as: "For it does not come into his heart, but rather into his stomach, and it goes out to the toilet, which cleanses all this is eaten." *Delitzsch*, 151

God, Peter exclaims to have never eaten anything common or unclean. If Jesus had taught that God's dietary standard was no longer relevant, Simon and the other eleven must have been strangely absent that day. Obviously Peter was under the impression (and had been for ten years) that God's menu was still binding and relevant. No doubt this was the example Yeshua himself set forth.

It should come as no surprise that the outgrowth of antinomian doctrines attached to passages like these has given the impression to Jews that Jesus was a law-breaking imposter who advocated and taught his disciples to forsake the Torah. This inaccurate portrayal of Yeshua comes straight from the pages of our own Christian doctrine. The picture of a lawless Christ that we have presented to the world is categorically flawed.

We must come to grips with the likelihood that our mischaracterization of Christ has contributed to Jewish rejection of Christ. Maybe we have given Jews all the evidence (and excuses) they think they need to reject their own Messiah.

Perhaps this is why our efforts to evangelize Jews have historically produced very little fruit. We've been trying to get them to reject the Scriptures that the Messiah clearly accepted and to accept a Messiah that Scripture clearly rejects. If Jesus was indeed a Torah breaker, Jews should reject Him and so should we. But if it is true that He upheld the Torah and taught others to as well, what should be rejected is our caricature of Jesus as a law-breaking, Torah-forsaking Messiah.

Conclusion

The traditional view that Jesus overturned the dietary laws of Leviticus 11 and Deuteronomy 14 is just that – a tradition. It is a tradition based on assumption and speculative translation. It is a tradition that replaces hermeneutics and sound Biblical interpretation with an un-contextualized hypothesis. It is a tradition that our church fathers have perpetuated until it has become the overwhelming popular position in Christian theology.

One can only arrive at this conclusion by reading Mark 7 backwards from the vantage of pagan culture. But read from a Jewish perspective, Yeshua's words categorically defend the Torah against Pharisaical corruption.

It should be noted that those who insist that Jesus voided the dietary requirements have no other verse in the Gospels beside this one to hang their hat on. This is their *coup de grace* - an unchallenged, creaky doctrine all from one thinly interpreted, out-of-context, three-word phrase. Since there is no credible evidence for this interpretation, it seems rather scandalous that almost every commentary repeats the same party line.

I find it ironic that a story where Jesus is rebuking Pharisees for confusing man's tradition with God's commands gets conflated into a doctrine that uses man's tradition to fundamentally undermine the commandments of God. How we've gone from a teaching about matters of the heart to a radical revision of Scripture is telling and troubling.

But it is the voice of Scripture that we need to attune our ear to. We are obligated to listen to it when it calls into account traditions and doctrines that undermine the word of God. We are compelled to speak up when cavernous gaps in context and careless mismanagements of the text are uncovered in our systematic theology.

All doctrines must be scrutinized and put to the test like any other, including those found in this book. When found to be consistent with Scripture they should be considered. But when inconsistencies are uncovered, it is our blind loyalty to these doctrines that must be questioned and reconsidered.

Could it be that we have fallen into the same ditch of the scribes and Pharisees? Are we blindly following the opinions of our theologians as the scribes and Pharisees of our time? Have we laid aside God's commands for the sake of our traditions and replaced the commandments of God with the teachings of man? Perhaps the

Pharisees are not the only ones guilty of adding to Scripture and misrepresenting God.

ACTS 10

Truth #14: *Peter's vision was about Gentiles and the gospel.*

When discussing the dietary laws, the first question I'm usually asked is: "What about Peter's vision of the sheet? Didn't God lift all dietary restrictions through this vision?" This is a legitimate question. Many believers are under the impression that the vision of Acts 10 expanded Peter's menu. Let's revisit the story.

> *"There was a certain man in Caesarea called Cornelius, a centurion of what was called the Italian Regiment, a devout man and one who feared God with all his household, who gave alms generously to the people, and prayed to God always. About the ninth hour of the day he saw clearly in a vision an angel of God coming in and saying to him, 'Cornelius!'*
>
> *And when he observed him, he was afraid, and said, 'What is it, lord?'*
>
> *'So he said to him, "Your prayers and your alms have come up for a memorial before God. Now send men to Joppa, and send for Simon whose surname is Peter. He is lodging with Simon, a tanner, whose house is by the sea. He will tell you what you must do." And when the angel who spoke to him had departed, Cornelius called two of his household servants and a devout soldier from among those who waited on him continually. So when he had explained all these things to them, he sent them to Joppa.*
>
> *The next day, as they went on their journey and drew near the city, Peter went up on the housetop to pray, about the sixth hour. Then he became very hungry and wanted to eat; but while they made ready, he fell into a trance and saw heaven opened and an object like a great sheet bound at the four corners, descending to him and let down to*

the earth. In it were all kinds of four-footed animals of the earth, wild beasts, creeping things, and birds of the air. And a voice came to him, 'Rise, Peter; kill and eat.'

But Peter said, 'Not so, Lord! For I have never eaten anything common or unclean.'

And a voice spoke to him again the second time, 'What God has cleansed you must not call common.' This was done three times. And the object was taken up into heaven again.

Now while Peter wondered within himself what this vision which he had seen meant, behold, the men who had been sent from Cornelius had made inquiry for Simon's house, and stood before the gate. And they called and asked whether Simon, whose surname was Peter, was lodging there.

While Peter thought about the vision, the Spirit said to him, 'Behold, three men are seeking you. Arise therefore, go down and go with them, doubting nothing; for I have sent them.'

Then Peter went down to the men who had been sent to him from Cornelius, and said, 'Yes, I am he whom you seek. For what reason have you come?'

And they said, 'Cornelius the centurion, a just man, one who fears God and has a good reputation among all the nation of the Jews, was divinely instructed by a holy angel to summon you to his house, and to hear words from you.' Then he invited them in and lodged them. On the next day Peter went away with them, and some brethren from Joppa accompanied him.

And the following day they entered Caesarea. Now Cornelius was waiting for them, and had called together his relatives and close friends. As Peter was coming in, Cornelius met him and fell down at his feet and worshiped him. But Peter lifted him up, saying, 'Stand up; I myself am also a man.' And as he talked with him, he went in and found many who had come together. Then he said to them, 'You know how unlawful it is for a Jewish man to keep company with or go to

ACTS 10

one of another nation. But God has shown me that I should not call any man common or unclean. Therefore I came without objection as soon as I was sent for. I ask, then, for what reason have you sent for me?'

So Cornelius said, 'Four days ago I was fasting until this hour; and at the ninth hour I prayed in my house, and behold, a man stood before me in bright clothing, and said, "Cornelius, your prayer has been heard, and your alms are remembered in the sight of God. Send therefore to Joppa and call Simon here, whose surname is Peter. He is lodging in the house of Simon, a tanner, by the sea. When he comes, he will speak to you." So I sent to you immediately, and you have done well to come. Now therefore, we are all present before God, to hear all the things commanded you by God.'

Then Peter opened his mouth and said: "In truth I perceive that God shows no partiality. But in every nation whoever fears Him and works righteousness is accepted by Him. The word which God sent to the children of Israel, preaching peace through Jesus Christ—He is Lord of all— that word you know, which was proclaimed throughout all Judea, and began from Galilee after the baptism which John preached: how God anointed Jesus of Nazareth with the Holy Spirit and with power, who went about doing good and healing all who were oppressed by the devil, for God was with Him. And we are witnesses of all things which He did both in the land of the Jews and in Jerusalem, whom they killed by hanging on a tree. Him God raised up on the third day, and showed Him openly, not to all the people, but to witnesses chosen before by God, even to us who ate and drank with Him after He arose from the dead. And He commanded us to preach to the people, and to testify that it is He who was ordained by God to be Judge of the living and the dead. To Him all the prophets witness that, through His name, whoever believes in Him will receive remission of sins.'

While Peter was still speaking these words, the Holy Spirit fell upon all those who heard the word. And those of the circumcision who believed were astonished, as many as came with Peter, because the gift of the Holy Spirit had been poured out on the Gentiles also. For they heard them speak with tongues and magnify God.

Then Peter answered, 'Can anyone forbid water, that these should not be baptized who have received the Holy Spirit just as we have?' And he commanded them to be baptized in the name of the Lord. Then they asked him to stay a few days." - Acts 10:1-48

Let's begin with a few observations.

1. *Up to this point, Peter had kept a strict Biblical diet.*

When told to rise, kill and eat, Peter retorts,

"Never, my Lord, because I have never eaten anything defiled or polluted." – Acts 10:14, Aramaic Bible in Plain English

You've got to hand it to Peter. He definitely had some *chutzpah*. He didn't just disagree with the heavenly voice but had the audacity to defy it. No doubt his bravado was due to both his strong commitment to Scripture and his observation of Yeshua's way of life.

Simon had been taught at a young age from the Scriptures what kinds of meat were fit for consumption, and he remained faithful to live within those parameters. According to his own admission, Peter had been keeping the dietary laws his entire life. When told to do something contrary to his convictions, to Scripture and to His Master, his response was essentially, *"Never! I have never. I would never!"*

Most scholars place Acts chapter 10 seven to ten years after the resurrection of Christ. By this time Peter would have been walking with Christ for the majority of his adult life. Yet he continued to follow Jesus and lead the church without ever entertaining the thought of eating unclean animals. Surely if Yeshua meant to discount the dietary stipulations found in the Torah, the Messiah would have taught it, demonstrated it or in the very least alluded to it with his disciples. There is no evidence of this whatsoever.

Based on his shock and response, abandoning the Bible's dietary standard was an outlandish proposal to Peter. The fact that Peter had avoided eating anything unclean or common his entire life, even after answering the call to discipleship, leads us to believe that (a) Peter never observed Jesus eating anything unclean, (b) Peter was never coached to discard the Torah's dietary guidelines, and (c) Peter, along with the other disciples, was expected to do likewise. Nowhere do we read of first-century believers eating unclean meats. Not. One. Place.

Peter's leadership would not only have a strong influence on the church but his actions would certainly reflect the practice of the apostles. This explains why Peter was so baffled by the vision. Why would the Heavenly Father order him to break the very dietary code that he himself had established and that Jesus exemplified? Never did Yeshua instruct nor expect his disciples to abandon the dietary laws.

Furthermore, if a dietary reform was forthcoming, we should expect to find a prophetic foreshadowing to it elsewhere in Scripture. An argument can be made that every new work of God is found in the Prophets. The promise of the Messiah, the destruction of Tyre, the rise of Alexander the Great, the reign of Cyrus, the fall of Jerusalem, the crucifixion of Yeshua, the betrayal of Judas - all were accurately predicted decades, some even centuries before these events.

If God had designs of a major overhaul and the phasing out of portions of His Torah, which he took painstaking and unprecedented measures to reveal, certainly it would be alluded to in the Prophets. It is no surprise that it is strangely absent. The Writings and the Prophets never so much as hint of a coming change in Torah's food standard. On the contrary, they reinforce it.

For example, speaking for the Lord, Isaiah writes,

> *"I spread out my hands all the day to a rebellious people who eat pigs flesh, and broth of tainted meat is in their vessels. Those who sanctify and purify themselves to go into the gardens, following one in the midst, eating pigs flesh and the abomination and mice, shall come to an end together, declares the Lord." - Isaiah 65:2a, 4b; 66:17 (ESV)*

Ezekiel adds,

> "You eat meat with blood, you lift up your eyes toward your idols, and shed blood. Should you then possess the land?" - Ezekiel 33:25

Solomon cautioned,

> "When you sit down to eat with a ruler, consider carefully what is before you; and put a knife to your throat if you are a man given to appetite. Do not desire his delicacies, for they are deceptive food. Do not mix with winebibbers or with gluttonous eaters of meat." - Proverbs 23:1-3, 20

It was Daniel who put these words into practice when he resolved to only eat vegetables so as not to defile himself at the king's table.

These passages support Scripture's guidelines regarding meat consumption. Both Yeshua and the Prophets uphold the authority of the Torah's food standard.

God isn't fickle. He doesn't change his expectations arbitrarily. Would He judge one generation for not upholding His dietary standard and reward another for ignoring it?

> "How could God, after generation upon generation of calling His people to Torah obedience, after book upon holy book of Scripture that exhorts His people to Torah, expect His people to suddenly follow a new way that jettisoned the Torah?"[1]

God doesn't punish his children for what he once praised them for and praise them for what he once punished them for. If he desired the Torah and its dietary boundaries to be moved, then he needs to apologize to the generations he judged and chastened for their violations of it.[2]

---

[1] D. Thomas Lancaster, "The Weekly eDrash," FFOZ, August, 29, 2013
[2] The Maccabean martyrs "stood firm and were resolved in their hearts not to eat unclean food" and "chose to die rather than be defiled by food or to profane the

Furthermore, there are no allusions of a new age of dietary lawlessness mentioned anywhere in the Torah, the Writings, the Prophets or by Christ. Jesus and the Prophets do hint at something ending, however. This happens to be what Peter needed a revelation of.

2. *Peter makes a distinction between common and unclean.*

In the vision were animals of all kinds – wild beasts, four-footed animals, creeping things and birds of the air. The sheet may have included some clean animals, but the implication is that these were primarily a mixture of animals – mostly animals unfit for human consumption. When told to eat, Peter confesses, "I have never eaten anything *common* or *unclean*" (v.14). Peter makes a distinction between common meat and unclean meat. What's the difference?

The word unclean or *akathartos* denotes something morally or physically impure.[3] This is the same word used when referencing 'unclean' spirits. *Akathartos*, along with its antonym *kathartos*, almost always refer to meat listed as unclean/clean if the context permits. In this case, the context fits.

Kathartos and *Akathartos* are the Greek words the Septuagint writers employed in Leviticus 11 and Deuteronomy 14 to distinguish clean from unclean. In light of the context, it is safe to assume that Peter is referencing food laws. Regarding unclean meats, Peter categorically denies ever eating anything unclean (*akathartos*).

Common (*koinos*) has a slightly different connotation. *Koinos* means ordinary or profane.[4] In the context of food, common meats are unclean meats, including permissible meat that has been cooked with, contaminated by, exposed to or somehow come into contact

---

holy covenant" (1 Maccabees 1:62-63). In Jewish history, both Tobit and Judith refused to be defiled by the "food of Gentiles" (Tobit 1:10-13, Judith 10; 12:1-20).
[3] *Strong's* #G169 ἀκάθαρτος; Brown, *The New International Dictionary*, Vol. 3, 102; *Thayer's*, Acts 10:14
[4] *Strong's* #G2839 κοινός; *Vine's*, "common"

with something deemed impermissible.[5] Common meats also refer to sacrificial meat that remained beyond the prescribed period of time, thus becoming unfit to eat.

In contrast to *akathartos*, *koinos* meats can be Biblically defined and acceptable meats (such as beef or lamb) but are considered defiled due to contact or exposure of some kind. Common meats can be unclean because of what they are, but they can also be unclean because of what they have touched. One purpose for common food laws is that they create fence laws to provide a line of protection from someone unintentionally eating something defiling.

To illustrate, suppose you order a bacon cheeseburger at your favorite bar and grill downtown. By removing the bacon before eating it, your burger might appear to be Biblically clean, but it would not be clean according to stricter standards. It is contaminated since it has come into contact with something unclean, let alone cooked in a non-kosher kitchen and served on the same plate with cheese! This is what Peter refers to as common or *koinos*. In addition to never eating anything Biblically unclean, Peter had never eaten anything common as well.

This is grossly oversimplified, but one could say that *koinos* is that which man makes unclean while *akathartos* is that which God makes unclean. In Peter's case, he had avoided both *akathartos* and *koinos* - that which was un-permitted by God and un-permitted by association. This had been his practice since birth, even a full decade after being baptized in the Holy Spirit. There is little doubt that this was also the practice of Jesus.

3. *Peter interprets the vision.*

Peter was initially perplexed as to what the vision meant, but the interpretation came sometime between Joppa and Caesarea. When he arrives, Peter declares,

---

[5] Bauer, Gingrich, Arndt & Danker, *A Greek-English Lexicon of the New Testament* (Chicago: The University of Chicago Press, 1979), Acts 10: See also Ben-Lyman HaNaviy, *Acts 10* [Online]. Available: graftedin.com

> *"You know how unlawful it is for a Jewish man to keep company with or go to one of another nation. But God has shown me that I should not call any man common or unclean. Therefore I came without objection as soon as I was sent for."* – Acts 10:28-29

He adds,

> *"In truth, I perceive that God shows no partiality, but in every nation anyone who fears him and does what is right is acceptable to him."* – Acts 10:34-35

Peter himself reveals the interpretation to the vision, which was not literal. He gained divine insight into what the vision was about, and it wasn't about eating clean or unclean animals. It was about the people the animals represent and with whom Peter should keep company.

God is speaking to Peter about Jewish exclusivity and Gentile inclusion in the kingdom of God. The vision confronts the traditional custom of Jews separating themselves from social contact with non-Jews, a practice that Peter faithfully observed. In fact, years later in Antioch, Peter relapses into this behavior, even influencing Barnabas to withdraw from eating with Gentile brothers. Because of it, Paul rebukes Peter for his hypocritical behavior.[6]

Peter references this Jewish custom when he says to Cornelius, "You know how <u>unlawful</u> it is for a Jewish man to keep company with or go to another nation" (v.28). The word unlawful here is not *anomia*, which would suggest a sin or transgression. The word is *athemitos*,[7] which means illegal, abominable or contrary to what is right.[8] *Athemitos* takes on the connotation of behavior unaccepted by the norm - a violation of man or a cultural taboo. It refers to things that just weren't typically done.[9] In Peter's case, it violated the standard

---

[6] Gal. 2:11-15
[7] *Strong's* #G111 ἀθέμιτος
[8] Louw, *Greek-English Lexicon, athemitos; Vine's*, "unlawful"
[9] Ben-Lyman HaNaviy, *Acts 10*

practice of his time, as most Jews considered the homes of Gentiles off limits.[10]

Peter is not suggesting that it was unlawfully sinful for Jews to interact with non-Jews. Nowhere does Scripture forbid Jews from associating with non-Jews.[11] He is merely citing Jewish culture that frowned upon social interaction with Gentiles.[12]

The reasons for Israelites avoiding table fellowship with non-Israelites were not unreasonable. Dr. H.D. Livingston writes,

> "As the meal provided an important opportunity for socialization in the ancient world, this injunction also served to establish protective barriers between Jews and their potential assimilation into the Greco-Roman world through social interaction and inter-marriage."[13]

When it came to Gentile interaction, a conscientious Jew likely ran the risk of becoming ritually unclean by entering the home of an idolater. Sharing a meal with a demon-worshipping barbarian or even a good-natured pagan could cause one to unknowingly eat foreign meat or drink wine that had been contaminated or dedicated to a deity through an incantation. Furthermore, certain sects within the Pharisees were concerned with the hyper-litigious stringencies of the Torah and opted not to eat with the general public for fear the food had not been properly tithed upon.[14]

Fellowship around the meal table meant something to Jews. Second century Jewish writings indicate that eating with a Gentile was

---

[10] *Oholot* 18.7
[11] Hegg, *Ten Persistent Questions,* 74: "Nowhere in the Torah is there a commandment to separate from Gentiles who have attached themselves to the God of Israel. Quite the contrary: the Torah regularly commands the native born Israelites to accept and welcome foreigners who desire to worship the One true God, and to treat them with equality as having the same covenant privileges and responsibilities as the native born Israelite (Ex. 12:19, Lev. 18:26, 24:16, Num. 9:14, 15:15, 16, 29, 19:10, Deut. 31:12)."
[12] Jubilees 22:16
[13] http://people.opposingviews.com/cultural-differences-jews-gentiles-9178.html
[14] D. Thomas Lancaster, *Torah Club,* Vol. 2 (Marshfield: FFOZ, 2006), 384

something that concerned the Jewish community. Some even suggest that eating with Gentiles posed a threat to Israel. We know this to be the case, because we find special instructions in the Talmud and in some ancient *halakhic* rulings about what to do when sharing a meal with a Gentile.[15]

Because Gentiles had morals that conflicted with Scripture, it was much safer for Jews to simply avoid social contact. For this reason, fence laws were generated to create boundaries around the commandments. These fence laws were meant to bring protection. Like anything else, however, good ideas and safeguarding principles can sometimes lose their wheels and wobble out of balance. Apparently, God wanted this train back on track.

There was a deep-seeded wall of separation that existed between Jew and Gentile in first-century Israel.[16] God was chipping away at it by addressing Peter's ethnocentricity. The vision was not a correction of Peter's eating habits or a revision of the rules regarding meat consumption. The Lord was putting his finger on Jewish nationalistic sentiments. If left unaddressed, they would ultimately hinder the advancement of the gospel. When it came to Gentiles, would Peter prove to be more loyal to Jewish custom or to the Scriptures?

When read carefully, we learn that the vision never commands Peter to eat forbidden animals. He was told to rise, kill and eat, but eat what? The vision does not specify. The answer to this question, however, can be found in the second instruction: "What God has cleansed you must not call common" (v.15). Note the precise words used here, for they are critical in hunting down this answer. The voice says, "What God has *katharizo*, you must not call *koinos*." In other words, what God had cleansed and permitted should not be considered unacceptable.

---

[15] *Tosapoth*, Jebamoth 94b, *Shulchan Aruch*, Yoreh Deah 152
[16] Animosity toward Jews also was a contributing factor. In the years leading up to the destruction of the temple, anti-Jewish sentiment grew increasingly stronger among Roman occupiers and the enemies of Israel.

In these words we see that God did not cleanse *akathartos*. He cleansed *koinos*. This is profoundly important. God was correcting Peter's definition of what is common, not his definition of what is unclean. Peter is being warned not to call common or unclean what God considers clean.

This distinction may seem small, but it is significant. The vision does not cleanse that which God deemed unclean. Rather, it cleanses that which Peter deemed common or unclean.

Even in the analogy of this vision, we can see that there is no change to what is considered unclean. No license was given to accept those things that are Biblically unacceptable. God neither retracts His established rules about what is unclean, nor reverses the guidelines of Leviticus 11. He was simply challenging the institutionalized policies that Peter was following.

We assume that the voice commanded Peter to eat from the entire group of animals he saw in the sheet. Based on his response, this is probably what Peter thought, too. But Peter was initially mistaken about the vision. Could he have been mistaken about what he was told to eat as well?

It is possible that Peter was not expected to eat any of the animals he saw in the vision, both literally or figuratively. The phrase "kill (θύω) and eat" in Greek rightly means to *kill and consume*, but its root is *to sacrifice*. It denotes "slaughtering for a sacrifice"[17] and is used in this fashion elsewhere.[18] With this in mind, the implication is that Peter was to include the unclean animals in a sacrifice to God. In being asked to slaughter defiled animals in preparation for a sacrifice, this could explain why Peter walked away from the encounter so perplexed. Perhaps it was a test to see where his allegiance lied.

It could also be that Peter was not being asked to offer these animals as a sacrifice but to call a sacrifice in which Gentiles were invited to

---

[17] Bauer, *A Greek-English Lexicon*, Acts 10:13
[18] Mark 14:12, Luke 22:7, Acts 14:13, 18, 1 Cor. 5:7, 10:20

the table. It might be that the voice was not asking him to eat the animals but to eat *with* the animals. In other words, Peter was not to consume Gentiles but was to offer peace offerings unto God and include Gentiles in a fellowship meal.

Those who argue that the vision gave Peter dietary liberty cannot deny that: (1) Peter never actually eats any of the forbidden animals in the sheet, and (2) God takes exception with Peter's use of *koinos*, not *akathartos*. If Peter was truly supposed to get down from that rooftop and eat some kind of meal involving meat, it would have had to have been a plate of common meat.

As he pondered and prayed about it, Peter understood the meaning of the vision and determined that it was not concerning food at all. The voice was admonishing him for calling something forbidden that God had accepted, namely, Gentiles. This was the "law" the vision was seeking to amend.

Using the language of this vision, the animals here represent the Gentile world. Because Jews treated Gentiles like they treated common meat, they were guilty of intentionally avoiding interaction with Gentiles in order to avoid being defiled. The Torah never calls Gentiles unclean or common. Whether with meat or with Gentiles, Jewish practice went beyond God's commandments and the gospel.

Peter was not instructed to eat Gentiles. That's morbid. Interpreting the vision in this way has some obvious flaws. God was calling Peter to invite to the table of the Lord those that were considered defiled. This was Peter's calling – to invite peoples of all kinds to worship God at Christ's table and to enjoy table fellowship with them, both physically and spiritually.

The vision also implies that Gentiles are not intrinsically unclean, for they could be cleansed from their sins just as Jews could. Whereas many Jews saw Gentiles as profane, God saw them as redeemable. Gentiles should not be regarded as a social taboo but as a mission field. Just as Cornelius had opened his door to Peter, the door of the gospel was now opened to the Gentiles as well. Those

Gentiles coming into the faith were to be accepted and recognized as bona fide children of Abraham.

The nationalistic posture of Israel had blinded Peter from this truth. By refusing to mingle with Gentiles, Peter's perpetuation of Jewish ethnocentricity was creating a barrier for the gospel to spread to every nation and tribe. It is my opinion that this vision was given to Peter not only because he was the one to whom Jesus had given the keys of the kingdom, but also because he was the worst offender. As we see in Galatians 2, he was also a repeat offender.

If Peter could abandon his opposition to Gentile interaction, the other disciples would follow suit and so steer the church. God knew he needed to adjust Peter's ethnocentric allegiance in order for the kingdom to advance. Boy, was he right!

Conclusion

In his great love, God wanted Peter to understand that Gentile interaction should not be considered offensive. Fellowshipping with a Gentile, in this case Cornelius and his family, would not make this disciple defiled. This revelation applied to both Peter personally and to the church corporately. The gospel had been extended to non-Jews. Soon Peter would be asked to embrace Gentile disciples as brothers in Christ and fellow citizens of the kingdom.

The immediate objective of the vision was that Peter should go with the men sent from the house of Cornelius. The lasting impact, however, was much broader. In the coming days and years Gentiles in Christ were not to be avoided, excluded or looked down upon. They were to be treated as cleansed in every sense of the word. They should be considered covenantal members in God's house without needing to submit to circumcision or any other Jewish rite in order to receive the promise of salvation.

It could be argued that Peter's vision was the greatest revelation given to the early believers. It catapulted them into an understanding that, in addition to Israel, people from all nations were included in God's plan of salvation. It paved the way for Paul to emerge as the apostle to the Gentiles. It was Paul who wrote about the mystery of the gospel, a term he used to refer to Gentile salvation.[19] Through Peter's vision and Paul's writings, God has now made known this mystery to us.

The conclusion of the matter is that there is no change to God's standard for meat, because the vision of the sheet is not about food. It's about you and me.

---

[19] Rom. 11:25, 16:25, Eph. 3:1-9, 6:9, Col. 1:26-27

Acts 11

Truth #15: *Peter never ate unclean animals.*

If Peter's vision were about food, it would become immediately evident. The author used precious parchment to recount the story. Luke would be sure to point out the implications that such an important revelation had upon Peter and the church. He would no doubt emphasize it, and we would observe Peter along with the other disciples expressing their newfound dietary liberty.

Peter's own actions confirm the interpretation. We do not find Peter in the next chapter immediately driving downtown to a diner to order bacon and eggs with a side of sausage for brunch. Nor did he attend a local crab fest or indulge himself in a ham sandwich. Nowhere do we read of the disciples eating unpermitted meats.

What we read instead is Peter preaching to the house of Cornelius and the message of the gospel multiplying among Gentiles. Luke devotes the rest of Acts to the spread of the gospel among the Gentiles. We find congregations with a mix of Jew and Gentile planted all around Asia Minor and multiplying across Europe.

The fruit of any revelation is always an indication of its interpretation. In this case the fruit was bountiful and beautiful Gentile conversions. The vision steered Peter and the church toward Gentile acceptance.

Interpretative Action

There is a position that speculates the vision has a dual purpose. The primary purpose was Gentile inclusion, but a secondary purpose was dietary liberty. It's a fair opinion. It has a soft underbelly, though.

Its weakness is that it lacks any consequential evidence. There is no action or change of conduct following Peter's vision that points to a food interpretation. Where do we find that Peter thought the vision to be about anything but Gentile inclusion? What evidence is there that the early believers, led by Peter, partook of unclean or even common meats? It is nonexistent.

Nowhere do we witness the congregations of the Way taking a doctrinal stance against Torah's dietary guidelines. This includes Paul's teaching in Romans 14 and 1 Corinthians 8. A departure from God's will concerning Biblical meats is plainly absent from the writings of the apostles, just as it is absent from the writings of the Prophets.

Evidence for a Gentile-inclusive interpretation, however, is overwhelming in the book of Acts, the Prophets and throughout the ministry of Yeshua himself. We find Jesus helping a Canaanite woman whose daughter was demon-possessed because of her great faith.[1] Yeshua showed compassion by healing the centurion's servant and casting demons out of the man of Gadarenes.[2] He ministered to the woman at the well and stayed with the Samaritans for two days.[3] Jesus alludes to Gentiles as the "other sheep I have which are not of this fold; them also I must bring and they will hear My voice; and there will be one flock and one shepherd" (John 10:16).

The Prophets also speak of Gentile inclusion. Isaiah writes,

> *"Also the sons of the foreigner who join themselves to the Lord, to serve Him and to love the name of the Lord, to be His servants – Everyone who keeps from defiling the Sabbath, and holds fast My covenant – even them I will bring to My holy mountain, and make them joyful in My house of prayer. Their burnt offerings and their sacrifices will be accepted on My altar; for My house will be called a house of prayer for all nations." - Isaiah 56:6-7*

---

[1] Matt. 15:21-28
[2] Mark 5
[3] John 4

Of the Messiah, he foretells,

> *"It is too small a thing that You should be my Servant to raise up the tribes of Jacob, and to restore the preserved ones of Israel; I will also give You as a light to the Gentiles, that you should be My salvation to the ends of the earth." - Isaiah 49:6*

Zechariah prophesied,

> *"Many nations will be joined to the Lord in that day, and they shall become My people. And I will dwell in your midst." - Zechariah 2:11*

Malachi adds,

> *"'For from the rising of the sun, even to its going down, My name shall be great among the Gentiles; in every place incense shall be offered to My name, and a pure offering; for My name shall be great among the nations,' says the Lord of hosts." - Malachi 1:11*

These words find their fulfillment with the apostles in Acts and beyond. Soon after the events of Acts 15, Paul received his Macedonian call and took the gospel to unreached Gentile nations. Imprisoned in Rome, Paul declared,

> *"Therefore let it be known to you that the salvation of God has been sent to the Gentiles, and they will hear it." - Acts 28:28*

The food interpretation falls flat, because it violates the fallacy of an argument from silence. An argument from silence is something that cannot be proven or disproven based on its absence of mention.

An example of this is how the Bible is silent on the number of Magi that came from the East to Joseph and Mary in Bethlehem. The traditional nativity pegs three wise men, but Scripture does not identify how many Magi there actually were. It cannot be proven or disproven that there were in fact three. There could have been three hundred or three thousand! In the same way, Biblical silence can neither prove nor disprove a doctrine.

As noted, the Bible is silent when it comes to any kind of coming change to the dietary laws, but it screams in announcing Gentile inclusion. The silence, as they say, is deafening.

Therefore, it should be logically concluded that due to the lack of silence and the overwhelming volume of material in Scripture, Gentile inclusion is the most supported, the most reasonable and the most obvious interpretation of Peter's vision. Taking into account Peter's own interpretation of the vision, the weight of the evidence is tremendously supportive of a Gentile interpretation. All other interpretations are unconvincing since they lack any concrete Biblical support.

Conclusion

The main point of contention with Peter's vision is not with its meaning but with its interpretation. Peter himself disagrees with those who draw a dietary interpretation from Acts 10. Obviously, his commentary is the best and most credible. It is the interpretation validated by the words of Christ, supported by the testimony of the Prophets and confirmed by the content that follows in Acts.

We also cannot deny Peter's after-the-fact behavior as evidence for its interpretation. He didn't climb down from the roof and phone-in a pepperoni pizza for takeout. What he did do was preach the gospel to a God-fearing Gentile and baptize his entire household after the Holy Spirit had fallen upon them all. Thank God the vision was not about food. Had Peter thought the vision was about dietary liberty, the gospel would not have been proclaimed in Caesarea that day.

Peter's statement about how unlawful it was for Jews to associate with Gentiles is telling and reveals how prevalent Gentile avoidance had become in the first century. It took a supernatural encounter for Peter to grasp that Gentile nations were included in God's plan of salvation and that God was grafting Gentiles into the covenant promises of Israel. It cannot be overstated how revolutionary this was at the time. The fact that no one today questions whether Gentiles can be saved demonstrates how significant Peter's vision was. It also exhibits how effectively God toppled this sacred cow.

God used his own dietary standards as a backdrop for this revelation, but we must be careful not to confuse the symbolism with the interpretation. Responsible readers will not read into the story something that it is not saying. Peter was to eat *with* the common, not eat the unclean.

Rich symbolism, however, can be found in the details of the vision. The sheet is representative of the burial cloth of our Lord Jesus Christ. Salvation comes to all nations through his death, burial and resurrection. The four corners of the sheet can represent the four corners of the earth where the gospel was soon to spread. Not only did it spread but thrived among Gentile nations. It still continues to thrive today.

Just as many believing Jews had overlooked the inclusion of Gentiles in God's plan of salvation, we must not overlook the inclusion of Torah in walking out our salvation. Peter chose to honor the Scriptures, in particular the dietary laws, even when a heavenly vision had seemingly instructed him to break them. From this we learn that God's word remains the final authority when it comes to all matters of life, including our salvation and the foods we enjoy.

There was no need for God to lift his dietary stipulations or to compromise his righteous standards just to accommodate Gentiles. God's standard brings a blessing to both the Jews and Gentiles alike. Today all nations are blessed that the barrier between Jew and Gentile has been broken and the mystery of the gospel has been revealed.

JEWS & GENTILES

Truth #16 – *The apostles clashed with Jewish ethnocentricity.*

As basic as it may sound to us today, the fact that uncircumcised Gentiles could be saved was a radical concept in the first century. The pervasive theology at the time was that atonement had only been made for Israel.[1] Since God covenanted with no other nation except Israel, it is reasoned that Gentiles must attach themselves in some manner to Israel in order to gain access to the covenant and secure the promises of the age to come.[2] One way this could be achieved is by becoming a Jewish proselyte or being a God-fearer (a Gentile worshipper of God like Cornelius).

It is impossible to try to reduce first century Jewish practice into one uniform doctrine. Judaism is not monolithic. Anyone who suggests otherwise is over-simplifying it a bit.[3] Just as Christianity today is replete with denominations and differing schools of thought, so was first century Palestinian Judaism.

Many Jews living in Israel were members of one of the various Jewish sectarian groups such as the Pharisees, Sadducees or Essenes. Divided by doctrine and differing in *halakha* (the way in which one lives out the Torah),[4] each sect had their own policies and way of interpreting the Torah. Yet even within these sects there was room for diversity.

---

[1] *Mishnah Sanhedrin* 10.1
[2] E.P. Sanders, *Paul and Palestinian Judaism* (Minneapolis: Fortress Press, 1977), 206-212
[3] G.F. Moore, *Judaism in the First Century of the Christian Era,* Vol. II (Cambridge: Schocken Books, 1927)
[4] The Hebrew word for *go* or *walk, halakha* means the way in which one walks out the Torah. It is a reference to the received traditions of the sages. Still today, a Jew's *halakha* governs their way of life and is often defined by their rabbi.

Covenantal Nomism

Recent scholarship suggests that the prevailing mindset of the first-century Judaisms was not legalistic but ethnocentric.[5] It was reasoned that an Israelite, whether native-born or a proselyte, had entered the covenant and was given automatic membership into the kingdom of God.

In writing about this subject, E. P. Sanders popularized the term *covenantal nomism*. Covenantal nomism is the view that "one's place in God's plan is established on the basis of the covenant and that the covenant requires the proper response of man's obedience to its commandments, while providing means of atonement for transgressions."[6] In his opinion, covenantal nomism dominated the Jewish mindset of the second-temple era.

As members of the covenant, Jews had privileged access to God and could secure a place in the world to come as God's chosen people. They were not so much obsessed with earning God's eternal favor through works-based righteousness, as Luther supposed. Instead, Israelites relied solely on their identity to procure the favor of God. In other words, Jews enjoyed all the promises given to Israel simply by being Jewish.[7]

From this perspective, Israelites did not obtain right standing with God through law keeping. Torah keeping was not generally considered as a means of earning God's grace but a way of maintaining their membership within God's covenant.[8] The issue was one of status, not works.[9]

First-century Jews were taught to rely on their status as an Israelite for their justification. However, it was their obedience to the Torah that made them righteous - a term used to designate obedient

---

[5] Sanders, *Paul and Palestinian Judaism*, 147-182
[6] Ibid; See also James Dunn, *The New Perspective on Paul* (Grand Rapids: Eerdmans, 2008), 6
[7] Dunn, *The New Perspective on Paul*, 6
[8] Sanders, *Paul and Palestinian Judaism*, 75, 236, 420, 544
[9] Tim Hegg, *Acts 15 & the Jerusalem Council* (Tacoma: TorahResource, 2008), 2

Israelites.[10] From this perspective, forgiveness was not attained through good works but given by a gracious God to those who repent.[11]

Simply stated, Jews and only Jews were in God's club. Those born into it were safe, and the only way out of it is by being a bad Jew. While Torah compliance was not a requirement to get in, practicing the Torah in a Jewish way was a requirement to stay in.[12] In this way, many of the Judaisms of the first century were not so much classically legalistic as they were ethnocentrically driven.

What about Gentiles?

For Gentiles to share in the blessings of God's covenant, it was commonly taught that they must be transferred into the covenant of Israel through some sort of ritual.[13] The ceremony for a proselyte gave one legal Jewish status. These rituals varied depending on region, rabbi and sect. Some involved a *mikvah* (baptism) or a sacrifice.[14] Almost all required males to be circumcised[15] and follow the Torah in a Jewish manner.[16]

Some scholars maintain that these rituals were Jewish conversion ceremonies for God-fearing Gentiles who wished to legally convert to being a Jew. Others view them as initiation rites for proselytes. In either case, adult ritual circumcision became practically synonymous with these Jewish customs.

The Torah did play a role in the covenantal-nomistic view, but not in the classic legalistic way. Many scholars feel there is strong evidence to support the claim that Torah keeping for the purpose of

---

[10] Sanders, *Paul and Palestinian Judaism*, 206
[11] Santala, *Paul*, 19
[12] Dunn, *The New Perspective*, 6
[13] *Minor Tractate: Gerim*
[14] Bernard Bamberger, *Proselytes in the Talmudic Period* (New York: KTAV Publishing House, 1939)
[15] *Tractate Yevamos* 46a-b, *Kerisos* 8b, 9a
[16] Sanders, *Paul and Palestinian Judaism*, 206

salvation was not widely held.[17] What was widely believed was that Israel was already saved and that good Jews were committed to living like a Jew. Among other things, this involved keeping the Torah as prescribed by their rabbi.

Because Torah observance couldn't earn a person Jewish status, the intention to obey the commandments did not earn an Israelite status with God, either. Neither was membership gained through good works. Keeping the Torah is what maintained and secured their position within the covenant. In other words, membership in the covenant was given through Jewish status and preserved through rabbinic Torah keeping. Commentaries that imply that Jews generally viewed Torah adherence as a kind of stairway to heaven are mistaken.

Oral Law

Jewish law often includes more than just the written Torah. When speaking of the law, most Jews are referring to the 613 laws of the Torah consisting of both Biblical and rabbinic laws, as well as the Mishnah. To a good many religious leaders, observing the law often meant keeping a long list of written and unwritten rules. Rabbinic customs and oral laws instituted by rabbis were considered just as binding as the Torah and were expected to be taken up as a part of being a proselyte or a native-born Israelite. Many rabbis, particularly those of the sects of the Pharisees and Essenes, required a strict adherence to the traditional regulations of the sages.

Ethics of the Fathers is a compilation of didactic Jewish teachings. In it, one rabbi believed that anyone who profanes holy things consecrated in the temple, degrades the feasts, humiliates a friend in public, abrogates the covenant of Abraham or interprets the Torah contrary to the accepted *halakha*, although he may possess knowledge and good deeds, he has no share in the world to come.[18]

---

[17] Sanders, *Paul and Palestinian Judaism*, 147-183. See also E.P. Sanders, *Paul, The Law, and the Jewish People* (Minneapolis: Fortress, 1983); N.T. Wright, *Paul* (Minneapolis: Fortress, 2009); Dunn, *The New Perspective On Paul*
[18] *Pirkei Avot*, Rabbi Elazar, 3:11

Still today, the oral Torah is considered by many Jews to be a second set of divine laws given to Moses to help interpret the written laws of Torah.

Avi ben Mordechai writes,

> "In the oral law, you will find detailed instructions on how to relieve yourself, how to put on your shoes every morning when you get up, how to pray and exactly what to say. The oral law turns the synagogue into a makeshift *Beit Hamikdash* (Temple). It turns your dining room table into an altar. The oral law tells you exactly how to live your life everyday according to how the Rabbis want you to live, and the list goes on with huge volumes of rules and regulations that define normative Jewish behavior and culture."[19]

Jews were expected to follow the Torah because they were Israelites, but how one followed the Torah could only be properly determined by the rabbis. This is where the oral law comes into play. Some rabbinic literature permitted uncircumcised Gentiles to learn the written Torah but restricted them from being taught the oral Torah. It was through the oral Torah that a good many Jews found their distinction. So, it was incumbent upon faithful Jews and proselytes to take up the Torah as interpreted by the rabbis to make a distinction.

Furthermore, whereas Jewish identity could give a Jew automatic access to God's covenant blessings, Torah observance, in and of itself, could not. An Israelite was first in God's kingdom through Jewish identity. They could, however, be shut out if they rejected the Torah or were apostate.[20]

To use modern Christian lingo, obeying the commandments did not get one saved, but following them and the many Jewish customs associated with them was expected of those who were saved. So, in

---

[19] Avi ben Mordechai, *Galatians* (Israel: Millennium 7000 Communications, 2005), 44-77), preface x
[20] Claude Montefiore, *Judaism and St. Paul* (New York: Arno Press, 1973)

the eyes of covenantal nomists, eternal security was automatically given to Israelites who faithfully kept the Torah.

Gentiles

Where does this leave Gentiles? Some taught that any righteous God-fearing Gentile who made a confession could have a place in the world to come.[21] To secure a place in Israel proper, however, allowances were made for non-Jews to be brought in. If a Gentile agreed to certain terms, they could be taught to properly practice the Torah and be legally recognized as a full Jewish convert (*ger tzedek*). In doing so, the Gentile would also be submitting themselves to rabbinic decrees and rabbinic authority.

Jewish rituals for Gentiles quickly became a hot topic for the leaders of the synagogue in the apostolic age. Under the preaching of Paul and others, there was a spike in the number of non-Jews attending the synagogue. Jewish leaders wrestled with what to do with these messianic Gentiles. The Pharisees were stricter in their soteriology than most. They wanted to shut the believing Gentiles out of the synagogue and out of the commonwealth of Israel unless they proved their sincerity. They insisted that Gentiles (1) change their status through circumcision and (2) agree to observe the Torah as taught by their rabbis.

> *"But some from the sect of the Pharisees who believed rose up, saying, 'It is necessary to circumcise them, and to command them to keep the law of Moses.'"* – Acts 15:5

As a result, tension was brewing in the messianic churches of the first century – a tension between Jewish leaders and Gentile converts. Social interaction between Jews and Greeks was already virtually non-existent. This posed a challenge to the diverse population of early believers. As Gentiles began turning to Christ in large numbers, it presented unique cultural and doctrinal obstacles. Increased Gentile involvement exposed the rift and widened the gap that already existed between Jew and Gentile.

---

[21] *Tractate Sanhedrin* 13.2

To a Gentile, Jewish nationalism may seem offensive. As God's chosen people, however, Jews felt an obligation to honor the Scriptures, respect their forefathers and preserve their history. This is to be commended.

Ancestry and pedigree are important to Israelites.[22] We should be grateful that the Hebrew people kept such scrupulous genealogical records, of which we can ascertain the lineage of Christ. However, Jewish exclusivity posed a problem for the message of repentance to spread to Gentile nations even before the apostolic age. Like he did with Jonah, God was putting his finger on it once again.

Conclusion

Peter had a similar calling to Jonah. He and the apostles were called to take God's message beyond the borders and mindsets of Israel. Peter's vision radically challenged the policies of covenantal nomism. It paved the way for Gentiles to be saved without being forced to succumb to Jewish rules and institutionalized ceremonies.

---

[22] Titus 3:9

ACTS 15:1-11

Truth #17: *Gentiles can be saved as Gentiles.*

The issue of Gentile inclusion was far from settled even ten years after Peter's visit to the house of Cornelius. It had been twenty years since Yeshua's ascension. What to do with Gentile believers still remained a point of contention. During this time persecution forced the believers living in Jerusalem to disperse, and the church at Antioch emerged as an influential community of disciples. While in Antioch, the Holy Spirit set aside Paul and Barnabas to take the gospel to the Gentile world. After a time of fasting, the elders laid hands on Barnabas and Paul and launched them on their first missionary endeavor.

Within the messianic community of Judea, however, there remained an influential contingency of Jewish believers who adamantly rejected uncircumcised Gentiles. They insisted that Gentiles must submit to Jewish ceremonial customs in order to be acknowledged and accepted into their communities of faith.

The dispute became contentious in Acts 15. Luke writes,

> *"And certain men came down from Judea and taught the brethren, 'Unless you are circumcised according to the custom of Moses, you cannot be saved.' Therefore, when Paul and Barnabas had no small dissension and dispute with them, they determined that Paul and Barnabas and certain others of them should go up to Jerusalem, to the apostles and elders, about this question." – Acts 15:1-2*

These men from Judea were insisting that in order for a Gentile to be saved, they must be circumcised. Of all things, why circumcision? This was not some legalistic enforcement of Torah. Neither was it to fulfill the circumcision of a male child on the eighth day. This circumcision was a Jewish custom that was required of a Gentile man wanting to be included in the covenant. It was standard operating procedure in those days and viewed much the same way many Catholics view baptism.

As noted in the previous chapter, it was widely held that in order for a Gentile to claim the blessings and promises of Abraham, they must obtain a Jewish status of sorts. A ceremony that included circumcision provided that. This is the circumcision spoken of in this passage.

In the eyes of these men from Judea, a God-fearing Gentile could enjoy the benefits of being a covenant member of Israel and secure a place in the world to come through circumcision. Ritual circumcision also gave the God-fearer access to the temple and membership rights in the synagogue. These circumcision rites became the entry point to the covenant for non-Jews in the eyes of many first-century rabbis.

Following the covenantal nomism of the time, the men from Judea expected believing Gentiles to become certified in order to authenticate their newfound faith in the Jewish Messiah. That certification required circumcision for males and often some combination of a sacrifice, *mikvah*, and taking on the written and oral Torah.[1] Once the requirements were fulfilled, a Gentile could be considered a member of the Jewish commonwealth.[2] In this case, ritual circumcision was the primary criteria chosen by these Judean men and by much of Israel.

In Acts, the men refer to the ritual as the custom of Moses, though there is no way to corroborate that this was actually the practice of Moses. *The custom of Moses* could refer to the process by which the circumcision was administered or the manner in which they were to take on the Torah. The fact that Scripture does not outline how one becomes a Jewish proselyte demonstrates that the rabbinic manner

---

[1] Chaim HaQoton, "Becoming A Jew" [Online]. Available: www.rchaimqoton.blogspot.com/2006/06/becoming-jew.html
[2] *HaYesod*, Student Workbook (Littleton: FFOZ, 2010), 7.12

of proselytization was entirely man-made.³ In submitting to it, however, the God-fearing Gentile was also submitting himself to an exhaustive list of written, oral and rabbinic requirements within a particular Jewish sectarian group.

Ritual Circumcision

It is helpful to realize that when circumcision is mentioned in the Apostolic Scriptures, it is typically not in reference to the commandment given in Torah. Because first-century racial tension is largely foreign to us, too often we confuse the circumcision spoken of here with the circumcision spoken of in the Torah. They are not the same. They are two different circumcisions with two separate motivations. One is the circumcision of male infants on the eighth day. The other is the circumcision of adult males. One is Biblical. The other is extra-Biblical.

The circumcision of infants is prescribed in Scripture for male children born to the house of Abraham.⁴ It is a precept given to parents for the consecration of their sons.⁵ Circumcising a male child on the eighth day is a sign of the covenant God made with Abraham.⁶

The type of circumcision spoken of in this passage and in much of Paul's writings, however, is ritual circumcision. It cannot be overemphasized that this type of circumcision was not a divine command but a man-made rite of passage bestowed upon Gentiles. There is no commandment in Scripture stating that a foreigner or stranger who desires to worship the God of Israel must be circumcised or undergo any kind of formal Jewish conversion.⁷ God

---

³ Hegg, *Acts 15 and the Jerusalem Council*, 2
⁴ Gen. 17:10-13
⁵ Lev. 12:1-3
⁶ Rom. 4:9-12
⁷ The only general ordinance for adult circumcision is of a foreigner who desired to partake of the sacrificial Passover lamb – Ex. 12:43-51. This does not prohibit uncircumcised Gentiles from celebrating Passover today. It was a specific injunction forbidding an uncircumcised male from eating the physical paschal lamb. Since a lamb cannot be sacrificed as a burnt offering in a modern Passover

offers no Biblical formula for how a Gentile could become a Jew, perhaps because He did not want Gentiles becoming Jews or Jews becoming Gentiles.

We do know that he desires a body of believers, both Jew and Gentile, righteously following Christ together. A non-Jew who submitted to adult circumcision was not doing so in accordance with the Torah but likely only to be in compliance with rabbinic requirements or at the insistence of covenantal nomists. You will find that most references to circumcision in the New Testament are a shorthand reference to these far more comprehensive Jewish rites.

In addition to the ceremony of the proselyte, circumcision was also a common way of gaining Jewish status. Circumcision is largely what differentiated a Jew from a Gentile in the first century and often still today. This is evidenced in Paul's letters. He commonly refers to Jews as *the Circumcised* and to Gentiles as *the Uncircumcised*.

In Acts 15, Paul and Barnabas together stood in opposition to requiring Gentiles to submit to the ritual of circumcision. They argued that Gentiles could be saved on the same condition as Jews without having to go under the knife, so to speak.

Luke continues,

> "When they had come to Jerusalem, they were received by the church and the apostles and the elders, and they reported all things that God had done with them. But some of the sect of the Pharisees who believed rose up, saying, 'It is necessary to circumcise them, and to command them to keep the law of Moses.'" – Acts 15:4-5

The context of the contention is salvation and Gentile inclusion, not holy living. This is a notable distinction. The question at hand is not if a believing Gentile man should ever be circumcised, or if he should circumcise his infant son on the eighth day. Neither does it address the expectation to follow God's commands as a matter of

---

festival, uncircumcised Gentiles are free to celebrate the feast and eat the commemorative Passover meal.

discipleship. Sanctification is not the topic here. No one was debating how Gentile Christians should conduct themselves in Christ. The tension centers solely on the qualifications of salvation for non-Jews.

Because the rabbis had created a religion that required non-Jews to become members, the sect of the Pharisees took the position that Gentiles needed to be initiated into Israel. These "believing" Pharisees wanted Gentile converts to jump through the traditional hoops handed down to them by their forefathers and to stick to the customary requirements that governed Jewish status. In their minds, circumcision and keeping the law were prerequisites and preconditions to Jewish social interaction. Once a Gentile was circumcised through their customs, only then could they gain access to what Jews possessed.

By enforcing circumcision, however, the Pharisees essentially believed that only the circumcised could be saved. If this doctrine had been tolerated, Jewish identity and circumcision would essentially replace faith as the primary evidence of salvation.

This doctrine didn't sit well with Paul. He had been given a heavenly revelation of Gentile inclusion. He adamantly preached that Gentiles could be saved as Gentiles. This is why he uses such strong language to oppose the practice of these Judeans.

Can a Gentile be Saved?

"Now the apostles and elders came together to consider this matter. And when there had been much dispute, Peter rose up and said to them: 'Men and brethren, you know that a good while ago God chose among us, that by my mouth the Gentiles should hear the word of the gospel and believe. So God, who knows the heart, acknowledged them by giving them the Holy Spirit, just as He did to us, and made no distinction between us and them, purifying their hearts by faith. Now therefore, why do you test God by putting a yoke on the neck of the disciples which neither our fathers nor we were able to bear? But we believe that through the grace of the Lord Jesus Christ we shall be saved in the same manner as they.'" – Acts 15:6-11

It is a common misconception that the purpose of the Jerusalem council was to determine if Gentiles needed to obey the Torah. This was not the case. No one was preaching salvation through good deeds in this passage, including the men from Judea.

In accordance with first-century mindsets and the context of this passage, the purpose of the Jerusalem council was to determine if Gentiles were required to submit to the Jewish ceremony of circumcision. They questioned whether Gentiles needed to be circumcised in order to validate their salvation and be assimilated into the faith community.

The questions at hand were: Can a non-Jew be saved? What qualified a person to be saved – ethnic status, circumcision or faith? What are the requirements for Gentiles seeking salvation? Are Jewish ceremonies a necessary prerequisite to salvation? Can a Gentile enter into a covenant relationship with God without becoming an Israelite? Must non-Jews submit to Jewish sectarian rites in order to secure a place within the age to come?

The answers to these questions may seem obvious to us today, but they weren't so obvious to them. There was no doubt a sharp difference of opinion over what expectations should be placed on Gentile converts coming to Christ. Since the first followers were almost all exclusively Jewish, the inclusion of Gentiles within their ranks was a precarious and not always welcomed development.

We must be careful not to flip the subject. The council met to determine what to do with Gentiles, not what to do with God's commandments. It was the doctrine of the circumcision party that was on trial, not the Torah.

The Unbearable Yoke

It is no coincidence that Peter was the one to stand up in defense of Gentile inclusion. Not only was he a leader among the brethren, but it was also his obedience to the vision at Joppa that paved the way for the gospel to spread among Gentile nations. Peter declares to the brethren:

> *"(God) made no distinction between us and them, purifying their hearts by faith. Now therefore, why do you test God by putting a yoke on the neck of the disciples which neither our fathers nor we were able to bear? But we believe that through the grace of the Lord Jesus Christ we shall be saved in the same manner as they." – Acts 15:9-11*

Many assume that the yoke to which Peter refers is the yoke of Torah obedience. This cannot be. Here's why. The subject matter of this passage is salvation. This is reinforced in verse 11 when Peter says, "We will be <u>saved</u> through the grace of the Lord Jesus, just as they will."

Luke reveals to us in what context Peter's comments should be taken. Peter is sticking to the topic at hand, namely salvation and determining what instructions should be given to Gentiles coming to Christ. The context is Gentile inclusion, not Torah exclusion. Peter is stating how a person comes to faith in Christ, not how a person expresses it. He advocates that Jews and Gentiles can be saved on the same condition.

The truth is that God's grace is given through faith in Christ, not ethnicity. For this reason, the yoke cannot be obedience to Torah commands. The yoke on the neck of the disciples was the rabbinic prerequisites (like ritual circumcision) that prevented Gentile converts from receiving the grace of God and entering into covenant relationship with God. It was Jewish mandates required by the rabbis and sewn into their proselyte ceremonies that was an unbearable yoke.

It should be pointed out that being faithful to God's commandments in response to his grace is always presented in a positive light in Scripture. The idea of an oppressive yoke of the law contrasting with the easy yoke of Christ is a figment of doctrinal imagination.

The easy yoke and the light burden that Yeshua speaks of in Matthew 11 is a reference to his manner of discipleship. His example of godliness is an achievable joy, and his life of love is kind. Like a husband pleasing his wife and fulfilling his vows, obeying God's commands as Jesus demonstrated is not a burden but a supreme act of committed love.

Additionally, Peter is not shy in bringing God's word into his presentation of the gospel in Acts 2. He makes a strong case from Scripture that Yeshua is the Messiah. Here we find Peter and the other apostles presenting the gospel within the framework of the Torah, not in opposition to it. How could the Torah keeping be the unbearable yoke if Peter bases the message of the good news upon the Torah?

The yoke that Peter refers to is undoubtedly the same yoke that Jesus identified as the heavy burden of the Pharisees in Matthew 23. It is the yoke of taking up fence laws, mechanical rule keeping and faithless customs in an effort to achieve the favor of God.

In contrast to the yoke of the Pharisees, the yoke of Christ is easy and light. It does not require a long list of additional or institutional embellishments. In this case, Peter wanted to protect Gentile converts from being required to take on faithless Jewish customs in their pursuit of Christ.[8]

Conclusion

Torah keeping does not factor into the equation of salvation and never has. It is the result of our salvation, not the means by which we are saved. Peter agrees with Paul and Barnabas that justification is by grace alone through faith.

Being justified before God is not achieved through Jewish identity or institutionalized policies. This was the doctrine of these Judean men.

---

[8] Paul also speaks of a yoke in his letters, referring to it as the *yoke of bondage*. Paul may be drawing from Lev. 26:13 in Gal. 5:1-3. Because the book of Galatians was written near the time of the events of Acts 15, some scholars conclude that it was penned around the same time of the decision of the Jerusalem council. I will go into more depth on this topic when we examine the book of Galatians, but the context here cannot be ignored. Paul is writing to a Gentile audience that is being pressured to succumb to mandated circumcision just as they were in Acts 15.

The yoke of trying to preserve salvation through man-made precepts is what Peter identifies as the unbearable yoke.

Gentile conversion through circumcision is a consistent theme addressed throughout the Apostolic Scriptures. In the book of Galatians, Paul is tackling the very same issues presented to the Jerusalem council. He is hammering home the point that submitting to circumcision ultimately rejects Christ as the Savior, because it professes that salvation comes not by faith but through Jewish identity.

The "whole law" that the Gentile becomes "a debtor to" includes a comprehensive list of oral, written and rabbinic law that was incumbent upon the proselyte. In the words of Paul, it is not the Torah but the doctrine of the circumcision party that is the liberty-stealing yoke of slavery.

ACTS 15:12-31

Truth #18: *The apostles instructed Gentile converts to keep Torah commands.*

After Paul and Barnabas share testimonies of genuine uncircumcised Gentile conversion, James stands up to give a ruling. This is not James the brother of John, one of the original Twelve. He was martyred by Herod. This is James the Just, the bishop of Jerusalem, the writer of the book of James and half-brother to Jesus.

> *"Therefore I judge that we should not trouble those from among the Gentiles who are turning to God, but that we write to them to abstain from things polluted by idols, from sexual immorality, from things strangled, and from blood. For Moses has had throughout many generations those who preach him in every city, being read in the synagogues every Sabbath." - Acts 15:19-21*

The antinomian perspective resolves that these verses conclusively release Gentile Christians from any obligation to follow Torah. It concludes that the Torah is troublesome to Gentiles who are turning to God, and expecting Gentile Christians to obey the Torah is contrary to the practice of the church of Acts. Let's analyze this passage further to see if this is accurate.

After testimonies are given, James agrees that the Gentiles need not be circumcised in order to follow Christ. He suggests they draft a letter instructing Gentile Christians to abstain from: (1) things polluted by idols, (2) sexual immorality, (3) things strangled and (4) blood. This is a curious list of prohibitions.

Of these four, three are specifically outlined and outlawed in the Torah – *idolatry* (Ex. 20:2-6, Lev. 19:4, 26:1, Deut. 4:15-31, 12:29-32), *sexual immorality* (Ex. 20:14, Lev. 18, Deut. 22:13-30), and *consuming* or *shedding blood* (Lev. 17:10-14, 19:26, Ex. 20:13). The fourth, *things strangled*, was an oral law that prohibited eating animals strangled to death, a Jewish kosher standard for meat.

Strangling an animal to death results in a certain amount of blood remaining in the meat. As a result, there was and still is a specific kosher method for slaughtering an animal that optimizes the drainage of blood. In Hebrew culture, eating an animal that had been strangled was generally not permitted in light of the commandment to "not eat any flesh with the blood in it" (Lev. 19:26 ESV).

If Gentiles were indeed released from obeying the Torah, as some argue, then how do we explain the apostles placing three Torah mandates and a Jewish kosher law on these new converts? Under the conventional interpretation of this passage, James would be guilty of placing them under a yoke of the law. What is more, he even mandated them to obey a Jewish oral law!

Something is obviously off. Our traditional definition of "yoke on the necks of the Gentiles" needs some adjusting.

Four Instructions

Why would James require the Gentile converts to submit to a Jewish custom? Our answer comes in understanding that these four instructions were tailored for a specific audience for a specific reason. These were a small list of expectations given to first-century Gentile converts. They are not an exhaustive list of discipleship requirements. Other instructions might be more appropriate for new converts in our culture, but these four were sufficient for that time and day.

Of all the initial requirements that could have been given, why were these four given in particular?

To begin with, these four activities were directly associated with temple paganism. They are representative of the many idolatrous practices that dominated the Gentile world at the time. Things polluted by idols, sexual immorality, strangled animal meat and blood all characterized the cult worship found in Greek temples. The pagan temples were dedicated to Roman gods and were a one-stop shop for indulging the flesh. They were a restaurant, brothel, shrine and city hall all rolled up into one. Often they were stationed at the heart of the city. Some Gentile Christians may still have frequented the local temples for legal or business purposes, even if they did not engage in all the festivities.

These four apostolic requirements urged Gentile believers to steer clear of anything to do with temple idolatry, including prostitution, blood sacrifices, blood soups, meat saturated with blood, murder and strangled flesh. Not only do these activities violate God's commands but they also aren't reflective of someone who worships the One True God. The apostles weren't prohibiting the Gentile converts from buying food from the marketplace. They were asking them to steer clear from attending idolatrous ceremonies and festivities at the pagan temples.

A modern equivalent to this injunction might be when a Hindu man hears the gospel, repents of his sin and comes to Christ. No doubt this new convert would be encouraged to cease to call upon the Hindu gods he once worshipped. In his discipleship, we might encourage him to no longer visit the Hindu temple, to remove all the idols from his home and to stop doing yoga.

Additionally, these four contributed to the social barriers that existed between Jew and Gentile. Three of these guidelines (*things polluted by idols, strangled meat* and *consuming blood*) are dietary prohibitions espoused by Jews but not regularly practiced by Gentiles.

Most Jews were less than willing to share a meal with a noted idolater. To avoid violating any laws regarding food, Jews simply found it easier to avoid pagan tables and Gentile food markets altogether. James reasons that by refusing meat that had been strangled or dedicated to a deity, a Jewish believer could share *koinonia* (fellowship) with a Gentile brother worry-free. In requesting Gentile converts to honor Jewish values, the social stigma was removed, and Jews could fellowship with non-proselytes in good conscience.

In this way, these prohibitions were practical and ethical. They were not just moral guidelines but social ones as well. By calling the converted Gentile to a higher standard of holiness, social disruption could be avoided and table fellowship could be enjoyed between the believing Jew and Gentile.

Notice that Scripture is not lowered to accommodate Gentile standards. The apostles raised the standard of the Gentile to meet the requirements of God's word. When it comes to Scripture, it is important that we do not compromise it for the sake of outreach, unity or evangelism. We don't stoop to the level of the world to entice them in. Neither do we compromise our convictions for one another. Instead, we call the new convert up out of their depravity and up into God's standard of righteousness.

Some teach that these four instructions were the only requirements expected of these Gentile believers going forward. The problem with this notion is how incomplete the list is. Theft, hatred, greed, jealousy, lying and drunkenness are all strangely absent from James' prohibition letter. If this was meant to be an exhaustive list of discipleship requirements given to Gentile believers, we have a bigger problem on our hands.

Following this line of thinking would make it acceptable for Christians to lie as long as they abstain from eating strangled meat. Or they could be permitted to cheat on their taxes so long as they don't cheat on their spouse. One might even reason that a Gentile Christian could be a wife-beating, casino-addicted drunkard so long as they eat a kosher diet!

Now, I have taken it to the ludicrous extreme, but you see my point. When pulled through, this interpretation cannot be sustained. We understand there is much more to sanctification and discipleship than just these four instructions.

Imagine if these four instructions were really the only moral guidelines for believers. Some clever Sunday school teacher would undoubtedly dub them the Big 4. We'd hold classes for new converts teaching them that Christian morality consisted only of abstaining from pagan meat, road kill, immorality and extremely rare steaks. Any other manner of behavior would be acceptable. Teaching these four guidelines would be the first order of every church's discipleship program. Hatred, sorcery, drunken rage – we don't care as long as you keep the Big 4. As ridiculous as this sounds, this represents the interpretation the church has traditionally held regarding this passage.

In examining the full teachings of the apostles, it can be concluded that they obviously understood there to be more to following Christ than these four given instructions. These four provided a baseline, not a finish line, at the onset of salvation for these Gentiles converting to Christ. You and I know full well that there is much more to following Christ than these four prohibitions. Any long-term discipleship expectations for maturing Christians should expand well beyond what is outlined in James' letter. In fact, there is ample scholarly evidence that the morality of the Torah was the norm for all believers in the first century.[1]

Some have suggested that these four represent the seven Noahide laws given to Noah and laid out in the Talmud. These seven laws were expected of Gentiles who wanted a place in the kingdom of heaven. They are identified as: (1) practicing justice, and abstaining from (2) blasphemy, (3) idolatry, (4) adultery, (5) robbery, (6) bloodshed, and (7) eating flesh torn from a live animal.[2]

I find this position porous for a few reasons. First, there is no reference to Noah or to this Talmudic teaching in this passage. Second, Noahide laws were not identified during the first century but came much later. Third, I do not see a connection here since blasphemy, robbery and injustice are absent from the list of prohibitions found in Acts 15. And lastly, God despises double

---

[1] Tim Hegg, *The Letter Writer* (Littleton: FFOZ, 2002), 265-266
[2] *Sanhedrin* 58b, *Tosefta*. There are some alternative lists presented by the rabbis.

standards.[3] I do not believe that Luke and the early apostles would support two separate standards of righteousness for the followers of Christ.

Moses on Sabbath

James continues.

> *"For Moses has had throughout many generations those who preach him in every city, being read in the synagogues every Sabbath."* – Acts 15:21

Why is verse 21 included? The inclusion of this verse suggests that additional obligations were required of Gentile converts. It also casts serious doubt on the opinion that the Torah does not apply to Gentile Christians. If Torah mattered not, then why would James make such a statement? Why did Luke include it in his narrative?

There is strong evidence that the congregation of the Way still gathered for Sabbath (*Shabbat*) in local synagogues even twenty years after Christ's ascension. James even employs the Greek word *synagōgue* to describe the gathering place of believers.[4] Being that Gentiles were largely ignorant of the Hebrew Scriptures, these Gentile converts could be integrated into the greater faith community and grow in their knowledge of the God of Israel through the weekly, public reading of the Torah in their local synagogue.

James informs us that the teachings of Moses were found in every city in the Roman Empire. Any Gentile Christian could hear for themselves what God required of them. It can only be that James and the apostles expected Gentile Christians to hear and follow the Torah as it was read in the synagogue each Sabbath. Since no Gentile was in possession of a Bible, a Gentile could personally hear the word of God each week and be folded into the messianic community as they continued their journey of faith in Christ.

---

[3] Prov. 20:10, 23
[4] James 2:2, *Strong's* #G4864 συναγωγή

Attending the synagogue was not for the purpose of evangelizing Jews. This was a part of their discipleship in Christ. This would help them grow in their newfound faith and in what God required of them. The four prohibitions ensured that these Gentile converts could attend their local synagogue in good standing and hear the word of God without being barred for being an idolater.

This is not too different from what we require today. We would not expect pastors to force newcomers to obey everything expected of them in Scripture on the first day of their visit. But once a new convert makes a commitment to Christ and comes to a place of maturity, there would be a growing expectation that they walk circumspectly and exemplify godly character.

The use of the word synagogue within the context of the early believers should not alarm us. Just as church (*ekklesia*) refers to a gathering of people and not the building itself, so it was with synagogues. Archaeological digs within Israel have revealed that private homes were more often used as synagogues than public buildings. Additionally, these synagogue homes were commonly referred to as places of prayer.[5] In fact, clues found in the Septuagint suggest that the words *ekklesia* and *synagōgue* may have been viewed as near synonyms at the time.[6]

No matter what city Gentile converts lived in, they would naturally want to gravitate to their local community of faith for fellowship and to learn how to live in a godly manner. Since church buildings did not exist at the time, James did not want them troubled and excluded from the messianic community simply because they refused Jewish rites. So, he gives them these four basic guidelines to help them navigate synagogue participation and Jewish interaction.

Today, we have tremendous access to Scripture. There is no lack of Christian fellowships that openly teach God's word. For this reason, Gentile participation in the local synagogue is not as common.

---

[5] Hegg, *The Letter Writer*, 72
[6] Ibid, 119

Perhaps this is why these four prohibitions are not the first order of discipleship for new believers in our culture.

Joseph Shulam offers a modern interpretation of verses 19-21. He writes,

> "Do not put obstacles in the way of the Gentiles while they are going through the process of turning from idolatry to God. Instead, let them use their spiritual energy in repentance. There will be plenty of opportunities later for them to absorb what Moses has to say."[7]

This seems to coincide with the *Didache's* instructions for Gentiles to bear all of the Torah when possible and "do what you are able to do."[8]

Conclusion

Acts 15 tells the story of how the early believers arrived at the conclusion that Gentiles could be saved as Gentiles. The apostles resolved that believing Gentiles were under no obligation to become Torah-observant Jews as a prerequisite to salvation. They agreed that both Jews and Gentiles could be saved by grace through faith. As basic as it sounds, this decision was revolutionary at the time and is still impacting us today.

---

[7] Stern, *Jewish New Testament Commentary*, 277
[8] Didache 6:2. Still today there are some within the messianic community that espouse that a person must have Jewish blood in their lineage to be a part of God's house. This doctrine, espoused by some within the *Two-House Movement* (also called the *Ephraimite Movement*), teaches that all believers are members of the lost tribe of Israel and will be reunited with the house of Judah under the new covenant. They maintain that every disciple of Yeshua has traces of Jewish blood in them and are really Jews in disguise descending from the house of Ephraim. Unfortunately, this position ignores the practice and doctrine of the apostolic church. This doctrine essentially advocates that only Jews can be saved, and that salvation comes through Jewish ancestry. It disregards the promise of Gentile conversion found in Scripture and advocates salvation through Jewish blood. It makes Jewish blood more efficacious than the blood of Yeshua. In this way, this teaching appears to side more with the position of the Pharisees than with the apostles. Because of this, I find this perspective unpersuasive.

Modern scholarship has produced a marked shift in our understanding of the second temple period. The world in which the apostles lived is coming into better focus. Reputable scholars now believe that the social dilemma of the first-century church was not about what role the Torah played in the new covenant, but about how Gentile Christians fit within the believing Jewish community. This makes sense in light of this passage.

The presumption that first-century Jews were legalistic in their theology is also no longer widely assumed. There is ample evidence to support the idea that Jews were covenantal nomists. This is a monumental shift in our understanding of the culture in which the New Testament was birthed.

Because circumcision essentially made a Gentile like a Jew, it posed a serious threat to the gospel. If the apostles had sided with the circumcision party, it would mean that salvation is by circumcision. Uncircumcised Gentiles would be left out in the cold. If the Judean men had their way, Gentile men today would still be required to gain legal, Jewish citizenship and submit to circumcision in order to be saved. Thankfully, the apostles arrived at another conclusion.

After hearing the testimonies of Paul, Barnabas and Peter, the Jerusalem council came together and established general rules for (a) Gentiles coming to Christ, (b) Jewish fellowship and (c) the protection of the entire messianic community. This is nothing more than what churches do today. James laid out general house rules to keep order and protect the congregation.

Opponents of this perspective use Acts 15 as proof that there are no additional Torah requirements needed for Gentile believers. A closer examination of the passage, however, suggests this to be a superficial reading. The issue at hand in Acts 15 was salvation, not sanctification.

In addition to initially adhering to a small list of written, oral and dietary prohibitions, the expectation was that Gentiles would hear the teachings of Moses read each Sabbath in the synagogues and to follow it going forward. Though the list was short, James was careful not to place large obstacles in the way of these Gentile believers as they turned from the practice of idolatry to the ways of God. Nowhere does this passage infer that Gentiles should be released from Torah obligations. On the contrary, it suggests that the Gentile disciples tied their discipleship to their knowledge of the Torah.

It was not the Torah that was troublesome to Gentiles seeking God. It was ritual circumcision and the doctrine of the Pharisees that was deemed troublesome. Obedience to God's commandments as a matter of discipleship is one thing, but taking on the complete written, oral and traditional rabbinic laws as a prerequisite to salvation is quite another. But if in their conversion to Christ the Torah helped to dictate the behavior of these Gentile believers, then it stands to reason that in their discipleship the Torah helped to dictate their behavior as well.

The church has come a long way since the Jerusalem council, so far that the pendulum has swung the opposite way. Whereas the basic problem in the first century was if a Gentile should identify as a Jew in order to be a Christian, nowadays people wonder if a Jew should become more like a Gentile in order to be a true Christian. Instead of expecting Gentile believers to submit to Jewish customs, we expect Jewish believers to shed their Hebrew heritage and behave more like Gentiles. How arrogant of us!

We've gone from Jews finding offense over Gentiles joining in to Gentiles being offended with anything that appears Jewish. While it is true that the nation of Israel has been partially hardened to the gospel until the times of the Gentiles is complete,[9] our Christian traditions are certainly not helping spread the good news freely among the Jewish people. I pray you and I are the ones who will bring about positive changes that will affect future generations for ages to come.

---

[9] Luke 21:24, Rom. 11:25

Romans 14, 1 Corinthians 8

Truth #19: *God has an opinion about food.*

Many of the significant events of the Bible involve food.

Adam and Eve disobeyed a dietary command. Melchizedek brought communion to Abram. Esau sold his birthright for a bowl of soup and then lost his father's blessing over a meal. Joseph rose to power during a famine. The Israelites ate the Passover before the Exodus. They ate quail and drank water from a rock. The spies brought back food spoils from the Promised Land. Elisha supernaturally multiplied the bread and healed the poisonous pot of stew. Jesus turned bath water into fine wine and fed fish sandwiches to the multitudes, not once but twice. Judas dipped his hand into the bowl at the last supper. John ate the scroll.

From Elijah's drought to the activities of the tabernacle, from manna to the marriage supper of the Lamb, food plays an important role in the Biblical narrative. It was no different for the apostolic church.

An issue arose over certain food items sold in the public markets. Leftover meat from pagan sacrifices was commonly sold in the local market, as well as wine that had been poured out as a libation.[1] Food or drink dedicated to Greek gods was considered by many to be idolatrous. Yeshua rebuked those in Pergamos who ate things sacrificed to idols,[2] and Paul also supported this view as well.[3]

---

[1] Virgil, *Aeneid*, VIII, 273 [Online]. Available: http://faculty.sgc.edu/rkelley/The%20Aeneid.pdf
[2] Rev. 2:14
[3] 1 Cor. 10:18-23

The problem, however, was that the origin of marketplace meat was not always known. This called into question meat and wine sold in the Greek markets.

Some felt that all marketplace meat was potentially dedicated to a pagan deity, thereby tainted. Consuming it violated their conscience. They strongly opposed any association with meat or drink that had been knowingly or unknowingly offered on a pagan altar.

Others were of the opinion that idols are worthless and eating food potentially dedicated to a pagan god is harmless. If one had unknowingly consumed sacrificial meat or wine poured out as an incantation, the food had no spiritual power over them. Since an idol is nothing in light of the One True God, they bought and ate meat from the pagan market in good conscience.

This clash was more heightened in cities where Jew and Gentile were integrated within the faith congregation, such as in Ephesus and Rome.

Paul addresses the topic in 1 Corinthians 8.

> *"Therefore concerning the eating of things offered to idols, we know that an idol is nothing in the world, and that there is no other God but one...However, there is not in everyone that knowledge; for some, with consciousness of the idol, until now eat it as a thing offered to an idol; and their conscience, being weak, is defiled." – 1 Corinthians 8:4,7*

To the Romans, he writes:

> *"Receive one who is weak in the faith, but not to dispute over doubtful things. For one believes he may eat all things, but he who is weak eats only vegetables. Let not him who eats despise him who does not eat, and let not him who does not eat judge him who eats; for God has received him. Who are you to judge another's servant? To his own master he stands or falls. Indeed, he will be made to stand, for God is able to make him stand." – Romans 14:1-4*

Pagan meat and wine offered to idols are the "doubtful things" that Paul is addressing here. Because there is no guidance given in Scripture concerning these matters, the apostle is seeking to bring perspective and instruction.

To Paul, an idol is powerless. "Whether in heaven or on earth," any "so-called god" is not the "the Father of whom *are* all things" and the "Lord Jesus Christ, through whom *are* all things, and through whom we *live*" (1 Cor. 8:5-6). With or without knowledge that a particular item was offered to a deity, an idol meant nothing to Paul and held no power over him. He never worshipped these idols and had no connection to them.

This was not the case for everyone. The "weak in the faith" were still coming out of these practices and coming into the full knowledge of the Most High. Evidently, there were some among them who avoided meat altogether and refused to eat any meat sold in the marketplace due to its possible connection with idols. Because their conscience was "weak," partaking of these things made them feel "defiled" (1 Cor. 8:7).

Paul urges the church to,

> *"Receive the one who is weak in the faith" and "eats only vegetables. Let not him who eats despise him who does not eat, and let not him who does not eat judge him who eats, for God has received him." - Romans 14:1-3*

He concludes that those weak in faith should not pass judgment on those who do eat. Likewise, those strong in faith should not despise those who don't.

> *"Therefore, let us pursue the things which make for peace, and the things by which one may edify one another." – Romans 14:19*

> *"For none of us lives to himself, and no one dies to himself...Therefore, let us not judge one another anymore, but rather resolve this, not to put a stumbling block or a cause to fall in our brother's way." – Romans 14:7,13*

In a fatherly tone, Paul urges them not to despise those who feel they cannot eat marketplace meat in good conscience. To Paul, if one had no prior knowledge of its connection to an idol, eating meat sold in pagan markets was acceptable. Those feeble in faith and convicted in conscience, however, should not be judged for their decision to abstain, because "food does not commend us to God; for neither if we eat are we the better; nor if we do not eat are we the worse" (1 Cor. 8:8).

In deciphering these passages, we must be mindful not to project our own cultural interpretation onto the text. Paul is not speaking to vegans or vegetarians. He is not addressing bacon, shrimp, alcoholic liberty or health dieting. These might be some of our own cultural issues, but they were not theirs. Nor is this a dissertation on dietary laws and unclean meats. The apostle clearly identifies the disputable matter as "eating things offered to idols" (1 Cor. 8:1,4).

The onus is on the stronger to protect the weaker. Those who knew that idols were nothing should not look down upon those who could not consciously eat food sold in the marketplace.

> *"Beware lest somehow this liberty of yours become a stumbling block to those who are weak. For if anyone sees you who have knowledge eating in an idol's temple, will not the conscience of him who is weak be emboldened to eat those things offered to idols? And because of your knowledge shall the weak brother perish, for whom Christ died? But when you thus sin against the brethren, and wound their weak conscience, you sin against Christ." – 1 Corinthians 8:9-12*

The one who knows God and does not have concern for idols must not use their freedom to cause the weaker to falter. If the liberated were found to be eating in a pagan temple, it could be perceived as participating in cult worship. It might encourage those feeble in faith to violate their conscience and fall into idolatry. Paul reasons that the stronger should not use their liberty to participate in anything that could be perceived as idolatrous for their own sake as well as for the sake of their brothers and sisters in Christ.

> *"Eat whatever is sold in the meat market, asking no questions for conscience' sake...If any of those who do not believe invites you to dinner, and you desire to go, eat whatever is set before you, asking no question for conscience' sake. But if anyone says to you, 'This was offered to idols,' do not eat it for the sake of the one who told you, and for conscience' sake...not your own, but that of the other...Give no offense either to the Jews or to the Greeks or to the church of God."* – 1 Cor. 10:25-31

Paul resolves to personally and permanently abstain from the practice of eating marketplace meat if it causes his brother to stumble.

> *"Therefore, if food makes my brother stumble, I will never again eat meat, lest I make my brother stumble."* – 1 Cor. 8:13

He reasons:

> *"If your brother is grieved because of your food, you are no longer walking in love. Do not destroy with your food the one for whom Christ died. Therefore do not let your good be spoken of as evil; for the kingdom of God is not eating and drinking, but righteousness and peace and joy in the Holy Spirit...It is good neither to eat meat nor drink wine nor do anything by which your brother stumbles or is offended or is made weak."* – Romans 14:15-17, 21

Our attitude should be the same when it comes to matters of individual conviction and preference. We are not at liberty to judge each other on matters not pertaining to eternal life or impertinent to Scripture. We are obligated to abstain from anything that has even the appearance of evil for the sake of love.[4] Our liberty is given to serve one another, not to serve ourselves.

What Day Is It?

In making his point, Paul draws an example from another doubtful thing.

---

[4] 1 Thess. 5:12

> *"One person esteems one day above another; another esteems every day alike. Let each be fully convinced in his own mind. He who observes the day, observes it to the Lord; and he who does not observe the day, to the Lord he does not observe it. He who eats, eats to the Lord, for he gives God thanks; and he who does not eat, to the Lord he does not eat, and gives God thanks."* – Romans 14:5-6

The assumption by many is that Paul is inserting Sabbath into the conversation, identifying its observation as a disputable matter. It has been traditionally interpreted and automatically presumed that "the day" Paul speaks of here is Sabbath. Some translations even capitalize Day to make this inference.

Theoretically, this could be the case. However, there are some difficulties with this interpretation.

For one, the word Sabbath isn't mentioned in this passage and is never used this way in Scripture. Never is Sabbath referred to as *the Day* or just *a day* in the Bible. It is speculative to conclude that Paul is referencing the Sabbath.

Two, the subject matter does not lend itself to the topic of Sabbath keeping. Would Paul intentionally compromise the integrity of one of the Ten Commandments with an off-hand remark used to support his argument about idol meat? Not likely. If he were, should we receive such teaching?

Let's not forget the context. The topic is meat sacrificed to idols in the marketplace, not Torah or Sabbath observance. These are pagan practices that Paul is speaking of. The two topics don't relate.

If the reference is not Sabbath, then what possible day could Paul be referring to? Any idea put forth is also conjecture, but he could be referring to fast days. We learn from Luke that the Pharisees fasted twice a week.[5] Since some of the early believers, including Paul, were Pharisees,[6] it's conceivable they continued the discipline of

---

[5] Luke 18:12
[6] John 3:1, Acts 15:1, Phil. 3:5

fasting. There is some evidence that the early apostolic church maintained the practice of weekly fasting.[7] Given the context, I am not sold on this explanation, but it is plausible.

It's also feasible that "day" is a reference to a pagan holy day. It should not surprise us to learn that the Jews are not the only culture to celebrate special days. We know that Romans held holy days of their own.

Brad Scott writes,

> "The Roman and Corinthians cultures had a myriad of superstitious days and times for everything under the sun. There were specific days that were best for marrying and asking for her hand in marriage. There were days above other days when it was time to wage war, to make love, to make a new friend, and to avoid certain foods, like only fish on Friday."[8]

Much like modern-day Ramadan, Lent and Christmas, first-century pagans celebrated festivals and holy days. While early believers likely did not actively participate in the many idolatrous Greek festivities, the question remained how a follower of Christ should approach pagan holidays. What were believers to do on that day?

Was it unlawful to do business on those days? If you owned a restaurant, was it acceptable to feed those gathered for a pagan feast? Is profiting off a pagan festival allowable? If a believer chose not to work or engage in business on a pagan holy day, would that be considered esteeming the day? If they did work, would their profits be contaminated as idolatrous-related income? Is it acceptable to keep your business open that day? Would it constitute celebration to take the entire day off? Perhaps these questions are what Paul is addressing with the Romans.

---

[7] Didache 8:1
[8] Brad Scott [Online]. Available: https://www.wildbranch.org/teachings/lessons/lesson64.html

Regardless of how we interpret Paul's words, the apostle did not endorse idolatrous practices or celebrating pagan holidays. He is also not addressing unclean meat or likely not even the Sabbath. He is most concerned with how they honored and loved one another, which is the context in which Romans 14 is written.

Nothing Unclean?

> *"I know and am convinced by the Lord Jesus that there is nothing unclean of itself; but to him who considers anything to be unclean, to him it is unclean." – Romans 14:14*

I used to read Romans chapter 14 thinking that Paul considered all animals fit for consumption and that God changed his mind about unclean animals. I was under the impression that those who took a Sabbath or refrained from unclean meats were weak in their faith. Doesn't the passage state this as such?

Unfortunately, I was the victim of my assumptions and my translation. The word used here for 'unclean' is *koinos* (unclean by association), not *akathartos* (Biblically unclean). As noted in chapter 14, *koinos* is not a reference to the clean and unclean animals of Leviticus 11 and Deuteronomy 14. Common infers something contaminated, desecrated or defiled. It is baffling as to why many translators translate this same word as 'uncommon' in Acts 10 yet render it 'unclean' here.

Koinos fits the context perfectly. *Akathartos* does not, which is why *koinos* is used. Paul is not undoing the clean and unclean dietary laws of the Torah in the slightest. Similar to the symbolism of Peter's vision, Paul is addressing common food considered defiled due to pagan handling. The apostle is not persuaded that eating any food unknowingly dedicated to an idol contaminates the soul. He is more concerned about any perceived or actual participation with an idol ritual and how this could affect the church community.[9]

---

[9] Hegg, *The Letter Writer*, 274

Hog Wild

In saying that there is "nothing unclean of itself" (Rom. 14:14), Paul is not suggesting everything in the world is acceptable and consumable. He is staying within the context that food as God defines it is acceptable if eaten without offense.

A similar contextual dilemma can be found in Genesis 9.

> *"Every moving thing that lives shall be food for you. I have given you all things, even as the green herbs." - Genesis 9:3*

At first glance it appears as if God is allowing Noah to eat any kind of plant or animal. However, we would be discriminatory if we removed this single verse from the context in which it is spoken.

True to form, the context of Genesis 9 is found in the previous two chapters. In Genesis 7 and 8 we learn that Noah knew the difference between clean and unclean animals, even before these classifications were codified in the Torah. Animal distinctions antedate the giving of the Torah. It appears as though God made known his will regarding these things, having already given Noah foreknowledge of animal groupings even before the time of Moses.

In the children's version of the flood account, animals file onto Noah's ark two-by-two. However, this is not factually accurate. According to Genesis, Noah brought one pair of every *unclean* animal and seven pairs of every *clean* animal onto the ark. That's a 7 to 1 ratio. The reasons for this are not given, but perhaps a surplus of clean animals was needed because (a) they were to be used for sacrifice, and (b) they were about to be given to mankind for consumption. All animals were to be preserved through the flood, but the value of unclean animals plays an important role in the narrative.

It may be that unclean animals are unfit for consumption for biological reasons. Crab, oysters, crayfish and lobsters are bottom-feeders. They clean our oceans and streams. Similarly, pigs clean up the farm. As an omnivore, a pig will eat anything from maggots to rotting vegetables to the decaying flesh of another animal, even their own feces. Because swine cannot sweat, their flesh absorbs the toxins of their diet. These poisons run down their legs and ooze pus from their feet. For this reason, a pig carries more than a dozen parasites and can transmit up to thirty diseases that can easily be passed on to whatever consumes its flesh.[10]

We can say with confidence that Noah did not interpret God's words to mean he should start marinating those snake and skunk steaks for his next family barbeque. If so, these animals would have been left without a mate and quickly gone extinct. The fact that alligators, eels, snails or any other unclean animal exist today is proof that Noah and his family were not given liberty to eat them.

Furthermore, to understand the first section of verse 3:

"Every moving thing that lives shall be food for you,"

We must consider to the last section of verse 3:

"I have given you all things, even as the green herbs."

Green herbs is a direct reference to Genesis 1:29-30. God gives Adam and Eve every seed-bearing herb, fruit and green herb "suitable for food." It was not every green herb but every green, seed-bearing herb *given as* food. This would rule out mistletoe and holly berries, since both are severely poisonous and would not be given as food. The stipulation was that the herb and fruit be both seed bearing and suitable for human consumption.

God's instructions to Noah 1,600 years later can only be correctly interpreted in light of the oral directives passed down to him from the beginning. *Everything* does not imply anything but only that which has been established as acceptable. It stands to reason, then, if the last part of verse 3 requires context to be understood, then so does the first.

---

[10] https://www.uncleanfoodsdietarylaws.com/unclean_foods_dietary_laws.html

We can conclude that not every life form that moves on the earth was appropriate for Noah to eat, but only that which had been previously established as acceptable for sacrifice. Could something be sacrificially unacceptable for God but acceptable for man? If God rejects it as unclean, so should we.

We should all be grateful that God instituted animal classifications. Today, we enjoy amazing unclean animals in the wild – lions, zebras, pandas, giraffes and so many more. It's the Creator's prerogative to create certain animals for consumption and certain animals to cleanse the earth. If we look at the diet of unclean animals, it may give us a clue as to why we are to avoid eating them.

Like Noah, you and I are permitted to bring to our table that which is accepted at the table of the Lord. If he really meant anything and everything that moves, God's guidelines for meat consumption given to Moses would be contradictory and compromise the consistency of his will as revealed in Scripture.

Swallowing Camels

In wrapping up this section, it may be surprising to learn that there are no passages found in the Apostolic Scriptures that deal specifically with the directives of Leviticus 11 and Deuteronomy 14. The apostles do not address the dietary laws in any formal way. Jesus contends with the Pharisees over bread. Peter's vision alludes to unclean animals but only symbolically. James introduces a small list of dietary prohibitions for the purpose of social interaction and avoiding paganism. Paul breaches the topic of meat sacrificed to idols.

The apostles neither challenged nor undermined God's food distinctions either in practice or in writing. Eating clean or unclean meats was simply not a point of contention for the apostolic church. God's dietary guidelines were accepted, embraced and expected to be followed.

Yeshua does make one more noted reference about the "diet" of the Pharisees.

> *"Woe to you, scribes and Pharisees, hypocrites. For you pay tithe of mint and anise and cumin, and have neglected the weightier matters of the Torah: justice and mercy and faith. These you ought to have done, without leaving the others undone. Blind guides, who strain out a gnat and swallow a camel."* – Matthew 23:23-24

I learned a song in preschool about an old lady who swallowed a horse. The lady:

Swallowed a donkey to catch a cow, swallowed a cow to catch a goat, swallowed a goat to catch a pig, swallowed a pig to catch a dog, swallowed a dog to catch a cat, swallowed a cat to catch a bird, swallowed a bird to catch a spider, swallowed a spider to catch a fly. I don't know why she swallowed the fly. Perhaps she'll die.

The old lady eventually swallows a horse and dies, of course. You know the song, but wow! Did this woman consume a lot of meat. No wonder she keeled over!

The moral of the story is that there are just some things that can't be stomached.

What I find hard to stomach is the extreme measures we have taken to eradicate God's dietary guidelines from our doctrine. We've deliberately turned a blind eye to those passages supporting God's dietary standard and audaciously interjected Torah abolishment into the teachings of Jesus and the apostles. We've weaponized the words of Paul against the word of God. Our doctrine and perhaps even our diet are killing us.

Our neglect of Sabbath has worn out our bodies prematurely. Our ignorance for God's appointed times has led us to adopt pagan holidays we were never designed to embrace. Our contempt for the Biblical dietary standard has weakened our immune systems and afflicted our bodies with diseases we were never designed to bear.

I once saw a sign on a Lutheran church advertising a Christian crab feed held at the free masonry building downtown. This is comically wrong for so many reasons and reveals the heart of the problem.

Gluttony is something we should be mindful of. You may be surprised to learn that from a Biblical perspective, gluttony entails both overeating as well as eating prohibited things. Our challenge is to prevent the church from becoming the old lady who dies swallowing a horse, or in Yeshua's words, a camel.

The scribes and Pharisees were neglecting the weightier matters of the Torah in favor of meticulous tithing. Yeshua admonishes them, "These you ought to have done, without leaving the others undone" (Matt. 23:23).

I do not know if Sabbath, the feasts and dietary laws are weightier matters to God or not, but I can say with confidence that Jesus does not want us to neglect them in our pursuit of justice, mercy and faith.

Conclusion

It should not surprise us to learn that God has an opinion on the foods we eat. Boundaries exist for all earthly appetites and pleasures - work, rest, money, marriage, sex. God does this to protect us and to protect that which he has given for us to enjoy.

It would be out of character for God to give guidelines on every other human activity except food, considering how important food is to our daily lives. He cares about what we eat, because he cares about us. Biblical parameters are not for our limitation but for our protection and enjoyment. God doesn't want what we consume to consume us.

Our Father created food to be enjoyed. We should be thankful that he has given us a dietary standard. Without any guidelines about anything, our society would eventually resort to devouring one another, in more ways than one.

SECTION III

ANIMAL SACRIFICES

Acts 21:15-26

Truth #20: *Paul offered sacrifices in the temple 20 years after his conversion.*

Acts Chapters 18-21 detail Paul's third missionary journey through Asia Minor and parts of Europe. After joining up with Timothy and Silas near the ancient city of Troy, Paul travels to several cities strengthening the brethren. Luke records that the apostle makes an effort to get back to Israel in time for Pentecost, for Paul was eager to go "up to Jerusalem to worship" (Acts 24:11).

Upon their arrival in Jerusalem, Paul and his company are greeted by James and the elders who rejoiced at the marvelous things God was doing among the Gentiles. The brothers spoke with Paul, saying:

> *"You see, brother, how many thousands of Jews have believed, and all of them are zealous for the law. They have been informed that you teach all the Jews who live among the Gentiles to turn away from Moses, telling them not to circumcise their children or live according to our customs. What shall we do? They will certainly hear that you have come." – Acts 21:20b-22 NIV*

News of Paul reached the ears of the Jerusalem church. It was reported that Paul was teaching Jews among the nations to "forsake Moses, saying that they ought not to circumcise their children nor walk according to the customs" (Acts 21:21). These allegations were false, but evidently it caused a stir, leading some to question Paul's apostolic authenticity.

These rumors unsettled the leaders enough that they requested Paul address them during his stay in the city. To prove that Paul was not teaching against the Law of Moses, they proposed he pay the expenses of four men who were fulfilling their Nazirite vows in the temple.

> *"We have four men who have taken a vow. Take them and be purified with them, and pay their expenses so that they may shave their heads, and that all may know that those things of which they were informed concerning you are nothing, but that you yourself also walk orderly and keep the law." – Acts 21:23b-24*

Paul's Nazirite Vow

Many suspect that Paul may have taken a Nazirite vow himself during his last missionary journey, which could explain why Paul "had his hair cut off at Cenchrea, for he had taken a vow" (Acts 18:18).[1] Numbers 6 instructs the Nazirite to not let a razor touch his head for the duration of the vow and to shave off his hair at the completion of the vow.[2] Sometimes, however, a man would shave his head at the beginning of the vow to allow his hair growth to symbolically represent the amount of time spent under the vow.[3] Often, if the vow were taken outside the land of Israel, the vow would be repeated while in the land and the head re-shaved.[4] It is proposed that Paul's prolonged stay in Corinth may have been a time consecrated to God under the vow of a Nazirite.

In addition to shaving his hair, the Torah requires the Nazirite to bring sacrifices to the tabernacle, or in this instance, the temple. Paul's visit to Jerusalem could have provided a convenient opportunity for him to complete his own Nazirite vow. If so, the apostle would have been fulfilling his vow in addition to assisting the four men with theirs.

---

[1] Scholars debate if the text implies Paul or Aquila shaved their heads. Augustine, Erasmus, Luther, Calvin, Jerome, Ramsay, Bruce, Baumgarten, Zeller, Beda and Calmet all see it as Paul, though not all agree that Paul's vow was a Nazirite vow.
[2] Num. 6:5-9
[3] *HaYesod*, 6.27
[4] *Mishnah*, m. Nazir, 3:6, 5:4; William Whiston, *The Life And Works Of Flavius Josephus* (Philadelphia, PA: The John C. Winston Company, 1957), *Wars of the Jews*, 2.15.1

Regardless of whether he had taken a Nazirite vow or not, Paul was asked to ritually purify himself in the temple. This included paying the expenses of these men and presenting to the priest the required burnt offerings, sin offerings, fellowship offerings and grain offerings. This he willingly did.

The sacrificial requirements for completing a Nazirite vow were involved and quite expensive, especially since Paul was footing the bill. If we include his own sacrifices, Paul would have needed to provide five unblemished yearling lambs, five unblemished yearling ewe lambs, five rams without defect, thirty-three liters of flour mixed with oil, two gallons of wine and five additional baskets of unleavened bread with oil.[5] The amount of animal sacrifices required of Paul was considerable - no less than twelve individual sacrifices and possibly up to thirty.[6] Yet, apparently, Paul did not consider temple sacrifices to be an affront to the work of Christ or in conflict with his faith in Yeshua.

It shouldn't startle us to read that Paul offered sacrifices in the temple some twenty years after his conversion to Christ. Paul followed the Torah closely enough to want to pilgrimage back to Jerusalem to complete his Nazirite vow and celebrate the Feast of Weeks with his fellow Jews. He even calls the observation of Pentecost an act of worship.

Zealous for the Torah

The accusations against Paul needed to be answered, so he agreed to purify himself with the others at the temple.

> *"Then Paul took the men, and the next day, having been purified with them, entered the temple to announce the expiration of the days of purification, at which time an offering should be made for each one of them." – Acts 21:26*

---

[5] Num. 6

[6] The number varies depending if Paul were offering sacrifices for himself and if the men were renewing their vows due to corpse contamination. See D. Thomas Lancaster, *King of the Jews* (Littleton: FFOZ, 2006), Chapter 15.

Paul joined with the thousands of believing "zealots for the Torah" (v.20) to lend his support for the temple, the Jewish people and the teachings of Moses. He did not give any credence to the accusation that he taught Jews to forsake Moses or to refuse to circumcise their sons. By offering sacrifices in the temple and contributing to the sacrificial system, Paul demonstrated to the brethren and to us that he neither taught against the Law of Moses nor against the temple.

It has been reasoned that Paul offered these sacrifices against his will out of respect for James, agreeing to it just to appease insistent Jews. As evidence of this evangelistic strategy, 1 Corinthians 9:20 is cited: "To the Jews I became as a Jew, to win the Jews."

This is a troubling portrait of Paul, is it not? Was Paul really that disingenuous and hypocritical? Those who read Paul know that he was not one to cave to peer pressure or practice evangelism by deceit.

If we can deduce anything about Paul, it's that he was anything but a man-pleaser. He did not acquiesce to public opinion and would not compromise his convictions just to placate the establishment. We read of him audaciously rebuking Peter, squabbling with Barnabas over Mark, proclaiming Christ unapologetically before a king and boldly laying down his life at the hands of an emperor. It is safe to say that Paul was not afraid to stand up for what he believed, even if it caused waves or went against the group-think majority.

While Paul would no doubt use common ground to relate to his audience, he would not denigrate the cross of Christ or twist Scripture just to win people over. It appears as if offering sacrifices at the temple presented no cacophony in his walk with Christ. If he felt that it was sacrilegious or improper to offer sacrifices in the temple, he would not have agreed to it.

Believers & Burnt Offerings

So, why would Paul bring burnt offerings to the temple? Didn't Jesus offer the final sacrifice? Weren't animal sacrifices done away with at the cross?

We must remember that the temple still stood for another forty years after the death and resurrection of Christ. Apparently, first-century messianic Jews living near the temple still continued to participate in temple activities, as this passage attests. Early believers had no reason to regard temple participation as something incongruent with being a disciple of Christ. Priestly duties and animal sacrifices posed no threat to their faith and no insult to the blood of Christ.

Worshipping God by bringing a sacrifice is understandably foreign to us, because we are far removed from ancient Israel and the world of animal sacrifices. It is widely assumed today that these sacrifices were an act of repentance and provided some sort of payment for sin for those alive before the time of Christ. Many are led to believe that God's forgiveness was predicated upon these sacrifices. Some even maintain that priestly offerings secured God's favor. They reason that at the death of Jesus, the whole system of sacrifice was voided and no longer offers any spiritual benefit.

This perception of animal sacrifices is oversimplified and presents a few theological problems for us. First, if animal sacrifices could really take away transgressions and provide some kind of payment for sin, then the blood of Yeshua was unnecessary. Forgiveness could be secured through the blood of an animal, something the writer of Hebrews specifically disavows.

> *"For it is not possible that the blood of bulls and goats could take away sins." – Hebrews 10:4*

If animal sacrifices could actually cleanse and remove sin, there would then exist two ways in which one could be made righteous – through animal sacrifices and through faith in Jesus. By default, this makes the death of Christ superfluous. The idea that someone could earn saving grace by bringing a sacrifice forces one into the position that there is an alternative path to salvation outside of the work of Christ. This concept, however, is unequivocally foreign to Scripture.

The blood of animals is insufficient in removing sin-guilt and is not a means of attaining righteousness. A wicked man could not just waltz into the temple, make a sacrifice and walk away righteous.

Solomon lets us know that "The sacrifice of the wicked is an abomination to the Lord; how much more when he brings it with evil intent" (Prov. 21:27 ESV).

Secondly, on more than one occasion God expresses his displeasure with the people's offerings and instructs them to no longer bring Him a sacrifice.

> "'To what purpose is the multitude of your sacrifices to Me?' says the Lord. 'I have had enough of burnt offerings and rams and the fat of fed cattle. I do not delight in the blood of bulls or of lambs or goats...Bring no more futile sacrifices.'" - Isaiah 1:11, 13a

> "Your burnt offerings are not acceptable, nor your sacrifices sweet to Me." - Jeremiah 6:20

> "For I desire mercy and not sacrifice and the knowledge of God more than burnt offerings." - Hosea 6:6

> "For You do not desire sacrifice, or else I would give it; You do not delight in burnt offering." - Psalms 51:6

If sacrifices were to be viewed as an act of repentance, why would God command his people to cease from bringing burnt offerings? He would be stopping them from repenting and denying them the only means toward restoration and forgiveness. This does not match the character of God. He desires to be reconciled with his children and for us to seek him humbly in repentance.

Thirdly, followers of the Way did not excuse themselves from temple life, as they met together daily "with one accord in the temple" (Acts 2:46). Peter and John apparently participated in temple services when they both "went up together to the temple at the hour of prayer" (Acts 3:1). As well, Paul spoke of spending time in the synagogues and being purified in the temple, telling Felix, "After many years I came to bring alms and offerings" (Acts 24:17). If animal sacrifices were contrary to the cross of Christ, how do we explain the apostles bringing offerings and participating in temple activities?

It must be that Paul, the apostles and the early believers saw no rivalry between burnt offerings, the temple and the work of Yeshua. James would not have encouraged Paul to engage in offerings at the temple if he thought temple sacrifices diminished the glory and finality of Christ's sacrifice. Peter and John would never have participated in temple activities if they felt it violated the spirit of grace. It can only be that for the apostles, animal sacrifices neither disregarded the sacrifice of Jesus nor distracted them from the finished work of Christ.

Who's to say that a sacrifice given from a sincere heart of worship didn't enrich their faith and enlarge their appreciation for Christ's sacrificial death? When a follower of Christ brought a burnt offering to the temple, perhaps it yielded a fresh revelation of the Lamb of God. Because it came from a heart fully alive, maybe the symbolism of the sacrifice became more alive as well.

Conclusion

Before his arrest, rumors circulated among the Jewish brethren that Paul was urging Jews to forsake Moses, cease from circumcising their children and abandon Jewish customs. These were false accusations leveled at Paul by his opponents, allegations later proven to be without merit. Refuting the lies of his critics, Paul claimed to be no opponent of the Torah, openly stating, "I worship the God of my fathers, believing all things which are written in the Law and in the Prophets" (Acts 24:14).

Peter warns about rushing to judge Paul, explaining that Paul's wisdom can be hard to understand (2 Peter 3:15-16). Today, it is still taught that Paul is anti-circumcision and anti-Torah. Apparently, western Christianity is not the only one confused by Paul's teachings. Even the first-century messianic church was as well.

In this passage, we also observe Paul contributing to the sacrificial system of the temple. In Paul's theology, there was no incongruence between temple participation and following Christ. In offering sacrifices and purifying himself in the temple, he sided with the thousands of believers who were zealous for the Torah.

ACTS 21:27-28

Truth #21: *Jesus did not do away with temple sacrifices.*

So, then, what was the purpose of animal sacrifices?

(1) Animal sacrifices revealed the *method* and the *means* by which God would redeem mankind. In offering a sacrifice, the worshipper could visibly and tangibly observe the manner in which God would deal with transgressions. Since only a few people in the history of the world would actually witness the Crucifixion, the slaughtering of an innocent animal offered a visual glimpse of the extent to which God would go to communicate his love. Through these prophetic acts, those who participated in these sacrifices could observe in a substantial way the agony and supreme price Yeshua would pay for our redemption.[1] This was as true for the priest as it was for the people.

Faith played a prominent role in God's acceptance of a sacrifice. The upright man who brought his gift to the altar did not place his faith in the offering but in God's faithfulness to forgive the penitent. It was not the burnt offering in itself that pleased the heart of God but the faith of the man bringing the offering, for "the just shall live by his faith" (Habakkuk 2:4). It is faith that justifies a man and makes him righteous. Only because of a person's faith in God would their offering be accepted.

(2) Animal sacrifices were not an avenue for salvation but an *act of worship.*[2] The Hebrew word for offering is *korban.*[3] Its root means *to bring near.*[4] In order to draw near to God and present oneself

---

[1] Hegg, *10 Persistent Questions*, 26-29
[2] Ps. 4:5, 27:6, 51:19, 66:15, 107:22, Mark 12:33
[3] *Strong's* H7133, קָרְבָּן
[4] *Strong's* #H7126, קָרַב

before him, the worshipper had to be cleansed. We know that sinful man cannot approach a holy God without an intercessor. Innocent blood spilled on the altar allowed the worshipper to come into the presence of God on the basis of the Promised One who would bear the sins of the world.

Drawing near to the Almighty is costly, and death is the price. The death of the animal was not so much a substitutionary act but done in proxy to allow the worshipper to draw near to God in his temple. The blood of the animal did not take away a person's sin. Rather, it was the method by which the Heavenly Father could be approached. Albeit temporarily, burnt offerings consecrated the flesh so that a person could worship God in the way He prescribes.

We should not view the sacrifice of Yeshua as identical or even a duplicate of the sacrifices of the temple. The priestly sacrificial system points us to Christ, but it could not accomplish what Yeshua did. The cross removes our sin and renders us righteous, something animal sacrifices were never designed or capable of doing. The two sacrifices were for two different purposes – one for worship and the other for redemption. In both cases, it is only by faith in the promises of God that righteousness could be attained. Because of this, there is no conflict of interest between the blood of Jesus and the blood of animal sacrifices.

For the apostles, temple activities did not diminish what Christ accomplished at Calvary, because priestly offerings were never designed to remove sins. Animal sacrifices are a prophetic act revealed in the Lamb of God. Theoretically, it should not matter if those sacrifices are before or after the death of Christ. Whether we are looking out of the windshield of the future or through the rearview mirror of history, animal sacrifices direct our attention to the Lamb of God who takes away our sin.

What the saints of old looked forward to, the apostolic church looks back on. For those living before Christ, the experience of the sacrifice assured them that a God-given sacrifice was forthcoming. For those living after Christ, the experience of the sacrifice reminds us that God's sacrifice has been accomplished. Either way, faith in the sacrificial Lamb appropriates the promises of God. For all of us, they are a precious reminder of the sacrifice of our Lord upon the cross. Perhaps this is why the apostles did not see animal sacrifices in opposition to the cross.

Paul's Reputation

The reputation of being anti-Torah dogged Paul throughout his ministry. While in Corinth, the Corinthian Jews rose up in one accord and charged him with persuading "men to worship God contrary to the law" (Acts 18:13).

Later, before Paul was arrested in Jerusalem, Jews from Asia stirred up the crowd, saying,

> *"This is the man who teaches all men everywhere against the people, the law, and this place; and furthermore, he also brought Greeks into the temple, and has defiled this holy place. (For they had previously seen Trophimus the Ephesian with him in the city, whom they supposed that Paul had brought into the temple)." - Acts 21:28-29*

Luke continues that the whole city was disturbed and together seized Paul, dragging him out of the temple. As they sought to kill him, Roman soldiers arrive on the scene and arrest Paul. When they discover that he was a Jew from Tarsus, they give him permission to address the crowd. Speaking in Hebrew, Paul shares his background and Damascus road experience. But it wasn't until he spoke of his mandate to take the gospel to the Gentiles that the mob became unruly, raising their voices and demanding that he be executed.[5]

It is interesting that the people took greater offense at Paul's mission to the Gentiles than his proclamation that Yeshua is the resurrected Messiah. The idea of God's covenant being extended to the Gentiles was so offensive that the crowd of angry Jews allowed Paul to preach until he professed that God was sending him to the Gentiles. It was as if Yeshua as Messiah was a tolerable position, but Gentiles integrated into the promises of Israel was abhorrent. It does serve to

---

[5] Acts 21-22

highlight the theological and social tension that existed between Jews and Greeks at that time.

Something similar happens to Stephen. Standing before the Sanhedrin, Stephen gives one of the boldest sermons recorded in Acts. Before a crowd of angry Jews and with the high priest looking on, he expounds upon Scripture. It wasn't until he called out their violent Torahlessness that they became enraged. His thunderous words proved to be prophetic.

> *"You stiff-necked and uncircumcised in heart and ears! You always resist the Holy Spirit; as your fathers did, so do you. Which of the prophets did your fathers not persecute? And they killed those who foretold the coming of the Just One, of whom you now have become the betrayers and murderers, who have received the law by the direction of angels and have not kept it." - Acts 7:51-53*

Stephen accuses them of being stiff-necked, Torah-breaking, Holy Spirit-resisting, murderous betrayers. It was as if the crowd accepted all that Stephen had to say until he pinned down their lawless hypocrisy.

Who were the Torah breakers according to Stephen? It wasn't the apostles or followers of the Way. Who were the ones resisting the Holy Spirit? It wasn't Stephen's brothers and sisters in Christ. The spiritless Torah breakers were the members of the Sanhedrin – the Pharisees, Sadducees and high priest. Stephen characterizes the religious leaders not as ultra Torah keepers as we have been led to believe, but as those who forsook the Torah. According to Stephen, it is not the Spirit-filled who are Torah breakers but those who reject the gospel and resist the Holy Spirit.

Laying Down the Law

Paul's enemies accused the apostle of persuading men to worship God contrary to the Torah and bringing Greeks into the Temple. Were they right?

We can say with confidence that the second part of the charge was false. Luke lets us know. Paul never actually brought Gentiles into the temple. The Jews only supposed that he had, because he was seen with Trophimus, who was Greek. Therefore, it stands to reason that if one part of the allegation is false, so might the other.

Paul confirms this to be the case himself, saying,

> *"I worship the God of my fathers, believing all things which are written in the Law and in the Prophets." - Acts 24:14*

And,

> *"Neither against the law of the Jews, nor against the temple, nor against Caesar have I offended in anything at all." - Acts 25:8*

Paul testifies about his life and doctrine in responding to his accusers. The apostle defends himself, saying that he is not against the Torah, the Prophets, the temple or Caesar. Like Yeshua, he believed and practiced all things written in the Torah and was in favor of everything that God had laid down in the Law of Moses.

In light of this, if we still hold to a belief that Paul was anti-Jew, anti-Torah or anti-temple, we are disagreeing with Paul's own words and with the Scriptures he defends. While we may pride ourselves in being pro-Paul, our theology sides more with those who persecuted the apostle. We may consider ourselves pro-gospel, but we actually stand in opposition to Paul's version of the good news.

Conclusion

Burnt offerings and sacrifices were never once a means of salvation. They have always been an act of worship that allowed the sinner to draw near to God in an earthly temple. The goal of animal sacrifices was to demonstrate the means and method by which God would redeem mankind. In this way, they lead us to a righteousness found only through Christ.

> *"To do righteousness and justice is more acceptable to the Lord than sacrifice."* - Proverbs 21:3 ESV

The sacrificial system was not designed to be a substitute for faith and obedience. Unfortunately, an inadequate view of the sacrificial system robs us of a fuller understanding of what Jesus did on the cross. The Biblical position has always been that it's the sacrifice of Yeshua, not the presentation of burnt offerings, that empowers us to walk in righteous obedience.

Thanks in part to Martin Luther, Paul holds the reputation of being for grace and against the law. The narrative that Paul advocated against the Torah conflicts with this story and finds its origins in the allegations of Acts 21. These kinds of misconceptions are regrettably still in circulation today.

Just as rumors spread that the apostle was teaching Jews to turn away from Moses and to not circumcise their sons, we have accused Paul of being critical of Moses. We also misunderstand the type of circumcision he was addressing among the Greeks. Remarkably, Paul's doctrine is just as misconstrued today as it was by these Judean brothers.

We must be careful not to allow Paul's enemies to shape how we view the apostle's life and letters. It was Paul's enemies who accused him of teaching against the Torah and temple. It was his adversaries who were responsible for spreading the rumors that, to this day, still continue to discredit his ministry. When we unfairly label Paul anti-Torah, not only do we twist his words to our own determent, as Peter describes, we also reinforce and legitimize the allegations of Paul's opponents.

How is it that the orthodox position of the church tends to side with the smear campaign hurled at Paul rather than with the confession of Paul himself? Who are we defending – Paul or his adversaries? When we spread the opinion that Paul's letters are anti-Torah, anti-Temple and anti-Jew, we are ultimately coming into agreement with his enemies and aligning ourselves with those who oppose the gospel of peace.

SECTION IV

PAUL & HIS EPISTLES

Paul's Life & Doctrine

Truth #22: *Paul used the Torah authoritatively in his letters.*

Before we dive into Paul's letters, it would be helpful to briefly examine the life of Paul and his Torah perspective. It is no exaggeration to say that Paul might be the most misunderstood of all the apostles, so it should come as no surprise that his writings are also sometimes misunderstood. Though straightforward and profound, Paul's writing style can be difficult to grasp, especially when factoring in time, translation and culture. Peter tells us as much.

> *"Our beloved brother Paul, according to the wisdom given to him, has written to you, as also in all his epistles, speaking in them these things, in which are some things hard to understand, which untaught and unstable people twist to their own destruction, as they do also the rest of the Scriptures." - 2 Peter 3:15-16*

This is probably truer today than it was in the first century.

Determining the doctrine of Paul as it relates to the Torah is no small feat. This is not because Paul is such a complicated guy, but because his theology about the law can appear to be inconsistent and contradictory. At times he glories in the Torah, while other times seems to take a negative stance against it. We find him exalting the law, praising its virtues, citing it authoritatively only to depict it elsewhere as a condemning burden.

Theologians have developed elaborate theories trying to figure out Paul's theology. There is no shortage of opinions. In spite of this, I aim to construct a rational, well-defined and workable consistency in Paul's doctrine regarding the law that is both honest with the text and doesn't convict Paul of contradictory thinking.

I have already laid some groundwork regarding Paul's Torah perspective in the last two chapters. In Acts 21, we read where Paul honors the Torah, the temple and the people of Israel upon his final visit to Jerusalem. Twenty years after his conversion, Paul is still walking according to the Torah. He upheld the Law of Moses and sided with those who were zealous for the law.[1]

During Paul's first missionary journey, he and Barnabas observed the Sabbath in a traditional Jewish way. H.L. Ellison maintains that Paul would not have been asked to speak in the synagogue had he not been wearing tassels (*tzitzit*).[2] As pointed out by Dr. David Fischer, they likely also dressed as traditional Jews. In order to be given a platform as a religious teacher, Paul would have been wearing traditional Pharisaic attire.[3] Paul and Barnabas seemed to share the message of the gospel while observing the Sabbath. This was Paul's practice throughout his ministry.[4]

Even toward the end of his life, Paul did not renounce the Torah or his Jewish heritage. While imprisoned in Rome, he tells the Jewish leaders, "I have done nothing against our people or the customs of our fathers" (Acts 28:17). He then "testified of the kingdom of God, persuading them concerning Jesus from both the Law of Moses and the prophets" (Acts 28:23).

Luke records Paul teaching from the Torah, celebrating a Biblical feast, observing the Sabbath, contributing to the sacrificial system, ritually purifying himself in the temple, financially supporting the men fulfilling their vows, honoring Jewish oral traditions and faithfully following all that is written in the law. This hardly sounds like Torah-defiance.

---

[1] Acts 21:20
[2] Daniel Juster referencing H.L Ellison, "Paul and the Law," in Gasque and Martin, *Apostolic History and the Gospel*
[3] David Friedman, *They Loved The Torah* (Clarksville: Lederer Books, 2001), 48-50
[4] Acts 16:11-15, 17:1-3, 17, 18:4, 19

New Perspective on Paul

There is a new perspective on Paul that has gained traction and garnered respect in academic circles over the past few decades. Advanced by the work of E.P. Sanders, as well as scholars like C.G. Montefiore, H.J. Schoeps, Krister Stendahl, N.T Wright, J.H. Yoder, James Dunn and others, this research presents an alternative perspective on the Judaisms of the first century. This perspective also sheds new light on Paul's doctrine regarding the works of the law.

The new perspective depicts first-century Palestinian Judaism not as a sterile, legalistic religion but as a community committed to covenantal nomism. Rabbis were not oriented toward classic legalism such as salvation by deeds. Nor did they believe that right standing with God could be attained through keeping the law. Their hope of securing the promises of the age to come was in remaining in the covenant. This could be only accomplished through being a descendant of Jacob accompanied by rabbinic Torah observation.

First-century Palestinian Jews viewed themselves as the people of the covenant. It was by God's sovereign grace that He elected Israel. Forgiveness was not earned through good works or human performance but given by a merciful God toward those who repent. Yet, the Torah was, and still is, something rabbis felt distinguished Israelites from Gentiles. In their eyes, Torah observation was only for the people of the covenant.

Sanders also notes that Paul's use of the word *righteous* breaks from the traditional Judaisms of his time. Whereas Jewish literature views righteousness as obedience to God, Paul uses righteousness to depict salvation. For Paul, righteousness meant being justified and made right before God.

Sanders writes,

> "Righteousness in Judaism is a term which implies the *maintenance of status* among the group of the elect; in Paul it is a *transfer term*. In Judaism, that is, commitment to the covenant put one 'in,' while

obedience (righteousness) subsequently keeps one in. In Paul's usage, 'be made righteous' ('be justified') is a term indicating getting in, not staying in the body of the saved."[5]

Whereas righteousness to Jews is right behavior, righteousness to Paul was being in right standing with God. This is helpful to remember when running across the concept of righteousness in Paul's letters.

This new perspective also challenges the conventional understanding of how Paul lived his life and expressed his faith in Christ. Many writers make a case for re-examining the traditional understanding of Saul of Tarsus. Under this new perspective, Paul is presented as a messianic Jew who lived in faithful obedience to the Torah and did not shun his Jewish heritage upon converting to Christ.[6]

It is a common misnomer that Paul founded and propagated a new religion called Christianity. The earliest followers of the Way never sought to distance themselves from Israel or start a new religion.[7] Instead, they were viewed as a sect of the Nazarenes who considered Yeshua of Nazareth the promised Jewish Messiah.[8]

It is also untrue that Paul changed his name from Saul to Paul to renounce Judaism and reflect his newfound religion. Unlike Simon Peter, Yeshua did not change Saul's name.

Having dual names was not an uncommon practice in the first century. It was customary for a Jew as a Roman citizen to possess both a Jewish name and a Roman name. In fact, Roman citizens usually possessed three names – a forename, family name and an additional name.[9] Because Paul was born a Jew and his father was a

---

[5] Sanders, *Paul And Palestinian Judaism*, 544
[6] Hegg, *The Letter Writer*; W.D. Davies, *Paul and Rabbinic Judaism* (New York: Harper Torchbooks, 1948); John Yoder, *The Politics of Jesus* (Grand Rapids: Eerdmans, 1994)
[7] Acts 9:2
[8] Acts 24:5
[9] Santala, *Paul*, 26

Roman citizen, Paul inherited Roman citizenship. He was given the Latin name *Paullus* at birth, which is Anglicized as *Paul*.[10]

After coming to Christ, Paul no longer relied on his identity as a Jew for his justification. His faith remained solely in Jesus Christ, and his letters ardently encouraged Gentile believers to do likewise.

Accepting this scholarship confronts Luther's depiction of Paul and first-century Judaism. Because Paul neither renounced his Hebrew heritage to become a Christian nor changed his name as an expression of his faith, it is quite reasonable to see why the apostle did not turn his back on the Torah. Paul was a non-rabbinic, messianic teacher called to take the gospel to the Gentile world. Perhaps this is one reason why he was so hated by the Jews.

Paul's Soapbox

After his encounter with Yeshua on the road to Damascus, Paul received a revelation that, in many ways, defined his ministry. Although he writes about many things pertaining to life and godliness, there is one topic that Paul was thrust into addressing and emerges in many of his letters. His epistle to the Galatians is one of his earliest and perhaps most profound arguments in defense of it.

Paul firmly believed that Jews and Gentiles could be saved on the same condition. Both could be grafted into the covenant promises of Israel through faith in Jesus Christ. Justification by faith may in fact have been the greatest discovery of his life.

This may sound academic to you and me. It is well established today that people are saved by grace through faith and that Gentiles need not become Jewish in order to be saved. While this is obvious to us, it wasn't to first-century minds. We have Paul to thank for it. He took the difficult and unpopular position that Gentiles could be saved as Gentiles and made it one of his defining messages. This was Paul's soapbox, if you will. It served him well in bringing the gospel to the Gentiles.

---

[10] F.F. Bruce, *The Spreading Flame* (Grand Rapids: Eerdmans, 1954), 90-91

What a remarkable calling it was! God plucked a young prodigy sitting under the tutelage of one of the most proficient Greek and Hebrew teachers in all of Israel and chose him to be His mouthpiece. Unknowingly, Gamaliel was preparing Saul of Tarsus to be an apostle to the Gentiles.

Paul's resume is exceptional. It is not a stretch to say that his upbringing and education uniquely qualified him for the task. Though educated in some of the most elite schools available, it cannot be overlooked that Paul thought and wrote from a Jewish perspective. There are several key passages and phrases found in his letters that are virtually incomprehensible to readers unfamiliar with Hebrew literature. This may yet be another reason why he is so often misunderstood.

At the time, what to do about believing Gentiles was a hotly debated subject. Paul's position regarding their inclusion in the promises of God was in the minority. He held the radical stance among his colleagues that God accepted believing Gentiles into the community of faith without any requirement of Jewish proselytization. A Gentile Christian could claim the covenant of Abraham and find redemption through faith in the work of Christ irrespective of any work of man.

Paul describes himself to the Philippians as "circumcised on the eighth day, of the stock of Israel, *of* the tribe of Benjamin, a Hebrew of the Hebrews; concerning the law, a Pharisee" (Philippians 3:5). Paul came from the sect of the Pharisees. This means that when it came to Torah observance, Paul once adhered to the Pharisees strict manner in which the Torah should be lived out.

The Pharisees, which derive their name from the Hebrew word *define* or *separate*, had the reputation of being scrupulous in their adherence to the law. They washed ritually, fasted twice a week, promoted ceremonial circumcision and strictly upheld the oral traditions of the Torah. Josephus describes them as "a body of Jews who profess to be more religious than the rest, and to explain the law more accurately."[11]

---

[11] Steve Mason, *Flavius Josephus on the Pharisees* (Boston: Brill, 2001), 107

The Pharisees drew up for the people numerous precepts not found in the Scriptures. This was Paul's upbringing. Paul's fellow Pharisees would no doubt have strongly opposed his message of Gentile inclusion into Israel.

Perhaps this is why Paul approaches the subject in Galatians and Romans like a prosecuting attorney using every angle possible to state his case – culture, creation, conviction, common sense, but chiefly, the Torah. He pounds home the claim that all can be saved by grace through faith in Yeshua, for the Jew and for the Gentile. This he proved, rather conclusively, from the Torah.

Gentile inclusion into Christ was not the only revelation given to Paul, but it was his most influential. Being that a Pharisee was preaching salvation to the Gentiles, the Holy Spirit used Paul to emphasize a truth that was under dispute and sorely needed.

This information is indispensable when reading the letters of Paul. The apostle is all-too-often misread and unfairly labeled as it relates to his position regarding the Torah. Simply understanding the environment in which Paul lived and wrote clears up many perceived inconsistencies and assumed discrepancies.

Torah Positive

Before we study Galatians and passages that seemingly cast a negative light on the Torah, let's take a quick glance at some of the positive things Paul has to say about the law.

> *"For not the hearers of the law are just in the sight of God, but the doers of the law will be justified." – Romans 2:13*

> *"Do we then make void the law through faith? Certainly not! On the contrary, we establish the law." – Romans 3:31*

> *"What shall we say then? Is the law sin? Certainly not! On the contrary, I would not have known sin except through the law. For I would not have known covetousness unless the law had said, "You shall not covet." – Romans 7:7*

> *"Therefore the law is holy, and the commandment holy and just and good." – Romans 7:12*
>
> *"For we know that the law is spiritual." – Romans 7:14*
>
> *"But we know that the law is good if one uses it lawfully." – 1 Timothy 1:8*
>
> *"The holy Scriptures, which are able to make you wise for salvation through faith which is in Christ Jesus." – 2 Timothy 3:15*

Lifting these verses from their context doesn't serve them justice. I will dissect each of these passages in fuller detail and in their proper context when tackling Romans and 2 Timothy. I will also be careful to give equal weight to the more derogatory statements Paul makes about the law. In seeking to reconcile all these verses together, I believe a solid construct regarding Paul's position about the Torah can be established.

At first glance, we cannot deny that Paul has some complimentary things to say about the Torah. In these verses, the apostle is shedding a positive light on the law. He portrays the Torah as holy, just, wise, good and spiritual. He believes it to be sound doctrine that rightly defines and condemns sin.[12] Furthermore, he states those who live by faith will establish the law as doers of the Torah.

This is not in isolation of Paul's seemingly negative statements, such as, "The strength of sin is the law" (1 Cor. 15:56) and, "the law is not made for a righteous person" (1 Tim. 1:9). Paul wrote, "Christ is the end of the law" (Rom. 8:4) and, "You also have become dead to the law through the body of Christ…so that we should serve in the newness of the Spirit and not the oldness of the letter" (Rom. 7:4,6).

In studying the writings of Paul, however, it has become apparent to me that Paul was not the anti-Torah cavalier some make him out to be. He considered all Scripture, including the Law of Moses, to be divinely inspired and useful for "teaching, rebuking, correcting and

---

[12] 1 Tim. 1:10

training in righteousness" (2 Tim. 3:16 NIV). He regarded the Torah and the Prophets as authoritative benchmarks for all subsequent writings and revelations.[13]

In addition to the many allusions and verbal parallels, Paul makes over one hundred direct quotes from the Hebrew Scriptures in his epistles.[14] The fact that Paul broke from the Jewish tradition of citing contemporary scholars and rabbinic literature to support his positions speaks to his strong inner value of Scripture. To Paul, the Hebrew Scriptures were the sole authority for his doctrine.

His overall view of Scripture rules out the notion that he sought the abolition of any part of it. Paul validates this by citing the Torah early and often. To argue that Paul sanctioned the cancellation of certain portions of Scripture, including the Torah, is to ignore the authoritative place he gives the Torah in his writings.

An honest reader will find Paul to be Torah-friendly. Never does he denigrate God's commandments or sanction disobedience within his congregations. Not once do we read of him discouraging Torah-obedience or advocating lawlessness. If he had, his critics would be rightly justified in labeling him a false teacher.

James Parkes writes,

> "We shall not have understood the meaning of [Paul's letters] until we have found an interpretation consistent with Paul's own belief that he was throughout a loyal and observant Jew."[15]

It comes as no surprise that the Jewish community today does not accept Paul's writings. This is partly due to our mischaracterization of him. We've made him out to be a law-breaking renegade, a brazen advocate of a lawless religion that dishonors God's established word. No wonder his work is rejected by many of his

---

[13] Acts 24:14
[14] Kurt and Barbara Aland, *The Greek New Testament* (UK: United Bible Society, 1983), 899-900
[15] James Parkes, *Judaism And Christianity* (London: Gollanez, 1948), 15

fellow countrymen. Paul is, once again, terribly misunderstood. If they could only see this apostle as a man who honored the Torah through his teachings and lived a life obedient to that honor, they might come to appreciate his work and benefit from his writings.

Conclusion

Paul honored the Torah in his personal life even after finding faith in Yeshua. Instructing Gentile believers that they can disobey the Torah in their faith walk would make him either a preacher of a double standard or a hypocrite. Paul was not a hypocrite. If the Torah were something that enriched his life in Christ, why would he freeze out Gentiles from enjoying the same blessings he did?

Neither did Paul preach a double standard. Nowhere in Paul's writings or in the Bible is there one standard by which Jews are accountable to and a separate but more relaxed standard for Gentiles. In Christ, there is one standard, one judgment and one Judge of all.

Early on in this journey I came to the conclusion Saul of Tarsus was not the anti-Torah teacher I had been led to believe. The idea that Gentiles have no obligation to God's commands is absent from his writings. The focus of the books of Galatians and Romans is Gentile justification and their inclusion in the covenant of Abraham. Any doctrine that claims Paul was anti-Torah is an argument from silence.

Though he wrote much about the law's inability to redeem us, he correctly identified the Torah's limited role in salvation. Paul does, however, lean heavily on the Torah to guide the new believer's behavior when addressing Christian living.

Paul's Letter To The Galatians

Truth #23: *The traditional interpretation of Galatians misreads the purpose of Paul's letter.*

When initially presented with the case for Torah-relevancy, the first place I turned to was the book of Galatians. Along with Romans, I once considered Paul's Epistle to the Galatians to be the strongest argument supporting antinomian grace. So as we turn our attention to Paul's letters, let's begin here.

Open to the book of Galatians in any study Bible. In the preface you will find a short synopsis of the letter. This contains information about the author, audience, time, background, occasion and outline of the book.[1] Regarding authorship, there is no real dispute. The writer of Galatians is clearly Sha'ul of Tarsus, as Paul identifies himself in the opening verse.

There is some debate on the intended audience and destination of Galatians, which influences when the letter is believed to have been written. A general timetable places the epistle close to the events of Acts 15, which some speculate occurred roughly 49-50 C.E. If written to the churches of the southern region of Galatia, it was likely penned just before or perhaps shortly after the decision of the Jerusalem council. If so, Paul would have written Galatians while in Syrian Antioch following his first missionary journey. If written to the churches in northern Galatia, a much later date is preferred.[2]

The date of Galatians deserves consideration. Addressed to the southern churches, Galatians would have been the first of Paul's Biblical epistles. If addressed to the northern churches, Galatians

---

[1] Often written by a textual editor
[2] Donald Guthrie, *New Testament Introduction* (Downers Drove: InterVarsity, 1990), 472-481

would have been written later in Paul's ministry, perhaps more than a decade after the decision of the Jerusalem council.

Some feel that because Paul's appeal makes no specific mention of the ruling of the Jerusalem council, a pre-Acts 15 date is desirable. The difference of opinion usually hinges upon how Paul's trip to Jerusalem in Galatians Chapter 2 is viewed. If Chapter 2 is recounting the same trip to Jerusalem that Paul took with Barnabas in Acts 15, Galatians would have been penned after the decision of the council. If not, an earlier date is preferred.

Regarding the audience, there is little doubt that the region of Galatia was primarily Gentile. Certainly some Jews lived in the area. A small representative of believing Jews could have been among the churches, but for the most part these believers were predominantly Gentile. Paul's letter to the Galatians clearly addresses Gentile issues with a primarily Gentile audience.

After determining the time, authorship and background, we turn to the purpose of the epistle. In most introductions and commentaries, something along these lines is written when discussing the occasion of Paul's letter:

> Judaizers were infiltrating this Gentile community of believers, insisting that converts adhere to Old Testament laws, including circumcision. These legalists were trying to bring the Galatian Christians under the yoke of the old covenant by forcing them to obey Mosaic Law. When Paul learned that the Galatians were already yielding to this bondage by observing Sabbath, feasts, new moon festivals and circumcision, he reaffirms that life and freedom in the Spirit is by faith and not through the law. He emphatically argues that a person is saved by grace through faith and insists that mixing grace with the law produces legalism. Any regression into the requirements of the law is evidence of being bewitched, living in the flesh and operating under a curse. He reassures his Gentile audience that Christ came to free them from mandated yokes of slavery to the law. Galatians is Paul's strongest and most impassioned rebuke of Torah keepers.

This introduction to Galatians is typical and unfortunate, because most Christians rely on these kinds of study notes to help them understand the Bible. The intent of Paul's letter, however, is not without dispute. Luther's reformed idea about Galatians, the interpretation uniformly taught today, is not without its deficiencies. A growing number of scholars are calling for and supporting an alternative view of Galatians. This is what I am presenting here.

Conclusion

In this section, I will put forth an historically and hermeneutically sound interpretation that stands in contrast to the widely accepted interpretation of Galatians. I am convinced that the traditional interpretation of Galatians misses the plain meaning of Paul's letter. I aim to establish a more precise premise in order to draw a more accurate conclusion.

GALATIANS 1

Truth #24: *The theme of Galatians is the gospel of man versus the gospel of Christ.*

> *"Paul, an apostle – sent not by men nor by a man, but by Jesus Christ and God the Father, who raised Him from the dead." – Galatians 1:1 NLT*

In the opening verse, Paul identifies himself in the usual manner as an apostle through the will of God the Father. Unique to this greeting, however, is Paul's caveat, "not from men nor through man" (v.1 NKJV). This phraseology is absent from all the other introductory statements of Paul's letters. This is by design. The apostle wastes no time hinting at his subject and striking at the core of the Galatian issue – man's rules vs. God's plan.

The issue at hand is that certain doctrines of men were being forced upon the Galatian congregation and were standing in the way of the teachings of God. Man-made rules, man-given philosophies and man-enforced policies were polluting and perverting the purity of the gospel given to Paul.

As we will see, the gospel of man opposing the gospel of Jesus Christ succinctly summarizes the crux of the Galatian dilemma. Whereas institutionalized religion requires the validation and endorsement of the establishment, the true gospel, the good news that Paul preaches, comes from God the Father and is validated through Jesus Christ.

Paul adds:

> *"For do I now persuade men, or God? Or do I seek to please men? For if I still pleased men, I would not be a bondservant of Christ. But I*

> *make known to you, brethren, that the gospel which was preached by me is not according to man. For I neither received it from man, nor was I taught it, but it came through the revelation of Jesus Christ." - Galatians 1:10-12*

And,

> *"I did not immediately confer with flesh and blood...I saw none of the other apostles except James." – Galatians 1:16,19*

From the onset we can ascertain that the apostle sought to guard the purity of his revelation and confront institutional rules that stood in opposition to the true gospel of Jesus Christ.

> *"I marvel that you are turning away so soon from Him who called you in the grace of Christ, to a different gospel, which is not another; but there are some who trouble you and want to pervert the gospel of Christ. But even if we, or an angel from heaven, preach any other gospel to you than what we have preached to you, let him be accursed. As we have said before, so now I say again, if anyone preaches any other gospel to you than what you have received, let him be accursed." – Galatians 1:6-9*

After greeting the church and giving glory to God, Paul's immediate concern was that some in the congregation were turning away to a different gospel. Troublers, as Paul defines them, were perverting the truth, insisting that believers be circumcised. He writes, "There are some who trouble you and want to pervert the gospel of Christ" (Gal. 1:7). "These would compel you to be circumcised, only that they may not suffer persecution for the cross of Christ" (Gal. 6:12-13). Paul calls out these troublesome men early in chapter 1 and throughout the rest of his epistle.

Troublemakers

Who were these troublers? They are not specifically identified here, but the same word used for trouble (*tarassō*) is the same word James employs in Acts 15:24 to describe the Judean Pharisees pushing circumcision.[1] The parallels between the two passages in scope and language cannot be ignored.[2] There is little doubt that Acts 15 and Galatians are tackling the very same issue, namely, Gentile inclusion and Jewish requirements for salvation. These troublers were likely from the same party of men who came down from Judea championing Jewish proselytization and ritual circumcision.

In chapter 2, Paul likens these troublers to a similar group of false brethren who "seemed to be something" (2:6) and secretly crept in to "spy out their liberty" and bring them "into bondage" (Gal. 2:4). "They zealously court you, but for no good; yes, they want to exclude you, that you may be zealous for them" (Gal. 4:17). Paul marvels that these young believers are so easily turning to a different gospel – a gospel not of grace but of covenantal membership. They were being coerced into submitting to a gospel not of God but of men.

The Galatian converts were being told that their conversion to Christ was not completely valid. To what can we liken this? Imagine being told that your initial water baptism was, for various reasons, illegitimate. Upon hearing this teaching, it caused you to question your faith. You became convinced that you needed to be re-baptized in a different church in accordance with this new teaching. By submitting to this doctrine, you would be calling into question your previous experience and renouncing what you had previously believed to be true.

In the same way, the troublemakers were sowing this kind of doubt among the new Gentile converts. The Galatian converts were being told their conversion experience was inadequate, illegitimate and that their faith in Jesus Christ was insufficient to secure eternal life. They were being compelled to be circumcised and re-identified as a member of the commonwealth of Israel.

---

[1] *Strong's* #G5015 ταράσσω; George Wigram, *The Englishman's Greek Concordance of the New Testament* (Peabody: Hendriksons, 1996)
[2] R. Alan Cole, *The Epistle of Paul to the Galatians* (Grand Rapids: Eerdmans, 1965)

The troublers may have been native-born Jews or perhaps proselytes themselves who had undergone circumcision. But because of the long-standing tradition of sectarian rituals, they no doubt considered themselves more informed on matters of covenant conversion.

It might be surprising to learn that first-century Jews didn't typically proselytize as we might expect. With the exception of the Pharisees, many Jews within second temple Judaism were indifferent to Gentile salvation. They were taught that any Gentile who truly wished to cling to the God of Israel would take it upon themselves to seek out the people of the covenant and learn the ways of Adonai.

For this reason, synagogues didn't typically launch missionary endeavors to convert Gentiles. While Pharisees did send out emissaries, their message was typically to Jews within the Jewish community, not Gentiles.[3] This put Paul, a Gentile sympathizer and apostle to the Gentiles, squarely at odds with the conventional thought and practice of his contemporaries.

The Jew-Gentile dilemma only grew worse as the gospel spread among the nations. With an influx of uncircumcised God-fearers among their ranks, the synagogues were flush with Gentiles. The troublers took it upon themselves to introduce and initiate the new converts into the way things operated. From their perspective, these Gentile Christians were newcomers to an old process and needed to be educated on how to follow proper protocol.

As previously sated, the prevailing mindset of the time was that only those within Israel proper could be God's chosen. A Gentile could not be in covenant with the God of Abraham, Isaac and Jacob without a re-identification. This meant that, in the eyes of the troublers, Gentiles seeking salvation were outside of the community of faith. They needed to be upgraded to legal Jewish status in order to prove their sincerity, finalize their conversion and access the covenant promises of Israel. The troublemakers were not promoting classical legalism as much as they were advocating Gentiles becoming covenant members through ritual circumcision.

---

[3] Friedman, *They Loved The Torah*, 50-51

In addition to circumcision, there was also an obligation to take on the full measure of the Torah and make oneself subject to rabbinic law. This was done in order to remain in the covenant. This involved keeping the Torah in the manner prescribed by their rabbis, which included an exhaustive list of written, oral and Jewish customs.

Of the troublers, Paul writes,

> *"They desire to have you circumcised that they may boast in your flesh." - Galatians 6:13*

Paul considered himself a Pharisee.[4] Given his background as a Pharisee and the son of a Pharisee, Paul was keenly aware of the motivation of these corrupters.[5] They were interested in more than preserving the sanctity of the synagogue or helping Gentiles secure a place in the world to come. These men wanted to brag about their proselytism and make Gentile converts "twice as much a son of hell" as they were.[6]

In the eyes of the troublemakers, the fundamental problem with these Gentiles was that they were not Jews! Through the custom of circumcision, these circumcision promoters sought to remedy the growing problem of Gentile influxation.

Taking Acts 15 and Galatians into account, we can gather some information about the troublers. In Acts 15, they are Pharisees (Acts 15:5) from Judea (Acts 15:1) who claimed to be Christ followers (Acts 15:5). In Galatians, they are false brothers (Gal. 2:4), who had their own gospel (Gal. 2:4) and were themselves Torah breakers (Gal. 6:12-13). Both were preaching salvation through mandated circumcision and rabbinic Torah keeping (Acts 15:1,5, Gal. 5:2-3). They sought to avoid persecution for associating with the Messiah (Gal. 5:11) and ultimately wanted to glory in circumcising Gentiles (Gal. 6:12-13).

---

[4] Acts 23:6
[5] Acts 23:6
[6] Matt. 23:15

It seems as though some of the Galatian brothers were planning to or had already undergone circumcision, which may be what predicated Paul's letter. In chapter 1, Paul is not only addressing the problem. He is addressing the problem-makers. He's writing to both the Galatian congregation and its agitators.

The gospel Paul preached, which he insisted was in accordance with the Heavenly Father, called for Gentiles to be accepted into the kingdom of God without reservation. It is a gospel that includes uncircumcised Gentiles within God's covenantal plan of salvation.

The "different gospel" that Paul mentions here is without question the gospel of the circumcision party. Also referenced in 2 Corinthians 11:4, the gospel of circumcision is a false gospel. This gospel was a different gospel, because it stood in direct opposition to the true gospel of faith that Paul himself received by revelation. It was a perverted gospel. It insisted on Gentiles submitting to proselyte circumcision and sectarian customs as a marker of their salvation.

There is little doubt that the subject of this letter is the gospel of salvation. This provides further evidence that Paul is dealing with matters of justification. The basic conflict within the Galatian church was not in how one approached the Torah or how Gentiles expressed their faith in terms of holiness. The prevailing issue was in determining what the true gospel was.

Is the gospel of the troublers the true gospel? Is salvation received through Jewish identity or by grace through faith in Jesus Christ? Is ritual circumcision part of the good news or an unnecessary work of the flesh? These were the questions pressing the Galatian believers.

Traditions of the Fathers

"For you have heard of my former conduct in Judaism, how I persecuted the church of God beyond measure and tried to destroy it. And I advanced in Judaism beyond many of my contemporaries in my nation, being more exceedingly zealous for the traditions of my fathers." - Galatians 1:13-14

The inclusion of Paul's credentials of having advanced in Judaism beyond his contemporaries is directed at Paul's counterparts and calls out a culture that regarded pedigree as having a direct bearing on one's spiritual status. This rings true with Sanders' depiction of covenantal nomism. Paul's apostolic authority is being challenged. He sought to remind the Galatians (and his opponents) of his qualifications.

In recounting his conversion to Christ and journey toward apostleship, Paul describes himself as one who was once very zealous for "the traditions of my fathers" (1:14). This is a reference to the rabbinic and oral laws he rigorously kept in his former life. These *traditions of the fathers* are what is now generically referred to as the oral law found in the Mishnah and elsewhere.

It was the Pharisees, of whom Paul was a member, who believed that the numerous traditions of the sages were just as binding as the written word of God. Josephus writes, "The Pharisees had passed on to the people certain regulations of the tradition of the fathers which are not recorded in the Laws of Moses."[7]

Paul is all too familiar with these customs, underscoring that he now contends against the same policies he once held. No doubt one of these policies was ritual circumcision for Gentile proselytes. Once a persecutor of the Way, Paul now was preaching the very gospel he sought to destroy (Gal. 1:23).

Paul resolutely rejects any institutionalized custom that pre-qualifies a person's justification and undermines the good news, both for himself and for his Gentile brethren. Like a protective father, Paul longs to shield these young Galatian believers from the constant noise coming from sectarian Judaism. These bitter debates would only seek to derail their pure and simple devotion to Christ.

The sentence syntax of this verse indicates that when Paul speaks of his former conduct, he is referencing his previous way of life, not his

---

[7] Santala, *Paul*, 18

previous Jewish life.[8] Paul never renounces his Jewish identity, nor did he leave his Jewish roots for a new Gentile-leaning religion. Paul was not ashamed of his Hebrew lineage. The shift he went through was not from one religion to another, or from Judaism to Christianity. The shift was in how righteousness could be attained and in Whom he placed his hope for eternal life.

Paul rejects the notion that being Jewish matters in terms of salvation and that imputed righteousness can be attained through it. Where Paul once thought in such ways, he breaks from that theology in an open rebuke to the troublers. As we will see, Paul wants to hammer home the point that God's covenant promises are not dependent on physical lineage but only grace through faith in Jesus Christ.

Conclusion

From the earliest portions of this letter, we can see a developing theme of Paul's epistle to the Galatians. In chapter 1, the apostle is addressing the gospel of the troublers. He identifies these troublesome men as false brethren wanting to glory in proselytizing and circumcising Gentile converts. Clearly, Paul is honing in on salvation and matters of conversion, not matters of Torah relevancy.

A Gentile's obligation to God's written word as a means of sanctification is not the principle topic of discussion here. Paul does address Christian living later in the epistle, which will, incidentally, reinforce the role Torah plays in our discipleship. But the subject matter of the first couple chapters is the gospel of salvation according to Jesus as revealed to Paul. In chapter 2, Paul firmly establishes there are no other prerequisites for salvation besides faith in Christ.

---

[8] Stern, *Jewish New Testament Commentary*, 522-523

GALATIANS 2:1-3

Truth #25: *The Galatian Christians were being pressured to submit to a circumcision not taught in Scripture.*

> *"Then after fourteen years I went up again to Jerusalem with Barnabas, and also took Titus with me. And I went up by revelation, and communicated to them that gospel which I preach among the Gentiles, but privately to those who were of reputation, lest by any means I might run, or had run, in vain. Yet not even Titus who was with me, being a Greek, was compelled to be circumcised."* - Galatians 2:1-3

Years after his encounter with the resurrected Messiah, Paul states that he went up to Jerusalem to be certain his teaching regarding Gentiles was sound. Because he places his message in submission to Peter and James, we can expect no contradiction between Paul's doctrine and the doctrine of the other apostles. Where they seem to be at odds with one another suggests a misperception on our part.

If we were not privy to the tensions that existed between Jews and Gentiles in first-century Israel, Paul's statement above regarding Titus would seem strangely out of place. He is talking about the purity of the gospel, his conversion to Christ, his message to the Gentiles and his interaction with the other apostles. Then, out of left field, Paul informs us that Titus did not feel compelled to be circumcised. What? Why does Paul thrust Titus and his refusal to be circumcised into this conversation? This is odd. And of all the laws of Torah, why is circumcision brought front and center?

The answer can only be that Paul is not speaking of infant circumcision or of any specific commandment about circumcision given in the Torah. As outlined in previous chapters, he is addressing the ritual of proselyte circumcision as taught by the rabbis and practiced by the troublers. This was not a Biblically-mandated practice but a rite-of-passage ritual invented by rabbis.

In bringing up Titus, Paul seeks to clarify his position regarding Gentile inclusion and justification. Titus was a full-grown adult. Infant circumcision, the type of circumcision outlined in the Torah, was not in play here.

Paul references Titus because his situation was germane to the topic at hand. Being Greek, Titus did not feel compelled to authenticate his salvation through a Jewish ritual at the insistence of these men. The pressure Titus felt to give in to the circumcision party was the same pressure being placed upon the Galatian believers. Paul thought it provided an excellent example of how the Galatians should handle the intimidation of the troublers.

Taking on the Law

It is important that we take into account the proper contextual background and to not misjudge the overall objective of Paul's argument. If, in this chapter, Paul were establishing a doctrinal position regarding Torah-obedience, the letter would read much more along the lines of the reformed interpretation of Galatians. Circumcision would then represent one of many laws outlined in the Torah that Paul was encouraging his audience to reject.

However, I humbly contend that the issues facing these Galatian believers were status-centered, not Torah-related. Paul is not addressing law obedience as we might define it. He is addressing the same situation and issues presented to the apostles in Acts 15 - the doctrine of ritual circumcision. Paul is giving answers to the same questions posed to the Jerusalem council, namely: What are the requirements for Gentiles seeking salvation? Is it necessary to become a Jewish proselyte? Can Gentiles inherit the promises of Abraham by faith alone without taking up ritual circumcision and a Jewish identity?

With the topic breached, circumcision now takes center stage in the rest of the epistle. Circumcision will become a major theme throughout this letter, as it represents the symbolic and physical sign of status conversion. Requiring circumcision of Gentile believers summed up the false gospel that Paul was dead set against.

It bears repeating that Paul is not citing the eight-day circumcision of infant boys prescribed in Leviticus 12. This requirement is seldom addressed in Paul's letters or in the Apostolic Scriptures. We know this to be true, because the troublemakers were neither pressuring the Galatians to circumcise their sons nor interested in passing along Abraham's heritage of faith. The context informs us that the Galatians were being compelled to submit to an adult conversion ritual of circumcision that was regarded as the custom of Moses.[1]

While many still regard circumcision as a marker of Jewish identity, it is not a marker of salvation. Following Christ has always been and will always be a decision of the will. Eight-day old boys do not choose to be circumcised.

Furthermore, when Paul speaks of circumcision, he is not merely referencing the physical act of circumcision but also the entire rabbinic ritual by which a Gentile could gain legal Jewish status. This involved much more than just the cutting of the foreskin. Among other things, it came with the obligation to keep an arduous list of written, oral and rabbinic regulations in order to maintain covenant membership.

To illustrate, when a person wishes to become a U.S. citizen, there is a long process they must undertake. This process includes completing an application, submitting photos, getting fingerprinted, being interviewed, taking a civics test and pledging an oath of allegiance to the country. One could say this process is a work of the law. In short, a person might simply say that they "took the oath" in reference to the final and symbolic step in gaining their citizenship.

In similar fashion, Paul distinguishes circumcision as part of the works of the law. Whereas the works of the law could be the whole process of citizenship, circumcision was *taking the oath*. Adult

---

[1] Acts 15:1

circumcision was not the only Jewish requirement for conversion, but it was the final, symbolic act of a man's proselytization. It was the physical sign of his entrance into the covenant. Instead of referring to the whole process, for brevity's sake, one could simply state that the proselyte was "circumcised."

Sometimes Paul uses circumcision in reference to Jews and the nation of Israel. The *Circumcised* and the *Uncircumcised* are colloquialisms for Jew and Gentile, respectively.[2] In his letters, "circumcised" is often a shorthanded way of saying *Jewish*. But in Galatians, Paul almost exclusively uses circumcision as a catchphrase for the doctrine of the circumcision party. Circumcision is the defining mark of a proselyte and the defining message of the troublemakers.

For example, in Paul's letter to Titus, he writes,

> *"For there are many insubordinate, both idle talkers and deceivers, especially those of the circumcision, whose mouths must be stopped, who subvert whole households, teaching things which they ought not, for the sake of dishonest gain. One of them, a prophet of their own, said, 'Cretans are always liars, evil beasts, lazy gluttons.' This testimony is true. Therefore rebuke them sharply, that they may be sound in the faith, not giving heed to Jewish fables and commandments of men who turn from the truth."* – Titus 1:10-14

The character of some of these circumcisers comes into sharper focus here. Paul describes them as insubordinate, idle talking deceivers who subvert households and seek dishonest gain. They had turned from the truth and were teaching things they ought not. They gave heed to Jewish fables and the commandments of men.

Because Paul did not compel Titus to be circumcised, some conclude that he was anti-circumcision; therefore, anti-Torah. However, if this was the case, why did Paul have Timothy circumcised in Lystra?[3] Paul's own actions are inconsistent with that

---

[2] Gal. 2:7-9, Eph. 2:11, Col. 4:11
[3] Acts 16:3

hypothesis. Timothy's circumcision had nothing to do with entering the kingdom of God, as he was already identified as a believer.[4] Timothy was circumcised in accordance with the Torah so that he could live his life as a messianic Jew and be able to minister among the Jewish community without offense.[5]

> "If Rabbi *Sha'ul* did not respect the Torah, then he would have had no reason to circumcise Timothy. The Torah is clear that every Jewish male needs to be circumcised (see Gen. 17:10-14). *Sha'ul*, in circumcising Timothy, was respecting and keeping the Torah."[6]

Clearly, Paul was not opposed to circumcision as a practice. Rather, Paul took issue with Gentiles being forced to undergo Jewish ceremonial rituals that involved circumcision for the purpose of gaining membership within Israel or any particular Jewish sect.

It could be said that it was not circumcision that irked Paul, but rather how circumcision was being used and abused. The apostle took issue with what they sought to accomplish through circumcision. Paul and the apostles were opposed to circumcision being hailed as something that could verify repentance. In their eyes, salvation came only by faith. Titus did not feel compelled to be circumcised, because he did not agree with the gospel of the circumcision party.

Jewish Status Quo

Why would a Gentile believer living in the first century want to become a Jewish proselyte in the first place? This is an intriguing question. There were some incentives for Greeks obtaining Jewish citizenship.

For starters, every Roman subject, small or great, was expected to acknowledge Caesar as a deity and give divine honors to the

---

[4] Acts 16:1
[5] For more on Timothy's circumcision, see Chapter 49
[6] Friedman, *They Loved The Torah*, 53

emperor.⁷ Emperors could be deified after their death or even during their reign, thereby elevating them to the status of a demigod. This included members of the imperial family, such as wives, sisters and daughters. Worship could also be directed to the emperor's guardian spirit, thereby requiring one to "swear by the genius of Caesar." Implements of imperial cult worship included temples, shrines, priests, sacrifices, feasts, hymns, altars, processions and incense.⁸

A strong expectation of social conformity governed Roman society. Families could choose to worship whatever god they desired so long as they fulfilled their civic duty. This duty involved bowing down to Caesar, burning incense to his image, paying homage to the gods of Rome, participating in Roman festivals, and/or bringing a token sacrifice to the Greek temple.

An atheist, for example, was socially tolerated so long as they performed their ritual duties once a year. In offering a token sacrifice or celebrating a pagan festival, however, one would have to question how true an atheist they really were. The same held true for Christians. Failure to perform these civic duties often resulted in social or material penalties, including ostracization and even imprisonment.⁹

Jews, however, were exempt from these obligatory customs. The practice of Judaism became a state-sanctioned religion under the reign of Claudius.¹⁰ Under Roman law, Jews had legal protection to freely practice their religion. Unfortunately, non-Jewish Christians were not given such liberties, leaving them conflicted when faced with the duty of imperial idolatry. For political and social reasons, becoming a member of a Jewish sect such as the Pharisees or Sadducees or Essenes was an attractive option for Gentiles who

---

[7] W.R.F. Browning, *A Dictionary of the Bible*, "Emperor Worship" [Online]. Available: www.oxfordbiblicalstudies.com
[8] https://www.oxfordbibliographies.com/view/document/obo9780195393361/obo-9780195393361-0030.xml
[9] Merrill Tenney, *The Zondervan Pictorial Encyclopedia Of The Bible*, Vol. II (Grand Rapids: Zondervan, 1975), 301-303
[10] H. Idris Bell, *Jews and Christians in Egypt* (San Francisco: Greenwood Press, 1972), 1924

wanted to worship the one true God but feared the Roman government.

Secondly, because they worshipped the God of Israel, followed a Jewish Messiah, and adhered to the Hebrew Scriptures, Gentile Christians looked very much like Jews to the pagan eye. For several decades there did not exist a discernible difference between Judaism and Christianity. Followers of the Way were seen more as a branch of Judaism than something separate and distinguishable. Many Christians found it easier to identify with Israel and the Jewish people than with the pagan culture around them.

Thirdly, there was a stigma attached to being a Gentile Christian in the eyes of first-century Israel. Though a Gentile believer had covenant access to God through faith in Yeshua, they were still rejected as a legitimate *ben Avraham* (son of Abraham) by the larger Jewish community. Rabbis did not recognize uncircumcised Gentiles as part of the commonwealth of Israel, because they weren't circumcised. This put Gentile believers in a precarious position. They weren't godless pagans anymore, yet they weren't fully Israelites, either.

For many God-fearing Gentiles, participating in Roman idolatry violated their conscience, yet they were given no legal recourse or religious exemption from it. Without securing Jewish status, Gentile Christians were left vulnerable to both Roman and Jewish persecution.

Fourthly, there was also a financial motivation for a Gentile to become a Jewish citizen. Rome had issued a special tax called the *fiscus Judaicus* in the early 70s C.E. The *fiscus Judaicus* was a tax imposed upon all Jews by the Roman Empire following the destruction of Jerusalem. It amounted to two days wages per person per household per year. The half-shekel temple tax that Jews normally brought to the temple in Jerusalem was collected by Caesar and diverted to the temple of Jupiter Capitolinus in Rome.[11]

---

[11] Josephus, *Jewish War* 7.218; Suetonius, *Life of Domitian* 12.1-2; Cassius Dio, 67.14.1-2

Paul penned his letter to the Galatians before Rome had instituted the *fiscus Judaicus*. Therefore, there was no financial penalty associated with being a Jew at that time. Jewish identity was still financially advantageous and politically attractive to a good many Greek believers. For this reason alone, there remained a strong incentive to gain legal, Jewish status.

All-too-often Gentile believers were marginalized by the Jews, persecuted by the Pharisees and in danger of the Roman Empire. Being circumcised and becoming a Jewish citizen was a convenient solution to these growing problems. Perhaps this is why Paul adds,

> *"If I still preach circumcision, why do I still suffer persecution? Then the offense of the cross has ceased." - Galatians 5:11*

And,

> *"These would compel you to be circumcised, only that they may not suffer persecution for the cross of Christ." – Galatians 6:12*

Agreeing to circumcision and becoming a legalized Jew alleviated much of the persecution they faced. It also guaranteed certain legal rights under Roman and Jewish law.

Perhaps the strongest argument for conversion was that holding Jewish citizenship eliminated some of the social ambiguities within their communities of faith. The church still met in home synagogues where Jews and Gentiles were thrust into interacting with one another, particularly in Jerusalem. Over time the messianic church became integrated, but in the early going Gentiles no doubt felt out of place without a sense of belonging. Becoming a Jewish proselyte or converting to Judaism put Gentiles in good standing with Jewish leaders. It also provided certain rights within the Jewish community, such as temple access and inner-marriage.

Because it was taught that access to God could only be gained through the covenants of Israel, God-fearing Gentiles who sought to worship the God of Israel found circumcision and Jewish citizenship attractive. For those wishing to avoid persecution and socially integrate, this offered an appealing route to God that required no faith.

Conclusion

We can surmise that proselyte circumcision, the kind spoken of in this chapter and in all of Galatians, stood in opposition to the gospel of grace. It was not representative of Christ or the Torah. It was a non-Biblical Jewish custom that was designed to re-identify non-Jews.

GALATIANS 2:4-5

Truth #26: *Paul did not liberate Gentiles from Torah mandates.*

> *"And this occurred because of false brethren secretly brought in (who came in by stealth to spy out our liberty which we have in Christ Jesus, that they might bring us into bondage), to whom we did not yield submission even for an hour, that the truth of the gospel might continue with you." - Galatians 2:4-5*

Paul is recounting his confrontation with the false brethren who were pressuring Titus and the brothers to succumb to circumcision when they were in Jerusalem. The false brothers spoken of here are not the same men that were troubling the Galatian churches. However, it is probable that the agitators troubling the Galatians belonged to the same party of men listed here and in Acts 15. The description and disposition are strikingly similar in these stories. Notice the parallels.

Galatian Troublers

"There are some who trouble you and want to pervert the gospel of Christ." - Galatians 1:6

"Compel you to be circumcised." - Galatians 6:12

"I could wish that those who trouble you would even cut themselves off!" - Galatians 5:12

False Brethren in Jerusalem (Galatians 2)

"False brethren secretly brought in to spy out our liberty." - Galatians 2:4

"Yet not even Titus who was with me, being a Greek, was compelled to be circumcised." - Galatians 2:3

"We did not yield submission even for an hour." - Galatians 2:5

Judean Circumcisers (Acts 15)

"Certain men came down by stealth." - Acts 15:1

"Taught the brethren, 'Unless you are circumcised according to the custom of Moses, you cannot be saved.'" - Acts 15:1

"Paul and Barnabas had no small dissension and dispute with them." - Acts 15:2

This helps to underscore the underlying conflict within the Galatian church and all the churches surrounding Palestine. It also uncovers who was responsible for attempting to steal their liberty and bring them into bondage.

In our pursuit of being honest with the text, our understanding of the terms *liberty* and *bondage* must fit within the content of the first two chapters of Galatians, not within the context of our choosing. It is often presumed that the "liberty" mentioned here is liberty *from* the Torah, and that "bondage" must be bondage *to* Torah-obedience. I suggest that Paul taught the exact opposite.

In light of the context and all of his writings, it is more accurate to say that Paul preached a liberty *to* obey God's word and that followers of Christ have been freed from the bondage of Torah-*dis*obedience. This is not the specific point Paul is proving here, but he does establish it elsewhere.[1]

Paul is fighting for the purity of the gospel. It took great boldness to stand up to the circumcision-driven orthodoxy well regarded as the "traditions of the fathers" (1:14). Paul was resolute. He knew all-too-well the bondage it would bring. He encouraged the Galatian

---

[1] Rom. 2:13, 3:31, 7:12, 8:1-2, 2 Tim. 3:15

disciples to rebuff the doctrine of these circumcisers. To Paul, any ideology that taught that God-fearing, Christ-following Gentiles must submit to rabbinic rites and Jewish rituals was unacceptable.

Conclusion

Context is not kind to the explanation that we are liberated from any obligation to obey the Torah. The subject matter of Galatians 1 and 2 is clearly the gospel of Jesus Christ, Gentile salvation and ritual circumcision. It is not simple Torah keeping. Paul was neither setting the Galatians free from Biblical mandates, nor dividing the Torah into three parts, excusing Gentiles from two of them. He is simply contending for a status-free gospel.

GALATIANS 2:11-15

Truth #27: *Paul rebuked Peter for being hypocritical about Gentile acceptance, not unclean food.*

> *"Now when Peter had come to Antioch, I withstood him to his face, because he was to be blamed; for before certain men came from James, he would eat with the Gentiles; but when they came, he withdrew and separated himself, fearing those who were of the circumcision. And the rest of the Jews also played the hypocrite with him, so that even Barnabas was carried away with their hypocrisy." –*
> Galatians 2:11-13

The Judaisms of the first century tended to divide the world into two categories - Jew and non-Jew. Good Jews didn't typically hang out with non-Jews. It may be that Peter still waffled in his posture toward Gentiles. As can be ascertained from this story, evidently Peter was still interested in being considered a good Jew.

Paul accuses Peter of withdrawing himself from Gentile believers out of fear. The men from James were no doubt stricter in their social interaction with Greeks. Peter was fearful of any confrontation about whether it was proper to eat with a Gentile. He simply found it easier to acquiesce. Peter tended to go with the customary flow of how Jews typically interacted with non-Jews than to get into an argument with fellow Jews that he was unprepared or unwilling to fight.

I do not think Peter was bigoted or consciously stood in solidarity with the doctrine of the circumcision party. It is more likely that he caved to the fear of man and conceded to those who remained loyal to traditional Jewish customs. This is not out of character for Peter.

This would not be the first time Peter displayed cowardly behavior when confronted in public.[1]

But by withdrawing from Gentiles, Peter was reinforcing the segregated lines of ethnocentricity and rebuilding the wall of separation between Jew and Gentile that he helped topple. He knew full well what he was doing but was probably oblivious to the gravity his decision would have upon the church and the gospel moving forward. To Paul's chagrin, Peter's spineless behavior influenced the rest of the Jewish brothers in Antioch. Paul nailed it. Peter was playing the hypocrite.

> *"But when I saw that they were not straightforward about the truth of the gospel, I said to Peter before them all, 'If you, being a Jew, live in the manner of Gentiles and not as the Jews, why do you compel Gentiles to live as Jews? We who are Jews by nature, and not sinners of the Gentiles." – Galatians 2:14-15*

Paul, on the other hand, was not afraid of confrontation. He was notably upset with Peter. After all, this was Simon Peter we're talking about. Of all people, Cephas should know better. He was one of the original Twelve. He walked on water with Jesus and was given the keys to the kingdom. He boldly proclaimed Christ on the day of Pentecost before the multitude and was given the groundbreaking vision of the sheet. His obedience brought the good news to Cornelius and paved the way for Gentile nations to hear the gospel.

Moreover, up to this point, Peter had been enjoying table fellowship with Gentiles seemingly without reservation. Why would Peter submit to these men from Jerusalem? This was no small matter to Paul.

---

[1] Matt. 26:69-75

GALATIANS 2:11-15

Living like a Gentile

Paul reminds Peter that Peter had been living "in the manner of Gentiles" (v.14). This wasn't a rebuke or a complement. This was a statement of fact more than anything.

In what way was Peter living like a Gentile? It wasn't in regards to idolatry, meat consumption or pagan festivals. This is not the substance of Paul's words. Nowhere do we witness Peter living in such ways.

Before the men arrived from Jerusalem, Peter had been living like a Gentile by setting aside Jewish social laws incumbent upon all Jews as it relates to pagans. He had come to the place where he could sit down over a meal and enjoy table fellowship with Gentiles, something most Jews would not comfortably do.

Paul calls out Peter for his hypocritical behavior. Before the men came, Peter had refused to take his cues from rabbinic Judaism. He was fraternizing with Greeks and socially interacting with Gentiles, just as Paul and the rest of the Jewish believers were. Upon their arrival, however, Peter gave in to the opinion of the circumcisers. He separated himself from table fellowship with Gentile brothers and influenced the other Jewish brothers to do likewise, including Barnabas.

Paul's rebuke was this: "If you, a Jewish man, disregard Jewish social standards by eating and worshipping with Greeks, how can you give in to the opinion of those who compel Gentiles to submit to Jewish policies for salvation?" Peter had been living in the manner of the Gentiles by sharing his meals with them. In changing course and separating himself from his Gentile brothers at mealtime, by default Peter was forcing his Gentile brothers to abide by Jewish laws. His actions insinuated that he was aligned with the doctrine of ritual circumcision.

Paul not only took issue with Peter's behavior but also with the ones who came from James, for "they were not straightforward about the truth of the gospel" (v.14). Paul did not approve of their stance on circumcision and Gentile interaction. We can only imagine what Paul said to them. Yet, it is curious that Paul also felt the need to call out Peter publically for his hypocrisy. He confronted the apostle for cowering before these men and not standing up for the truth.

In his rebuke, Paul also accused Peter of compelling "Gentiles to live as Jews" (v.14). In other words, if Peter had rejected the Jewish policies for Gentile interaction and had been living like a Gentile in the eyes of scrutinizing Jews, why then was he now making Gentiles abide by the policies he had previously abandoned? Paul is perplexed as to why Peter would force Gentiles to submit to Jewish customs as it pertains to social matters if he knew they need not submit to Jewish customs as it pertains to salvation.

Just as Jews are not justified by Jewish identity, neither circumcision nor Jewish affiliation justifies Gentiles. If racial lines have no bearing on the greater matter of salvation, then why would racial lines have any bearing on the smaller issue of fellowship?

It should be noted that the word compel (*anagkazo*) used here is the same word used earlier when Paul insists that even Titus was not compelled (*anagkazo*) to be circumcised.[2] It is also the word employed in Galatians 6:12 to describe the actions of the troublers.[3] These are the only three places this word appears in the book of Galatians. This could indicate that the nature of Paul's accusation against Peter was identical to what the troublemakers were compelling Titus, the Jerusalem and Galatian believers to do.

Paul was right to condemn Peter's actions. Consciously or not, Peter was siding with the circumcision-promoters and ultimately corrupting the gospel.

---

[2] Gal. 2:3
[3] *Strong's* #G315 ἀναγκάζω

Galatians 2:11-15

Telling Stories

J. Vernon McGee comments on this passage in his radio commentary series entitled *Thru The Bible*. I like McGee's colorful personality. He is witty and entertaining, for sure.

Unfortunately, McGee fails to recognize how strong the cultural tension between Jew and Greek was at the time. Instead of seeing Gentile inclusion, Christian unity and Peter's hypocrisy as the main points of Paul's confrontation, McGee reduces the argument to mere bickering over meat matters, forcibly and mistakenly injecting the dietary laws of Leviticus 11 into the narrative.

McGee presumes that there were two tables at the church in Antioch – a kosher table and a Gentile table. This is a supposition of McGee's, not an historical fact. Since Peter and the other Jews withdrew from the Gentiles at mealtime, he reasons that there was a "Jew only" table separate from the main table. This is plausible, I guess.

McGee, however, supposes that only kosher meats were being served at the Jewish table, while meats of all kinds, including unclean animals and animals sacrificed to idols, were served at the Gentile table. This is unlikely.

Days before the men arrive from Jerusalem, he imagines Peter eating only with Jews at the kosher table and Paul eating unclean meats and fellowshipping with Greeks at the Gentile table. In a made-up scenario, he supposes that one evening after supper Peter takes a stroll with Paul. Peter asks Paul about the pork roast that had been served over at the Gentile table that night. McGee tells his story:

"Paul, I noticed you eat at the Gentile table," Peter says.

Paul responds, *"Yes."*

Peter, *"I saw that you ate pork tonight."*

Paul, *"Yes."*

Peter asks, *"Well, by the way, is it good? I've never tasted it."*

"It's delicious!" exclaims Paul.

Peter, *"Do you think it would be alright if I ate over there?"*

Paul, *"Well, it's my understanding that we're gonna have some nice pork chops in the morning for breakfast."*

Peter, *"Oh, I think I'd like to come."*

So, in the morning, Peter sits down gingerly, asks rather reluctantly and takes a pork chop. He tastes it, reaches over and says to Paul, *"It's delicious, isn't it?"*

Paul said, *"Yes, because after all, under grace, you can either eat it or you cannot eat it. It doesn't make any difference. Meat doesn't commend you to God."*

And so Simon Peter said, *"I'll be here tonight. I understand that you're gonna have some ham tonight. I wanna try that."*

McGee adds, "So that night, Peter starts rushing in, looks over and sees in attendance some of the elders from the church of Jerusalem. They came to visit also. And Simon Peter played musical chairs. He went all the way around that Gentile table and sat down at the kosher table like a little whipped puppy. Peter sits down with these brethren rather sheepishly, and Paul saw it."

McGee concludes, "It was alright for Peter to go to either table. He could sit down and eat kosher or the other. But when he had been eating at the Gentile table and for fear of these brethren, he comes in and goes back, he is saying by substance and by act that eating at the Gentile table is wrong and that Gentiles should come over and eat at this other table. He's saying that the kosher table is the right one, and he goes back from the liberty that we have in Christ to legalism and Judaism."[4]

---

[4] J. Vernon McGee, *Thru The Bible*, Radio Commentary, Gal. 2

This commentary epitomizes the typical narrative that is perpetuated about this interaction between Peter and Paul. As Bible teachers, if we are going to create fictional scenarios and conversations between two apostles in an attempt to reconstruct the story and teach doctrine, we'd better make sure our facts are airtight. While it does provide entertaining fodder, McGee's story has more than a slow leak.

The first puncture is that he incorrectly identifies food as the point of contention. The issue in Galatians 2 was not the meal, as the menu is never mentioned in the passage. The dispute was a procedural one regarding intrapersonal contact with Gentiles. Before the men arrived, Peter enjoyed fellowship with uncircumcised Greek believers. Table fellowship was important to the early communities of Yeshua, as this is where they shared the Lord's Supper.[5]

After the men arrived, however, Peter reverted back to Jewish policies governing social interaction with non-Jews. Paul makes no specific mention of two segregated tables or the type of food served on the table. It is Peter's reaction to the people sitting around the table that is the issue, not his reaction to the served meal.

The second perforation is the assumption that the Gentile Christians were all eating pork while the Jewish believers were eating kosher meat. Not only is this absent from the story, so is the assumption that both Paul and Peter were eating unpermitted animals. Where is this found in the text or anywhere else in the Apostolic Scriptures?

I understand creative license, but even by modern standards this is slanderous. He accuses two of the most venerated apostles of disregarding the practice of our Lord, discounting the word of God and indulging in pork flesh. He characterizes Paul as a law-breaking rebel and Peter as secretly coveting swine. Despite it being brazenly unbiblical, it is backhanded character assassination.

McGee's third rupture is doctrinal. He envisions Paul saying, "Under grace, you can either eat it or you cannot eat it. It doesn't

---

[5] Juster, *Jewish Roots,* 110

make any difference. Meat doesn't commend you to God." If Paul were talking about salvation, McGee's supposition here would be correct. Food doesn't commend us to God's grace. Adherence to any of God's commands, including the dietary laws, cannot earn anyone salvation.

But under McGee's stated scenario, Peter and Paul are discussing food items around the Christian table. This makes McGee's supposed conversation about matters of sanctification (victory over sin), not justification (reconciliation to God). In other words, McGee mysteriously changes the established context of the book of Galatians from Gentile interaction and what is required of them for salvation to dietary liberty and acceptable Christian behavior. This is an oversight.

Since McGee incorrectly makes holiness, not salvation, the subject matter, he finds himself supporting the precarious position that a Christian's response to God's word does not factor into their relationship with God in any way. Whether purposely or accidentally, he confuses saving grace with one's loving obligation to God's grace.

This kind of abuse of the doctrine of grace is used as justification for all kinds of immoral behavior within Christendom today. It turns the idea of *It doesn't matter what you've done* into *It doesn't matter what you do*. This approach insists that a believer's actions matter not to God, or in McGee's words, do not commend them to God. Clearly, this suggestion mishandles the spirit of grace and the teachings of Christ.

Lastly, when Paul wrote "food does not commend us to God" (1 Cor. 8:8), he is addressing food offered to idols, not eating unclean meats. McGee mistakenly takes a quote from Paul out of context to address a problem that he takes out of context.

McGee misses the point as to why Paul recounts this story to the Galatian believers. Paul tells the story to tie his authority as an apostle (Chapter 1) to the message of faith (Chapter 3). He uses it to reinforce his argument that the gospel of the troublemakers is a gospel of hypocrisy. To Paul, these Jewish policies stem not from the true gospel of Jesus Christ but from the gospel of man. The bottom line is that Paul does not want the Galatian believers to be duped into submitting to circumcision.

Conclusion

The social, ethnic and political tension that existed at the time between Jew and Greek cannot be understated. Today, we have no problem with Gentiles being saved. After all, most of the world is Gentile. But many Jews struggled with seeing beyond the long-standing customs of their fathers and accepting as equals the people that still occupied the Promised Land.

Paul sets out to prove that the gospel of the troublers is not the true gospel of Jesus Christ. It is a man-made, status-driven gospel that forces one into believing that salvation comes through Jewish identity and practice. He shares the example of Titus and his rebuke of Peter to illustrate that the Galatians should resist being forced into submitting to any of the Jewish circumcision customs in their conversion to Christ.

While it may be easy for us to be critical of Peter's hypocrisy, this story can help us come to terms with our own blind spots. To a certain extent, the Christian community has given into the fear of man and been hesitant to break with traditional orthodoxy, particularly as it relates to the subject matter of this book. Many of us have discarded the Torah in favor of long-standing church positions regarding the law. Sometimes it takes someone like Paul to stand up and say, "Hey, wait a second. Do you see what's happening here? We are not being straightforward with the truth." I am grateful someone did this for me. I'm confident Peter was as well.

GALATIANS 2:16 – PART I

Truth #28: *The Dead Sea Scrolls help define Paul's works of the law.*

"Knowing that a man is not justified by the works of the law but by faith in Jesus Christ, even we have believed in Christ Jesus, that we might be justified by faith in Christ and not by the works of the law; for by the works of the law no flesh shall be justified." – Galatians 2:16

Verse 16 introduces a new phrase to the vocabulary of Paul's argument – *works of the law*. Assuming Galatians was written before Paul's letter to the Romans, chronologically this is the first mention of the term in the Bible. Paul is still recounting his rebuke of Peter.

This phrase deserves focused attention, so I want to slow-play this section of Galatians. Understanding the term *works of the law* is important in seeking to understand the book of Galatians.

The key to this term is found in the context of Paul's words. If Paul is straying from his main premise of circumcision, *works of the law* means what it traditionally has always meant. But if Paul is continuing with his argument for Gentile inclusion, the phrase takes on a whole different connotation.

The phrase *works of the law* (more literal *works of law*) is exclusive to Paul in the New Testament. It reads *ergon nomos* in the Greek – *ergon* (works)[1] *nomos* (law).[2] Since no other New Testament writer employs this phrase, it has long been considered a term coined by Paul. For centuries readers have assumed it was Paul's general term

---

[1] *Strong's* #G2041 ἔργον
[2] *Strong's* #G3551 νόμος; Marshall, *The Interlinear Greek-English New Testament*, 746

for keeping the Torah, but some scholars are beginning to question that postulation. As it turns out, the meaning may not be as simple as we have presumed.

I'm going to ask you to lay aside any preconceived ideas you may have formed about this familiar phrase. I have come to realize that it is not settled that *works of the law* means *keeping the commandments of Torah*. There is more to consider.

4QMMT

The debate over the meaning of *works of the law* is not new but has newly resurfaced. This stems from the fact that no other reference to this phrase had ever been found anywhere in antiquity, that is, until the discovery of the Dead Sea Scrolls. Up until 1947, scholars assumed *works of the law* was exclusive and specialized Pauline terminology.

But found in cave 4 among the ancient documents of Qumran were six fragments of a document that bear the title in Hebrew: *Miksat Ma'asei HaTorah*. Scholars Elisha Qimon and John Strugnell, whose work helped to publish this document, translated this title as "Some of the Works of the Law."[3] Although a better translation might be "Important (or Pertinent) Works of Torah."[4]

This ancient manuscript has been catalogued as document 4QMMT of the Dead Sea Scrolls. Since its official release in 1994, the public has been given direct access to this manuscript. This scroll is a monumental discovery for many reasons. For us, it signifies the first time the term *works of the law* has been found somewhere outside of Paul's writings.[5]

---

[3] Elisha Qimon and John Strugnell, "An Unpublished Halakhic Letter from Qumran" *Israel Museum Journal,* 1985
[4] Martin Abegg, *Paul, Works of the Law and MMT,* Dead Sea Scrolls, *Biblical Archaeology Review,* Nov-Dec 1994
[5] In 1994, the Israel Antiquities Authority took major steps toward advancing the publication of the Dead Sea Scrolls. Discovered by a young Bedouin shepherd in 1947, the Dead Sea Scrolls have offered unmatched insight into 2nd temple Judaism. Previously, the scroll fragments extracted from the caves of Qumran had

In reading 4QMMT (MMT for short), the contents surprisingly have little if nothing to do with the topics of law and grace.[6] The body of the text consists of twenty or so policy measures concerning purity procedures, priestly boundaries, calendar computations and legal interpretations of Jewish law. It addresses issues such as the right handling of sacrifices, the genealogical purity of the priesthood, admitting Gentile corn, Gentile offerings and the blind into the temple, the cleansing of lepers, the transmission of impurity by the flow of water, plowing with diverse animals, the intermixture of wool with linen, cooking sacrificial meat in impure vessels, and the intermarriage of priests with commoners.[7]

Most of the rulings found in the scroll relate in some manner to the Torah but are not specific to Torah proper. They are external rules that address oral customs and fence laws. MMT concerns itself primarily with the proper interpretation and observation of rabbinic and Mosaic amplifications.

There is no consensus among scholars about who wrote the ancient letter and to whom it was written. Most experts do agree, however, that there is an external and internal component to the letter.

Externally, it is an argument written to persuade a prominent leader to agree with the writer's opinion. MMT seems to represent the doctrinal position of some particular Jewish sect. Because the author has a strong opinion regarding rabbinic law and priestly protocols, scholars speculate that it was written to someone outside the community explaining the position of the community and seeking to convince the reader to their point of view.[8]

---

only been available to a handful of international scholars. But since 2001, most of the documents have been published and can be accessed in academic libraries. Since their discovery and release, a recent explosion of new scholarship has emerged regarding first-century Judaism and how it relates to the New Testament.
[6] Jeff Dryden, "4QMMT," 2011, 2-4. [Online]. Available: www.tyndale.cam.ac.uk/tyndale/staff/Head/4QMMT.htm
[7] Abegg, *Paul, Works of the Law and MMT*, 2
[8] As an external document, the letter may hold clues as to why the sect had separated itself from the general society. It could be that the document was written to reconcile an intra-communal dispute between those with whom this sect had

Some suspect the leader of the Qumran community might have penned MMT. If so, the document likely belonged to the Essene sect dwelling in Qumran near the Dead Sea. It would then have been written to an influential religious leader outside of the community.[9] Others propose that the scrolls were not written in the caves themselves but produced in Jerusalem and hidden in the desert by a group of Pharisees or Sadducees.[10]

Even if the Dead Sea Scrolls did not originate with the Essenes, we can ascertain that the group responsible for 4QMMT was conservative, exclusive and homogenous, as the writer of this letter was very much concerned with unholy mixture. As a persuasive letter, it discusses, rather dogmatically, how certain Jewish fence laws should be observed and put into practice. In other words, it deals almost exclusively with Jewish *halakha* (the correct manner in which the Torah should be lived out).

The position of this document dictated who was allowed in the community, who was out and how members should conduct themselves. This could describe the Pharisees, who had grown to an estimated 6,000 before the destruction of the temple.[11] It also fits what we know about the Essene community who commonly referred

---

separated themselves from. Because *Miksat Ma'asei HaTorah* strongly admonishes its recipient, it aims to persuade a colleague to reconsider his position on certain policy matters and to take a specific course of action. Dryden writes, "The purpose of the epistle is for the recipient to adopt or reaffirm practices advocated in section B. Whoever the recipient is, he is the leader of some group of influence in Israel, since he has the power to make such a decision for the group and that this will not only affect him and his group but all of Israel, since the very end of MMT says that this decision is 'for your welfare and for the welfare of Israel'". He adds that because the bulk of the material concerns priestly matters, it most likely was written to the high priest of the temple. (Dryden, "4QMMT," 2-4)
[9] James Vanderkam, "The People of the Dead Sea Scrolls: Essenes or Sadducees?"
[10] Lawrence Schiffman, "The Saducceean Origins of the Dead Sea Scrolls Sect", cited by Hershel Shanks, *Understanding the Dead Sea Scrolls* (Reno: Random House, 1992); Norman Golb, *Who Wrote the Dead Sea Scrolls?* (New York: Simon and Schuster, 1995)
[11] According to Josephus and Philo; *Pharisee* derives from the Hebrew word *parash*, which means "to separate"

to themselves as 'workers of the law' and were considered even stricter in their interpretation of the law than the Pharisees.[12]

Internally, the letter reads like a church membership handbook of sorts. The scroll, also referred to as the *Halakhic Letter*, appears to represent the doctrinal position of the community and define the sociological boundaries of this particular sect. In this way, it may have served as the official doctrinal position of the community, outlining institutional requirements expected of members or individuals wishing to be an active member within the community.[13]

It is rather curious that 4QMMT does not concern itself with keeping the Torah as we might expect but with matters relating to specific rulings regarding priestly, rabbinic and calendar matters. There is no question that MMT assumes the reader will keep the Torah. What that looks like and what it means to be orthodox, however, is what is being argued.

For example, the issues raised in the document are not whether the Biblical holidays should be observed, but what is the correct way to compute the days of the Hebrew calendar. It does not question the authority of temple priests, but how these priests were selected and how they should behave. In other words, MMT seeks to clarify the proper position on certain matters of appropriate behavior and to convince the reader that he and his people should adopt this same viewpoint.

---

[12] Professor David Flusser, Hebrew University of Jerusalem

[13] 4QMMT is divided into three main sections - Section A: A Hebrew calendar. Section B: Jewish halakhic discussions. Section C: An exhortation. Martinez and Tigchelaar, *The Dead Sea Scrolls Study Edition*; Dryden, *4QMMT*, 1. There are still a lot of unanswered questions about the people that produced the Dead Sea Scrolls. Many believe that they were Essenes (Vanderkam), Sadducees (Schiffman) or perhaps even Pharisees. (Josephus and Philo) If one takes the position that the Essenes produced the Dead Sea Scrolls, it would explain the impassioned appeal of this letter. Essene members of the Qumran community were considered even stricter in their interpretation of the law than the Pharisees. There is no consensus on what is meant by the Essenes referring to as 'workers of the Torah', but it could have some connection to 'works of the law.' See H. Ringgren, *Theological Dictionary of the Old Testament* (Grand Rapids: Eerdmans, 2001), 11:402

It is no coincidence that MMT uses language similar to Paul, as scholars believe parts of it were written around the same time the apostle was writing to the churches. In addition to employing the term *works of the law*, the phrase *counted as righteousness* is also found in 4QMMT, a term common in Paul's letters.

According to Martin Abegg,

> "MMT provides the 'smoking gun' for which students have been searching for generations, not from the pages of rabbinic literature but from the sectarian teachings of Qumran. MMT demonstrates that Paul was not jousting with windmills, but was indeed squared off in a dramatic duel – not with mainstream Judaism but with sectarian theology – that ultimately defined Christianity. If I have understood rightly, the importance of MMT for New Testament research is nothing short of revolutionary."[14]

Now that the phrase *works of law* has been found outside of Paul's letters, we are obligated to reconsider what the term meant to Paul's audience and to first century believers. There is no evidence that Paul read or had access to this *Halakhic Letter,* but it does not rule out the possibility that some members of the letter's community or those familiar with the term *works of the law* had come to faith in Yeshua of Nazareth. In light of MMT's discovery, Paul and his audience may well have understood the term differently than we have.

Defining *Works of the Law*

In light of the discovery of 4QMMT, many ideas have been presented as to what *works of law* meant to the Galatians, to Paul and to first century Jews. These range anywhere from "doing things to earn salvation" to "those things which were added to the Torah by the scribes" to "the different gospel that Paul speaks of." Here are some diverse perspectives.

---

[14] Abegg, "Paul, Works of the Law and MMT"

James Dunn in his book, *The New Perspective On Paul*, contends that the phrase *works of the law* is narrower and more restricted than simply "the deeds of the Torah." He sees *ergon nomos* as markers of Jewish identity that define covenantal works and exclusive sociological boundaries. He writes,

> "Works of the law are not to be understood as restricted to circumcision, food laws and Sabbath issues. 'Works of the law' characterize the whole mindset of 'covenantal nomism' – this is, the conviction that status within the covenant (= righteousness) is maintained by doing what the law requires."[15]

Noting the link between Galatians and 4QMMT, he adds,

> "I was stunned by the astonishing parallel which it provided with Galatians. 'Works of the law' are used in reference to various halakhoth described earlier in the letter; clearly implicit is the claim that the law was only properly observed at these points when the Qumran interpretations of the law were followed. The letter's conclusion clearly implies that righteousness will be reckoned (echoing Gen. 15:6) only to those who perform these works of the law."[16]

N.T Wright regards *works of the law* not as "the moral 'good works' which the Reformation tradition loves to hate. They are the things which divide Jew from Gentile."[17]

E.P. Sanders writes,

> "In the phrase 'not by works of law' the emphasis is not on *works* abstractly conceived but on *law,* that is, the Mosaic law. The argument is that one need not be Jewish to be 'righteous' and is thus against the standard Jewish view that accepting and living by the law is a sign and condition of favored status...Paul's statement 'not by

---

[15] Dunn, *The New Perspective On Paul*, 213-214
[16] Ibid, 15
[17] N.T. Wright, *Justification: God's Plan and Paul's Vision* (Downers Grove: InterVarsity, 1995), 116-117

works of law' has to do with entry into the body of Christ. It is not at all inconsistent that he expects correct behavior on the part of those who are in Christ."[18]

D. Thomas Lancaster considers *works of law* ceremonial matters of the Torah that deal with a specific subset of Torah's commandments.[19]

Brad Scott defines them as "all works and attempts to gain salvation through or by your own merit."[20]

David Stern deduces that,

> "In every instance, *erga nomou* means not deeds done in virtue of following the Torah in the way God intended, but deeds done in consequence of perverting the Torah into a set of rules, which, it is presumed, can be obeyed mechanically, automatically, legalistically, without having faith, without having trust in God, without having love for God or man, and without having being empowered by the Holy Spirit."[21]

Ben-Lyman HaNaviy suggests that *works of law* are a shorthand way of referring to the proselyte policies of circumcision. In his eyes, he sees similarities between *works of law* and *works of conversion*, as Paul does seem to use them as synonyms. In this way, they serve as the physical works that provided an entry point into the covenant blessings of Abraham in the eyes of first-century rabbis.[22]

Tim Hegg likens *ergon nomos* to group membership identity, identifying them as a "specific set of rules or halachah which a given group required in terms of its self-definition."[23] In other words, he sees *works of Torah* as a technical phrase that refers to both the

---

[18] Sanders, *Paul, the Law and the Jewish People*, 46, 105
[19] Lancaster, *The Holy Epistle To The Galatians* (Littleton: FFOZ, 2011)
[20] Brad Scott, *Galatians 4:8-10* [Online]. Available: www.wildbranch.org
[21] *Jewish New Testament Commentary*, 537
[22] Ariel ben-Lyman HaNaviy, *Exegeting Galatians* [Online]. Available: www.graftedin.com
[23] Hegg, *Paul's Epistle to the Galatians* (Tacoma: TorahResource, 2005), 127

requirements imposed upon an individual wishing to join a closed group and rules that distinguish a particular community from others. Often the goal with these kinds of rules isn't so much to adhere to Scripture as it is an attempt to practice Torah and rabbinic tradition in the manner prescribed by the group. Their purpose is to keep members in good standing with God and leadership. This seems to square with how 4QMMT portrays them.

Defining *works of the law* is not as clean and simple as once assumed. Considering the parity and wide range of perspectives, it is not out of the question to think of *works of law* similar to how the *Halakhic Letter* portrays them: (1) localized group requirements placed on those joining a Jewish community and (2) membership policies imposed on those coming into a Jewish sect. We know that sectarian groups and a system of status-related rules governed first-century Israel. Bearing in mind the setting, *ergon nomos* may simply be referring to these Jewish sectarian-related regulations.

Within the culture of the synagogue today, it is well known that there are rabbinic regulations for just about everything. From how to tie the knots of your tassels to the correct dimensions of your sukkah to the proper way in which cattle should be slaughtered, the rabbis have an opinion on anything and everything related to the Torah. It should come as no surprise to learn that this was true in first century Israel as well.

In light of 4QMMT and the setting in which Galatians was written, it is reasonable to deduce that *ergon nomos* is terminology for these Torah-related regulations. Broadly defined, the works of the law are works added to the Torah – works that go above and beyond God's law. In the world of sectarian Judaism, they would include (a) entrance requirements, (b) policies and conditions for members, (c) observing the Torah in a specific manner, and (d) practicing those traditions held by the group in order to maintain membership.

If the Qumran community had policy measures and membership procedures that were commonly known as *works of Torah*, it is likely that other sectarian leaders and groups (like the Pharisees) employed similar language. In this way, we could liken *works of law* to the modern practice of church membership. *Ergon nomos* could very well represent the church membership policies and expectations of the sectarian system of first-century Israel.

It may have been to one of Israel's leaders that 4QMMT was originally written. As an insider, Paul certainly would be familiar with this dialogue. Perhaps this is where he picks up the terminology.

Why does Paul bring this terminology into his letter to the Galatians? In pressuring Gentile converts to commit to ritual circumcision, *works of law* could very well describe the group *halakha* of the circumcision party. The Galatian converts were being told that through circumcision, Jewish affiliation and practicing the rabbinic Torah, one could gain identity within the sect. More broadly, a Gentile could gain favored status within the covenant of Israel through *works of law*.

Can of Corn

Given my love for baseball, perhaps *works of the law* can be better understood as it relates to America's pastime. I liken *works of law* to the baseball term *can of corn*.

To the world outside of sports, a can of corn is a vegetable addition to a bachelor's dinner plate. Everyone knows that a can of corn is corn in a can, right? But in baseball vernacular, a can of corn takes on an entirely different connotation. In baseball, a *can of corn* is a lazy fly ball to an outfielder. In this way, the term *can of corn* becomes specialized and takes on a whole new meaning when placed within the context of the game of baseball.

In the same way, *works of law* is specialized lingo when placed within the context and backdrop of the second-temple period. To those of us living outside of that culture and two thousand years removed from its customs, the definition seems obvious. *Works of the law* can mean nothing other than doing the law. But to Paul's audience, *works of law* takes on an entirely different connotation. When put in the context of the world in which Paul and the apostolic church emerged, it becomes a *can of corn* – a specific and specialized term.

Using this analogy, we can define the *works of the law* as the specific and specialized term Paul uses for the rabbinic regulations that governed Palestinian Judaism. It is these regulations for entering the covenant that the new Gentile converts were being pressured to honor. Much like the policy measures laid out in 4QMMT, these rules governed who was in, who was out and what was required of a member. For Gentiles, these *works* included circumcision.

Not only does the context permit such an approach, so do all the passages in Paul's epistles that use the term *works of law*. Since Paul never once uses the word proselyte in his letters,[24] perhaps *works of law* is the phrase he prefers when referencing the procedure of becoming a proselyte.

Conclusion

The *Halakhic Letter* discovered in cave 4 at Qumran sheds new light on an old phrase. It bears the unique and uncanny title *Works of the Law,* a phrase found only in Pauls' letters to Galatia and Rome. In it the author warns against unholy mixture.

It is no coincidence that unholy mixture was the predominant posture taken by second-temple Judaism regarding non-Jews. Gentiles interacting with Israelites would no doubt have been considered an unholy mixture in the eyes of most sectarian leaders. Perhaps this is the reason why strict entrance policies were initiated and a code of ethics was enforced. These codes are now known as *the works of the law*.

As it turns out, the phrase *works of the law* is not Paul-speak after all and likely does not mean what we have traditionally defined it to mean. In light of 4QMMT, it takes on a whole new connotation.

---

[24] *Strong's* #G4339 *prosēlytos*

To MMT's exclusive Jewish settlement, *ergon nomos* did not imply a wholesale keeping of the commandments of the Torah. Rather, it defined the doctrinal position of the community and the correct manner in which their policies were to be observed. *Works of the law* helped identify the rules that governed Jewish law and Torah-observation. These rules determined who was in, who was out and how insiders were expected to conduct themselves.

GALATIANS 2:16 - PART II

Truth #29: *The works of the law are not the commandments of the Torah.*

Paul uses the specific phrase *ergon nomos* (works of law) a total of ten times in his letters – six times in Galatians and four in Romans. Here is the full list:

Galatians 2:16 – "A man is not justified by ergon nomos but by faith in Jesus Christ, even we have believed in Christ Jesus, that we might be justified by faith in Jesus Christ and not by ergon nomos; for by ergon nomos no flesh shall be justified."

Galatians 3:2 – "Did you receive the Spirit by ergon nomos, or by the hearing of faith?"

Galatians 3:5 – "He who supplies the Spirit to you and works miracles among you, does He do it by ergon nomos, or by the hearing of faith?"

Galatians 3:10 – "For as many as are of ergon nomos are under the curse; for it is written, 'Cursed is everyone who does not continue in all things which are written in the book of the law, to do them.'"

Romans 3:20 – "Therefore by ergon nomos no flesh will be justified in His sight."

Romans 3:27-28 – "Where is the boasting then? It is excluded. By what law? Of ergon? No, but by the nomos of faith. Therefore we conclude that a man is justified by faith apart from ergon nomos."

Romans 9:32 – "They did not seek it by faith, but as it were, by ergon nomos."

From these verses we can make a couple initial assumptions about Paul's doctrine:

Position A: Paul believed that *works of law* are insufficient for justification. Four times he states that no man can be justified (or saved) through *ergon nomos*.

Position B: The opposite of *works of law* is *hearing by faith*. Paul contrasts faith with *ergon nomos* in all but two of these verses.

Interpretation Battle

In determining the most accurate reading of these verses, let's play a round of Interpretation Battle to see which interpretation best lines up with Paul's doctrine and agrees with Scripture.

Let's start with Contestant #1: Works of law = Obeying Torah commands.

Question 1 – Does Contestant #1's interpretation agree with Paul's Position A that *works of* law, as defined as obeying Torah commands, are unable to justify us before God?

/*ding, ding, ding*

Yes it does. You are correct!

/*studio audience applauds*

Obeying God's commands is not sufficient to save or justify us before God. This interpretation agrees with Paul's Position A.

Question 2 – Does Contestant #1's interpretation agree with Paul's Position B that *works of law*, as defined as obeying Torah commands, is the opposite of hearing by faith?

/*buzz*

No. I'm sorry. Your answer does not line up with Scripture.

/*studio audience: "Awwww"*

Keeping Torah commands is not the opposite of faith. Hebrews 11 disproves this notion, as does the books of James, 1 John and the Gospels. In fact, it is our faith in Jesus Christ that helps us obey God's commands and keeps us from straying from His word. Lying, stealing, adultery and murder are neither the fruit of the Spirit, nor the fruit of true believers. They are the fruit of unbelievers and the product of unbelief. Therefore, obeying God's commands can only be the fruit of the faithful. This interpretation disagrees with Paul's Position B; therefore, it disagrees with Paul's doctrine.

Now onto Contestant #2: Works of law = Circumcision and group *halakha*

Question 1 – Does Contestant #2's interpretation agree with Paul's Position A that *works of law*, as defined as circumcision and group *halakha*, are unable to justify us before God?

/*ding, ding, ding*

Yes it does. You are correct.

/*audience applauds*

Circumcision and keeping the rabbinic Torah are unable to justify us before God. Being a Jew or obtaining Jewish status is not sufficient enough to take away sin. This interpretation agrees with Paul's Position A.

Question 2 – Does Contestant #2's interpretation agree with Paul's Position B that *works of* law, as defined as circumcision and group *halakha*, is the opposite of hearing by faith?

/*ding, ding, ding*

Yes. Right again!

/*audience cheers*

Without a doubt Paul viewed seeking salvation through Jewish affiliation, ritual circumcision, status-related *halakha* or even Torah keeping to be in direct contrast to hearing by faith. In light of the stated context of Galatians, adhering to the doctrine of the troublers is most certainly a false gospel that opposes the gospel of faith. This interpretation agrees with Paul's Position B. Therefore, this interpretation agrees with Paul's doctrine.

Of course this does not prove conclusively that *ergon nomos* is in fact faithless actions done in an effort to enter and remain in the covenant, but it does offer some credibility and plausibility to that definition. This deduction fits the content of 4QMMT. It squares with Paul's theology and the rest of Scripture. While it does not substantiate that circumcision and status-related *halakha* is the correct interpretation, it does put a dent in the notion that Paul defines *works of law* as actions done in obedience to the Torah.

Good Works vs. Works of the Law

Faith and law are not at odds. Paul never contrasts faith with law. He contrasts faith (*pistis*) with <u>works of</u> law (*ergon nomos*). This distinction is noteworthy.

To Paul, there is something particular about the phrase *ergon nomos* that is distinct from simply law (*nomos*). The addition of the word *ergon* suggests Paul sees faith in conflict with something other than the Torah or Torah keeping.

When Paul wants to express the idea of Torah keeping in his letters, he favors other phrases such as *keeping the law, doing the law, keeping the commandments* or *good works*.

For example, he writes to the Ephesians,

> *"For by grace you have been saved through faith, and that not of yourselves; it is a gift of God, not of <u>works</u>, lest anyone boast. For we are His workmanship, created in Christ Jesus for <u>good works</u>, which God prepared beforehand what we should in them." – Ephesians 2:8-10*

"Works" and "good works" are distinct here and obviously not equivalent to Paul. *Works* is his reference to the works of the law. This is evident by his inclusion of the phrase "lest anyone boast." Boasting is consistently how Paul describes those who preach circumcision and rely on Jewish status for their justification.[1]

Good works is the term Paul prefers here for Torah-obedience and holy living. He notes that these works have been prepared beforehand through the giving of the Torah.

Some other examples of the phrases Paul prefers are:

> *"Circumcision is nothing and uncircumcision is nothing, but keeping the commandments of God is what matters." - 1 Corinthians 7:19*

> *"For not the hearers of the law are just in the sight of God, but the doers of the law will be justified." - Romans 2:13*

> *"For circumcision is indeed profitable if you keep the law; but if you are a breaker of the law, your circumcision has become uncircumcision." - Romans 2:25*

> *"If an uncircumcised man keeps the righteous requirements of the law, will not his uncircumcision be counted as circumcision?" - Romans 2:26*

> *"For not even those who are circumcised keep the law, but they desire to have you circumcised that they may boast in your flesh." - Galatians 6:13*

> *"The good works of some are clearly evident, and those that are otherwise cannot be hidden." - 1 Timothy 5:25*

> *"Be rich in good works, ready to give, willing to share." - 1 Tim. 6:18*

---

[1] Gal. 6:13-14, Rom. 2:17, 23, 4:2, 11:18

> "They profess to know God, but in works they deny Him, being abominable, disobedient, and disqualified for every good work." - Titus 1:16

> "In all things showing yourself to be a pattern of good works; in doctrine showing integrity, reverence, incorruptibility." - Titus 2:7

> "Those who have believed in God should be careful to maintain good works. These things are good and profitable to men." - Titus 3:8

> "And let our people also learn to maintain good works, to meet urgent needs, that they may not be unfruitful." - Titus 3:14

Why does Paul avoid these phrases in Galatians and favors the more technical term *ergon nomos*? Perhaps it is because these terms are not identical. *Works of law* should be distinguished from the word *works* and the word *law*.

If the subject matter of Galatians were Torah obedience as we have traditionally defined it, the topic of keeping the Torah would be relevant to the Galatian dilemma. But if the context is indeed the pressure to conform to circumcision rites, *works of law* would no doubt take on an entirely different connotation than these other definitions.

> "Even we have believed in Christ Jesus, that we might be justified by faith in Christ" – Galatians 2:16

The "we" Paul speaks of are Israelites, referring to himself, Peter and to all messianic Jews. He is arguing that even Israelites who find faith in Yeshua should know that their justification does not come from Jewish lineage, sectarian policies, circumcision or anyone's *halakha*. Reconciliation to God only comes through faith in Yeshua. Jews have the temple, the Torah and the pedigree. The apostle knew even this is not sufficient enough to secure a place in eternity.

Paul argues that if Jews must be justified through faith, why wouldn't it be true for Gentiles as well? If Gentiles need *not* be circumcised to enter the kingdom, why require them to adhere to policy works of the law for their justification?

N.T. Wright surmises,

> "But it was precisely in that context, the entry of Gentiles into God's people and the question of whether they had to be circumcised or whether they could be full members as they were, that Paul developed his doctrine of justification by faith, to meet (in other words) a situation which, for good reasons, Jesus had not himself faced. It is ironic that some within the 'old perspective' on Paul, by continuing to promote the wrong view of justification as conversion, as the moment of personal salvation and coming of faith rather than God's declaration *about* faith, have reinforced as well a polarization between Jesus and Paul which a more historically grounded and theologically astute reading can and must avoid."[2]

This revised definition of *ergon nomos* meshes with Paul's line of reasoning and fits the context of Galatians perfectly. The same cannot be said of the traditional definition.

For these reasons, it is entirely plausible that Paul's *works of the law* is not a blanket statement for the laws of Torah but a specific reference to the status-based regulations of the circumcision party. *Ergon nomos* may well have been the first-century term for covenantal nomism, incorporating the policies of ritual circumcision, rabbinic *halakha* and group membership requirements. In my assessment, I can see how *works of law* could have represented the majority view on how one entered the covenant and how the Torah was expected to be observed.

Broadly, the works of the law encompassed the man-made system of law-related policies outlining covenantal behavior and institutional membership. Narrowly, they could be defined as Jewish regulations. This definition is complicated, I realize. Perhaps this is why it was easier for Paul to simply refer to them as *works of law*.

---

[2] Wright, *Paul*, 159-160

Plugging in this understanding, Galatians 2:16 might read something like this:

> *"A man is not justified by covenantal circumcision but by faith in Jesus Christ, even we have believed in Christ Jesus, that we might be justified by faith in Christ and not by Jewish affiliation; for by man's regulations no flesh shall be justified."* – Galatians 2:16, paraphrased

Hypocrisy & Legalism

By separating himself from Gentile fellowship, Peter was siding with the doctrine of the troublemakers. Paul accused Peter of inadvertently lending his support for status-driven policies – *works of the law*. In abiding by the Jewish rules that governed Gentile relations, Peter was endorsing the doctrine of those who insisted upon ritual circumcision and rabbinic regulations.

If it takes faith to save Jews, then according to Paul's logic, it takes faith for Gentiles to be saved as well. Yet it takes no faith whatsoever to submit to Jewish regulations. In doing so, Peter was guilty of denying the gospel of faith.

People often use this portion of Galatians to confront legalism within Christianity. Galatians 2 does find an application when dealing with classic legalism. It counters legalism in saying that adherence to God's law or to any code of behavior cannot atone for sins. Right standing with God can only be secured through faith in Jesus Christ. Moral deeds or good works cannot earn God's favor as it relates to our redemption. I trust we can all agree on this point.

While factually right, however, the above application is contextually wrong. Trying to obey the law in order to self-righteously save oneself is what we call legalism. But this is not what Paul had in mind. This is evidenced by the fact that first-century Jews did not believe eternal life could be attained through good works. Paul may in fact be confronting legalism but of a different breed. Even though the traditional application of this verse may be theologically accurate, it is accidentally accurate.

Conclusion

The consensus opinion for centuries has been that *works of the law* means legalistically obeying the commandments of the Torah. I have learned that the consensus is often wrong.

Interpreting *works of the law* to mean *obeying the Torah* in this verse and in the book of Romans is problematic on several counts and for several critical reasons. Perhaps some preached salvation through legalistic Torah compliance in the first century, but this wasn't the kind of legalism that the Galatian church was contending with. Commentaries implying that Jewish rabbis regarded the Torah as a stairway to heaven are misinformed. Even the Pharisees did not believe that obeying all of the Torah merited eternal life.

What did merit a place in the age to come according to the Judaisms of the first century was favored, Jewish status accompanied by rabbinic Torah keeping. This guaranteed a member good standing within the covenant. In the opinion of the troublemakers, for Gentiles to secure a righteous status within the covenant, it required an official and long-standing ceremony that involved circumcision and taking on the recommended *halakha*. All of this encompassed what Paul regarded as *works of the law*.

Paul is not being critical of Jews or discouraging Gentiles from keeping God's commandments. Torah pursuance is not in opposition to the gospel of faith according to his doctrine. A Gentile Christian who took on Jewish citizenship was not necessarily putting himself back under sin. Paul is simply maintaining that ritual circumcision and Torah keeping are not the mechanism of salvation.

Salvation is by grace alone through faith in the Messiah. If Gentiles could truly be saved as uncircumcised Gentiles, then they don't need the status-based *works of the law* to validate the sincerity of their conversion or initiate them into covenant relationship with the God of Israel.

Galatians 2:17-21

Truth #30: *The Torah cannot redeem sinners.*

"But if, while we seek to be justified by Christ, we ourselves also are found sinners, is Christ therefore a minister of sin? Certainly not!" – Galatians 2:17

Paul continues his argument against Peter and against those perverting the gospel. It appears that the circumcision party regarded as sinners those Jewish believers who openly fellowshipped with Greeks and willingly disregarded traditional racial boundary lines. In their minds, a non-Jew was a pagan and eating with a pagan was on par with being a sinner.

Jesus became a target of this mentality as well when the scribes and Pharisees needled Him, saying, "Why do You eat and drink with tax collectors and sinners" (Luke 5:30)? The Galatian troublers were of this persuasion. Likely so were the Judean men of Acts 15.

The irony, of course, is that those who racially shunned Greeks wagged their fingers at those who didn't, accusing them of sin. In actuality, perhaps it was the separatists who were in sin. They were blind to their own hypocrisy. Nowhere in Scripture is a Jew interacting with a Gentile considered a transgression. A stronger case can be made that a Jew or Gentile who refuses to interact with another of like faith because of race is guilty of bigotry.

So, any transgression in this story starts with those Jewish believers who refused to interact with non-Jewish brothers in Christ because of their ethnicity. The racial animosity of these Jews toward Gentiles was inherently wrong, hypocritical and stood in opposition to the Holy Spirit.

> *"For if I build again those things which I destroyed, I make myself a transgressor." – Galatians 2:18*

What things did Paul destroy? It wasn't the Torah. It was the dividing line of separation between Jew and Gentile that was destroyed and should not be rebuilt. Peter broke through this wall, and Paul followed behind barreling through with the gospel. To revert back to the traditional, institution laws that governed Gentile association was, in Paul mind, a transgression.

Paul's point is that if the rabbinic rules that governed Gentile interaction were truly perverted, then it must true that the rabbinic rules that governed Gentile salvation were also corrupt. To slide back into seeking to be justified through policies and ceremonies is a transgression and a public endorsement of those who enforced the discriminatory rules governing Gentile contact. Along with Peter, the men from James were validating the doctrine of the circumcision party and reinstituting lines of segregation.

Through the Law *to* the Law

> *"For I through the law died to the law that I might live to God. I have been crucified with Christ; it is no longer I who live, but Christ lives in me; and the life which I now live in the flesh I live by faith in the Son of God, who loved me and gave Himself for me. I do not set aside the grace of God; for if righteousness comes through the law, then Christ died in vain." - Galatians 2:19-21*

From these verses it has been supposed that Paul formerly tried to earn his salvation *by* the law *for* the law *through* the law. Exasperated, he eventually succumbed to the foregone conclusion that the law's impossible standards were too high for anyone to reach. When he met Christ, he found his righteousness in Christ, died to the law and quit trying to obey it.

Reading Galatians 2:19-21 through this lens does seem as though Paul is being scornful of the Torah. It offers an explanation as to what Paul means by dying *to the law*. But Paul never admitted to trying to earn his salvation *by* the law, and a workable explanation is often not included as to what he means by dying *through* the law. A more sensible interpretation reconciles the two phrases and provides an explanation as to what he is communicating.

One sensible explanation is that since this is the first place in Galatians that Paul uses *law* separately from *works of law*, it may be a shorthand reference to the full term *ergon nomos*, a practice not uncommon in ancient literature. It may be that Paul is not straying from the topic of Jewish identity but referencing the law of the circumcisers. For all intents and purposes, Jewish law, including the oral, written and rabbinic rulings, was the law of the Pharisees. Having already established that the troublers had a law unto themselves, this could certainly apply.

The word *law* in the Apostolic Scriptures has a much broader meaning than just the Torah or the first five books of the Bible. The Greek word *nomos* often refers to the Torah but not always. It can allude to any kind of law - civil, civic, common or religious. Considering the subject matter of the prior verses, dying *to the law through the law* could be understood to mean Paul would never go back to the institutional policies he broke free from. Whereas he once thought being Jewish could save someone, Paul no longer relied on his Jewish status for salvation.

Another explanation is that Paul is bringing the condemnatory nature of the law into the conversation to strengthen his argument. Since he does continue to use *nomos* separately from *ergon* in the next chapter, this is a logical fit.

If this is the case, he would be saying something along the lines of:

"Ancestry does not give Jews a leg-up with God as it relates to salvation, since they are 'found to be sinners' (v.17). Jews, as well as Gentiles, still stand accused by the law and face the judgment of God regardless of whatever law they adhere to. Man-made laws, even God's Torah, cannot save anyone from destruction."

In this way, the law that Paul died *to* and *through* was the condemnatory aspect of the Torah of which all find themselves under. According to Paul, right standing with God as it relates to salvation could not be attained through any kind of Torah, but only by grace through faith in Jesus Christ.

It should be noted that Paul states he *died to the law*, not *the law is dead to me*. The one dying in this verse is not the law but Paul. He was crucified with Christ, and so are we. It's not the Torah that expires. It's Paul's sinful nature (and ours) that passes away.

It is not accurate to deduce from these verses that Paul is disregarding the Torah or that he regards the law as something that has expired. The apostle makes no mention of the law ending. He is merely pointing out that the law condemns everyone while justifying no one. In order to be free from its verdict, one must die to their sin through Christ and be resurrected with Him.

Praise God that all who are in Christ have been freed from their transgressions and are liberated from the accusation of the law. We have died to what is fruitless, sinful and condemning. We are free from those things condemned by the law and condemned by man. This perspective fits the overall context of the letter and avoids condemning Paul as a Scripture-denier.

It is helpful to remember that Paul's use of the word *righteousness* infers being made right before God. To Paul, righteousness was a transfer term that brought a person into right standing and covenant relationship with God. This helps us when interpreting this verse. According to Paul, both the law and the law of circumcision most definitely do not justify a person before God.

Conclusion

The Torah cannot redeem anyone from sin. No one can be regenerated *by* the law *through* the law *under* the law or *over* the law. Just as circumcision cannot make anyone righteous, neither can the law.

The Torah does prophesy, as with all of Scripture, the coming One who is the emancipator of our soul and the propitiation for our sins.

He is Seed of the woman who crushes the head of the serpent (Gen. 3:15), the perfect Passover lamb (Ex. 12:1-11) and the Prophet who speaks "all that I command" (Deut. 18:18).

Paul's position 100% agrees with the Torah. It is the law that tells us we stand guilty before God as sinners. The only remedy for a guilty conscience is not the Torah itself but the Living Torah. Jesus fulfilled the law to redeem sinners who are under condemnation for their sin. Only through Him can the death verdict of the law be broken and right standing with the Father be gained.

In this way, the Torah is not an end in itself. It is a means to an end. That end is faith in Yeshua the Messiah.

GALATIANS 3:1-5

Truth #31: *Flesh is the opposite of spirit.*

> *"O foolish Galatians! Who has bewitched you that you should not obey the truth, before whose eyes Jesus Christ was clearly portrayed among you as crucified? This only I want to learn from you: Did you receive the Spirit by the works of the law, or by the hearing of faith? Are you so foolish? Having begun in the Spirit, are you now being made perfect by the flesh? Have you suffered so many things in vain-- if indeed it was in vain? Therefore He who supplies the Spirit to you and works miracles among you, does He do it by the works of the law, or by the hearing of faith?" – Galatians 3:1-5*

For centuries Christians have understood Galatians 3 without much difficulty. Isn't the meaning obvious? Paul is clearly stating that law and faith are opposites and that keeping the Torah is at odds with walking in the Spirit. This explanation has worked for much of church history. The only problem is – it doesn't work. It has never worked. It doesn't work, because it violates the context and contradicts Scripture. Let me explain.

In this chapter, Paul neither changes his argument nor deviates from the topic. He wasn't addressing Torah abolition in the first two chapters, and he isn't here, either.

There is much to decipher here, so let's dissect this section verse-by-verse.

> *"O foolish Galatians! Who has bewitched you that you should not obey the truth, before whose eyes Jesus Christ was clearly portrayed among you as crucified?" – Galatians 3:1*

Paul warns the Galatians against disobeying the truth, particularly in light of Christ crucified. He echoes this later:

> *"You ran well. Who has hindered you from obeying the truth?"* - *Galatians 5:7*

The issue is that the gospel of truth (as it relates to salvation) was being compromised. Compulsion to obey God's commandments cannot be the culprit. Here's why.

(1) *All Scripture, including the Torah, establishes God's truth and the truth about the Messiah.* If keeping the commandments of the Torah is the message responsible for leading these Galatians away from truth, how could obeying God's truth lead them away from obeying God's truth? This is circular reasoning.

Whoever is bewitching them is leading them away from Biblical truth. Since the Torah, as is all Scripture, is God's truth, the bewitchers could not be leading them closer to the written word of God. They must be leading them further. Any demand to obey God's commands does not match this description and cannot be the crux of the message troubling the Galatians. If truth really begets truth, then we can safely say that the Galatians were being pushed to accept something other than the truth found in God's word.

(2) *Are we comfortable maintaining that the Ten Commandments, which God established and audibly spoke, are likened to the spell of a witch?* Even if one were to only discount the so-called ceremonial laws of the Torah, they are still God's word and God's spoken truth. Do we really believe that those who seek to earnestly practice Scripture are instead practicing witchcraft? Was this Paul's theology? Is this our position?

Witchcraft can't bring a person closer to God's truth. It does the exact opposite! Moses obeyed the Torah, as did David. Was Moses opposed to God's truth? Did David practice witchcraft?

It can only be that the troublemakers were preaching something other than obedience to God's word. They were teaching an extra-

Biblical doctrine that distracted the Galatians from the real truth and turned them away from the purity of Holy Scripture.

(3) *The Galatians were bewitched by someone, not something.* Paul asks, "*Who* has bewitched you?" and "*Who* has hindered you?" Someone was responsible for bewitching the Galatians and throwing them off course. The Torah is not responsible for this, because the Torah is not a *someone*. Paul is holding people accountable here, not the law.

No doubt these people are the same troublers identified in chapters 1 and 2. These men were treating the kingdom of God like some exclusive club, making it their self-appointed duty to determine who was in and who was out. In true form, Paul takes them and their doctrine to task. It is these corrupt men who are on trial here, not the word of God.

Cross Examination

Paul reminds them that Yeshua was clearly portrayed as crucified, a death that was significant for so many reasons. But these corrupters did not see the significance. Their doctrine taught that salvation ultimately came through Jewish identity and affiliation. Whether intentionally or not, this made the cross of Christ insignificant. If redemption could be attained outside of His death and resurrection, then Yeshua's sacrifice was pointless.

But we know Jesus did not die in vain. Redemption can only be found in Him, which means it cannot be attained through circumcision or the works of the law.

> *"This only I want to learn from you: Did you receive the Spirit by the works of the law, or by the hearing of faith?"* – Galatians 3:2

Perhaps you have heard it taught that the law is the opposite of faith or that the Spirit opposes the law? Law versus faith or Torah versus Spirit is a popular tug of war perpetuated today.

But have we ever considered that when we say this we are discrediting the very Scriptures we seek to uphold? In doing this we are saying that the Spirit was absent from the story of creation and that it took no faith for Noah to build the ark. We are asserting that the Holy Spirit was opposed to the giving of the Torah and that Jesus violated the spirit of faith when He observed Sabbath and Passover. But none of this is true.

In actuality, there is no substantive conflict between faith, God's Spirit and his commandments. They all derive from the Heavenly Father. They're all Biblical and should all be active in the life of a believer. There is no need to pit one against the other, as if one is current and the other is outdated. Paul is not teaching this, and this verse makes no such claim. Obedience, faith and the Holy Spirit are not at war with one another. They have been in operation since the beginning of mankind.

What Paul is communicating is that salvation comes through receiving the message in faith. He purposely sets the term *ergon nomos* in opposition to "hearing by faith." It is not *nomos* in general but specifically *works of nomos* that opposes hearing by faith. He identifies a specific target, a specific term. This is intentional.

Paul doesn't pit faith against the Torah. He is contrasting believing the message of salvation (hearing by faith) with man-made rules for achieving such salvation (works of law). Do you see the difference? The law is not the bad guy here and keeping it is not a bad thing. What is bad and what stands in direct contrast to the message of faith is seeking to be justified through institutional rules. Faith is how the Galatians came to Christ, and by faith is how they received the Spirit of God.

In terms of justification, works of any kind cannot do what faith does. In terms of discipleship, however, faith will never displace or replace loving obedience. Keeping God's commands is evidence that faith is at work in our hearts.

Speaking to the house of Israel, Ezekiel prophesies:

> *"I will put My Spirit within you and cause you to walk in My statutes, and you will keep My judgments and do them."* - Ezekiel 36:27

This passage demonstrates that God's Spirit and God's Torah work in conjunction with one another. It is God's Spirit that enables us to obey His word, and it is our heartfelt response to God's word that communicates our love for Him. So, just as the law is not the opposite of faith, the Torah is not at odds with the Spirit.

What, then, is the opposite of the Spirit? Paul gives the answer in the next verse.

> *"Are you so foolish? Having begun in the Spirit, are you now being made perfect by the flesh?"* – Galatians 3:3

According to Paul, the opposite of Spirit is not law but flesh.[1] Given the context, flesh here is likely a reference to the fleshly cutting away of the foreskin. From a physical standpoint, there is no more obvious work of the flesh than ritual circumcision. It constitutes a literal attempt to be "made perfect by the flesh." In addition to faith in Jesus Christ, the Galatians were being told they must complete their salvation through the fleshly work of circumcision.

Cross Contamination

While the circumcision pushers may have believed that faith in Yeshua was a good starting point, they did not believe it was sufficient enough to secure the promises of God. In their minds, these Galatians needed a Jewish affiliation.

The message that concerned Paul was not:

Jesus + the Torah = salvation.

The troubling message was:

Circumcision + works of the law = salvation.

---

[1] *Strong's* #G4561 *sarx*

If Jesus had to be thrown into the mix, the troublers were cool with it.

Paul, however, saw through this smokescreen. The Galatian Gentiles had already come to a place of salvation by grace through faith. If these converts would have followed the doctrine of the circumcision party and submitted to an additional, after-the-fact conversion ceremony, they would be admitting that the cross was not sufficient for grace. They would be confessing that salvation is more rightly attained through a status-based religion.

Paul is reminding them that they received the Spirit and experienced miracles through repentance and faith, not rites and rituals. They didn't need a Jewish group or ceremony to confirm it. The Spirit among them should be evidence enough that their redemption had been satisfied and secured.

Suffering in Vain

"Have you suffered so many things in vain-- if indeed it was in vain?"
– Galatians 3:4

This verse seems out of place and makes little sense under the reformed reading of Galatians. What were the Galatians suffering and why? Was it persecution? And if so, how is it connected to the topic at hand?

It all makes perfect sense in light of the proper context, as this verse contains a dual application. For those who had already become proselytes through circumcision, they had indeed suffered in vain. The physical pain of circumcision afforded them no redemptive value. Their ritual conversion did not make them more saved or justified with God. Neither did it bring them into the covenant of Abraham. It may have brought them earthly status and some legal protections but not without a whole lot of unnecessary pain. Nothing of redemptive consequence was secured through the process.

Those who refused a Jewish conversion suffered as well. They had to endure ridicule from Jews and persecution from Rome. Was their suffering in vain? Not in the least, according to Paul. This kind of persecution is par for the course for the followers of Yeshua. It is a badge of honor for those who bear the cross of Christ, for it is an opportunity to share in the sufferings of Christ.

This verse is clear in light of this perspective. For those who submitted to rabbinical circumcision, their physical suffering had indeed been in vain. To those who refused to be circumcised at the coercion of these troublemakers, however, their suffering of persecution had not been in vain. You will find that the reformed interpretation offers very little logical explanation as to what this verse contextually means.

> *"Therefore He who supplies the Spirit to you and works miracles among you, does He do it by the works of the law, or by the hearing of faith?" – Galatians 3:5*

Paul again specifically identifies *ergon nomos*, not Torah in general, as the faithless opposition to the work of the Spirit. It takes no faith to be circumcised and adhere to a code of ethics, but it does take faith to work miracles. Evidence that the Galatians had genuine and lasting covenantal status is the fact that the Holy Spirit was working in and among them. If faith supplied the Spirit and worked miracles, then what real benefit was there in securing Jewish status through circumcision?

Conclusion

It is not completely accurate to say that there is nothing to be gained through circumcision. Timothy was circumcised as an adult. The Bible does not chastise those wanting to be circumcised as a sign of their ethnicity or faith in Christ. The problem here was the motive, not the act.

The pressure placed on the Galatians by the troublers to be ritually circumcised was not a decision of discipleship. It was an entrance requirement enforced by those who did not see the Son as the only way to the Father. Paul was not opposed to Biblical circumcision. He opposed the manner in which circumcision was being leveraged.

GALATIANS 3:6-14

Truth #32: *Christ liberated us from the curse of the law, not the law itself.*

"Just as Abraham 'believed God, and it was accounted to him for righteousness.' Therefore know that only those who are of faith are sons of Abraham. And the Scripture, foreseeing that God would justify the Gentiles by faith, preached the gospel to Abraham beforehand, saying, 'In you all the nations shall be blessed.' So then those who are of faith are blessed with believing Abraham." - Galatians 3:6-9

Using Abraham as an example, Paul assures the Galatians that a person is justified by faith alone. As a Gentile, it was Abraham's faith, not his circumcision, that gave him right standing with God and secured the blessings of the covenant. As the first Hebrew, there was no Jewish advantage to speak of.

Just as Abraham was justified through faith, so are "those who are of faith" (v.7,9). The true offspring of Abraham come not through status conversion or Hebrew ethnicity but through faith in Jesus Christ.

A son of Abraham or *ben Avraham* (בֶּן אַקְבְהם) was a common term used for a Gentile that underwent a legal conversion to Judaism.[1] A *ben Avraham* was viewed as a child of the covenant. Seeing the obvious correlation, Paul seizes upon this definition and distinguishes how one becomes a *ben Avraham* in God's eyes.

Whether Jew or Gentile, those who trust God for their justification as Abraham did, are legitimate sons of Abraham and true sons of

---

[1] *HaYesod*, 7.10

God. In this way, Abraham is the father of those who possess his spiritual DNA more than his physical DNA.

Faith vs. Flesh

The phrase "those who are of faith" (v.7,9) is worth mentioning. The tussle is not between 'those who are of faith' and 'those who are of Torah.' It is with those who are of *faith* and those who are of *flesh*. Paul reiterates that flesh, not Torah, is the opposite of faith. Since the law had not been codified in Abraham's day, Paul likely is not breaching the topic of Torah legalism here.

> *"For as many as are of the works of the law are under the curse; for it is written, 'Cursed is everyone who does not continue in all things which are written in the book of the law, to do them.' – Galatians 3:10*

Emphasis can be found on the word *written* as it appears twice in this verse. Paul places it in contrast to the unwritten rules of the works of law. The troublers strayed from what was written by God and were guilty of championing what was esteemed by man. Paul's message for these men and their followers is that their works of the law could not redeem them from the curse of the law.

Notice that the curse of the law does not apply to everyone. It applies only to those who "are of the works of the law" (v.10). Since the works of the law cannot atone for sin, those who rely on them are still under the curse of the law.

Paul's doctrine is that those who rely on Jewish and rabbinic regulations are not *of faith*. They still bear the weight of their sin under the curse of the law. Gentiles faithlessly submitting to institutional rules were liable to the full weight and punishment of sin spelled out in Torah. Paul wants those seeking the blessing of Jewish identity to consider the consequences that come with that pursuit. While they might receive certain blessings that come upon the nation of Israel, they would equally receive all the curses as well.

If Paul truly believed that following the Torah places one under a curse, then he cursed himself when he sacrificed in the Temple (Acts 21) and encouraged the Corinthians to celebrate the Feast of Unleavened Bread. (1 Corinthians 5:8). Was Paul living and ministering under the curse of the law? According to the antinomian definition of the phrase, he was. We know better. Keeping God's commands is never a curse, and forsaking his commands is not how the curse is broken.

> *"But that no one is justified by the law in the sight of God is evident, for 'the just shall live by faith.' Yet the law is not of faith, but 'the man who does them shall live by them.'"* – *Galatians 3:11-12*

"The law is not of faith," indicates that the Torah is not redemptive. The law justifies no one. It is not of faith, because it requires no faith to obey it. Yet without faith, it is impossible to keep all the laws of the Torah perfectly.

But Jesus Christ fully obeyed the laws of the Torah. He is "the Man" who did them and lived by them. Only through him can we live out the commands of the Torah properly.

No one is made right before God through Torah observation, but it is going beyond the text to say that the Torah cannot guide the behavior of an individual or society. Paul cites not one but two proof texts to state that he who obeys the Torah is a righteous man who lives by faith. Faith evidenced by actions - this is the Biblical picture of godly behavior. The troublers somehow squeezed faith out of the equation.

In defiance, Paul saw that those teaching that righteousness came by Jewish identity and faithless Torah compliance were still under the curse of the law. He uses the law to validate his point, which means, of course, that he cannot be disparaging the Torah. If he wanted to invalidate the Torah, it would be irrational to quote the Torah to validate his invalidation. The apostle quotes the Torah authoritatively five times in a span of nine verses. This is hardly the practice of someone seeking to undermine the law and liberate Gentiles from it.

> *"Christ has redeemed us from the curse of the law, having become a curse for us (for it is written, 'Cursed is everyone who hangs on a tree'), that the blessing of Abraham might come upon the Gentiles in Christ Jesus, that we might receive the promise of the Spirit through faith."* – Galatians 3:13-14

Ironically, some teach that anyone attempting to obey the Torah is accursed. This is a misreading of Paul. Even though followers of Christ are imperfect in following all of the Torah, they are not under the curse of the law. Those in Christ have been redeemed. Unlike those still under the old covenant, they are not condemned for failing to perfectly keep all that is written in the law. So, it is not believers but unbelievers who find themselves under the law's harsh penalty for sin.

Conclusion

Do not make the mistake of equating the Torah with the curse of the law. The curse of the law is not the law. It is from the curse of the law, not the law, that we have been freed.

The fact that we have been redeemed from the curse does not excuse us from our obligation to the Torah. It simply means that (1) we are not condemned for failing to obey the law flawlessly, and (2) God will not count our transgressions against us.

Galatians 3:19-22

Truth #33: *The Torah defines sin and reveals our need for a savior.*

Galatians 3:15-18 is covered in the section on the new covenant, so we turn to Galatians 3:19-22

> *"What purpose does the law serve? It was added because of transgressions, till the Seed should come to whom the promise was made, and it was appointed through angels by the hand of a mediator. Now a mediator does not mediate for one only, but God is one. Is the law then against the promises of God? Certainly not! For if there had been a law given which could have given life, truly righteousness would have been by the law. But the Scripture has confined all under sin, that the promise by faith in Jesus Christ might be given to those who believe." – Galatians 3:19-22*

Paul recounts the role that the Torah plays in our coming to Christ – to specify, measure and condemn sin. The law was added "because of transgressions" (v.19) in order to properly define sin. At the same time, it also reveals our need for a Savior and points us to a divine remedy for our fallen state.

God's laws entrust us with the holiness of God by properly identifying and condemning all that is found to be unholy. Being that a transgression is a violation of a standard, the Torah provides that objective standard by which all violations are measured.

In the Torah is also found the revelation of God and His godliness. By distinguishing between good and evil, God's law creates boundaries for what is pure and life giving in the sight of God. Anything falling outside those boundary lines falls short of God's standard of holiness. In doing so, the law reveals the human flaw.

The fact that Abraham came before Moses demonstrates that from the beginning the Torah was never a faith-giving document, for "the law could not impart life" (v.21 NIV). When applied correctly, the Torah convicts us of sin and leads us to faith in Christ. When misapplied, however, much error can occur.

> *"What purpose does the law serve? It was added because of transgressions, till the Seed should come." – Galatians 3:19*

The phrase "till the Seed should come" has been used by some to essentially cut the Torah out of the hands of believing Christians. It is concluded that with the coming of Christ, the law no longer serves a purpose.

I'm disinclined to believe this viewpoint. The Seed does not liberate us from the Torah but from the condemnation that the Torah prescribes for Torah breakers. Before Christ, the law served to highlight our transgression. After Christ, it guides the behavior of those who find faith in the Messiah and possess the Spirit of God. In this way, only believers in Yeshua can properly follow the Torah without condemnation.

"Till" or "until" marks a point in time.[1] It does not necessarily imply the subject is no longer relevant. It means rather that the subject accomplished its goal. In this case, it implies the mission has been accomplished. The law has accomplished the goal of leading us to Christ.

To illustrate this point, suppose you instructed your children to observe you build a campfire. You would not give them instruction unless you had in mind that in their observation they would learn how to build a fire for themselves. You are essentially asking them to observe you *until* they are ready and confident enough to try it on their own. It does not imply that once your fire is built they should cease learning the art of fire building or cease learning from you altogether. Rather, the goal of your instruction is that they would learn from you through observation.

---

[1] *Strong's* #G891 *axri*

This is how "till" is used. The law condemned us *until* the Messiah came. As followers of Jesus, the Torah still convicts us of sin. It still is a lamp to our feet and a light to our path. However, those in Christ are no longer under its condemnation. Through Yeshua, we are free to allow God's word to illuminate our steps and navigate our behavior.

The law was given to measure sin and reveal Christ. It exposes our transgression and points the sinner to a sinless Messiah. This is the consequential aspect of the law as it relates to our salvation, but it is not the sole purpose of it. The Torah offers much more to us.

The Torah was added "because of transgressions" simply means that the Torah was given to demonstrate how God would redeem those bound in their transgressions. Through the sacrifice of the Lamb our sins would be forgiven, and we could gain victory over them.

Conclusion

Paul uses covenantal language in this chapter to combat covenantal nomism and support the eternal truth that salvation comes by faith. He reminds us that God's covenant with Abraham came 430 years before the giving of the Torah. Just as Abraham came before Moses, so faith comes before the law. If Abraham was saved by faith (and not by the law), then so is everyone that comes after him.

The law is not at odds with a life of faith and did not come to an end with the coming of the Seed. *Till the Seed should come* means that Jesus beautifully and masterfully made faith and obedience a tangible reality for us. When faith in Christ (covenant of Abraham) and heartfelt obedience to his commandments (covenant at Sinai) come together, we have a clearer picture of who Christ is and how God wants us to live under the new covenant.

The purpose of the law in terms of our justification is to bring us to the realization that we are sinners in need of redemption. The Torah reveals that we cannot be saved through the Torah, by Jewish identity or by the works of the law. Instead, the law most effectively directs us to Christ, our saving Redeemer. He is our only hope of glory. As the redeemed, the standard of the law no longer condemns us for our unrighteousness but serves to instruct us in how to live righteously.

GALATIANS 3:23-29

Truth #34: *Under the law means under the condemnation of the law.*

"But before faith came, we were kept under the law, shut up unto the faith which should afterwards be revealed." – Galatians 3:23 KJV

Under Law

Paul's first mention of the term *under the law* is found here. "Before faith came, we were kept under (*hypo*) the law (*nomos*)" (v.23). This is another important phrase to consider, as Paul uses *hypo nomos* (under the law) a total of 11 times in his epistles - 5 times in Galatians, 3 times in 1 Corinthians and 3 more in Romans.

> *"Before faith came, we were kept <u>under guard by the law</u> (hypo nomos), kept for the faith which would afterward be revealed." – Galatians 3:23*

> *"But when the fullness of the time had come, God sent forth His Son, born of a woman, born <u>under the law</u> (hypo nomos), to redeem those who were <u>under the law</u> (hypo nomos), that we might receive the adoption as sons." – Galatians 4:4-5*

> *"Tell me, you who desire to be <u>under the law</u> (hypo nomos), do you not hear the law?" – Galatians 4:21*

> *"But if you are led by the Spirit, you are not <u>under the law</u> (hypo nomos)." – Galatians 5:18*

> *"To the Jews I became as a Jew, that I might win Jews; to those who are <u>under the law</u> (hypo nomos), as <u>under the law</u> (hypo nomos), that I might win those who are <u>under the law</u> (hypo nomos)." – 1 Corinthians 9:20*

> *"But now the righteousness of God apart from the law is revealed, being witnessed <u>by the Law</u> (hypo nomos) and the Prophets." – Romans 3:21*

> *"For sin shall not have dominion over you, for you are not <u>under law</u> (hypo nomos) but under grace. What then? Shall we sin because we are not <u>under law</u> (hypo nomos) but under grace? Certainly not!" – Romans 6:14-15*

The traditional definition of *under the law* reads something along the lines of: (1) servitude to the Torah, (2) bondage to obeying the Old Testament, (3) returning to the old covenant, or (4) legalistically observing the Law of Moses.

It is generally understood as under the obligation to obey the law.

This definition has merit. Those living *under law* are obligated to obey the Torah just as all are. It is fundamentally true that salvation cannot be attained through faithless deeds or self-righteous legalism. There is no benefit in returning to the old covenant. That being said, the traditional definition could use some expanding.

In the previous verse, Paul uses the *hypo nomos* but worded differently.

> *"But the <u>Scripture has confined all under sin</u>, that the promise of faith in Jesus Christ might be given to those who believe. But before faith came, we were <u>kept under guard by the law</u>, kept for the faith which would afterward be revealed." – Galatians 3:22-23*

In Paul's argument, "Scripture has confined all under sin" is equivalent to "kept under guard by the law." These phrases are synonymous and express the same concept. *Under the law* is merely a shorter version of this sentiment.

> *"Before faith came, <u>we</u> were kept under guard by the law." – Galatians 3:23*

By including "we" the apostle is referring to those with knowledge of the law. This includes Israel, God-fearing Gentiles and himself, of course. All are under law and under sin.

Taking this into consideration, we can see where the traditional interpretation of *hypo nomos* becomes limited. As Greeks, there was never a moment "before faith came" when these Galatians had legalistically sought to earn their salvation through obeying the commands of a Hebrew book. They were not Jews. They were lawless pagans. The knowledge of what Moses taught was largely foreign to them. Any exposure they had to the law before coming to Christ was at best minimal. While some may have been God-fearing synagogue attenders before coming to Christ, those percentages decreased as the gospel rapidly spread among them.

Unlike Israel, God has made no covenant with Gentile nations. It is impossible that these Greeks had ever felt an obligation to obey the Hebrew Torah before they had come to faith in Christ. How could the Galatians return to an old covenant that they were never under in the first place?

It is reasonable to opine that the pressure placed on the Galatians to oblige the law was much more than simply *sola Scriptura*. In seeking a definition for *under law,* the motivation for coming and remaining under the law must be accounted for. To which laws they were being coerced to uphold needs to be explored.

The newly circumcised were expected to observe the oral, written and rabbinic laws of Israel by the prevailing sect of the troublers. In addition, Gentile proselytes were also expected to take on the complete magnitude of the Torah – blessings and curses alike.

Those agreeing to circumcision were agreeing to the full weight and consequences of those under the old covenant. They rashly indebted themselves to the rabbinic Torah, which provided no redemptive benefit. What they assumed was protecting them was actually obligating them to Torah perfection. It subjected them further to God's wrath and prevented them from experiencing the true grace of God. In short, they were still under sin and still condemned as sinners. Gentiles heeding the message of the circumcisers were foolishly following the wrong Torah for all the wrong reasons.

Any definition of *under the law* should take into account the provision of condemnation that the law prescribes for those who possess knowledge of the law. For this reason, *hypo nomos* must mean more than simply *under the obligation to obey the law*.

For this reason, I have found a better definition for *under the law* to be *under the full weight and condemnation of the law*. This takes into account the text and the context.

Let's revisit the above verses again. This time let's read *under the law* not as 'under the obligation to obey the law' but as 'under the full weight and condemnation of the law.'

> "Before faith came, we were kept <u>under the full weight and condemnation of the Torah</u> *(hypo nomos)*, kept for the faith which would afterward be revealed." – Galatians 3:23

> "But when the fullness of the time had come, God sent forth His Son, born of a woman, born <u>under the full weight of the Torah</u> *(hypo nomos)*, to redeem those who were <u>under the condemnation of the Torah</u> *(hypo nomos)*, that we might receive the adoption as sons." – Galatians 4:4-5

> "Tell me, you who desire to be <u>under the full weight of the Torah</u> *(hypo nomos)*, do you not hear the law?" – Galatians 4:21

> "But if you are led by the Spirit, you are not <u>under the weight and condemnation of the Torah</u> *(hypo nomos)*." – Galatians 5:18

> "To the Jews I became as a Jew, that I might win Jews; to those who are <u>under the weight and condemnation of the Torah</u> *(hypo nomos)*, as <u>under the weight and condemnation of the Torah</u> *(hypo nomos)*, that I might win those who are <u>under the weight and condemnation of the Torah</u> *(hypo nomos)*; to those who are without law, as without law (not being without law toward God, but under law toward

Christ), that I might win those who are without law." – 1 Corinthians 9:20-21

"Now we know that whatever the law says, it says to those who are <u>under the full weight and condemnation of the Torah</u> (hypo nomos), that every mouth may be stopped, and all the world may become guilty before God. Therefore by the deeds of the law no flesh will be justified in His sight, for by the law is the knowledge of sin." – Romans 3:19-20

"For sin shall not have dominion over you, for you are not <u>under the weight and condemnation of the Torah</u> (hypo nomos) but under grace. What then? Shall we sin because we are not <u>under the weight and condemnation of the Torah</u> (hypo nomos) but under grace? Certainly not!" – Romans 6:14-15

Judge for yourself which is the proper definition.

In my view, this rendering accentuates and brilliantly advances Paul's argument laid out in chapters 1-3. The circumcisers sought Jewish identity under the protective hand of the Torah but instead were left condemned under the heavy hand of the law. Outside of Christ, they still found themselves convicted of law breaking, rejecting the redemptive blood of Yeshua.

It could be said that *under law* is essentially attempting to keep the Torah outside of faith in Christ. Plug this into the above verses, and it works. Plug the conventional definition into the above verses, and we are left with doctrinal confusion that misconstrues Paul's position.

Torah Tutor

"Therefore the law was our tutor to bring us to Christ, that we might be justified by faith. But after faith has come, we are no longer under a tutor." – Galatians 3:24-25

Paul isn't saying anything different in these verses than he was in the previous verse. Paul is still explaining *hypo nomos* and uses the analogy of a tutor to illustrate his point. "Our" and "we" is a reference to the Jews or to those under the law.

"Tutor" is the Greek word *paidagogos*. From it we derive the English word 'pedagogue'. A modern-day pedagogue is an educator or teacher. An ancient pedagogue, however, was less a teacher and more a caretaker entrusted with supervising and directing a child's moral conduct. It was not uncommon for well-to-do families to hire someone to be an attendant to their child or assign a household slave as their pedagogue. This person was tasked with escorting the child to the schoolroom, sometimes even carrying their writing utensils and wax tablet.[1]

From the writings of Plato and Yenophan we learn that a *paidagogos* did anything from escorting the child to and from school, to supervising their behavior, to serving as their guidance counselor. They were sometimes a bodyguard, sometimes a warden, often a chaperone, but always entrusted with some degree of responsibility for the child.[2]

It should be noted that an ancient pedagogue was a child's caretaker, not their jailer. For this reason "kept under guard by the law" might be a bit strong here. Alternate translations render it "enclosed", "kept safe" or "protected." Still, there is an aspect of Torah that holds one captive, as Paul indicates in Romans.

> "*Is the law sin? Certainly not! On the contrary, I would not have known sin except through the law. For I would not have known covetousness unless the law had said, 'You shall not covet.' But sin, taking opportunity by the commandment, produced in me all manner of evil desire. For apart from the law sin was dead. I was alive once without the law, but when the commandment came, sin revived and I died. And the commandment, which was to bring life, I found to bring death. For sin, taking occasion by the commandment, deceived me and by it killed me. Therefore the law is holy, and the commandment holy and just and good.*" - Romans 7:7-12

---

[1] Santala, *Paul*, 25
[2] BAG, *Greek-English Lexicon of the New Testament, Paidagwgov*

The condemnation of the Torah toward sinners is brutally consequential.

> *"If a person sins, and commits any of these things which are forbidden to be done by the commandments of the LORD, though he does not know it, yet he is guilty and shall bear his iniquity." - Leviticus 5:17*
>
> *"But it shall come to pass, if you do not one the voice of the LORD your God, to observe carefully all His commandments and His statutes which I command you today, that all these curses will come upon you and overtake you." - Deut. 28:15*
>
> *"For whoever shall keep the whole law, and yet stumble in one, he is guilty of all." - James 2:10*
>
> *The Torah condemns sin and informs sinners they are being held at gunpoint by their sin. For transgressors, the law is a death sentence. But to the righteous, it "rejuvenates" our soul and shows us how to "dance to the tune of your revelation." (Ps. 119:50,70, MSG).*

The law itself is neither the death-giver nor the life-bringer. It is Christ who gives life and sin that brings death. The Torah merely shines a light upon our sinful state. It points all of us to Christ, revealing death to the sinner and life to the righteous.

Using Paul's metaphor, the Torah is our tutor, teaching us the ways of life. It is the job of this tutor to bring us to full faith and maturity in Christ.

> *"But after faith has come, we are no longer under a tutor." – Galatians 3:25*

Here, the term *under law* is used again, except said as "under a tutor." In this way, the Torah also serves as a tutor. In Romans, Paul addresses the supposition that there is no need for the Torah now that we have found faith in Christ.

> *"Do we make void the law through faith? Certainly not! On the contrary, we establish it."* - Romans 3:31

Paul did not view the law as something void. Rather, he viewed it as something established and complete. Christ re-established it with grace.

Our faith for redemption is in Christ, not the law. No longer are we under the condemnation that comes with Torah perfection. Since a living Shepherd has come, we are now under His care. There is no salvation related reason for Gentiles to be circumcised or place themselves under the full weight and consequence of the Torah.

Like a caretaker supervising a child and directing their moral conduct, the pedagogue escorts a child to the schoolmaster and gives a full report of their behavior. Once safely delivered to the teacher's care, the pedagogue is released from keeping a record of the child's wrongdoings.

In similar fashion, the Torah is the guidance counselor that escorts us to Yeshua our Schoolmaster. Under His care, we are no longer strong-armed by the Torah and condemned by its watchful eye. We are released from the record of our previous wrongdoing. God's commandments lead us to the only begotten Remedy for our wayward ways. He in turn teaches us how to walk them out without condemnation.

Christlikeness is the goal here. However, this does not imply the Torah cannot help us in knowing Christ and becoming more like Him. Jesus is our living example of how to walk in the Spirit and live a life of obedience. It's the Holy Spirit who uses the Torah to help us navigate our journey toward Christ and Christlikeness.

Using this definition of *hypo nomos*, let's plug it into these verses.

> *"But before faith came, we were under <u>the weight and condemnation of the law</u>, kept for the faith which would afterward be revealed. Therefore the law was our <u>supervisor</u> to bring us to Christ, that we might be justified by faith. But after faith has come, we are no longer*

under *the scrutinizing eye of the guardian.*" – Galatians 3:23-25, paraphrased

Paul's metaphor need not be taken further than it was designed to. "No longer under a tutor" is not equivalent to Torah cancellation. It is a synonym for being *under the law. Hypo nomos* is a phrase which implies one is still condemned by the Torah and bound to a covenant where one is obligated to perfect compliance.

The Torah will never be un-established. It does not cease to guide, protect, instruct and escort us to Christ. What ceases is the scrutinizing eye of the pedagogue. We become free from its condemnation by staying under the care of our life-giving Schoolmaster. It's His judgment that is the final analysis of our conduct.

Conclusion

Historically, Paul's use of the terms *circumcision, works of the law* and *under the law* have been terribly misunderstood and tragically misused. But there is no reason to continue in such a misunderstanding. Those who seek an accurate understanding of these phrases can repair much of the damage that has been done by those who misread Paul and misrepresent his doctrine.

I have come to appreciate that *hypo nomos* implies more than simply seeking to live within the framework of the Torah. For the Galatians, it meant intentionally placing oneself under a Jewish expression of the Torah for the purpose of validating their salvation and securing a place in the age to come. It meant taking on the full weight, measure and judgments of the law. It was an attempt to gain right standing with God and right standing within a particular Jewish sect outside the cross.

In agreeing to circumcision and submitting to a conversion ceremony, the proselyte took on every provision of the Torah found within the traditions of Judaism. In doing so, those who placed themselves *under the law* were not *under grace* but were still *under sin*; thus they were still *under the condemnation* that the law prescribes for sinners.

Praise God in Christ this is not our story!

GALATIANS 4

Truth #35: *The Law of Moses is not bondage. The law of sin is.*

> "Now I say that the heir, as long as he is a child, does not differ at all from a slave, though he is master of all, but is under guardians and stewards until the time appointed by the father. Even so we, when we were children, were in bondage under the elements of the world. But when the fullness of the time had come, God sent forth His Son, born of a woman, born under the law, to redeem those who were under the law, that we might receive the adoption as sons." – Galatians 4:1-5

Paul states that Jesus was born *under law,* meaning He was born under the full weight and condemnation of the Torah. His birth came to redeem those who also are *under law.*

You may have heard it taught that Jesus was born obligated to obey the Torah to redeem those who are obligated to obey the Torah. They add that now that we are sons of God, we are no longer slaves to Torah obedience.

If Paul had written that Jesus was "born of a Torah keeper" or "born of a Jew" or "born into a culture subservient to the law," this interpretation might have value. But in saying that Jesus was "born of a woman," Paul's point snaps into place.

Yeshua was born human, born of a sinner, born of a descendant of Adam for the express purpose of redeeming sinners born under the condemnation of Adam's sin. As sinners, all are enslaved to sin and subject to their sinful nature until the Father's appointed time. It is not the law that keeps people in bondage. It is sin. The law is simply the mirror that reveals our sinful state and reflects our fallen glory.

Fighting the Elements

"Even so we, when we were children, were in bondage under the elements of the world." – Galatians 4:3

The use of "under the elements of the world" is comparable to how Paul uses *under the law* and *under a tutor* but with distinction. Being *under law* is to be under the full weight and condemnation of the Torah. It is a faithless attempt to find righteousness outside of faith in Christ.

Similarly, being *under the elements* is being under the full power and deception of worldly idolatrous philosophies. It is the faithless adherence to mystical creeds and man-made religion in hopes of gaining spiritual rewards. Both adhere to a strict code of conduct, yet both are futile in terms of salvation.

This is the first mention of "under the elements (*stoicheion*) of the world (*kosmos*)" in Galatians but not the only in Paul's letters. Paul uses this terminology twice in Colossians and again in verse 9.

> *"As you, therefore, have received Christ Jesus the Lord, so walk in Him, rooted and built up in Him and established in the faith, as you have been taught, abounding in it with thanksgiving. Beware lest anyone cheat you through philosophy and empty deceit, according to the tradition of men, according to the basic <u>principles</u> (stoicheion) <u>of the world</u> (kosmos), and not according to Christ." - Colossians 2:6-8*

> *"Therefore, if you died with Christ from the basic <u>principles</u> (stoicheion) <u>of the world</u> (kosmos), why, as though living in the world, do you subject yourselves to regulations-- "Do not touch, do not taste, do not handle," which all concern things which perish with the using-- according to the commandments and doctrines of men? These things indeed have an appearance of wisdom in self-imposed religion, false humility, and neglect of the body, but are of no value against the indulgence of the flesh." - Colossians 2:20-23*

Weymouth translates *stoicheion kosmos* as 'the world's rudimentary notions'. NIV has it 'elemental spiritual forces'. The NLT renders it 'the spiritual powers of the world', while the New King James reads 'elements' or 'principles of the world.'

Paul's use of *stoicheion kosmos* in Colossians helps us better grasp what he is communicating to the Galatians. From this passage, we can deduce that the elemental principles of the world are institutionalized codes of conduct that are powerless to overcome the flesh, break the bondage of sin or create any kind of pathway to God. They are likened to the ascetic superstitions of the Gnostics that forbid the touching, tasting and handling of certain foods and pleasures. These regulations are man-made philosophies, embraced by false religions and are unable to conquer sinful flesh. Being under these elemental principles is being under the judgment of the fallen world.

In the context of the Apostolic Scriptures, it is entirely possible that these elemental principles were connected to a particular Jewish sect such as the Pharisees or Essenes. The Essenes, in particular, were quite rigid in their interpretation of the law, even stricter than the Pharisees. Essenes were known to practice celibacy and hold all property in common.[1] They also maintained distinct entrance requirements. There was a 2-3 year probationary period for prospective members, finalized in an oath vowing to obey all the standards, practices and beliefs of the community.[2] Asceticism was characteristic of Essene members, whose membership in Philo's time had reached 4,000.[3]

The Essenes were also meticulous in their calculation of the Hebrew calendar and genealogies. Paul warns Timothy to give no "heed to fables and endless genealogies" (1 Tim. 1:4) and "avoid foolish disputes, genealogies, contentions and strivings about the law; for they are unprofitable and useless" (2 Tim. 3:9). Perhaps it was the

---

[1] Josephus, *Jewish Wars*, 2.8.2.120-121; Philo, *Hypothetica*, 11.14
[2] Spencer Tucker, *The Encyclopedia of the Arab-Israeli Conflict*, Vol. I (Santa Barbara: ABC-CLIO, 2010), 839
[3] Timothy Lim and John Collins, *The Oxford Handbook of the Dead Sea Scrolls* (England: Oxford University Press, 2010), 174

Essenes who were behind all the trouble in the region of Galatia and beyond.

Some contend that "do not touch, do not taste, do not handle" (Col. 2:21) describes the laws of Torah. While this might appear to be the case, it is not very convincing. Paul depicts these basic principles as "philosophy and empty deceit, according to the tradition of man" (Col. 2:8) having "an appearance of wisdom in self-imposed religion, false humility and neglect of the body, but are of no value against the indulgence of the flesh" (Col. 2:23). Self-imposed, contrived wisdom, empty deceit, false humility, body-neglect and traditions of man are not accurate descriptors of God's Biblical instructions. What they do describe, however, are the customs of sectarian Judaism and the idolatrous practices of the pagans.

We know this to be the case, because Paul is changing the argument in verse 8 from the traditions of the Jews to the traditions of the world.

> *"But then, indeed, when you did not know God, you served those which by nature are not gods." - Galatians 4:8*

The argument now shifts from Jewish rites and rituals to worldly doctrines and philosophies. Paul speaks of their past life before Christ "when you did not know God" (v.8). The Galatian believers were still coming out of bondage to pagan practices. Why then embrace the bondage of Jewish practices? Incredulously, they were trying to break free from one bondage only to subject themselves to another. This is what doctors refer to as symptom substitution.

> *"But now after you have known God, or rather are known by God, how is it that you turn again to the weak and beggarly elements (stoicheion), to which you desire again to be in bondage? You observe days and months and seasons and years. I am afraid for you, lest I have labored for you in vain." - Galatians 4:9-11*

Galatians 4:10-11 is included in the section on Sabbath & the feasts. I will not repeat what is written there, except to say that the *days, months, seasons and years* here are not a reference to Sabbath, feasts or jubilee years. They refer to the many holidays of the Greek culture.

Evidently, these new Christians still struggled with separating themselves from their past, turning "again to the weak and beggarly elements." These weak and beggarly principles of the world are clearly something they came out of and were being tempted to return to. This categorically rules out a reference to the Torah. Pagan idolatry and Greek festivals is a better fit.

Is "weak and beggarly" really how Paul and the Holy Spirit would portray God's Word? How could they return to a Torah they never followed in the first place?

These elements are weak and beggarly, because they provide no victory over the flesh. Much like the tower of Babel, the vain and godless philosophies of man are the building blocks of all man-centered religions. These principles can be found in the religions of the world just as they can be found within the traditions of Judaism.

Conclusion

When archeologists discover ancient civilizations, it often requires much excavation. This is because societies tend to bury that which was in order to build that which is. Take a trip to Israel. Many of the spiritual landmarks of the Bible have been covered by structures, churches and buildings.

We've done the same with the ancient paths of our spiritual forefathers. We've covered them with doctrinal buildings and buried them under religious structures. It is man-made religion that seeks to prevent us from discovering our true roots, but with some digging, unlimited treasures await those willing to go a little deeper.

Paul warns the Galatians not to return to their old religious ways. Let us take a lesson from this. Perhaps it is time for all of us to make a clean break from the pagan Christian holidays the church has adopted and from any form of idolatry that still remains among us. If we are willing to dig past that which is synthetic, we will come to that which is authentic.

GALATIANS 5

Truth #36: *Man-made religion is the yoke of bondage.*

> *"Stand fast therefore in the liberty by which Christ has made us free, and do not be entangled again with a yoke of bondage." – Galatians 5:1-6*

What is the 'yoke of bondage?' It is presumed that the Torah itself is the yoke of bondage. One commentary reads,

> "The liberty here, is that freedom from the law, of which the apostle hath been speaking all along in this Epistle; for the curse of the moral law, and from the co-action of it; and principally from the ceremonial law contained in ordinances."[1]

Another adds,

> "The law of Moses, which he was cautioning them to avoid, was a yoke of the same kind with that under which they had groaned while heathen…with this difference, that none of them are of divine appointment."[2]

Faithless Torah legalism can certainly be a yoke of bondage. If this is what the Galatian believers were being persuaded to do, it would indeed be a yoke they should break free of.

But is this what Paul is referring to? Thankfully, he answers this question for us in the following verses.

---

[1] *Jamieson-Fausset-Brown Bible Commentary* (Electronic Version, Biblehub.com), Gal. 5:1

[2] Macknight, *Benson Commentary*, Gal. 5:1 [Online]. Available: www.biblehub.com

> *"Stand fast therefore in the liberty by which Christ has made us free, and do not be entangled again with a yoke of bondage. Indeed I, Paul, say to you that if you become circumcised, Christ will profit you nothing. And I testify again to every man who becomes circumcised that he is a debtor to keep the whole law. You have become estranged from Christ, you who attempt to be justified by law; you have fallen from grace." – Galatians 5:2-4*

Verse 1 - *"Do not be entangled again with a yoke of bondage."*

Verse 2 - *"If you become circumcised..."*

Verse 3 – *"...debtor to keep the whole law."*

Verse 4 - *"...you who attempt to be justified by law."*

These phrases together perfectly describe the yoke of bondage. The yoke is: Circumcision + keeping the whole law flawlessly + attempting to be justified through the Torah.

In agreeing to circumcision, the Gentile was attempting to be justified by the works of law instead of through faith in Jesus Christ. Previously, they had been under the yoke of paganism. Now the Galatians were in danger of coming under another type of bondage - the yoke of Jewish rites and rituals. This bondage-producing yoke takes on the full weight and condemnation of the law through the fleshly act of circumcision.

The Galatian believers were already sons of Abraham by faith. They were children of Sarah. Why become children of Hagar? They had successfully come out of slavery to paganism. Taking on another unnecessary yoke of bondage would be foolish.

The law (in general) and Torah keeping (specifically) cannot be the yoke of bondage spoken of here. The yoke Paul speaks of is man given, not God given. God's commandments are most definitely God-given. It was the circumcision promoters who were pushing systemic laws on the Galatians.

Remember that it was fifty days after the Exodus that God gave the Torah at Sinai. The question we must ask is: Would God have taken Israel out from under the yoke of slavery (Egypt) only to place them under another yoke of slavery (Torah) in a matter of days? If we are to assume that the Torah is a yoke of bondage, God would be guilty of doing to Israel what Paul was warning the Galatians to reject. Would God want Gentiles under a yoke of bondage?

It is apparent that the traditional understanding of the yoke of bondage needs to be re-examined. A more sensible understanding is that those men troubling the Galatians were pushing something other than simple obedience to God's commands.

Faith, Love & Obedience

> *"For in Christ Jesus neither circumcision nor uncircumcision avails anything, but <u>faith working through love</u>." – Galatians 5:6*

This is not the only time we find such a statement. Later in Galatians, Paul writes something similar,

> *"For in Christ Jesus neither circumcision nor uncircumcision avails anything, but <u>a new creation</u>." – Galatians 6:15*

And in 1 Corinthians,

> *"Circumcision is nothing and uncircumcision is nothing, but <u>keeping the commandments of God</u> is what matters." – 1 Corinthians 7:19*

What does faith working through love look like practically? Paul answers this when we combine all three of these verses. Putting these three together, it reads:

"For in Christ Jesus neither circumcision nor uncircumcision is anything, but faith working through love, being a new creation and keeping the commandments of God is what matters."

Faith working through love is the result of a new creation. Only those who have been made new can truly love as Christ loves. We love according to our faith by keeping the commandments of God.

In terms of salvation, neither Jewish lineage nor Gentile blood matters. What matters is faith, love and obedience. A new creation breeds a love-filled, faithful life that is demonstrated through obeying God's commandments. Proof that I am a new creation is found in my heartfelt response to his love. Paul's opinion is that when I am not keeping God's commands, I am not living a life of loving faith.

> *"And I, brethren, if I still preach circumcision, why do I still suffer persecution? Then the offense of the cross has ceased. I could wish that those who trouble you would even cut themselves off!"* – Galatians 5:11-12

Paul admits he used to preach circumcision but was now suffering persecution for abandoning it. Evidently, Paul's message of Gentile inclusion was not popular with his former companions.

The offense of the cross is that all have sinned, all must repent and all are in need of a Redeemer, both for the Jew and the Gentile. The cross is offensive to Jews, because they don't get a free pass for being a Jew. They must humble themselves, pick up their cross and follow Yeshua like everyone else.

Jewish offense could also be found in Paul's insistence that Gentiles could be saved on the same condition as Jews. It disrespected the custom of the rabbis that a Gentile could be grafted into Israel and enjoy the blessings of Abraham for free without submitting to circumcision. Using the language of circumcision, Paul wished the troublers would cut themselves off from the Galatian congregation altogether!

Love is Law Fulfilled

> *"For you, brethren, have been called to liberty; only do not use liberty as an opportunity for the flesh, but through love serve one*

> *another. For all the law is fulfilled in one word, even in this: 'You shall love your neighbor as yourself.'"* – *Galatians 5:13-14*

Paul breaks from the subject of salvation here to address godly living. In light of all of this, what is required of these Gentiles? Are they under no obligation to God's law?

Paul doesn't dismiss the Torah here. Again, he turns to the law as his textbook.

> *"You shall love your neighbor as yourself."* – *v.14, quoting Leviticus 19:18*

Paul uses the Torah to sum up the Torah. In using Leviticus 19:18 as a model for Christian living, the apostle places the Torah as a current, applicable and relevant authority over our lives. Contrary to the antinomian position, Paul expected the Galatian believers to abide by God's laws.

God gave liberated Israel His Torah. Why would He not give liberated sinners like you and me the same instructions?

The beauty in this walk is that there is no guesswork in what pleases the Father. God lays it out for us in clear and simple terms. It is the Torah that teaches us how to live a life of love as God defines it. If my ox gores your ox, "I'm sorry about that" is not good enough. Love is giving you my ox or paying for your loss. It is the Torah that teaches us what true justice looks like.

> *"I say then: Walk in the Spirit, and you shall not fulfill the lust of the flesh. For the flesh lusts against the Spirit, and the Spirit against the flesh; and these are contrary to one another, so that you do not do the things that you wish. But if you are led by the Spirit, you are not under the law."* - *Galatians 5:16-18*

The opposite of the Spirit is the flesh. The opposite of the flesh is the Spirit. The Spirit of God: (1) walks with us, (2) keeps us from fulfilling the lusts of the flesh, (3) wars against our flesh, and (4) delivers us from the condemnation of the law.

Conclusion

"For he who sows to his flesh will of the flesh reap corruption, but he who sows to the Spirit will of the Spirit reap everlasting life" - *Galatians 6:8.*

Unless we have the Spirit of God actively working in our lives, we will not be victorious over sin and the lusts of the flesh. Those who were preaching spiritless circumcision to the Galatians had no victory over sin and no supernatural ability to curb their sinful appetites. If their message didn't work for them, why did they think it would work for others?

Yeshua is our ultimate example. He was led by the Spirit and obeyed the Torah perfectly. In my opinion, any spirit that leads us to disobey the Torah is not the Spirit of God. Any interpretation that implies we are not under any obligation to keep the Torah, in light of the life of Christ, should be categorically rejected.

Galatians 6

Truth #37: *The law of Christ is the Law of Moses.*

> *"Brethren, if a man is overtaken in any trespass, you who are spiritual restore such a one in a spirit of gentleness, considering yourself lest you also be tempted." – Galatians 6:1*

How were the Galatian believers to know what was a transgression? You guessed it - the Torah. Given this verse, Paul could *not* have wanted the Galatians to discard the Torah. If the law were cancelled, then the definition of a transgression would also be cancelled. There would be nothing in place to restore another from or to.

In Paul's estimation, Christians clearly are capable of sinning. But how can sin be identified or defined if not for the Torah? A person cannot be restored from sin if the law that defines sin no longer is relevant.

Torah of Christ

> *"Bear one another's burdens, and so fulfill the law of Christ." – Galatians 6:2*

Some suppose that the law of Christ is a new law of love instituted by the Messiah that replaces the old Law of Moses. One commentary reads,

> "The law of Christ; which is the law of love to one another (John 13:34) in opposition to the law of Moses, the Judaizing Galatians were so fond of, and by which Christ's disciples may be distinguished from those of Moses, or any others."[1]

---

[1] John Gill, *Gill's Exposition of the Entire Bible*, Gal. 6:2 [Online]. Available: https://www.biblestudytools.com

I understand why this position is taken. I also understand why some are skeptical of this opinion. I share this skepticism. This viewpoint doesn't resonate, because in my estimation, it is not honest with Scripture.

Yeshua gave us a new commandment to love one another[2] and to treat others as we wish to be treated.[3] These work in conjunction with the Law of Moses, not in contrast. The law of Christ is the same as the Law of Moses, because the instruction to love others originates in the Torah. Both call for loving God and loving our neighbor.[4] Both require love and obedience. In this way, the Law of Moses is not loveless, and the love of Christ is not lawless.

There is no *new* Torah established by Jesus that replaces the Torah of God. Jesus didn't invent a new law and give it to his disciples. The law of Christ is nothing more than the commandments of God taught and explained by Yeshua. To fulfill the law of Christ is to consider the Law of Moses in light of the instructions of Christ and rightly apply it to our lives. Only through Christ can the law truly be fulfilled.

When we bear one another's burdens and show sympathy to those in distress best, we fulfill the instructions of our Lord. Just as the words of our Lord do not replace God's commands, the law of Christ does not replace the Law of Moses.

In Matthew 5:17, Yeshua states that He came to fulfill the law. Those who maintain that Jesus ended the law when he fulfilled it run into some problems when interpreting Galatians 6:2. Since Paul is instructing us to fulfill the law of Christ, to be consistent, they must also maintain that we end the law of Christ when we fulfill it. If one chooses to translate fulfill as *bring to an end*, then, according to this logic, Paul wants to bring the law of Christ to an end as well. This cannot be what Paul is inferring. This definition of *fulfill* falls short, and so does this interpretation.

---

[2] John 13:34, 15:12,17
[3] Matt. 7:12, Luke 6:31
[4] Deut. 6:5, 11:1, Lev. 19:18, Matt. 22:36-40, Mark 12:28-34, Luke 10-25-28

Fulfill means *to do and act in obedience.* Just as Yeshua acted in obedience to the Law of Moses, so we seek also to obey the Torah in conjunction with the teachings of our Master.

> *"As many as desire to make a good showing in the flesh, these would compel you to be circumcised, only that they may not suffer persecution for the cross of Christ. For not even those who are circumcised keep the law, but they desire to have you circumcised that they may boast in your flesh. But God forbid that I should boast except in the cross of our Lord Jesus Christ, by whom the world has been crucified to me, and I to the world." - Galatians 6:12-14*

The troublemakers were very eager to convince the Gentiles to submit to circumcision. Paul was equally eager to reveal their motivation. Their motivation was to (1) make a good showing in the flesh, (2) avoid persecution, and (3) boast in their proselytization. Their driving motive wasn't love and care for these young Gentile believers. They had an agenda. They sought to make a boastful showing in the eyes of the larger Jewish community.

Paul's motive was devoid of such boasting. He had no interest in bragging about another convert or adding another disciple to his tally. He was not looking to build upon his resume or take up a larger collection. Like a true father, he fought for them and for all that Christ suffered for.

> *"For in Christ Jesus neither circumcision nor uncircumcision avails anything, but a new creation." – Galatians 6:15*

Paul echoes this sentiment in Galatians 5:6 and 1 Corinthians 7:19 but with a twist. Here, Paul is saying that circumcision and Jewish identity afford a person no advantage in terms of justification. What matters for salvation is becoming a new creation in Christ.

Conclusion

> *"From now on let no one trouble me, for I bear in my body the marks of the Lord Jesus." – Galatians 6:17*

In his closing remarks, Paul does not hide the fact that he was a circumcised Jew, but his boast is not in this detail. From circumcision to beatings to persecution, the apostle was a marked man! But the marks on his body that he cherished most were the scars he had from preaching the good news and sharing in the sufferings of Christ. Unless the circumcision-pushing troublers were willing to lay down their lives for these Gentile brothers as Paul did and bear the sufferings of Christ, the Galatians need not listen to their teaching or allow them to trouble them any longer.

Paul's Letter To The Romans

Truth #38: *The book of Romans is pro-Torah.*

Many consider Paul's epistle to the Romans the greatest book of the New Testament. It is thought of as the most profound, most fundamental and most comprehensive doctrinal statements of the entire Bible. Arguably, no epistle has influenced Christian theology more than Romans.

There is no need to be intimidated by the book of Romans. While Paul's letter is meaty, it is more than digestible if given the right context. You might find Romans to be easier to comprehend and more Torah positive than its reputation holds.

The book of Romans serves as a longer and more far-reaching commentary than the shorter book of Galatians. If Galatians is the concentrate, Romans is the juice. Think of Romans as a comprehensive apology for Paul's overall doctrine and Galatians as a more concentrated argument. They both share similar content, but Romans expands the argument further and wider. Now that you've already braved Galatians, Romans will be easier to navigate.

If you're looking for an exhaustive, in-depth study of Paul's epistle to the Romans, you may be disappointed with my effort. I offer only a brief overview of Romans, but it will be sufficient for our purposes. We did most of the heavy lifting in the Galatians section, so I will only address those topics that have not already been covered there. Please keep in mind that I refine my attention to the portions of Romans that specifically address the Torah.

Authorship

Paul identifies himself as the author in the very first verse. He likely dictated this letter to his friend Tertius sometime around A.D. 55-58 while in Corinth at the end of his third missionary journey. It appears that the letter was designed to prepare the Romans for his visit and explain the gospel of Jesus Christ as he proclaims it.

"To all who are in Rome, beloved of God, called to be saints." – Romans 1:7a

Paul is writing to the believers in Rome, a church he did not establish and had not personally visited. Though Rome was in his heart,[1] the apostle had never been to the city at this point. He was motivated to preach the gospel to the Romans,[2] for he carried with him a heavenly promise that he would one day bear witness to Christ in Rome.[3] This could explain why Paul does not address the church of Rome as a whole but writes to individual house churches and believers within the region.

In the last chapter of his letter, Paul sends a personal greeting to twenty-six individuals and their households. He mentions twenty-four by name. Some scholars feel that chapter 16 is an addendum sent along with his original letter to Rome, which offers an explanation as to why Paul greets so many people. What matters most in our study is that Paul's letter is addressed to both Jews and Gentiles in Christ.

---

[1] Rom. 1:11
[2] Acts 19:21, Rom. 1:15
[3] Acts 23:11

ROMANS 1-2

Truth #39: *Doers of the law are justified in God's sight.*

> *"Paul, a bondservant of Jesus Christ, called to be an apostle, separated to the gospel of God which He promised before through His prophets in the Holy Scriptures, concerning His Son Jesus Christ our Lord." – Romans 1:1-3*

Paul sets an early precedent. Established Scripture is his launch point. Paul's doctrine does not run counter to what has already been written and established in the Holy Scriptures. The gospel of Jesus Christ is a promise that is revealed through the Prophets and now proclaimed by the apostles. It is not by accident that Paul references the Hebrew Scriptures 57 times in the book of Romans, not including the many numerous indirect allusions.

In the first couple chapters, Paul addresses sin, judgment and the wrath of God. He quotes Psalm 62:12 and Proverbs 24:12 to say that the Almighty will "render to each one according to his deeds" (2:6) and judge those who "do not obey the truth" (2:8). Those who make a practice of doing good will be rewarded with "glory, honor and immortality" (2:7). Those who continue in "self-seeking" and "obey unrighteousness" will be given "wrath, "tribulation and anguish…to the Jew first and also to the Greek. For there is no partiality with God" (2:8-11).

> *"For as many as have sinned without law will also perish without law, and as many as have sinned in the law will be judged by the law." – Romans 2:12*

The news is not encouraging for us sinners. Moral man cannot live up to his own conscience, and no man can live up to the Torah. Those who sin without the law will die lawless. Those who sin with the law will be judged by the law. Both miss the mark, as Paul famously pronounces, "All fall short of the glory of God" (3:23).

Hearers & Doers

"For not the hearers of the law are just in the sight of God, but the doers of the law will be justified." – Romans 2:13

What a second. Stop the bus. What is this? What is Paul saying here? Did he just say that doers of the law will be justified? Shouldn't it say those who hear by faith are justified? Is Paul insinuating that a person can be justified through keeping the Torah?

Paul is not advocating salvation through good deeds. He is calling out those who boasted in their knowledge of Scripture as security for their right standing with God. They knew the word of God, but the God of the word did not know them. They had the word, but the Word did not have them.

Knowledge of God is not sufficient enough proof of anyone's faith in God. A Sunday school education of Jesus and the Bible will not suffice. Active obedience to God's word is the primary evidence of our faith in Jesus Christ. This is Paul's point.

From a Hebraic standpoint, listening involves more than just hearing. It implies *hearing with the intent to obey.*[1] When God called out to young Samuel in the tabernacle, his response was, "Speak, for your servant hears (*shama*)" (1 Sam. 3:10). Something similar is said of Abraham. "Abraham obeyed (*shama*) My voice and kept My charge, My commandments, My statutes, and My laws" (Gen. 26:5). The same word *shama* is translated as both *hearing* and *obedience* on separate occasions. Paul seems to characterize "hearers and doers" in this same sense.

---

[1] Samuel Tregelles, *Gesenius's Hebrew and Chaldee Lexicon* (London: Samuel Bagster & Sons, 1857), H8085; Harris, Archer & Walke, *Theological Wordbook of the Old Testament*, Vol. II (Chicago: Moody Press, 1980), 938

A person who hears but does not act is just as guilty as the one who never hears and never acts. In fact, they may be worse off. Yeshua likens this kind of person to a fool who builds his house on sand. When the wind and rain come, his house falls. But the one who hears and does is the wise man whose foundation is built upon the rock. His house will endure through the storms of life.[2]

In Yeshua's parable of the two sons, the father instructs both sons to work in the vineyard. The first son is defiant. He refuses to obey, but later has a change of heart and works in the field. The second son is compliant but deceptive. After agreeing to work, he never actually does. Jesus then asks the question, "Which of the two sons did the will of the father?" The answer is obvious. Both heard the word of the father, but only one son pleased him (Matt. 21:28-32).

Our life in God must go beyond knowledge, family background and mental ascent. Being a minister or an orthodox Jew doesn't score extra points with God. Attending church or reciting a prayer ought to be met with consistent and sincere follow through. Whether He finds us compliant or defiant, our *creeds* can never replace our *deeds*. The absolute test of whether we possess genuine faith is how we live out what we profess. This is what I believe Paul is getting at here.

Salvation is more than a one-time experience. Paul himself taught that salvation is past, present and future.

Past	Present	Future
We have been saved	We are being saved	We will be saved
Eph. 2:8 – "For by grace you *have been saved* through faith."	1 Cor. 1:18 - "For the message of the cross is foolishness to those who are perishing, but to us who *are being saved* it is the power of God."	Rom. 10:9 - "If you confess with your mouth the Lord Jesus and believe in your heart that God has raised Him from the dead, you *will be saved*."
Justification	Sanctification	Glorification

---

[2] Matt. 7:24,26

The redemption of our soul is threefold: Justification, Sanctification and Glorification. All three contribute to our complete salvation. We have been *justified* and declared not guilty of our sins (past). We are being *sanctified* and set-apart from sin (present), and we will one day be *glorified* and completely delivered from the power of sin (future).

New Covenant Gentiles

> *"For when Gentiles, who do not have the law, by nature do the things in the law, these, although not having the law, are a law to themselves, who show the work of the law written in their hearts, their conscience also bearing witness, and between themselves their thoughts accusing or else excusing* them) *in the day when God will judge the secrets of men by Jesus Christ, according to my gospel." –* Romans 2:14-16

From these verses, much dialogue surfaces about the manner in which God will judge those who never hear the good news and don't know the truth. I will not add to that discussion, except only to say that a person is accountable to the Torah that is written upon their heart. This is as true for the Jew as it is for the Gentile.

The Torah, the same law written on our hearts, will judge us all. According to "Paul's gospel," (v.16) not only are Jews and Gentiles saved in like manner (by grace through faith in Christ), they will also be judged in like manner by the same standard.[3]

Who are these Gentiles that Paul references, who "do the things in the Torah" and have "the Torah written in their hearts?" Pagans? God-fearers? Aborigines living in a primitive land? Given the context, it is likely that these are new covenant Gentile believers that have the Torah written on their hearts.

When a believing Gentile keeps that which is written in the Torah, they demonstrate that they have the Torah written on their heart.

---

[3] Tim Hegg, *Paul's Epistle to the Romans*, Vol. I (Tacoma: TorahResource, 2007), 49

Isn't this the very goal of the new covenant? Even though a Gentile's upbringing and culture might be far removed from the Torah, hearing and doing God's word is proof of their faith in Christ. If indeed this is whom Paul is referring to, the day of reckoning will smile favorably on Christians who aim to keep God's commandments.

> *"Indeed you are called a Jew, and rest on the law, and make your boast in God, and know His will, and approve the things that are excellent, being instructed out of the law, and are confident that you yourself are a guide to the blind, a light to those who are in darkness, an instructor of the foolish, a teacher of babes, having the form of knowledge and truth in the law. You, therefore, who teach another, do you not teach yourself? You who preach that a man should not steal, do you steal? You who say, "Do not commit adultery," do you commit adultery? You who abhor idols, do you rob temples? You who make your boast in the law, do you dishonor God through breaking the law? For 'The name of God is blasphemed among the Gentiles because of you,' as it is written." – Romans 2:17-24*

Paul now addresses the religious Jew who relies on his Jewish status for right standing with God. He reiterates that breaking God's law dishonors God and blasphemes the name of God. This is just as true for the Israelite as it is for the Catholic, Evangelical, Pentecostal, Irish priest or pastor's kid. Our affiliation does not count. Our association matters not. Bible education cannot do what simple faith and obedience does. In the end, God is more honored through our personal attention to his commandments than our knowledge or proclamation of them.

Circum-Decision

> *"For circumcision is indeed profitable if you keep the law; but if you are a breaker of the law, your circumcision has become uncircumcision. Therefore, if an uncircumcised man keeps the righteous requirements of the law, will not his uncircumcision be counted as circumcision? And will not the physically uncircumcised, if he fulfills the law, judge you who, even with your written code and circumcision, are a transgressor of the law? For he is not a Jew who*

is one outwardly, nor is circumcision that which is outward in the flesh; but he is a Jew who is one inwardly; and circumcision is that of the heart, in the Spirit, not in the letter; whose praise is not from men but from God." – Romans 2:25-29

In the context of Jewish boasting, Paul now brings circumcision into the conversation. Those circumcised in the flesh (Jews and proselytes) reveal that they have an uncircumcised heart (pagan) when they consistently break the Torah. Their Jewishness is counted as un-Jewishness when they make a practice of disobedience.

But those *un*circumcised in the flesh will be regarded by God as circumcised when they keep the "righteous requirements of the law." (v.26) Those who honor the Torah, maybe not in perfection but certainly in practice, will be a character witness on judgment day. They will, in the words of Cranfield, be "evidence of what the Jew ought to have been and could have been."[4]

Paul clearly does not view uncircumcised Christians as breaking the Torah. An uncircumcised Gentile believer is one who simply resisted giving in to the rabbinic ritual of circumcision. Whether circumcised or uncircumcised, fulfilling the Torah as Yeshua did is what makes one a true Israelite. For Gentile believers, faith and obedience are for us an inward circumcision of the heart.

This does not throw out the value of circumcision. Circumcision is profitable, because it is still a sign of the Messiah. How so?

When Abram was ninety-nine years old, the Lord appeared to him and changed his name. God gave him a promise and established a covenant with him. Abraham and his household were circumcised, which predicated the miracle birth of Isaac. It is not by accident that the sign of circumcision applies directly to the male reproductive organ. Just as Abraham and Sarah miraculously bore a child after their childbearing years, so the Messiah was conceived and brought

---

[4] C.E.B. Cranfield, *A Critical and Exegetical Commentary on The Epistle to the Romans,* Vol. 1 (Edinburgh: T&T Clark, 1975), 174

forth through miraculous means – the virgin birth. As it was with Isaac, so it is with Christ.

Yeshua is the supernatural promise and fulfillment of that covenant. Circumcision still remains a seal of the covenant of faith and points the world to Yeshua, the Seed of Abraham.

Conclusion

Through two chapters of the book of Romans there is no anti-Torah sentiment found in Paul's doctrine. On the contrary, Paul is quite complementary of the Law of Moses.

ROMANS 3

Truth #40: *We use our freedom in Christ to establish the Torah.*

> *"What advantage then has the Jew, or what is the profit of circumcision? Much in every way! Chiefly because to them were committed the oracles of God...What then? Are we better than they? Not at all. For we have previously charged both Jews and Greeks that they are all under sin." – Romans 3:1-2, 9*

As in all of his writings, Paul holds the Scriptures in high regard. Referred to here as "the oracles of God," the apostle continually praises Holy Scripture throughout his letter to the Romans.

Paul does not speak of Jews derogatorily. To Paul, there is still great value to being a Jew. Israel has been given a sacred trust and entrusted with the very words of God. This godly heritage has brought salvation to every nation on earth, of which we all are indebted.

While being a Jew is advantageous as it relates to the oracles of God, there is no advantage as it relates to redemption or the forgiveness of sin. A Jew can waste this advantage by being boastful in their Jewish status or hypocritical in their application of the Torah.[1] Because Jews and Gentiles are both natural-born sinners, circumcision affords no superiority to those seeking to be made righteous through it.

> *"Now we know that whatever the law says, it says to those who are under the law (hoses nomos), that every mouth may be stopped, and all the world may become guilty before God." – Romans 3:19*

---

[1] Stern, *Jewish New Testament Commentary,* 336

"Under the law" is poorly translated here. This is not the same under the law (*hypo nomos*) found in Galatians, 1 Corinthians and later in Romans 6. This is *hosos nomos*, which implies "those living within the framework of the law."[2] It denotes those who take on or have possession of the Torah.[3] This phrase is also found in Romans 2:12, "As many as (*hosos*) have sinned in the law (*nomos*) will be judged by the law."

With this in mind, this verse addresses people who have heard or possess the Torah, namely, Israel. Sin is an equal-opportunity destroyer. Just as Israel was found guilty of violating the Torah, so are we. There is no legal defense for our unjust behavior. Every self-justifying mouth will be silenced, and God will have His day in court. Paul is saying that if the Jews, who are guided by the Torah, stand guilty before God, how much more will those nations that are not guided by the Torah.

Works or Works of Law?

> *"Therefore by the deeds of the law (ergon nomos) no flesh will be justified in His sight, for by the law is the knowledge of sin." – Romans 3:20*

Paul quotes David, "For in your sight no one living is righteous," (Ps. 143:2) attaching to it the term *ergon nomos*. Why does he paint *works of law* in this manner?

It is possible Paul is saying that no person can be justified in God's sight through the good deeds of the Torah. Because all have sinned and have been born into sin, imperfect people cannot obey the Torah perfectly. If no one is good enough, then doing good cannot be a means of salvation.

We know that even under the purest of intentions, sinners cannot obey the Torah suffiently to bring them into right standing with God.

---

[2] Ibid 334, 343; Heinrich Meyer, *Meyer's New Testament Commentary*, Vol. 5 (New York: Funk & Wagnalls, 1886), Rom. 3:19
[3] Hegg, *Paul's Epistle to the Romans*, 69

A person cannot manufacture a righteousness that atones for sin with even the most scrupulous adherence to Scripture. No amount of obedience can do what Christ's obedience has done for us.

It is also possible that Paul is implying something else. I've noted that Paul prefers the phrases *good works, keeping the law* or *doers of the law* when referencing commandment keeping. The fact that he uses *ergon nomos* instead could indicate that he is not discussing the topic of Torah keeping at all; rather, he may be referring specifically to those who sought to enter the covenant of Abraham through circumcision. Since it's equally true to say that no person can be justified in God's sight through Jewish regulations, both explanations are plausible.

I'm of the opinion that when Paul uses *works* in Romans and Galatians, it is a shorthand reference to *works of the law*. This does seem to be Paul's pattern throughout Romans and when using *works of law* later in the letter.

Law of the Redeemed

"But now the righteousness of God apart from the law is revealed, being witnessed by the Law and the Prophets, even the righteousness of God, through faith in Jesus Christ, to all and on all who believe. For there is no difference; for all have sinned and fall short of the glory of God." – Romans 3:21-23

Righteousness "apart from the law" (v.21) is necessary, because the righteousness that comes through the Torah cannot make anyone innocent of sin. The Torah does not redeem us. It prepares us for redemption and for how to live as the redeemed.

What the law couldn't accomplish, Yeshua did. While the Torah is limited, the grace of God through Yeshua is unlimited. The Torah and the Prophets give witness to a righteousness apart from the Torah that comes through faith in Jesus Christ.

Being delivered from our sin is likened to when God delivered the children of Israel from Egypt. They were slaves; so were we. They were in bondage; so were we. The blood of the lamb protected them from death; so does the blood of Yeshua. They passed through the waters of the Red Sea; we pass through the waters of baptism.

It was by design that the Lord gave the Torah to Israel after they had been freed from Egypt and passed through the Red Sea. As slaves in Egypt, they could not physically observe the Sabbath or His festivals. They did not have the liberty to worship God in the way He prescribed due to their Egyptian bondage. This was Moses' reasoning before Pharaoh as to why all of Israel must leave to go into the wilderness.[4]

In the same way, it is impossible for us to obey all of God's laws when we are still enslaved to our sins. We must first break free from the bondage of sin and be baptized. Our newfound freedom liberates us to meet the Lord on the Mount Zion and receive his instructions.

The Torah came after redemption, not before. This suggests that the Torah has always been for the redeemed.

> *"Where is boasting then? It is excluded. By what law? Of works? No, but by the law of faith. Therefore we conclude that a man is justified by faith apart from the deeds of the law. Or is He the God of the Jews only? Is He not also the God of the Gentiles? Yes, of the Gentiles also, since there is one God who will justify the circumcised by faith and the uncircumcised through faith. Do we then make void the law through faith? Certainly not! On the contrary, we establish the law."*
> *– Romans 3:27-31*

This boasting came from those taking pride in their circumcision. Citing the works of law, Paul communicates that faithless adherence to any set of rules, whether civil, spiritual or rabbinic, can never achieve what Christ accomplished for us. The Jewish man cannot boast in his Jewish identity, just as the proselyte cannot boast in his ceremonial circumcision.

---

[4] Ex. 5:1

Some presume that because we are not saved through the law, the Torah has no purpose. Paul's response to this is: "By no means!" or "Certainly not" (v.31). Setting aside God's commands is lawlessness cleverly disguised as Christian liberty. Law and grace are not enemies. The opposite of grace is lawlessness, not law.

The apostle refuses to play the grace card here. Legalism insists, "I obey in order to be saved." Grace replies, "I obey, because I am saved." Paul does not teach a shoddy grace or endorse living a life of sin under the guise of living free in the Spirit. The true enemy of the Spirit is the flesh, not the law.[5]

Avoid A Void

"Do we then make void the law through faith?" – Romans 3:31

The phrase "make void" is the Greek word *katargeō*. It is translated elsewhere: *abolish, cease, destroy, vanish, do away with* or *make of no effect*.[6] Literally and figuratively, *katargeō* means *to render ineffective* or *to cause to cease*.[7]

When it comes to the Torah and the new covenant, this is the ultimate question. If salvation comes by faith, does the law have any authority over me? This is the question we've historically tripped over and are still grappling with.

Paul answers it resoundingly for us.

"Certainly not! On the contrary, we establish the law." – Romans 3:31

Establish implies *to set in place, uphold* or *to cause to stand*.[8] According to Paul, our liberty does not free us from upholding the

---

[5] Rom 3:19, 1 Cor. 9:20, Gal. 4:4, 21, 5:18
[6] *Strong's* #G2673; *Thayer's*, καταργέω
[7] Hegg, *Paul's Epistle to the Romans*, Vol. I, 80; Pierce, *The Outline Of Biblical Usage*, Rom.3:31
[8] *Strong's* #G2476 ἵστημι; Zodhiates, *The Complete Word Study*, 911

Torah. Now that we are free in Christ, what are we free to do? We are free to establish the Torah by upholding it and setting it up in a prominent place in our lives.

Conclusion

Paul's doctrine agrees with the words of Yeshua. The law is not destroyed. Upon finding faith in Christ, our goal is to establish the Torah and allow it to take hold of our lives. God's law no longer works against us. It works for us.

Romans 4

Truth #41: *Christ died, not the law.*

> *"What then shall we say that Abraham our father has found according to the flesh? For if Abraham was justified by works, he has something to boast about, but not before God. For what does the Scripture say? 'Abraham believed God, and it was accounted to him for righteousness.' Now to him who works, the wages are not counted as grace but as debt. But to him who does not work but believes on Him who justifies the ungodly, his faith is accounted for righteousness." – Romans 4:1-5*

The works of Abraham are not his good deeds or any specific upright behavior. This is evident by the precise words that Paul uses here. He contrasts *flesh, works, boasting* with *faith, grace, justification* and *imputed righteousness*. The specific work of Abraham that Paul is targeting is the circumcision he received as an adult.

The sign of circumcision was given after Abraham placed his faith in the Lord, not before.

> *"He received the sign of circumcision, a seal of the righteousness of the faith which he had while still uncircumcised, that he might be the father of all those who believe, though they are uncircumcised, that righteousness might be imputed to them also." – Romans 4:11*

The work of circumcision did not play a role in Abraham's justification. Because he believed God and was declared righteous before circumcision, Abraham was saved by faith, not by the fleshly work of circumcision.

In Paul's day, Jews and proselytes that boasted in their circumcision were relying on the sign of the covenant instead of the Seed that the sign points to. In their human effort to identify themselves as children of Abraham, they made themselves debtors to circumcision and the works of the flesh. Ironically, Gentiles who model Abraham's faith and believe in Abraham's Seed are more children of Abraham than those who are circumcised but faithless. Paul's point is that the promise of salvation comes through faith, not the ritual of circumcision.

It is an interesting side note that Abraham was circumcised after Ishmael was conceived, not before. This analogizes that Ishmael was brought forth before Abraham was consecrated. Ishmael was not the son of promise. He came about through fleshly means and was a work of the flesh. Symbolically, it illustrates that these circumcisers were trying to receive the promises of God through fleshly means.

But Yeshua, the promised son of Abraham, is a work of the Spirit and was brought forth through supernatural means. Our salvation is secured through a work of the Spirit, not a work of the flesh. Consequently, Israel was guilty of worshipping circumcision, which was the sign, instead of worshipping the Seed.

> *"Just as David also describes the blessedness of the man to whom God imputes righteousness apart from works: 'Blessed are those whose lawless deeds are forgiven, and whose sins are covered; Blessed is the man to whom the Lord shall not impute sin.'"* – Romans 4:6-8

Paul quotes David, saying, "Blessed are those whose lawless deeds are forgiven." He does not say, "Blessed are those who are no longer obligated to the law." This is because we have been forgiven and released from our actions *against* the Torah. We are not released *from* the Torah. To return again to these actions would bring us back into bondage and violate the spirit of grace.

Both Abraham and David found grace in the eyes of God. One had the law. The other didn't. David was circumcised. He had the Torah and found grace in God's eyes. Abraham was not circumcised. He did not have the Torah but also found grace.

From this we can glean that our salvation is irrespective of the Torah. Whether a person has full knowledge of God's commandments or not, the Torah does not factor into their salvation either way.

Upon a closer examination, the Torah is not really the subject matter of this passage, because the topic at hand is salvation. We misunderstand Paul and Romans if we think the Torah is on trial here. The *works* Paul speaks of are not the commandments of God as it relates to the Torah. There is a strong indication that they are a shorthand reference to *the works of the law* – the rabbinic mechanism by which a Gentile was considered brought into the covenant of Abraham.

In this we can deduce that since our justification does not come through the law, the law is not a hindrance to our salvation. The Torah does not need to be removed in order for God to remove our sin. What dies is not the lawful standard. Instead, it is Yeshua who died to satisfy the penalty of our lawless rebellion.

> *"For if those who are of the law are heirs, faith is made void and the promise of no effect, because the law brings about wrath for where there is no law there is no transgression." – Romans 4:14-15*

Those who are of the law are those trusting in circumcision, Jewish identity or the manner in which they follow the Torah to make them righteous before God. In reality, they are missing out on Abraham's inheritance. By seeking righteousness without faith, they still remain under sin and are outside of the promises of God. The same law that they seek to be under is the same law that judges them for being a faithless transgressor of the law.

Conclusion

Those who believe that the law is done away give themselves convenient liberty to engage in lawlessness. If there is no law, there is no law to break, right?

But Christ did not forgive our lawless deeds by doing away with the law. He paid the penalty for us. Through faith in Him we become the children of promise.

While the Torah does not give us legal justification before God, it does not contradict the promise given to Abraham. If it were possible to be saved through Jewish ceremonies, then salvation could be gained through some other means than faith.

Romans 6

Truth #42: *The law is not the enemy of grace.*

> *"For sin shall not have dominion over you, for you are not under law (hypo nomos) but under grace. What then? Shall we sin because we are not under law (hypo nomos) but under grace? Certainly not!"* – Romans 6:15

I have already presented my thoughts on what it means to be under the law in chapter 34. You may want to reference that section of Galatians for a more thorough analysis on this topic.

To recap briefly, we've traditionally read this verse to mean: "Now that you are freed from the law, your only obligation is to enjoy God's grace."

No doubt Paul is championing the glory of God's grace. However, he is not implying that this grace cancels the law or makes all things lawful. Grace is neither the opposite nor the enemy of the law. Being under grace simply means we are no longer judged by the law and no longer under the covenantal requirement to obey the Torah perfectly.

A conventional definition of *under law* maintains that we are not under the obligation to obey the Torah. Our working definition of *hypo nomos*, however, is that we are no longer under the condemnation that the Torah prescribes for lawbreakers. A better paraphrase of verse 15a might read:

> *"For sin shall not have dominion over you, for you are no longer under the condemnation of the law but are free from sin and given God's favor by an act of His loving kindness."* – Romans 6:15a, paraphrase

When we equate the term *under law* with Torah keeping, we make faith, Spirit and the Word incongruent with one another. We inadvertently brand anyone who remains committed to God's commandments as faithless and Spiritless. This is problematic considering that Yeshua faithfully kept the Torah. He was not the Torah-breaking cavalier that the Pharisees readily accused Him of.

It also flies in the face of the men and women of Hebrews 11 who by faith faithfully upheld the Torah in their devotion to God. Their salvation, so to speak, was achieved by faith. But it was their deeds done in accordance to God's word that proved their faith.

Noah, for example, received favor (grace) from God, but it was his actions that saved him. If he didn't act upon the grace given to him, he would have drowned with the rest of the world.

Scholars are beginning to realize that there was more going on in the first-century church than simply Judaizers forcing Gentiles to keep the Torah. If the traditional context for which Paul wrote is inaccurate, then it stands to reason that we should rework our definition of *under the law*. For this reason, an alternative understanding of *hypo nomos* is worth considering.

> *"For just as you presented your members as slaves of uncleanness, and of lawlessness leading to more lawlessness, so now present your members as slaves of righteousness for holiness."* – Romans 6:19b

Paul characterizes a life of sin as *lawlessness leading to more lawlessness*, or more literally, *Torah breaking to Torah breaking*. This being the case, the opposite must hold true for the righteous. We go from *Torah keeping to more Torah keeping*.

Never did it cross Paul's mind that we should abandon God's law now that it no longer condemns us. It was our lawless behavior that led us into slavery in the first place. Why would we turn again to the same mentality that leads us into bondage again? Yet, there is a bondage that actually frees us.

Romans 6

Life, Liberty & the Law

It may be beneficial to define freedom here. Paul's notion of freedom is not the liberty to do whatever we please. He writes,

> *"And having been set free from sin, you became slaves of righteousness."* – Romans 6:18

Our freedom in Christ still carries with it an obligation. In this case, we exchange one type of slavery (sin) for another type of slavery (righteousness). In Paul's definition, our freedom surprisingly still involves a form of slavery.

Biblical freedom is not defined as, "I get to do whatever I want." True freedom is to want what we need. Under these terms, the truly free person not only knows what they need, but doesn't crave those things that lead to sinful bondage. They desire only those things that are beneficial and life giving.

Suppose a person you know says, "I may be addicted to alcohol and cigarettes, but I'm free to do whatever I want." True, they may have the lawful and moral freedom to make their own choices in life, even if those choices make them an addict. But are they free in their soul? They are not truly free, because they crave something that leads them into bondage and produces death.

It is those who desire to do the will of God that are the ones who are genuinely free. What they crave leads to life. They are free to do good!

When we truly love God, we should never want to do anything that breaks his heart or violates his will. Our love motivates us to please the One we love. In this way, those who truly love God can do whatever they want to. So long as God dictates every desire of your heart, you and I are free to do whatever pleases us. When his heart is in yours, the desires of your heart are his desires.

Law & *Dis*grace

The concept of grace should be seen in the same way. Our modern version of grace is much too weak. We confess the grace of God is something we all need, because God's standard of righteousness is just too difficult to match. Therefore, we need his grace.

Grace, however, is much stronger and more marvelous than that. God's grace does not lower the standard of his righteousness. It empowers us to reach his higher standard of righteousness and truth. It is his grace that elevates us to reach for godliness. We misunderstand grace when it does not motivate us to heartfelt, loving obedience.

Adopting a *weak* grace accepts a defeated life where sin continues to have dominion over us. It provides no motivation to rise from the ashes and live a victorious life. It carries little hope of ever becoming like our Master.

Strong grace, however, calls us to a higher place. It enables us to "reckon ourselves dead to sin" and does "not let sin reign in our mortal body, that we should obey it in its lusts" (Rom. 6:11-12). With victorious grace, we "present ourselves to God as being alive from the dead and our members as instruments of righteousness to God." (Rom. 6:13). Whereas weak grace gives an excuse for continuing in sin, strong grace arms us with the power to defeat it.

Paul seems to agree.

> *"What then? Shall we sin because we are not under law but under grace? Certainly not! Do you not know that to whom you present yourselves slaves to obey, you are that one's slaves whom you obey, whether of sin leading to death, or of obedience leading to righteousness? But God be thanked that though you were slaves of sin, yet you obeyed from the heart that form of doctrine to which you were delivered. And having been set free from sin, you became slaves of righteousness." - Romans 6:15-18*

The slavery imagery in this passage need not trouble us. It communicates that our servitude to godliness is stronger than our former subjection to sin; that our flesh is subservient to our spirit; that righteousness is stronger than wickedness. God's grace frees us from slavery to mortal sin and makes us slaves of obedience leading to righteousness. Compared to the bad the world is enslaved to, God's grace makes us better, stronger and more faithful servants of all that is good.

Conclusion

There are those today trying to earn God's grace. This is unfortunate. Far more prevalent, however, are those taking advantage of God's grace. This grieves me.

Under law does not contrast grace with obedience. It contrasts grace with condemnation. When it comes to the law, the emphasis should be on shunning its condemnation, not its obligation. True grace restrains us from continuing to break the very law that necessitates our need for grace. It frees us from the judgment of the Torah and empowers us to live within its confines.

It is not necessary to choose between law and grace, because grace and law are not opposites. The law does not bully grace. Neither should grace bully the law.

Law without grace is legalism. Grace without law is lawlessness. But the law of grace sets us free.

Romans 7:1-13

Truth #43: *The law is not crucified with Christ. We are.*

> *"Or do you not know, brethren (for I speak to those who know the law), that the law has dominion over a man as long as he lives? For the woman who has a husband is bound by the law to her husband as long as he lives. But if the husband dies, she is released from the law of her husband. So then if, while her husband lives, she marries another man, she will be called an adulteress; but if her husband dies, she is free from that law, so that she is no adulteress, though she has married another man. Therefore, my brethren, you also have become dead to the law through the body of Christ, that you may be married to another-- to Him who was raised from the dead, that we should bear fruit to God. For when we were in the flesh, the sinful passions which were aroused by the law were at work in our members to bear fruit to death. But now we have been delivered from the law, having died to what we were held by, so that we should serve in the newness of the Spirit and not in the oldness of the letter." – Romans 7:1-6*

Translators insert subtitles at the beginning of certain portions of Scripture in an attempt to describe the content presented and enhance the reading experience. I like this, so long as these subtitles are accurate. The subtitle for Romans chapter 7 typically reads: "Freed from the Law" or "Released from the Law." This subtitle is accurate. However, the law you have been freed from may not be the law you have been told you are free from.

Here's Paul's analogy: A married woman decides to marry another man. If her original husband were still living, she would be guilty of breaking the law of marriage. She would be considered an adulteress. But if her original husband had already died, she would be released from her marital vows and free to remarry.

In this scenario, you and I are the woman. Our first husband is the law, and our second husband is Christ. Because we have broken the law, we are guilty of sin. We are lawbreakers. In order to come to Christ lawfully, someone needs to die. A death is necessary in order to free us from the condemnation of our first husband.

We naturally might think that our first spouse, the law, must die. Surprisingly, it is not the law that dies. It is us who dies! We died with Christ so that we could lawfully be joined together with Him.

Let me repeat. In this illustration, the law never dies. We die! Paul writes,

> "<u>You</u> also have become dead to the law through the body of Christ, that you may be married to another - to Him who was raised from the dead, that we should bear fruit to God." – Romans 7:4

You and I have been crucified with Christ (Gal. 2:20). So, while we are counted as dead, the law lives on. He adds,

> "Do you not know, brethren, that the law has dominion over a man <u>as long as he lives</u>?" – Romans 7:1

The dominion of the law is the condemnation of the law. Upon our death, the condemnation for our sin also passes.

The purpose of our divorce from the law, if you will, is not so that we walk away from the Torah like people walk away from a previous marriage. The purpose is that we die to our former life of sin and walk away from the condemnation that the law prescribes for lawbreakers.

Verse 6 then shows us what our new purpose is:

> "But now we have been delivered from the law, having died to what we were held by, so that we should <u>serve</u> in the newness of the Spirit and not in the oldness of the letter." – Romans 7:6

Our new purpose is to serve. Serve what? Dare I say that Paul infers that we now serve the law! He supports this later, writing:

> *"With the mind I myself serve the law of God, but with the flesh serve the law of sin." –Romans 7:25*

Some translations render it:

> *"I myself am a slave to God's law." (NIV)*

And,

> *"I am a Servant of The Law of God." (Aramaic Bible In Plain English)*

This is not to say that we don't serve Christ. We absolutely do. But Paul clearly means that as followers of Christ, we serve the Torah. We now walk in God's ways by the power of the Spirit with our new husband.

This interpretation can be verified easily. By adding "law" and "Christ" into the text, we can determine which one serves the context best.

First, let's add *Christ*:

> *"We should serve [Christ] in the newness of the Spirit and not [serve Christ] in the oldness of the letter."*

This cannot be the intention of the verse. The *gramma* (letter of the law) is the Torah devoid of the revelation of Christ. It is impossible to serve Christ in the oldness of the letter.

Now, let's add the *law*:

> *"We should serve [the law] in the newness of the Spirit and not [serve the law] in the oldness of the letter."*

Or some might prefer:

> *"We should serve [Christ] in the newness of the Spirit and not [serve the law] in the oldness of the letter."*

The thought of serving the Torah should not offend us. If Christ is the Word made flesh, the living Torah, then we serve the Torah when we serve Him. So long we have faith in Jesus the Messiah, we serve Him when we serve the Torah. Serving the living Word of God should lead us to serving the written Word of God.

> *"We should serve in the newness of the Spirit and not in the oldness of the letter."* – Romans 7:6

Serving the Torah in the oldness of the letter means attempting to be reconciled to God through faithless adherence to *works of law* and the Torah. This accurately described Jews and proselytes placing themselves under rabbinic rituals and regulations.

Serving the Torah in the newness of the Spirit means walking out the word in the power of the Spirit. This attests that eternal life cannot be acquired through the syntax or grammar (letter) of the Torah.

Yeshua said of the Jews persecuting Him:

> *"You search the Scriptures, for in them you think you have eternal life; and these are they which testify of Me."* – John 5:39

They were searching the Scriptures from the letter, not the Spirit. Jesus informs that the Scriptures devoid of Him do not produce life in and of themselves. He is the life-giver![1]

The Law is a Level

> *"What shall we say then? Is the law sin? Certainly not! On the contrary, I would not have known sin except through the law. For I would not have known covetousness unless the law had said, 'You*

---

[1] See Chapter 50 for a more detailed analysis of the letter of the law versus the spirit of the law.

shall not covet.' But sin, taking opportunity by the commandment, produced in me all manner of evil desire. For apart from the law sin was dead. I was alive once without the law, but when the commandment came, sin revived and I died. And the commandment, which was to bring life, I found to bring death. For sin, taking occasion by the commandment, deceived me, and by it killed me. Therefore the law is holy, and the commandment holy and just and good. Has then what is good become death to me? Certainly not! But sin, that it might appear sin, was producing death in me through what is good, so that sin through the commandment might become exceedingly sinful." – Romans 7:7-13

With the law comes the knowledge of sin. Sin was present in us before the commandment came, but knowledge of right and wrong in God's eyes cannot be fully realized or perfected outside the Torah. It is only through God's word we can know what behavior leads to life and what leads to death.

Paul affirms the Torah as "holy and just and good." Having our sins exposed is never comfortable, but it is beneficial. It gives us the opportunity to repent and change our ways. It is not the commandment that produces death in us. The commandment reveals that sin produces death, for sin "was producing death in me through what is good" (v. 13).

The Torah is like a carpenter's level. It reveals those things that are straight and true. Yet, this is not the only purpose of this tool. We also use a level to determine when our wall or picture frame is not level. It shows us what's off so we know how to adjust things and make them straight. The level, then, has a dual purpose. We use it to show us when our picture is straight and when it's not.

When I hung the mirror in our bathroom crookedly, it was not my level's fault. It was my fault for not consulting the level first. The level confirmed what I suspected - that the mirror was not straight. I did not ask the level to fix the problem. Fixing it was my job. The level's job is to give me information that I need in order to complete my project. To throw out my level once my mirror is corrected would be foolish. How would I know how to adjust the mirror if it ever became crooked again?

In the same way, the law of God reveals those things in our lives that are crooked and warped. It is not the job of the law to fix the problem. With the help of the Holy Spirit, that is our job. We take the wisdom that the Torah gives and apply it to our condition. To throw out the Torah once we are on the straight and narrow would be foolish. How would we know how to make adjustments when we find ourselves out of alignment?

Conclusion

The law is perfect. As a by-product, it reveals things that are not perfect, namely, you and me. To not consult with the Torah when making decisions in life would be unwise. It is God's word that encourages us and keeps us on the straight and narrow.

ROMANS 7:14-25

Truth #44: *The law of the Spirit sets us free from the law of sin.*

"For we know that the law is spiritual, but I am carnal, sold under sin. For what I am doing, I do not understand. For what I will to do, that I do not practice; but what I hate, that I do. If, then, I do what I will not to do, I agree with the law that it is good. But now, it is no longer I who do it, but sin that dwells in me. For I know that in me (that is, in my flesh) nothing good dwells; for to will is present with me, but how to perform what is good I do not find. For the good that I will to do, I do not do; but the evil I will not to do, that I practice. Now if I do what I will not to do, it is no longer I who do it, but sin that dwells in me. I find then a law, that evil is present with me, the one who wills to do good. For I delight in the law of God according to the inward man. But I see another law in my members, warring against the law of my mind, and bringing me into captivity to the law of sin which is in my members." – Romans 7:14-23

This portion of Romans 7 garners a lot of attention. What is Paul communicating here? Two opinions usually emerge:

Interpretation #1: *Paul reveals the great struggle with sin he fought as a believer. He admits that he has no power to conquer it.*

Interpretation #2: *Paul reveals the great struggle with sin he had before he became a believer. Before Christ, Paul continually gave into sin.*

There are drawbacks to each of these interpretations. Critics of the first question, "Was Paul exaggerating his struggle or was he continually falling into habitual sin? Did he really have no power to resist his sinful urges?" It casts doubt on the character of this venerated apostle.

Critics of the second point out that the passage is written in the present tense. Paul writes, "I am doing...I will to do." Paul does seem to be talking about his current life in Christ, not his life before Christ. Wouldn't Paul use the past tense if he were referring to his old life?

There are obvious problems with both of these conclusions. Paul clearly is revealing a current issue, not a past one. He does indeed use the present tense. Yet, are we prepared to say that the writer of two-thirds of the Apostolic Scriptures, a true follower and apostle of Christ, was a serial sinner with no victory over his flesh?

Thankfully, there is a third interpretation to consider.

Interpretation #3: *Paul reveals his great struggle with sin when trying to overcome his flesh through willpower.*

Seven times Paul refers to his *will*.

> "For what <u>I will</u> to do, that I do not practice; but what I hate, that I do. If, then, I do what <u>I will</u> not to do, I agree with the law that it is good...for <u>to will</u> is present with me, but how to perform what is good I do not find. For the good that <u>I will</u> to do, I do not do; but the evil <u>I will</u> not to do, that I practice. Now if I do what <u>I will</u> not to do, it is no longer I who do it, but sin that dwells in me. I find then a law, that evil is present with me, the one who <u>wills</u> to do good." – Romans 7:15-21

The word is *thelō*. It means *to will, have in mind, desire, resolve, wish* or *intend*.[1] Paul is saying that while he may be resolved in his will to practice righteousness and resist evil, his will is not powerful enough in itself to accomplish it.

It is Paul's position that while the intent of those seeking to please God outside of faith in Christ may be noble, their pursuit will prove to be frustrating and fruitless. This means that Israelites and proselytes without faith in Yeshua are still under the old covenant. Any effort to overcome sin through willpower, self-righteousness or

---

[1] *Strong's* #G2309 θέλω; Pierce, *The Outline Of Biblical Usage,* Rom. 7:15

circumcision is futile. Why? Because there is another law at work within all of us – the law of sin.

> *"I find then a law, that evil is present with me, the one who wills to do good. For I delight in the law of God according to the inward man. But I see another law in my members, warring against the law of my mind, and bringing me into captivity to the law of sin which is in my members." – Romans 7:21-23*

The law of sin is like the law of gravity. If you held the chair or couch you are sitting in over your head, you could hold it up in the air for some time. One could say that you are overcoming the law of gravity through your willpower. This may be true, but for how long? The weight of the chair and your endurance would ultimately determine how long you could hold it up. Eventually, gravity wins and the chair will fall. In this instance, the law of gravity always prevails.

Like gravity, the law of sin always prevails. It cannot be overcome through fleshly effort or willpower alone. Any attempt at being godly through self-righteous determination or observing the Torah will ultimately come crashing down on our heads. This is because sin is a law.

Paul characterizes this law as "evil present within me warring against the law of my mind and bringing me into captivity to the law of sin which is in my members." (v.21-23) Even well intentioned sinners are doomed.

Jews under the law and Gentiles relying on circumcision are subject to the law of sin. So, any kind of man-made religion devoid of the Spirit of God is ineffective, unproductive and exhausting.

So, what's the solution? Are we ruined?

Thankfully, there is a way to overcome a law. The only way to overcome a law is to introduce a new law. It takes a stronger law to supersede an existing law. In this case, a law stronger than our sin nature is needed and exists.

Imagine now swimming to the bottom of a pool holding a basketball. If you were to release the ball from the bottom of the pool, would it rise or sink? Contrary to gravity, it would rise. Why? A greater law has come into the play. In this instance, the law of buoyancy overcomes the law of gravity.

In the same way, a greater law overcomes the law of sin. Paul calls this law *the law of the Spirit of life in Christ Jesus*. He explains:

> *"For I delight in the law of God according to the inward man. But I see another law in my members, warring against the law of my mind, and bringing me into captivity to the law of sin which is in my members. O wretched man that I am! Who will deliver me from this body of death? I thank God-- through Jesus Christ our Lord! So then, with the mind I myself serve the law of God, but with the flesh the law of sin. There is therefore now no condemnation to those who are in Christ Jesus, who do not walk according to the flesh, but according to the Spirit. For the law of the Spirit of life in Christ Jesus has made me free from the law of sin and death." - Romans 7:22 - 8:2*

The law of the Spirit is greater than the law of sin. Only through Christ can the weight and condemnation of the law be released. Where the law of the sin weighs us down, the law of the Spirit buoys us up above sin and death.

Conclusion

Like some religions today, the Essenes believed human wretchedness could be conquered through good works, asceticism and body mortification.[2] This was not Paul's belief. Because sin is a law, it cannot be defeated through stricter laws. It can only be conquered through a greater law.

Sixteen times the Holy Spirit is referenced in Romans 8. The Spirit of God has a law, and it is full of the Spirit. It is called the law of the spirit of life in Christ Jesus. Through it, we are delivered from the law of sin, condemnation and death. There is one stipulation,

---

[2] Santala, *Paul*, 137, 156

however, for achieving this victory. It requires that we no longer "walk according to the flesh" (8:1).

For us, flesh may be viewed as attempting to defeat sin and temptation through willpower or self-righteous determination. To the Roman, however, flesh was a direct reference to the fleshly work of circumcision and Jewish regulations. For all of us, the answer is the same. Our human flesh and our sin nature can only be conquered through the Spirit of the Living God.

ROMANS 10:4

Truth #45: *Christ is the goal of the Torah.*

> *"Brethren, my heart's desire and prayer to God for Israel is that they may be saved. For I hear them witness that they have a zeal for God, but not according to knowledge. For they are ignorant of God's righteousness, and seeking to establish their own righteousness, have not submitted to the righteousness of God. <u>For Christ is the end of the law for righteousness to everyone who believes.</u>"* – Romans 10:1-4

Here it is written plainly. Paul finally comes out and says it. He waits until chapter 10 to state the obvious - the Torah has expired. Christ put an end to the law!

Not so fast.

The word *is* does not appear in the original text but is inserted for English readability. Without this *is,* Paul's statement reads differently, does it not?

The word used for "end" is *telos. Telos* can mean *terminate* or *finish.*[1] It can also mean *aim, goal* or *purpose.*[2] How is Paul meaning it here?

Peter uses *telos* in 1 Peter. He writes,

> *"The genuineness of your faith, being much more precious than gold that perishes, though it is tested by fire, may be found to praise, honor and glory at the revelation of Jesus Christ, whom having not seen you love. Though now you do not see Him, yet believing, you rejoice with*

---

[1] *Strong's* #G5056 τέλος
[2] *Vine's, telos;* Stern, *Jewish New Testament Commentary,* 395-396; Hegg, *Paul's Epistle to the Romans,* Vol. II, 54-57

> *joy inexpressible and full of glory, receiving <u>the end (telos) of your faith</u> – the salvation of your souls." – 1 Peter 1:7-9*

Many have pointed out that *telos* means *goal* in this context.[3] Peter is not implying that faith, which he values more than gold, is terminated once we are saved. He means that the aim and purpose of our faith is "the salvation of our souls" (v.9).

Peter and Paul use *telos* in the same manner. Just as no one would take the position that our faith is terminated once we come to Christ, so the Torah does not terminate upon salvation. Faith and the Torah do not come to an end. They have a goal – Jesus Christ. Yeshua is the aim of the Torah and the target of our faith. In the words of N.T. Wright, Christ is the "climax of the covenant."[4]

Conclusion

The Torah is not on trial in this passage. The context is Israel seeking righteousness through righteous membership. In seeking to establish their own righteousness, they did so without knowledge and became ignorant of God's righteousness. What does this have to do with the Torah?

Israel sought to obtain right standing with God through Jewish identity and observing the Torah in a particular manner. In their pursuit of righteousness, they missed the purpose of the Torah – to save us out of man-made religion and bring us to Christ. The law exists to show us that we cannot obtain right standing with God through bloodlines or Torah righteousness. Our righteousness is found only in the Lamb of God who takes away our sin.

---

[3] Juster, *Jewish Roots,* 126
[4] N.T. Wright, *The Climax of the Covenant* (Minneapolis: Fortress, 1993)

PHILIPPIANS 3:2-9

Truth #46: *The Torah teaches us how to live a godly life.*

> *"Beware of dogs, beware of evil workers, beware of the mutilation! For we are the circumcision, who worship God in the Spirit, rejoice in Christ Jesus, and have no confidence in the flesh, though I also might have confidence in the flesh." – Philippians 3:2-4a*

The doctrinal influence of the circumcision party was not isolated to Rome and the province of Galatia. The church of Philippi was also under the same pressure to conform to circumcision rites, as these verses indicate. *Dogs, evil workers* and *the mutilation* are terms Paul uses to describe those pushing circumcision rituals.

The truly circumcised, according to Paul, are not those who identify as Jewish. The circumcised are those "who worship God in the Spirit, rejoice in Christ Jesus" and place "no confidence" in ethnicity or fleshly circumcision for their justification. They have been "circumcised with the circumcision made without hands, by putting off the body of the sins of the flesh, by the circumcision of Christ." (Col. 2:11) Those seeking justification through circumcision or Jewish identity may in fact be physically circumcised but are not, in Paul's words, circumcised "of the heart" (Rom. 2:29).

The mutilation likely consisted of both native-born Jews and Gentile proselytes who sought to boast in their recruiting numbers. Paul points out that if any man had reason to boast in his positional identity or circumcised state, it was he.

> *"If anyone else thinks he may have confidence in the flesh, I more so: circumcised the eighth day, of the stock of Israel, of the tribe of Benjamin, a Hebrew of the Hebrews; concerning the law, a Pharisee; concerning zeal, persecuting the church; concerning the righteousness which is in the law, blameless." – Phil. 3:4b-6*

Saul of Tarsus was an Israelite through and through. Circumcised on the eighth day; of the tribe of Benjamin, Torah observant; a Pharisee, a zealot and a Hebrew-speaking Yeshua denier. In describing himself formerly as blameless, Paul knew the rules and kept them all. He was a faithful Jew who followed the Jewish, rabbinic and oral laws to perfection. Having been trained as a Pharisee, Paul had more reason to boast in his Jewish identity than anyone else.

> *"But what things were gain to me, these I have counted loss for Christ. Yet indeed I also count all things loss for the excellence of the knowledge of Christ Jesus my Lord, for whom I have suffered the loss of all things, and count them as rubbish, that I may gain Christ and be found in Him, not having my own righteousness, which is from the law, but that which is through faith in Christ, the righteousness which is from God by faith." – Phil 3:7-9*

In his conversion to Christ, the apostle did not stop being an Israelite from the tribe of Benjamin. He was still a circumcised Pharisee dedicated to the Scriptures. None of this changed. What changed was the object of his zeal. No longer was he zealous for the "traditions of my fathers" (Gal. 1:14) or in "persecuting the church" (v.6). He now was zealous in his proclamation of Yeshua the Messiah.

Paul considered those things that were advantageous to him in the flesh as dung compared to the knowledge of Christ. Whereas Paul was once himself an arrogant troubler preaching circumcision, boasting in his Jewish identity, persecuting believers and giving his approval of Stephen's death, he left those nets behind to follow the call of Christ.

Conclusion

> *"Concerning the righteousness which is in the law, blameless...not having my own righteousness, which is from the law but that which is through faith in Christ, the righteousness which is from God by faith." – Phil 3:6,9*

Paul admits that there is a righteousness that comes from the Torah. This righteousness, however, is not adequate to cleanse sin or redeem the soul. It is *practical* righteousness (righteous behavior), and if done outside of faith, it is self-righteousness. Whereas the Torah teaches us how to live righteously, it cannot position us as righteous before God. *Positional* righteousness, that which Yeshua secures for us, comes only "from God by faith" (v.9) in Jesus Christ.

COLOSSIANS 2:11-14

Truth #47: *The Torah was not nailed to the cross.*

"In Him you were also circumcised with the circumcision made without hands, by putting off the body of the sins of the flesh, by the circumcision of Christ, buried with Him in baptism, in which you also were raised with Him through faith in the working of God, who raised Him from the dead." – Col. 2:11-12

Colossae was not far from the province of Galatia. Those preaching circumcision were hounding the Colossians in similar fashion. Paul again asserts that there exists a circumcision available to uncircumcised Gentiles – the circumcision of Christ. We who have put "off the body of the sins of the flesh" have been spiritually circumcised, buried and resurrected with Christ. Physical circumcision cannot replace the cross and is meaningless if it is not accompanied by faith in Yeshua.

Some take this to mean that Christians have the liberty to spiritualize and neglect any commandment of their choosing, such as idolatry, tattoos, tassels, Sabbath or the Ten Commandments. However, Paul is not spiritualizing the *commandment* of circumcision spoken of in the Bible or of any written instruction of God. He is spiritualizing the non-Biblical Jewish proselyte *ritual* of circumcision. He does this to illustrate that Gentiles in Yeshua are forgiven of their sins and given new life irrespective of circumcision.

This is supported in the following verse when he writes that we are "buried with [Christ] in baptism" (Col. 2:12). Paul links circumcision with baptism, a direct correlation to the Jewish ceremonies that often included both circumcision and an immersion (*mikvah*). His point is that non-Jews have a circumcision and a baptism available to them in Christ that allows them to inherit the covenant promises of God.

> *"And you, being dead in your trespasses and the uncircumcision of your flesh, He has made alive together with Him, having forgiven you all trespasses, having wiped out the handwriting of requirements that was against us, which was contrary to us. And He has taken it out of the way, having nailed it to the cross." – Col. 2:13-14*

The Greek for "handwriting of requirements" is *cheirographon dogma*.[1] It means a certificate of debt or a bill of indebtedness. Like an ancient I.O.U., these notes were common in the Greco-Roman world and legally binding.[2] They were often written in one's own handwriting as proof of obligation. Spiritually speaking, Jews were taught that God kept an account of man's moral debt and imposed a just judgment based on records from His heavenly ledger.[3]

It was also customary in Greek culture for a criminal to have his or her sentence written and hung above their prison cell. When they had served their time, the charges were then blotted out. Similarly, a list of crimes committed was attached to the execution stake of criminals sentenced to death much like the sign affixed atop the cross of Yeshua.[4] In addition to being a bill of indebtedness, *cheirographon* may also be a reference to this Roman practice. No doubt Paul is using this kind of metaphor here.

Like circumcision, our sins have been cut off and discarded. Like baptism, our transgressions have been buried with Christ, and like an acquitted criminal our crimes have been paid for. We are free from any I.O.U. with God. No longer is there a written record of our wrongdoing. Our violations against God's ordinances have been nailed to the cross. Through Christ our criminal record has been blotted out. We are released from our sentence of guilt.

---

[1] *Strong's* #G5498 χειρόγραφον and #G1378 δόγμα; Zodhiates, *The Complete Word Study New Testament*, 663, 898
[2] *HaYesod*, 7.15-6
[3] Peter O'Brien, *Word Biblical Commentary*, Vol. 44 (Nashville: Thomas Nelson, 1982), Col. 2
[4] Stern, *Jewish New Testament Commentary,* Col. 2; Scott, *A Concordance of the Law*, 268

This verse is erroneously used to conclude that the Law of Moses was nailed to the cross and died with Yeshua. I can see how this conclusion is drawn, but the context and the Greek certainly beg to differ. It is our sin record that has been eradicated and nailed to the cross, not the law.

Conclusion

The righteous Judge did not choose to take away his lawful standard in offering us forgiveness. Rather, He sacrificed His Son to meet that lawful standard and pay the price for our crimes. Yeshua pardoned our sin so that we could be forgiven and God's righteous standard could be upheld.

1 & 2 TIMOTHY

Truth #48: *Paul considered the Torah sound doctrine.*

> *"As I urged you when I went into Macedonia—remain in Ephesus that you may charge some that they teach no other doctrine, nor give heed to fables and endless genealogies, which cause disputes rather than godly edification which is in faith. Now the purpose of the commandment is love from a pure heart, from a good conscience, and from sincere faith, from which some, having strayed, have turned aside to idle talk, desiring to be teachers of the law, understanding neither what they say nor the things which they affirm."* – 1 Timothy 1:3-7

In the first of what is known as the Pastoral Epistles (1 & 2 Timothy and Titus), Paul urges Timothy to instruct the Ephesian leaders to teach sound doctrine and to not "give heed to fables and endless genealogies, which cause disputes" (v.4).

A large colony of Jews lived in Ephesus. Aquila, Priscilla, Apollos, John the apostle and Mary the mother of Jesus all resided in the city at one time or another. Much like Timothy himself, the church of Ephesus was a mix of Jew and Gentile. Evidently, the pedigree of Jewish bloodline caused some quarrels among them. Some had even "strayed" from the faith and "turned aside to idle talk" (v.6), projecting themselves in their ignorance as teachers of the Torah (v.7).

Timothy, a native of Lystra, became one of Paul's closest traveling companions. Paul left Timothy in Ephesus with specific instructions to appoint elders in the church and contest false teaching.

> *"But we know that the law (nomos) is good if one uses it lawfully, knowing this: that the law (nomos) is not made for a righteous person, but for the lawless and insubordinate, for the ungodly and for*

sinners, for the unholy and profane, for murderers of fathers and murderers of mothers, for manslayers, for fornicators, for sodomites, for kidnappers, for liars, for perjurers, and if there is any other thing that is contrary to sound doctrine, according to the glorious gospel of the blessed God which was committed to my trust." – 1 Timothy 1:8-11

We can draw a couple conclusions about the Torah from these verses.

(1) *Paul considered the Torah good.*

Kalos, one of the Greek words for good, means *beautiful, excellent, precious, useful, noble, honorable* and *favorable*.[1] The Torah is good so long as it is used well. If used beautifully, the Torah is beautiful. If used nobly, it is excellent. If used honorably, it is useful, but if used dishonorably, it can be destructive. It seems that some were twisting and abusing the Torah for their own purposes and to their own detriment.

Some opine that *nomos* (v.8,9) is not a reference to the Torah here but to some other kind of law. This is not likely since the behavior listed clearly references the Torah. These violations are "contrary to sound doctrine" (v.10), which means that the Torah, according to Paul, teaches sound doctrine. The false teachers influencing the Ephesian church were not advocating Biblical doctrines but something superfluous to Scripture.

(2) *The Torah detects and defines sin.*

The law leaves no one innocent, as there is no escaping the long arm of God's law. The insubordinate, the ungodly, the unholy, the profane, the murderer, the fornicator, the sodomite, the kidnapper, the liar and the perjurer - all are guilty of sin and lawlessness.

---

[1] *Strong's* #G2570; Thayer's καλός; Pierce, *Outline of Biblical Usage*, 1 Tim. 1:8; Woodhouse, *English-Greek Dictionary*, 366

> *"The law (nomos) is not made for a righteous person, but for the lawless." – 1 Timothy 1:9*

In saying that "the law is not made for a righteous person," it is tempting to conclude that Paul is restricting the Torah to a single-use document that offers no spiritual guidance to the righteous person. This leads some to the conclusion that the Law of Moses holds nothing beneficial to new covenant believers. Is the Torah only useful for sinners?

Paul himself, incidentally, refutes this notion and in his second letter to Timothy, nonetheless. He writes,

> *"From childhood you have known <u>the Holy Scriptures</u>, which are able to make you <u>wise for salvation through faith</u> which is Christ Jesus. All Scripture is given by <u>inspiration of God</u>, and is <u>profitable for doctrine, for reproof, for correction, for instruction in righteousness</u>, that the man of God may be <u>complete, thoroughly equipped for every good work</u>." – 2 Timothy 3:15-17*

This verse contradicts what Paul writes in 1 Timothy, or does it? Is Paul schizophrenic?

What Paul means is that our first encounter with God's law is always as a sinner, not as the righteous. No one can approach the Torah and walk away blameless. It kicks away every self-righteous crutch we lean upon. It topples every sanctimonious kingdom we build. It pulls out from under us every religious rug we rely. We cannot come to Christ and be made righteous until we first come face to face with our own degeneracy and confront the utter depravity of souls.

The first step in our redemption is to admit that we are hopelessly drowning in our own vomitus sin and utterly lost without a Savior. Coming to grips with our proud, selfish hearts draws us to receive the gracious gift of God with gratitude and appreciate the redemptive work of Christ.

If we are honest, we already know what Paul is getting at here. It's not Torah cancellation. It's that the lawless person stands condemned and judged by God's standard of behavior. Paul's negativity is directed at man's sinful nature more than the mirror that points it out.

> *"Now the Spirit expressly says that in latter times some will depart from the faith; giving heed to deceiving spirits and doctrines of demons, speaking lies in hypocrisy, having their own conscience seared with a hot iron, forbidding to marry, and commanding to abstain from foods which God created to be received with thanksgiving by those who believe and know the truth. For every creature of God is good, and nothing is to be refused if it is received with thanksgiving; for it is sanctified by the word of God and prayer."*
> *– 1 Timothy 4:1-5*

The Essenes of Palestine and the Therapeutae of Egypt were both Jewish sects that repudiated marriage and taught meritorious celibacy.[2] Philo observed that, "None of the Essenes marry."[3] Pliny writes that the Essenes were, "A people without a single woman, for they renounce marriage."[4]

The Essenes also practiced extreme dietary restrictions, abstaining from wine and animal meat.[5] Their meals consisted of a piece of bread and vegetables prepared by consecrated officers to assure that it would be free of contamination. Lightfoot writes that even upon excommunication, an ousted Essene was reduced to eating the grass of the field and often died of starvation due to having made a vow to not eat food prepared by defiled hands.[6] Years later, these same doctrines of celibacy and dietary extremes were adopted by the Gnostics.[7]

The word used in this passage for foods is *brōma*. This is the same word Yeshua uses in Mark 7. Some translate *brōma* as *meat*, but it is

---

[2] Bell, *Jews and Christians in Egypt*, ii. 8, 2; Philo, *Vit. Contempla*te § 4
[3] Philo, *Fragment*, 633
[4] Pliny the Elder, *The Natural History of Pliny*, 5:15
[5] Vincent, *Vincent's Word Studies in the New Testament*, 1 Tim. 4:1-5
[6] Spence and Exell, *The Pulpit commentary*, Book 48, 89
[7] Ellicott, *Ellicott's Commentary for English Readers*, 1 Tim. 4:3

better understood as *food of all kinds*.⁸ In this case, Paul may be referring to animal meat, although it can be distinguished from the distinctive animal meats of the Torah. In addition to various Jewish sects, the Gnostics, such as the Encratites and the Purists under Tatian, had themselves developed a systematic rule of abstinence from animal meat.⁹ It is likely that Paul is referring to the Essenes and/or the Gnostics in these verses.

Conclusion

Even among reformed scholars, there is little doubt that these verses are not talking about the Torah but about marriage and dietary restrictions beyond Scripture – Essene, Gnostic or otherwise. Those who believe and know the truth of God's word cannot knowingly, in good conscience, receive with thanksgiving something forbidden by Scripture.

---

⁸ Louw, *Greek-English Lexicon of the New Testament*, brōma
⁹ A.E. Humphreys, *Cambridge Bible* (UK: Cambridge University Press, 1895), 1 Tim. 4:4

Timothy's Circumcision

Truth #49: *Paul had Timothy circumcised, because he wanted Timothy to be Torah compliant.*

> *"Then he came to Derbe and Lystra. And behold, a certain disciple was there, named Timothy, the son of a certain Jewish woman who believed, but his father was Greek. He was well spoken of by the brethren who were at Lystra and Iconium. Paul wanted to have him go on with him. And he took him and circumcised him because of the Jews who were in that region, for they all knew that his father was Greek." – Acts 16:1-3*

Timothy was circumcised as an adult in Acts 16. This takes place immediately after Paul's confrontation with the Judean Pharisees in Jerusalem and the apostolic decision to allow Gentiles to remain uncircumcised.[1] Luke records that Paul had Timothy circumcised "because of the Jews who were in that region" (v.3).

This is an odd occurrence. In light of the verdict of the Jerusalem council, Paul's strident letter to the Galatians, and Titus' refusal to be circumcised, why would Paul insist on circumcising Timothy? Was Paul being inconsistent? Was he suddenly abandoning the doctrine of justification by faith?

There are several theories posed as to why Paul circumcised Timothy. We can rule out with a high degree of certainty that Paul capitulated to the circumcision party. In light of all we know about Paul, there is zero chance of this happening. There are other viable explanations.

One theory holds that unbelieving Jews would be scandalized if they knew Paul had an uncircumcised man as a traveling partner. Some

---

[1] Acts 15

speculate that circumcising Timothy was a spur-of-the-moment decision done as a favor to the Jews to avoid opposition and the reproach of Paul's countrymen.

Another proposes that Paul was being sensitive to Timothy as the "weaker" brother in Christ. If Timothy wished to cling to an antiquated practice of the Jews, Paul would extend liberty to the weaker-faithed brother and not stand in his way.

Many draw the conclusion that this was part of Paul's evangelistic strategy. The apostle insisted Timothy adopt the maxim: "To the Jews I became as a Jew, that I might win Jews" (I Cor. 9:20). Uneager to offend his Jewish counterparts, Paul hoped to opportunistically score points with the Jews and heighten his influence among them.

One even suggests that Paul wanted Timothy to be like him in his own circumcised state and imbibe the spirit of his mentor.

In my estimation, all of these explanations leave something to be desired. Would Paul circumcise another man simply because he was concerned about what other Jews thought of him? Was Paul one to avoid opposition and offense? If circumcision could increase the likelihood of salvation among Jews, shouldn't Paul advocate circumcision for every Christian minister? Did Paul view Timothy as weak in faith? Would an apostle to the Gentiles compromise his convictions to win over the Jews?

These explanations leave more questions than answers. There is a more logical explanation for Timothy being circumcised as an adult.

(1) *Timothy was a Jew.*

Timothy was the son of a mixed marriage, though some suggest that his parents may not have been married. Timothy's father was Greek, and his mother, Eunice, was a Jew, as was his grandmother Lois. In Judaism, the responsibility of circumcision rests with the father, but because Timothy's father was Greek, Timothy remained uncircumcised.

Being the son of a Jewish woman knowing "the Holy Scriptures from childhood" (2 Tim 3:15), Timothy was likely given a Jewish upbringing and education. It could be that Eunice did not wish to circumcise her son against his father's wishes. Perhaps this is why Timothy remained uncircumcised into adulthood.

For all intents and purposes, Timothy was to be considered a Jew. In Hebrew culture, a son received legal entitlements and inheritance from his father, but rabbinic code recognized the child of a Jewish mother as a Jew.[2] David Stern writes,

> "Jewish and non-Jewish descent are invariably traced through the mother, not the father. The child of a Jewish mother and Gentile father is Jewish, and the child of a Gentile mother and Jewish father is Gentile. If a Gentile mother converts to Judaism, she is a Jew and her subsequent children are likewise Jewish."[3]

Determining Jewish ethnicity through the mother's line can be traced as far back as the 5th century B.C.E.[4]

There is some debate as to whether Timothy should be considered a Gentile. If he was a Gentile, however, Paul's decision to have him circumcised is illogical and suspect. There would be no justification for Paul's actions in light of his position regarding proselyte circumcision. Why not circumcise Titus or any other Gentile Christian for that matter? Paul's decision only makes sense if both Paul and Timothy viewed Timothy as having a claim to Jewish heritage. Because Paul had Timothy circumcised, it is clear that they both considered Timothy a Jew.

(2) *Paul wanted Timothy to be Torah compliant.*

It is one thing for a Gentile to be uncircumcised, but quite another for a Jew. God spoke to Israel:

---

[2] *Talmud*, T.J. Yebamoth, ii. 6
[3] Stern, *Jewish New Testament Commentary*, 281-283
[4] Lawrence Schiffman, *Who Was A Jew?* (Hoboken: Ktav, 1985), 16

> *"This is My covenant which you shall keep, between Me and you and your descendants after you: Every male child among you shall be circumcised; and you shall be circumcised in the flesh of your foreskins, and it shall be a sign of the covenant between Me and you. He who is eight days old among you shall be circumcised, every male child in your generations, he who is born in your house or bought with money from any foreigner who is not your descendant. He who is born in your house and he who is bought with your money must be circumcised, and My covenant shall be in your flesh for an everlasting covenant. And the uncircumcised male child, who is not circumcised in the flesh of his foreskin, that person shall be cut off from his people; he has broken My covenant."* – Genesis 17:10-14

An uncircumcised Jew is in violation of the covenant. Paul wanted Timothy to fulfill the Torah as a descendant of Abraham. It is not clear as to why Timothy had delayed his circumcision up to this point in his life. Perhaps his father had recently died or the occasion to travel with Paul presented the opportunity. What is clear is that Paul had Timothy circumcised because of the Torah, not in spite of it.

(3) *Timothy was put forth as a teacher of the law.*

As Paul's co-laborer, Timothy's authority to teach would have been met with objection, as it is a reproach for a Jew to be uncircumcised.[5] All the Jews in that region knew that Timothy's father was Greek and that he was uncircumcised. Bringing Timothy along with him could hinder Paul's ministry and impede his ability to proclaim the gospel to the Jew first. By being circumcised, Paul and Timothy would be given a place to teach in the synagogues.

Conclusion

When considering Timothy's circumcision and Titus' non-circumcision, there is no inconsistency in Paul's position. Titus was

---

[5] Josh. 5:1-9

a Gentile. Timothy was a Jew. Whereas Timothy had Biblical reasons to be circumcised, there was no Biblical obligation for Titus.

Paul's commitment to the Torah is resolute. He does not instruct Titus to remain uncircumcised. He simply states that Titus was not "compelled to be circumcised" at the insistence of the troublers (Gal. 2:3). Timothy, on the other hand, was circumcised at Paul's insistence. Whether he took him to a *mohel*[6] or performed the circumcision himself, Paul is directly responsible for Timothy's circumcision. Apparently, Paul was not fundamentally opposed to adult circumcision.

---

[6] A person trained to perform a circumcision.

2 Corinthians 3:5-11

Truth #50: *The Holy Spirit brings life to the letter of the law.*

"The letter kills, but the spirit gives life." – 2 Corinthians 3:6b

We are familiar with the terms *letter of the law* and *spirit of the law*. In English, these phrases are used to explain laws, the reason behind them and why it's sometimes necessary to break a written law.

For example, if you completely followed your mother's instructions to never talk to strangers, you would never meet anyone new for the rest of your life. This would be tragic, especially if you planned to make friends and get married! We understand the spirit of her rule. While the letter of mom's law is to never talk to strangers, the spirit of the rule is to be guarded when approached by a stranger.

This is how we use *letter* and *spirit* of the law in our culture, but we must not presume this is what Paul means here. As it turns out, this is not at all how these phrases are to be understood Biblically.

In 2 Corinthians chapter 3, Paul's apostolic authority was being challenged, and the Corinthian church provided proof of his ministry credentials. Paul is complementing the Corinthians for being a living recommendation letter of his ministry.

> *"Do we begin again to commend ourselves? Or do we need, as some others, epistles of commendation to you or letters of commendation from you? You are our epistle written in our hearts, known and read by all men; clearly you are an epistle of Christ, ministered by us, written not with ink but by the Spirit of the living God, not on tablets of stone but on tablets of flesh, that is, of the heart. And we have such trust through Christ toward God." – 2 Corinthians 3:1-4*

It is in this context that Paul expands his analogy of letter versus spirit.

> *"Our sufficiency is from God, who also made us sufficient as ministers of the new covenant, not of the letter but of the Spirit; for the letter kills, but the Spirit gives life." – 2 Corinthians 3:5b-6*

Paul ties his comments about his ministry and letters of commendation to the ministry of the Spirit. Just as the Corinthians were a living epistle of Paul, so followers of Yeshua are living epistles of Christ.

"Letter" is the word *gramma* from which we derive the word grammar.[1] It is translated as *document, drawing, alphabetical character* or *written record*.[2] *Gramma* is a bill in the parable of the shrewd manager (Luke 16:6-7), a grammatical letter in Galatians (Gal. 6:11), the words written over Jesus on the cross (Luke 23:38), Yeshua's knowledge of Scripture (John 7:15), Paul's learnedness (Acts 26:24), written reports (Acts 28:21), and Scripture (2 Tim. 3:15). It is used similarly in Romans 2 and 7 as it is here.

Even though *nomos* is not found in this passage or anywhere in this epistle, the *letter* of the law here refers to the writings of Moses. The letter or *gramma* of the law is simply the Torah without the Spirit. It is the words of Moses devoid of the Spirit and life of Jesus – the law bereft of Christ.

Paul's argument is that the Torah is not a life-giving document unless Yeshua is revealed in it. Without God's Spirit, the Torah is just another book, reduced to mere characters on a page. It is spiritless, and without Christ, it is less glorious.

"The Spirit gives life," means that believers have been regenerated through the indwelling of the Holy Spirit. Those who walk according to the Spirit live a Spirit-filled, obedient life, for it is

---

[1] *Strong's* #G1121 γράμμα
[2] *Thayer's, gramma;* https://www.etymonline.com/word/-gram?ref=etymonlinecrossrefer-ence

God's Spirit that empowers us to live righteously. Through the revelation of the Messiah, the Spirit breathes new life into us and illuminates God's word in our hearts. One beautiful aspect of the new covenant is that the Torah is being written on our hearts – not with ink or on tablets of stone but "by the Spirit of the Living God" (v.3).

Those who live by the *gramma* and only pursue the letter of the Torah are lost and without hope. They have no revelation of Jesus and therefore seek God and His word without the aid of the Spirit. According to Paul, studying Scripture yet failing to see Yeshua as the central target of the Torah is futile and ultimately fatal.

To sum up, this is how we should view Paul's use of the terms letter and spirit of the law:

<u>Letter of the law</u>: The words of the Torah read without faith in Christ and without the illumination of God's Spirit.

<u>Spirit of the law</u>: The words of the Torah read with faith in Christ and with the illumination of the God's Spirit.

> *"But if the ministry of death, written and engraved in stones, was glorious, so that the children of Israel could not steadfastly behold the face of Moses for the glory of his countenance; which glory was to be done away: How shall not the ministry of the Spirit be more glorious? For if the ministry of condemnation had glory, much more shall the ministry of righteousness abound in glory. For even that which was made glorious had no glory in this respect, by reason of the glory that excels. For if that which is done away was glorious, much more that which remains is glorious." - 2 Corinthians 3:7-11 King James 2000 Bible*

For those outside of Christ, the letter of the law is a "ministry of death and condemnation." A person who attempts to keep the entire Law or looks to Moses for their redemption is still judged and condemned as a sinner *by* the Law of Moses. The letter kills even the one giving the strictest attention to the Torah.

But the Torah is a ministry of life to those who look to Christ and walk in the Spirit. Whereas the letter of the law brings judgment, the Spirit of the law brings righteousness. It is life to those who believe and death to those who don't. In an odd twist, the Torah is well suited, perhaps even better suited, for followers of Christ who walk according to the Spirit.

Conclusion

Paul admits that the old covenant has glory. It was so glorious that Moses' face radiated at its giving. Yet, what was to come would be even more glorious. Moses simply caught a glimpse of it.

The ministry of the Spirit through Yeshua is more glorious than the letter of the law. This doesn't minimize the life of Moses as much as it amplifies the ministry of Jesus. Like shining a flashlight directly into the sun, the glory of Mount Sinai was dim compared to the glory of Calvary.

For believers, death and condemnation have been "done away" with (v.11). Praise be to God! Those who find faith and glory in the Son of God have been completely separated from the ministry of condemnation and death.

2 THESSALONIANS 2:7-8

Truth #51: *Anti-Torah is anti-Christ.*

Paul writes of several mysteries in his letters. There's *the mystery of faith* (1 Tim. 3:9), *the mystery of godliness* (1 Tim. 3:16) *the mystery of Christ and the church* (Eph. 5:32), *the mystery of the resurrection of the dead* (1 Cor. 15:51), and *the mystery of the gospel* (Rom. 11:25, Eph. 3:9, Col. 1:26-27), which is also *the mystery of Christ* (Col. 4:3). This is the mystery that reveals Gentiles are co-heirs and included in God's plan of salvation.

But there is another mystery that Paul identifies as *the mystery of lawlessness*.

> *"For the mystery of lawlessness (anomia) is already at work; only He who now restrains will do so until He is taken out of the way. And then the lawless one (anomos) will be revealed, whom the Lord will consume with the breath of His mouth and destroy with the brightness of His coming." - 2 Thessalonians 2:7-8*

Spiritual Lawlessness

It is tempting to think of lawlessness in civic terms here; that Paul is foreseeing a time marked by chaos, violence and anarchy. This may be, but there is little doubt the apostle is describing lawlessness of the heart. The last days will bring a full manifestation of sinful rebellion and the shunning of God's ways proliferated by the lawless one. While end-time lawlessness may include civil lawlessness, first and foremost it must entail moral lawlessness, for lawless behavior comes from a lawless heart.

The Greek word for lawlessness is *anomia*.[1] It means to *violate, be ignorant of, hold contempt for* or *distance oneself from the law*.[2] *Anomia* is often translated *wickedness, iniquity, unrighteousness* and *transgression*.

Paul uses *anomia* elsewhere.

> "For just as you presented your members as slaves of uncleanness, and of lawlessness (anomia) leading to more lawlessness (anomia), so now present your members as slaves of righteousness for holiness." - Romans 6:19

> "Do not be unequally yoked together with unbelievers. For what fellowship has righteousness with lawlessness (anomia)? And what communion has light with darkness?" - 2 Corinthians 6:14

Quoting Psalm 32,

> "Blessed are those whose lawless deeds (anomia) are forgiven, and whose sins are covered." - Romans 4:7

And to Titus,

> "Who gave himself for us, that He might redeem us from every lawless deed (anomia) and purify for Himself His own special people, zealous for good works." - Titus 2:14

Civil disobedience is not adequate enough to explain Paul's use of the word. *Anomia* is spiritual rebellion. Lawless deeds are deeds of darkness, and lawlessness is likened to unholy, unrighteous behavior. According to Paul, it is from lawlessness that we have been redeemed, and it is out of lawlessness that we have been called.

---

[1] *Strong's* #G458 ἀνομία
[2] Friedman, *They Loved The Torah*, 32; Barclay, *New Testament Words*, 123; *Thayer's, anomia*

2 Thessalonians 2:7-8

Losing my Lawlessness

Jesus speaks of lawlessness in such terms in the parable of the Wheat and Tares.

> *"The Son of Man will send out His angels, and they will gather out of His kingdom all things that offend, and those who practice <u>lawlessness</u> (anomia)." - Matthew 13:41*

Elsewhere to the scribes and Pharisees,

> *"Even so you also outwardly appear righteous to men, but inside you are full of hypocrisy and <u>lawlessness</u> (anomia)." - Matthew 23:28*

And about the end times,

> *"And because <u>lawlessness</u> (anomia) will abound, the love of many will grow cold." - Matthew 24:12*

And,

> *"Not everyone who says to me, 'Lord, Lord,' shall enter the kingdom of heaven, but he who does the will of My Father in heaven. Many will say to me in that day, 'Lord, Lord, have we not prophesied in Your name, cast out demons in Your name, and done many wonders in Your name?' And then I will declare to them, 'I never knew you, depart from Me, you who practice <u>lawlessness</u> (anomia).'" Matthew 7:21-23*

This last reference might be the most haunting. Yeshua takes us forward to the Day when all will stand before Him. Many will call Him *Lord* but cast out His presence. They prophesied. They expelled demons. They performed miracles in His name, but He will declare to them,

> *"I never knew you. Depart from Me, you who practice anomia." (v.23)*

Some make a practice of defying Scripture to their own demise. They drift away from God's word and subsequently drift away from his heart. But in rejecting God's word we reject God, and in forsaking his commands we forsake Christ. These ones thought their lives and spiritual gifts pleased him. How wrong they were and will be!

It is possible to profess God's name but profane his will. Jesus emphasized *doing* the will of the Father above miracles, knowledge, authority and proclamation. Calling Jesus *Lord* is not sufficient enough proof that he is truly the lord of our lives.

Obedience is the pathway to the kingdom of Heaven. It is not enough to tell others what to believe if we do not practice what we profess. Those who willfully make a practice of neglecting God's commandments and choose to live lawlessly will ultimately and eternally be separated from God. This is a sharp reminder that even powerfully gifted ministers and prophetic churches can fall prey to the deception of lawlessness.

You who practice lawlessness is the oft-neglected part of this passage, yet the most revealing. These ministers were not civil anarchists inciting reckless violence in the streets. They were barred from the kingdom of heaven for being morally lawless. Yeshua's words are sobering, and only in the context of moral lawlessness do they make sense.

What should be our attitude toward lawlessness? We should treat lawlessness the same way we treat sin. John writes,

> "*Whoever commits sin also commits lawlessness (anomia), and sin is lawlessness (anomia).*" - 1 John 3:4

From a Biblical perspective, sin is lawlessness, and lawlessness is Torahlessness. Torahlessness is lawless in that it opposes the laws of God. Just as civil lawlessness shakes its fist in defiance of authority, spiritual lawlessness shakes its fist in defiance of God's Word. We flirt with the sin of *anomia* when we harbor contempt for the Torah and make a practice of violating it.

Conclusion

Yeshua is God's Torah – the living, breathing, walking Word of God. To be anti-Torah is to be anti-Christ. Paul reveals that one glaring characteristic of the anti-Christ and those who walk in the spirit of the anti-Christ is disdain for the Torah of God. The teaching that Yeshua and Paul stood against the Torah carelessly accuses them of being like the anti-Christ. But how can Christ be anti-Christ?

Torahlessness is not to be taken lightly. The mystery of lawlessness was already at work in Paul's time and is an evil that will fully manifest in the last days. When society and ministers distance themselves from the Torah, we distance ourselves from Christ. We must remain vigilant to weed lawlessness out of every area of our lives – out of our hearts, minds, churches and theology.

Section V

Sabbath & The Feasts

1 Corinthians 5

Truth #52: *Paul instructed the Corinthians to observe Passover.*

"Christ, our Passover, was sacrificed for us. Therefore let us keep the feast." – 1 Cor. 5:7-8

In this verse, Paul is encouraging the believers to celebrate the Passover and keep the Feast of Unleavened Bread. In fact, Paul had an expectation that the believers of Corinth, a church he planted, would observe Passover and the seven-day Festival of Unleavened Bread.

William Conybeare writes,

> "There seems no difficulty in supposing the Gentile Christians joined with the Jewish Christians in celebrating the Paschal feast after the Jewish manner, at least to the extent of abstaining from leaven in the love-feasts. And we see that St. Paul still observed the 'days of unleavened bread' at this period of his life, from Act xx.6"[1]

Many scholars believe Paul penned 1 Corinthians around 55 A.D. Given the reference to Passover, it is reasoned that Paul's letter may have been written or received around the time of the Feast of Unleavened Bread. It is remarkable that even twenty-five years after the ascension of Christ a predominantly Gentile church was observing the oldest known Biblical holiday. The thought of ignoring or removing the celebration of Passover for Gentile converts never seemed to cross Paul's mind. Instead, the apostle takes the time to teach about the meaning of this festival to his Gentile audience.

---

[1] William Conybeare, *The Life and Epistle of St. Paul* (Grand Rapids: Eerdmans, 1978), 390

Scripture proclaims that Passover is an "everlasting ordinance" (Ex. 12:14) that will be observed "forever" (Ex. 12:24). In other words, it's a holy day that is not going away.

Communion of the Feast

When we serve the bread and wine in our meetings, let us not forget its origins. It was in the context of Passover that Yeshua ate the bread and drank the wine with his disciples. The Last Supper was a Passover meal. One could say that the original communion is Passover, and it is observed annually.

When Jesus says, "Do this in remembrance of me," He is not just speaking of eating the bread and drinking the wine. He is speaking of Passover. For the followers of Christ, the connection between the Passover and communion is forever intertwined. Communion cannot be separated from the context of Passover. Let us remember His example and the symbolism, not forsaking one for the other.

Later in this letter, Paul mentions another feast.

> *"I will tarry in Ephesus until Pentecost." – 1 Corinthians 16:8*

The fact that Paul references both Pentecost and Passover in the same epistle indicates that God's appointed times served as markers in time for the early church and for Paul. If Paul observed these festivals and referenced them with those that had little former familiarity with the Jewish calendar, it stands to reason that time was kept by the Corinthian church in accordance with the majority Jewish calendar.

It also indicates that these converts had already been instructed in the feasts of the Lord. Combined with the fact that Paul personally celebrated the Feast of Weeks and contributed to the sacrificial system of the temple, it is reasonable to conclude that Paul honored the Biblical holidays and extended that expectation to those he discipled.

Is there Biblical evidence that early believers kept the Biblical festivals and observed Sabbath?
Luke writes,

> *"When the day of Pentecost had fully come, they were all with one accord in one place" - Acts 2:1*

The 120 in the upper room were gathered on the day of Pentecost. Among them were Yeshua's disciples, mother and brothers. They were all together in one place for the festival of Pentecost (*Shavuot*). Since Pentecost is the anniversary of the giving of the Torah on Mount Sinai, it is significant that the outpouring of the Holy Spirit occurred at the precise moment the Feast of Pentecost was being celebrated.

One reference notes,

> "The New Testament shows clearly that Pentecost was celebrated in the first century and that it came to have a special Christian significance. In writing to the Corinthians, Paul says that he plans to stay in Ephesus until Pentecost (1 Cor. 16:8). Apparently, he expects his readers to understand his meaning, a fact that has led some interpreters to suggest that Pentecost had become a Christian observance as early as Paul's time."[2]

On several occasions in the book of Acts, Luke refers to the festivals of the Lord. He specifically mentions Passover and the Feast of Unleavened Bread twice.[3] He refers to *Yom Kippur* (the Day of Atonement) as "the Fast."[4] The fact that Luke would use the feasts as calendar markers shows that these festivals were not foreign to him or to Theophilus.

It cannot be denied that the feasts play a significant role in our Christian history. Jesus was crucified on Passover. He was raised to

---

[2] Paul Achtemier, *Harper's Bible Dictionary* (San Francisco: Harper and Row, 1985), "Pentecost"
[3] Acts 12:3-4; 20:6
[4] Acts 27:9

life on First Fruits and during the Feast of Unleavened Bread. The disciples were baptized in the Holy Spirit on the day of Pentecost. Some assert that Yeshua was born during the Feast of Tabernacles (*Succot*) and will return around the Feast of Trumpets (*Yom Teruah*).

The holidays found in the Apostolic Scriptures are the ones we read about in the Hebrew Scriptures - Passover, Pentecost, the Feast of Tabernacles, Feast of Trumpets, Feast of Unleavened Bread, First Fruits and Day of Atonement. Through the ministry of Christ and the outpouring of the Holy Spirit, our spiritual history and our life in the Spirit are indelibly and eternally linked to God's appointed times.

Why is it that we don't, in general, observe the same holidays today as our spiritual forefathers did?

I once saw a giant sign on a Catholic church inviting the public to a Feast of the Assumption mass. "What is this?" I thought. I don't remember reading about this feast in Scripture. Obviously, I did not grow up Catholic.

It is our "assumption" that God has given us new Christian holidays that replace the feasts of the Lord. This is only assumption. In reality, Christian holidays foreign to the Bible are secular feasts and might fall more in line with the pagan holy days of our culture than with the Bible.

Many acknowledge the prophetic symbolism of Yeshua in the Biblical feasts, but when these festivals come around annually they often quietly escape us. Because we are not in the practice of observing God's appointed times, we lose the richness of these great festivals and in the process lose our connection with the apostolic church. I wonder if we have also lost our cadence with God and the divine appointments Heaven has scheduled with earth. Could this be one of the contributing reasons why the western church today lacks the power and influence of the church of Acts?

Sabbath

During Paul's missionary journeys, we also read that he and his companions regularly attended the synagogue on the Sabbath. In Antioch Pisidia, they "went into the synagogue on the Sabbath day and sat down" (Acts 13:14). After the reading of the Torah and the Prophets, Paul was given the floor and preached Christ to those in attendance. Afterward, "the Gentiles begged that these words might be preached to them the next Sabbath...On the next Sabbath almost the whole city came together to hear the word of God" (Acts 13:42,44).

Upon receiving his Macedonian call, Paul sailed to the city of Philippi. Together with Silas, Timothy and Luke, they went out to the riverside on Sabbath "where prayer was customarily made" (Acts 16:13). In Thessalonica, there was a synagogue. "Paul, as his custom was, went in to them, and for three Sabbaths reasoned with them from the Scriptures" (Acts 17:2). This resulted in a great multitude of devout Greeks, including women, joining Paul and Silas. In Corinth, we read that Paul "reasoned in the synagogues every Sabbath, and persuaded both Jews and Greeks" (Acts 18:4).

From these verses we can draw a couple conclusions. (1) It was customary for Paul to attend the synagogue each Sabbath in the city he was visiting. (2) Paul's Jewish and Gentile companions attended Sabbath services with him during his missionary journeys. (3) Both Jews and God-fearing Greeks were found in these synagogues. (4) Believing Jews and believing Gentiles gathered each Shabbat to pray and to hear the preached word. (5) Paul's company adhered to the Jewish calendar.

Because Jesus and Paul both regularly attended the synagogue on the Sabbath, we can conclude that it was their practice to observe the Sabbath day.

In bringing this to light, I am not suggesting that we make a mass exodus from our churches and return to the synagogue. What I am suggesting is that the Sabbath day should be given a greater place of prominence in our churches, lifestyle and worship. Yeshua proclaimed,

> *"The Sabbath was made for man, and not man for the Sabbath. Therefore, the son of man is also Lord of the Sabbath." – Mark 2:27-28*

God has given us a gift – the gift of Sabbath. It is a gift to our minds for rest, to our bodies for recovery and to our spirits for rejuvenation. When we disregard the Sabbath day, we miss out on this wonderful gift from God.

Yeshua is the Lord of every day, especially the Sabbath. It is His day, but it is also ours. The Creator has given this day from the very beginning to all mankind. The Father has set aside the seventh day for our benefit. We don't live in bondage to the Sabbath. The Sabbath lives to serve us.

Since Jesus is Lord of the Sabbath, it stands to reason that He would not identify Himself as Lord of something He meant to abolish. He still keeps the Sabbath with us and will continue to do so in the kingdom of God. Isaiah prophesies,

> *"'And it shall come to pass that from one New Moon to another, and from one Sabbath to another, all flesh shall come to worship before Me,' says the Lord." - Isaiah 66:23*

The Sabbath is an eternal commission.[5] It was at creation, during Abraham, before Sinai, after Babylonian captivity, before Christ, at the time of Yeshua, after the resurrection, in the church of Acts, during the end times and in the Millennium. In observing the Sabbath, we are proclaiming creationism to an evolutionary world and prophesying that the Torah will still be observed in the age to come.[6]

---

[5] Ex. 31:16
[6] Deut. 30:1-10, Is. 2:2-3, Jer. 31:33, Ezek. 36:26-27, 37:24, Micah 4:2, Zech. 8:23, 14:16-18, Rev. 12:17, 14:12

Conclusion

In Scripture, the feasts of the Lord are never called the feasts of Israel. This is man's title. As well, there is no direct instruction in the Bible that discontinues the Sabbath day or replaces it with Sunday. This is also our doing.

Funny how there is radio silence from our pulpits regarding Sabbath, the feasts and a Biblical diet but volumes of sermons about tithing. Yet both instructions come from the very same Scriptures we confess to regard.

In ancient times, you knew what god a person worshipped by observing what festivals they regarded. If we took a step back and took a good look at ourselves, I wonder what could be said of us.

GALATIANS 4:10-11

Truth #53: *Paul calls the Galatians out of pagan holidays, not Biblical holidays.*

> *"When you did not know God, you served those which by nature are not gods...How is it that you turn again to the weak and beggarly elements, to which you desire again to be in bondage? <u>You observe days and months and seasons and years.</u> I am afraid for you, lest I have labored for you in vain." Galatians 4:8-11*

It is likely you have been taught that Sabbath, feasts, Jubilee years and new moon festivals are the observations that Paul is referencing here. Since Judaism does have its fair share of holy days, it is easy to see the correlation. Some reason that the Galatians were being persuaded by Judaizers to celebrate "Jewish" holidays.

The pushback to this position, however, is that Paul describes these observances as having "an appearance of wisdom in self-imposed religion, false humility and neglect of the body, but are of no value against the indulgence of the flesh" (Col. 2:23). He calls them "the weak and beggarly elements" which bring bondage (Gal. 4:9). Are Biblical holy days self-imposed with false humility and body-neglect? Were God's appointed times weak and beggarly when He established them? This does not seem to be a very accurate description of the God-ordained, joyous celebrations of worship given to us in Scripture.

Almost every Biblical scholar agrees that the church of Galatia was predominantly Gentile and had come out of paganism. Yet almost every commentary interprets Paul's days, months, seasons and years as Jewish holidays. How could those who never served the God of Israel or followed the Torah return to something they never practiced in the first place? It is impossible for these Galatian Gentiles, who previously served idols and did not know the God of Israel, to backslide into Jewish practices and Biblical holidays. They had never observed Sabbath, new moon festivals or the feasts in their former life of sin. How could they return to a Jewish calendar that they never once observed?

It doesn't take much digging to uncover that Israel is not the only culture to observe holy calendar days. In addition to calendar observances found within the Egyptian and Babylonian cultures, such as the Feast of Drunkenness (Egyptian Tekh Festival) or the months of the Babylonia calendar, the Greeks were extremely religious and quite superstitious in their celebration of the gods.

The ancient Greeks were known to hold festivals throughout the year. There was the Panathena of Athens held in observance of Athena's birthday. It involved a processional through the city of Acropolis that included priests, animal sacrifices, chariots, athletes and maidens.[1] There was the Great Dionysia, which took place in March and was held in honor of Dionysus, the god of wine.[2] At this festival, participants formed a parade carrying sacred objects and phallic symbols made of wood or bronze. At the end of the parade bloodless offerings were made and animal sacrifices were performed.[3] There was also the festivals of Boedromia (in honor of Apollo), Thargelia (in honor of Artemis), Thesmorphia (in honor of Demeter and Persephone), Hermaea (in honor of Hermes), Heracleia (in honor of Hercules), Bouphonia (a sacrificial ceremony), Apaturia (mid-October to mid-November), the family festival of Amphidromia, the feast of Adonia (in honor of Aphrodite and Adonis) and the 3-day festival of Anthesteria.

Notice that Paul lists days, months, seasons and years. While the Biblical calendar does hinge on the Sabbath, holy days, as outlined in Scripture, are measured by weeks and groupings of seven. They are not measured by months, seasons and years. It should be pointed

---

[1] http://factsanddetails.com/world/cat56/sub406/entry-6197.html
[2] *Encyclopedia Britannica*, "Great Dionysia: Greek Festival" [Online]. Available: www.britannica.com
[3] http://www.reneeoconnorfan.pixel51.com/xenaera/greekholidays/index.html

out that weeks, which is predominant in the Hebrew calendar, is notably absent from Paul's list of calendar observances.

Given that the context is about those things that the Galatian Christians were turning again to, it is unlikely that Paul is referring to any Biblical feast specifically or to any Biblical festival whatsoever. Pagan days, months and seasons of the Greek festivals are a better fit here. These Gentile converts once observed these pagan festivals. The apostle is concerned that they are not letting go of these worldly observances now that they have turned to Christ.

Conclusion

Paul is not opposed to Sabbath, Passover and the feasts of the Lord. After all, he himself observed these his entire life, even after his conversion to Christ. It is pagan festivals that alarmed Paul. To put it in a modern context, perhaps we should be less alarmed with Christians observing Passover and more distressed that believers would participate in Christmas, Easter, Halloween and a Burning Man festival.

Colossians 2:16-23

Truth #54: *The Colossian believers were being judged for how they observed the Torah.*

> *"So let no one judge you in food or in drink, or regarding a festival or a new moon or sabbaths, which are a shadow of things to come, but the substance is of Christ." – Col. 2:16-17*

There are two ways to interpret these verses. One is that the Colossian believers were not actively observing Biblical holy days and dietary restrictions. They were subsequently being judged for not doing so. This position follows that Judaizers were pressuring them to take up oppressive commandments, which predicates Paul's instruction. The apostle comes to the defense of those resisting this brand of Jewish legalism. In an attempt to belittle the feasts, Paul relates external Torah observation to a shifting shadow in light of the substance of the Messiah.

The other way to read it is that the Colossians were actively participating in these holy days already and being judged for how they went about it. The young church, under the direction of Paul, did not align itself with rabbinic or sectarian Judaism. It follows that the church of Colossae was constantly under the watchful eye of scrutinizing Jews and proselytes who took it upon themselves to critique the way in which these new synagogue-attending Gentiles walked out their faith.

This position reasons that some liberty was given for personal conviction within the congregation of believers. One group of disciples were stricter in their observance of the appointed times than another. Others were inclined to observe new moon festivals and the like. As a whole, the church was likely more accepting of pagan meat (meat bought in pagan marketplaces) than the Jewish community. Paul urges the Colossians to neither judge one another in these matters nor allow outsiders to place judgments upon them. He reminds them that Christ is the source of all revelation, not the revelation itself.

The key to interpreting these verses is to first determine who is doing the judging. Most presume that opinionated Jews were doing the judging, but an adequate answer is never provided as to why they were judging these Gentile converts. Were these a group of Judaizers insisting Gentiles keep the Torah, or were they sectarian Jews scrutinizing them for the manner in which they kept the Torah?

Peace, Love & Torah

When Meljoné and I stopped eating unclean animals and started observing Sabbath and the Biblical feasts, we got some sideway stares from some friends and family. "Why are you putting yourself under the law? Are you trying to be a Jew? Don't you know about the new covenant?" Some were skeptical of our new commitment to Scripture and feared that we were falling into Jewish legalism. We understood and appreciated their concern.

If our Torah expression had been under the microscope of the Jewish community, criticism would also have been measured out for the manner in which we were attempting to walk out the Scriptures. In seeking to embrace the commandments, we were quickly introduced to the "house rules" for honoring the seventh day. We discovered that there was, in the eyes of some, a correct and incorrect way to observe the feasts. We were caught in a tug-of-war between those who accepted the majority calendar and those who rejected it, between Two-house, One-law and Sacred-Namers. Do I even need to mention the manifold opinions on what is considered a kosher diet? While one group was curious as to *why* we were obeying these commandments, another could have easily judged us for *how* we were obeying them.

I have little doubt that this is the kind of judgment that these believers were experiencing. These young Christians were likely being bombarded by both the pagan and Jewish communities.

Paul's primary focus in Colossians 2 is on the arrows coming from the Jewish camp. The circumcisers were not judging them for upholding the Torah as much as for *how* they were upholding it. Paul encourages them to follow the example of Christ and not give heed to excessive scrutiny coming from without or within.

Shadow of Coming Things

It is not a given that *food* in this passage is a reference to the clean and unclean meats of the Torah. Because Paul includes food and *drink*, a reference to the Bible's dietary guidelines is unlikely since there are no beverage restrictions listed in Leviticus 11 or Deuteronomy 14. He is more likely referencing meat and wine dedicated to an idol much like he does in Romans 14 and 1 Corinthians 8.

Realizing that the circumcisers belonged to a Jewish sect that imposed stringent requirements on its members is helpful in deciphering this passage. These groups adhered to scrupulous regulations on everything including Sabbath, the calendar, new moon festivals, and pagan food and drink. Given that the context of Colossians 2 is human tradition, those committed to these regulations were placing these same expectations upon the Colossian church.

The scrutinizers were not judging the Christians for refusing to obey the Torah as much as they were judging them for how they were obeying the Torah. As it was with all the churches, Paul feels the constant need to protect his converts from the narrow rules and faithless customs of institutionalized religion that sought to catapult them past the living Torah.

> *"Which are a shadow of the coming things, and the body* is *of the Christ." – Col. 2:17 (Young's Literal Translation)*

I prefer Young's translation of this verse for several reasons. First, some versions mistakenly translate "coming things" in the past tense. These versions render it as *things that were to come* (NIV), *were going to come* (NIRV) or *was to come* (The Message). This implies that these things are bygone and irrelevant. The original, however, is in the future tense and better understood as *things to come* (KJV, ESV), *what is to come* (NASV) or *coming things* (Young's).

Secondly, some translators inexplicably introduce a dismissive adjective before the word "shadow," such as "*mere* shadow" (NASB) and "*only* shadows" (NLT). This also is erroneously done in Hebrews 10:1.[1] By inserting *mere* or *only*, the reader is forced to belittle those things as something that should be dismissed. You should be aware that *mere* and *only* are absent from the Greek text.

Thirdly, Young prefers to use *and* over *but* and correctly includes the word *body* in the text, which some translations shy away from, even though it is present in the original Greek.

So, *a shadow of the coming things* appears to hit the mark in my opinion.

Gnosticism

"Let no one cheat you of your reward, taking delight in false humility and worship of angels, intruding into those things which he has not seen, vainly puffed up by his fleshly mind, and not holding fast to the Head, from whom all the body, nourished and knit together by joints and ligaments, grows with the increase that is from God. Therefore, if you died with Christ from the basic principles of the world, why, as though living in the world, do you subject yourselves to regulations—'Do not touch, do not taste, do not handle,' which all concern things which perish with the using—according to the commandments and doctrines of men? These things indeed have an appearance of wisdom in self-imposed religion, false humility, and neglect of the body, but are of no value against the indulgence of the flesh." – Colossians 2:18-23

In addition to Jewish regulations, the church of Colossae also wrestled with Gnostic and pagan influences. "Basic principles"

---

[1] "For the law is *only* a shadow of the good things that are coming." – NIV

could very well be a reference to the mystical practices of a particular Jewish sect, such as the Essenes. More likely, however, they are Gnostic related and address the problem of pagan influences within the church.

Some maintain that Paul is describing Torah commands here. Because the previous verses deal with Torah-related topics such as Sabbath and the feasts, it is assumed that the next verses also are Torah linked.

Running through the list, however, it becomes apparent that most do not apply to the Torah, which makes this conclusion less appealing.

Let's take a look at Paul's description of "basic principles" in this passage to determine if the apostle is disparaging the Torah or combating Gnosticism.

"*False humility*" fits the self-abasing, extreme asceticism prevalent within Gnosticism. Consequently, this phrase does not accurately describe the Torah. While rabbis and Torah teachers can certainly be falsely humble, God's word does not encourage it. The Torah comes from God. Can anything false come from God?

"*The worship of angels*" was a common practice among the Gnostics. The Torah does not encourage angel worship.

"*Intruding into those things which he has not seen*" can be indicative of the visions and meditative experiences invoked by Gnostics. Dreams and prophetic visions are certainly found in the Torah. However, they are God-given and cannot be conjured up through human effort, which seems to be what Paul is implying.

"*Vainly puffed up by his fleshly mind*" accurately describes the exaltation of secretive divine knowledge that Gnosticism boasted in. Certainly a person can be vainly puffed up by their fleshly mind in their Torah observance, but the Bible does praise vanity and pride as godly virtues.

"The basic principles of the world," as referenced in Galatians 4:3, are the hollow philosophies and vain systems of organized and institutional religion of which Gnosticism finds its origins. This rules out the Torah since the Torah consists of neither principles nor worldly values.

"Do not touch, do not taste, do not handle" was the mantra of the Gnostics. Extreme dieting, sexual abstinence and ritual fasting were distinguishing traits within Gnosticism and represent their dualistic view of matter. It could be argued that the Torah contains laws that forbid touching, tasting and handling. There could be some application here, but this is not how many would summarize the commandments of God.

"Commandments and doctrines of man" reveals that all man-made religions, Gnosticism included, have their own set of commandments and doctrines. The Torah has commandments, but the second phrase does not apply, since the Torah is not a doctrine of man but a doctrine of God. Some consider Paul's letters a doctrine of man. Would Paul consider his writings less a doctrine of man than the Torah?

"An appearance of wisdom" relates to the Gnostic belief that esoteric knowledge empowered the redemption of the human spirit. This somewhat applies to the Torah. It can give you the appearance of wisdom since it is full of God's wisdom.

"Self-imposed religion" is the man-made attempt to find spiritual freedom and harmony. There is a vast difference between self-imposed and God-imposed. The Torah is the latter.

"Neglect of the body" involves the severe treatment of the body common among the Gnostics. There is not much relation to the Torah here. There is much more feasting than fasting in the Torah, as there is only one day of fasting commanded in the Bible.

"No value against the indulgence of the flesh" demonstrates the futility of Gnosticism (or any Babel-based religion) to conquer sin. It

is true that the Torah cannot cure our sinful appetites, but it can help to curb them.

So, the overwhelming evidence points to the conclusion that which was 'cheating" the Colossians out of their reward was something other than God's Torah.

Conclusion

There are some good scholars who maintain that Paul is describing the Qumran society of the Essenes with their hermit-like, ultra-ascetic, hyper purity. The Essenes were known to be even stricter than the Pharisees in their interpretation of the Torah relating to dietary restrictions and purification regulations. Their doctrine of fasting and angels was unique and demanding.[2] There is also some evidence that the Essenes sought to worship God through mystical experiences with the aid of angels, even developing a liturgy they regarded as the pattern of heaven. It is not out of the realm of possibility that this list points to the Essenes as the circumcisers and/or those holding to the basic principles of the world.

---

[2] Santala, *Paul*, 148-9

Section VI

New Covenant

GALATIANS 3:15-22

Truth #55: *The covenant of Moses builds upon the covenant of Abraham.*

> *"Brethren, I speak in the manner of men: <u>Though it is only a man's covenant, yet if it is confirmed, no one annuls or adds to it.</u> Now to Abraham and his Seed were the promises made. He does not say, 'And to seeds' as of many, but as of one 'And to your Seed,'" who is Christ. And this I say, that <u>the law, which was four hundred and thirty years later, cannot annul the covenant</u> that was confirmed before God in Christ, that it should make the promise of no effect. For if the inheritance is of the law, it is no longer of promise, but God gave it to Abraham by promise."* – Galatians 3:15-18

We seldom use the word covenant in our culture. With the exception of marriage, covenants are largely a foreign concept to us. We are more familiar with contracts. To ancient civilizations, however, covenants were not uncommon and were commonly understood.

Whereas a contract is a legally binding *agreement* between two or more parties, a covenant is a legally binding *relationship* between two or more parties. A contract has an expiration date. A covenant is perpetual, trans-generational and when divinely initiated, eternal. Contracts, such as sports or business contracts, can be voided and replaced by newer contracts. Not so with covenants. When cutting a covenant, a more recent covenant cannot cancel a previously established one, and upon confirmation a covenant cannot be amended.

Book of Covenants

A common misconception is that there are only two covenants in the Bible. In actuality, the whole Bible is woven together by several covenants and unified in Christ. The Bible is actually a series of compounding covenants that reaffirm one another and follow the lineage of Christ, culminating with the New Covenant. By my count, there are nine covenants initiated and established by God in Scripture - Noah (Gen. 8-9), Abraham (Gen. 12-17), Isaac (Gen. 26), Jacob (Gen. 28), Sinai (Ex. 19-20), Aaron (Num. 18), Phineas (Num. 25), David (2 Sam. 7), and the New Covenant (Jer. 31).

Covenants in Scripture contain many of the same elements found in ancient Semitic covenants. Biblical covenants are perpetual, spiritual, transgenerational, eternal, and build upon one another. Most were instituted with a ceremony, have a sign and include the terms and conditions of the covenant.

For example, God's covenant with Noah is transgenerational ("you and your descendants" - Gen. 9:9), perpetual ("perpetual generations" - Gen. 9:12) and included terms and conditions for both parties (*God* - Gen. 8:21, 9:15, *Noah* - Gen. 9:1-4). This covenant was instituted with a ceremony that included sacrifices and burnt offerings (Gen. 8:20) with the rainbow serving as the sign of the covenant (Gen. 9:13).

The Abrahamic covenant follows a similar pattern. It is transgenerational ("To your descendants I give this land" – Gen. 12:7), perpetual ("Between you and Me and your descendants" – Gen. 17:7), and eternal ("I give you and your descendants this land forever" – Gen. 13:15). The terms and conditions were clearly outlined (Gen. 12:1-3, 13:14-17, 15:1-6, 22:18). A ceremony was performed (Gen. 15:7-21), and Abraham built an altar to the Lord to commemorate the covenant (Gen. 12:7). Circumcision is given as a sign of this covenant (Gen. 17:9-14).

The covenant made at Sinai, also known as the Mosaic covenant, is also transgenerational ("You shall be to Me a kingdom of priests and a holy nation" - Ex. 19:6) and eternal ("That the people may hear when I speak to you and believe you forever" - Ex. 19:9). God laid out His terms and conditions, promising to bless, heal, protect, provide and supply His presence. Israel pledged to obey all that the Lord had spoken (Ex. 24:7). Moses built a ceremonial altar and set up 12 pillars (Ex.24:4). Sabbath was given as a sign of this covenant (Ex. 31:13,17).

Like every covenant God establishes in Scripture, His covenant with Abraham was legally binding, perpetual, trans-generational and eternal. Because the Abrahamic covenant preceded the Mosaic covenant, the covenant made at Sinai could never set aside or do away with God's promises given to Abraham. In this way, the words of Moses must affirm and confirm God's covenant with Abraham.

Paul uses the fact that Abraham preceded Moses to illustrate that salvation comes through faith regardless of the law. Paul sought to teach the Gentiles that the first step in their conversion was genuine faith in Christ. Once they fully appreciated and understood that their righteousness was reckoned to them and not earned, only then would they be able to appreciate the value and necessity of God's righteous instructions.

Because Abraham came before Moses and not the other way around, it means that faith must precede obedience. The order is crucial. Torah pursuance and faith are not incompatible. So long as they are placed in proper order, faith and obedience complement one another.

Those troubling the Galatian believers took the opposite approach to salvation. They taught that salvation came first through works (physical circumcision) and then by an expression of their Jewish identity. This is contrary to the order in which Abraham received it. Abraham had faith, and then he was given circumcision. In Abraham's case, circumcision did not cancel the promises received by faith. Because it came afterward, it was not a requirement for justification.

In the same way, the Mosaic covenant could never cancel the covenant made with Abraham or any other covenant that preceded it. Salvation by faith had already been established, which means that the covenant at Sinai was never God's intended way of achieving salvation. The giving of the Torah was meant to build upon Abraham's promise, not tear it down.

Simply put, faith must come before obedience, and obedience does not cancel out faith. Our actions confirm our faith, just as Abraham's did.

Antinomian doctrine presumes that salvation could at one time be achieved through Torah observation, and that God through Christ provided a better way. This is one of the main arguments for why the Torah is no longer relevant. However, this admits that salvation could be attained outside of the work of Christ, something Paul adamantly refutes. This runs counter to Scripture and the order of the covenants.

There is not and has never been two competing paths to eternal life. There is and has always been only one – by grace through faith. Even for the saints of old, salvation was by faith, for "the just shall live by faith" (Hab. 2:4). Abraham found it. David walked it. So did all those whose names are listed in Hebrews 11. God did not start with salvation by faith, move to salvation by works, and then move back to salvation by faith. It has always been salvation by faith, even before Christ.

The righteous who lived before the coming of Christ trusted God for their salvation and looked ahead to a future Messiah for their redemption. We who live after Christ also trust God for our salvation, looking back on His finished work and looking unto our risen Lord. Like Abraham, we all now anticipate the coming of our Messiah who will restore all things as we eagerly await a city "whose builder and maker is God" (Heb. 11:10).

> *"For if the inheritance is of the law, it is no longer of promise, but God gave it to Abraham by promise." – Gal. 3:18*

If the covenant of salvation comes only to those who are Jewish and take up a faithless obligation to the Torah, as was being taught by the circumcision party, then it no longer comes by promise to all nations. Paul essentially asks, "If salvation comes by promise and not by Jewish identity, then what is the point of a Jewish conversion?"

Conclusion

The circumcisers worshipped the sign of the covenant (circumcision) instead of the Seed that it points to (Christ). In their theology, salvation could be gained through *ergon nomos*, making faith unnecessary.

What requires faith is obedience to God in response to his love through Christ. Being faithful to God and giving attention to his commands is not the opposite of faith. It is what it means to be a person of faith.

GALATIANS 4:21-31

Truth #56: *The new covenant does not abolish an established covenant.*

> *"Tell me, you who desire to be under the law, do you not hear the law? For it is written that Abraham had two sons: the one by a bondwoman, the other by a freewoman. But he who was of the bondwoman was born according to the flesh, and he of the freewoman through promise, which things are symbolic. For these are the two covenants: the one from Mount Sinai which gives birth to bondage, which is Hagar--for this Hagar is Mount Sinai in Arabia, and corresponds to Jerusalem which now is, and is in bondage with her children--but the Jerusalem above is free, which is the mother of us all. For it is written: "Rejoice, O barren, you who do not bear! Break forth and shout, you who are not in labor! For the desolate has many more children than she who has a husband." Now we, brethren, as Isaac was, are children of promise. But, as he who was born according to the flesh then persecuted him who was born according to the Spirit, even so it is now. Nevertheless what does the Scripture say? "Cast out the bondwoman and her son, for the son of the bondwoman shall not be heir with the son of the freewoman." So then, brethren, we are not children of the bondwoman but of the free."*
> Galatians 4:21-31

For those who sought justification through Jewish membership and desired to live under the terms of the old covenant, Paul gives an illustration from the Torah. His midrash of Genesis 15-18 is of two women, two covenants and two outcomes.

Traditionally, it has been taught that the bondwoman is the old covenant and the freewoman is the new covenant. The bondwoman is born of the flesh, representing Hagar and physical Israel. The freewoman is born of promise, representing Sarah and spiritual Israel. Those born of Hagar are cursed, but those who are the children of promise are free. It has served as a staple for celebrating our liberty from the law. It also infers that Jews are cursed and Torah keepers are in bondage to the flesh.

This section of Galatians is often misinterpreted - not because of what it says, but because of what it doesn't say. You will not find the terms *old* and *new covenant* in these verses. Yet almost every commentary interprets it along these lines.

Old & *Older* Covenant

The problem with the standard interpretation is that it incorrectly identifies the participants. The two covenants are not the old and the new covenants. Paul is contrasting the old covenant and the *older* covenant, specifically the covenants of Sinai and Abraham. These are the covenants in his illustration.

Let's consider.

Abraham had two sons, representing two covenants. Ishmael is the covenant at Sinai. He was born of a slave woman and brought forth through fleshly effort. Jerusalem, at that time, was likened to Ishmael. The nation of Israel, as a whole, was under this broken Sinaitic covenant and in condemnation for violating the terms of the covenant. That term was to obey everything commanded of them.[1] The covenant at Sinai was not able to free them from the bondage of sin, nor was it designed to. Ishmael represents those still in sin, condemned by the law and legally bound by covenant to obey the Torah perfectly.

Paul identifies those seeking the promises of God through circumcision and the works of the law as the children of Hagar. Gentiles turning to ritual circumcision for their justification were just as much in bondage as Jews relying on their ethnicity. Both sought God's promise by fleshly means. Both were still bound to the old covenant. Both resulted in slavery.

---

[1] Ex. 19:7

Isaac, however, represents the covenant of Abraham. He was born of promise and was brought forth through the free woman. Unlike Ishmael, his birth came by supernatural means. This symbolizes those being justified by faith. Uncircumcised Gentiles who have come to faith in Christ are free to claim the promise given to Abraham that "all nations will be blessed in your Seed." (Gen. 22:18).

The covenant of Abraham is a covenant of salvation, accessed through faith. The covenant of Sinai, however, is not a covenant of salvation. It is a covenant of sanctification and obedience. It was given to Israel so that the promises given to Abraham could come to fruition. Any participation in the covenant at Sinai outside of faith in the Seed of Abraham would not and could never insure justification. Nor could it secure the promises given to Abraham. Because Abraham was both a Gentile and a Hebrew, Jews and Gentiles gain access to God through Abraham's covenant and find right standing with God through his Seed.

This means that those who rely on their Jewish status for salvation are still in bondage to the old covenant and still carry the guilt of their sin. But those who find salvation through faith in the Seed of Abraham are children of the free. Just as Abraham was declared righteous by his faith, our salvation is brought forth not through a work of the flesh (circumcision) but through the promise of the Spirit. We belong to heavenly Jerusalem, which is the inheritance of all who are in Christ.

Notice that Mount Sinai gave birth to two women – the "free woman above" and the "slave woman below." Sarah represents mountaintop revelation and all who are birthed from above. She is the mother of promise who gives birth to the free. She signifies those who receive the Torah by faith in the presence of God.

Hagar represents bottom-of-the-mountain bondage and all who are of the flesh. She is the mother of those who write off Moses and worship the golden calf of manufactured religion. She signifies those who assume to know how God wants to be worshipped and are condemned by the Torah. This brand of religion breeds bondage.

The offspring of these two women represent two different kinds of Gentiles found within the Galatian congregation - the Gentile relying on Jewish conversion through circumcision and the Gentile relying on faith in Christ alone for salvation. While one futilely seeks to enter Abraham's family through a physical act (circumcision), the other successfully finds it through a supernatural act (faith in Christ).

Hagar cannot replace Sarah, just as Sinai cannot replace Abraham. Salvation is through the covenant of Abraham, sanctification through the covenant at Sinai. Paul disagrees with those who maintain that the Torah has been abolished, for he taught that an established covenant cannot be abolished by a newer covenant. Unfortunately, antinomianism serves to nullify the work of sanctification in the life of a Christian and diminish those who obey God's word in faith.

Paul's illustration depicts promise versus works, flesh versus spirit, that which is born of faith versus that which is born of flesh. The contrast is between heavenly promise and man-made effort.

Since Paul is advocating salvation by faith in the face of the gospel of circumcision, this interpretation is the most contextually responsible. It is consistent with the stated purpose of Paul's letter and avoids inserting a foreign and confusing narrative into the text.

> *"But as he who was born according to the flesh then persecuted him who was born according to the spirit, even so it is now." – Galatians 4:29*

This is yet another reference to the troublers. The Judean Pharisees pushing circumcision were taunting, criticizing and even persecuting these uncircumcised Gentile believers. Just as it was with Sarah and Hagar, so it was with them.

Rock, Paper, Spirit

The story of the Torah did not end with Moses' generation. What was initially written on stone soon went to paper. In the centuries following, scribes meticulously transcribed the Torah onto scrolls of parchment, which preserved the writings of Moses.

While the words of the Torah are available for all to read, the original stone tablets of the Ten Commandments have been hidden from us. Even Indiana Jones couldn't find them if he tried, because the location of the Ark of the Covenant is still yet unknown. But they are not lost to us. God has burned these words upon our hearts.

Speaking of a new covenant, Jeremiah writes,

> *"But this is the covenant I will make with the house of Israel after those days, says the Lord. I will put my law (Torah) in their minds, and write it on their hearts." - Jeremiah 31:33*

The journey of the Torah is as simple as *Rock-Paper-Spirit*. God's words were inscribed on *rock*, copied to *paper*, and are now being written by the *Spirit* upon our hearts. The written Torah is no longer confined to ink and paper. It is now a part of us. We are becoming one with God's word. The Holy Spirit is implanting it in our thoughts and etching it upon our hearts.

Even though the tablets are lost to us, God's word lives on. It lives on in you and me. In this sense, we have become a word from heaven sent to earth to accomplish what He sent it to do.

Which laws are being written on our hearts? The answer can only be all of them. The Holy Spirit doesn't accept some only to discard others. Just as Jesus embodied all of God's commands, all of God's words are being inscribed upon our hearts and minds, even the ones we tend to discount today.

Since Jesus represents all that comes from the Father, including the Torah, He then is the manifest Word of God. He is the Torah with skin and bones. Following Him means we also follow the laws that He had a hand in writing.

We may ask, "How can anyone obey all of God's laws?" We try, but we fall short. This is why we need a Savior. However, this shouldn't discourage us in our quest for Christlikeness. "As He is, so are we in this world" (1 John 4:17). Like Jesus, it is not impossible to be fully pleasing to the Lord in all our ways. We have the power to live a blameless life, because He showed us the way.

When Israel received the Torah, it was given to them *after* their deliverance from Egypt, not before. Why after and not before? This was because God's people had to come out of captivity first and pass through the Red Sea before they could receive the Torah. As Egyptian slaves, they could not fully obey God's commandments. They were still being held in bondage to Pharaoh and did not have the liberty to rest one day a week, care for a tabernacle or observe a holy day.

Similarly, we too have come out of the land of Egypt. We have been delivered from slavery to sin and have passed through the waters of baptism. The blood of Jesus, our Passover Lamb, is smeared over the doorpost of our hearts. We have escaped death and are en route to our Promised Land.

Before Christ we were held captive to sin and were incapable of obeying God's commands. But a sacrifice has been made. A baptism has occurred. And our deliverance has come. We are now free - free to hear his voice, free to receive his instructions and free to become like Christ. We are emancipated from our slavery and liberated to respond to his love. Sin can no longer keep us from the narrow path.

In this way, the Torah is for the redeemed, not the unredeemed; for the free, not the slave. God's laws are first and foremost for the people of God. Through the commandments we can know the will of our Father, and in the Torah we have been entrusted with the very words of our Creator.

Conclusion

Redemption always precedes commandment. We now can view the law from a post-salvation perspective. Our response to His mercy is not a legalistic obligation but a voluntary debt of love. Obedience to the Torah has never been factored into the equation of our salvation, but it still remains a targeted outcome of the saved.

For the disciple of Christ, Torah keeping is not an attempt to add to the work of Christ. It is our joyful response to the work of Christ. It is our heartfelt endeavor to be like Him. He is the beautiful completion of the Torah – the substance of the law. Just like in the Exodus, obedience is perfected after our deliverance, not before. If before, it is legalism, but if after, it is love.

D.L Moody said,

> "God, being a perfect God, had to give a perfect Law, and the Law was not given to save men but to measure them."[2]

Well said, Mr. Moody. The law lifts up our standard of living but is unable to lift us up to that standard because of our imperfection. While it is perfect, it cannot perfect us.

The Torah could never save us. It never will. This is not its function, and it is futile to attempt to earn salvation through Torah observance.

The Torah, rather, is God's plumb line for all of humanity. It measures us, directs us to a loving Savior and shows us how to walk in His righteousness in response to God's saving grace.

---

[2] Ray Comfort, *The Evidence Bible* (Gainesville: Bridge Logos, 2001), 594

2 CORINTHIANS 3:12-18

Truth #57: *Jesus reveals the glory of the Torah.*

> *"Therefore, since we have such hope, we use great boldness of speech—unlike Moses, who put a veil over his face so that the children of Israel could not look steadily at the end of what was passing away. But their minds were blinded. For until this day the same veil remains unlifted in the reading of the <u>Old Testament</u>, because the* veil *is taken away in Christ. But even to this day, when Moses is read, a veil lies on their heart. Nevertheless when one turns to the Lord, the veil is taken away." – 2 Corinthians 3:12-16*

It might shock you to learn that this is the only place in the Bible where the term *old testament* (or its synonym *old covenant*) is found. Nowhere else is it used. Furthermore, when Paul speaks of an old testament, he is not referring to the Hebrew Scriptures, since the Old Testament was not called the Old Testament in Paul's day. The old testament/covenant reference here specifically refers to the Torah of Moses.

Old & New Alike

Before we examine the differences between the old and new covenants, there are some similarities. Both covenants are between God and Israel. Both are eternal, trans-generational and ceremonial. The Torah is central to each, and both contain terms, conditions and a sign.

Mosaic Covenant

Eternal: "That the people may hear when I speak to you and believe you forever" (Ex. 19:9).

Transgenerational: "You shall be to Me a kingdom of priests and a holy nation" (Ex. 19:6).

Ceremony: Moses "built an altar at the foot of the mountain, and twelve pillars according to the twelve tribes of Israel" (Ex. 24:4).
Terms and Conditions: God promised to bless, heal, protect, provide and supply His presence. Israel pledged, "All that the LORD has said we will do, and be obedient" (Ex. 24:7).

Sign: The Sabbath. "My Sabbaths you shall keep, for it *is* a sign between Me and you throughout your generations…It *is* a sign between Me and the children of Israel forever; for *in* six days the LORD made the heavens and the earth, and on the seventh day He rested'" (Ex. 31:13,17).

New Covenant

Eternal: The sun, moon, stars and sea bear witness that "the seed of Israel shall (never) cease from being a nation before Me forever" (Jer. 3:35-36).

Transgenerational: "You *are* a chosen generation, a royal priesthood, a holy nation" (1 Peter 2:9).

Ceremony: The Passover Communion. "Then He took the cup, and gave *it* to them, saying, 'Drink from it, all of you. For this is My blood of the new covenant, which is shed for many for the remission of sins'" (Matt. 26:27-28).

Terms and Conditions: God will put the Torah upon hearts and minds. Israel will be God's people. All will know the Lord, and their sins will be forgiven (Jer. 31:33-34).

Sign: The resurrection. "So the Jews answered and said to Him, 'What sign do You show to us, since You do these things?' Jesus answered and said to them, 'Destroy this temple, and in three days I will raise it up'" (John 2:18-19). "Then some of the scribes and Pharisees answered, saying, 'Teacher, we want to see a sign from You.' But He answered and said to them, 'An evil and adulterous generation seeks after a sign, and no sign will be given except the sign of the prophet Jonah. For as Jonah was three days and three nights in the belly of the great fish, so will the Son of Man be three days and three nights in the heart of the earth'" (Matt. 12:38-40).

Kainos Covenant

Some refer to the new covenant as the *renewed covenant*. It is reasoned that the new covenant restores the broken old covenant. There is some linguistic reasoning behind this.

(1) There are two words in Greek for "new": *neos*[1] and *kainos*.[2] *Neos* means new in time or youthful.[3] It infers something that is brand new or has never existed.[4] *Kainos* means new in quality. It carries overtones of freshness, sometimes even renewing something that already exists.[5] An example of this is found in Matthew 9, "They put new (*neos*) wine into new (*kainos*) wineskins, and both are preserved." (Matt. 9:17)

(2) The Hebrew word "new" in Jeremiah 31:31 to describe the new covenant is *chadash*.[6] The writer of Hebrews and the Septuagint (LXX) translators chose to translate the Hebrew word *chadash* using the Greek word *kainos*. Furthermore, with the exception of Hebrews 12:24, *kainos* is always used for the new covenant in the Apostolic Scriptures[7], including here in 2 Corinthians 3.

Eight times the new covenant is called the *kainos* covenant. Once it is referred to as the *neos* covenant. This could indicate that the difference between *neos* and *kainos* is not as wide as some assert. Perhaps they are more similar than distinct. There must, however, be some distinction since they are used separately.

---

[1] *Strong's* #G3501 νέος
[2] *Strong's* #G2537 καινός
[3] *Vine's, neos;* Pierce, *Outline of Biblical Usage, neos*
[4] *Thayer's*, νέος
[5] *Vine's, kainos;* *Thayer's*, καινός
[6] *Strong's* #H2319 חָדָשׁ
[7] Matt. 26:28, Mark 14:24, Luke 22:20, 1 Cor. 11:25, 2 Cor. 3:6, Heb. 3:6, 8:8, 8:13, 9:15

In my estimation, the best translation is *new* covenant. However, a case can be made for calling it the *renewed* covenant. From this perspective, the new covenant is the old covenant made fresh again by the Holy Spirit.

Wedding Veil

> *"My covenant which they broke, though I was a husband to them." - Jeremiah 31:32*

God uses marital language to describe His original covenant with Israel. Marriage might be the best modern example of a covenant relationship. We find the elements of ancient Semitic covenants interwoven within the ceremonies in traditional weddings.

A traditional western wedding often takes place in a church with a minister, ceremony and reception. This is similar to ancient near Eastern covenants. Ancient covenant cutting involved a ceremony with a sacrifice and a shared meal.

Like a covenant, marriage is designed to be eternal. Two people unite two families forever. The union is transgenerational, as their offspring are family-tied blood relatives. There is an exchange of names, which was commonplace in covenant making. The traditional wedding vows are the terms and conditions of this covenant. The inclusion of "Till death do us part" indicates that covenants are until death. In theory, the two parties pledge to die before breaking the covenant. The token or sign of this covenant is the wedding ring.

In these verses, Paul refers to a veil but is actually talking about reading of the Torah. There were two groups of people reading the Torah – those approaching it with a veiled heart and those approaching it with an unveiled heart. Those with a veiled heart are those who read the letter of the law without faith and without the benefit of the Spirit. For them, the Torah produces death and condemnation. Just as Moses veiled his face and hid the people from the glory of Christ, their minds are blinded from seeing the glory of

Yeshua. In this way, the old covenant becomes symbolic for attempting to keep God's commandments outside of faith in Christ.

Today, when the Torah is taken out and read in the synagogue, a veil still remains over the eyes of unbelieving Jews. Israel, as a whole, is blinded from the truth written in the very pages of the Torah about Jesus the Messiah. When the Torah is studied without faith and without the Spirit, Yeshua is hidden. A veil is drawn so that Israel cannot see what Moses and the elders saw.

> *"Moses went up, also Aaron, Nadab, and Abihu, and seventy of the elders of Israel, and they saw the God of Israel. And there was under His feet as it were a paved work of sapphire stone...They saw God, and they ate and drank." - Exodus 24:9-11*

Moses and the leaders saw God in bodily form. They spoke and ate with the Anointed One on that holy mountain. Quite literally, the glory that rested upon Moses was the glory and revelation of the Messiah. According to Paul, Moses veiled Israel from seeing this glory not because he was embarrassed by his glowing face or because the people were afraid. He veiled his face because the time of Christ had not yet come. Just as Yeshua veiled his teachings with parables, so the glory of Christ is veiled from Israel.

For those in Yeshua, however, the veil has been removed. Our spiritual eyes have been opened. We are being transformed into the image of the Son. We see by faith what Moses saw in the natural. We see what Paul describes a few verses later – "the light of the gospel of the glory of God in the face of Christ" (2 Cor. 4:4,6).

Notice that both the veiled and the unveiled are reading and hearing the same Torah. The person reading the Torah by faith is reading the same Torah as the person reading it without faith. It is not the Torah that changes but the faith of the reader.

The letter of the law is written with ink, but the Torah of the Spirit is written by the Spirit upon our hearts. The letter on stone brings condemnation, but the Spirit on the soul brings life. Where the Torah was once dead to us, the Spirit of the Torah is now alive within us. Where it once killed, it is now endowed with the life of the Spirit.

The Holy Spirit is the key that unlocks the Scriptures to us. Only God's Spirit can give life to the Torah. He opens our eyes to see Christ on every page. He illuminates our hearts to the truth about our Savior. The words of the Bible are spiritless to the person bereft of the Spirit, but they are spiritual to those who walk in the Spirit. It is the Spirit of God that takes away the veil. When He takes it away, we see Yeshua everywhere in Scripture, including in the Torah.

> *"Now the Lord is the Spirit; and where the Spirit of the Lord is, there is liberty. But we all, with unveiled face, beholding as in a mirror the glory of the Lord, are being transformed into the same image from glory to glory, just as by the Spirit of the Lord." – 2 Corinthians 3:17-18*

Mirrors in the Bible can symbolize the written word of God.[8] In this way we are being transformed into the image of Christ through the word and the Spirit. With unveiled faces we now see what Moses saw – the glory of the Messiah. Our liberty is not from the Torah but to the Torah. Our freedom is not from the obligation of the law but from the condemnation of it. We have gone from glory to greater glory.

Conclusion

As dangerous as it is to embrace the Torah without the Spirit, it is equally destructive to embrace the Spirit without honoring God's word. Paul offers a word of wisdom to both sides. Our challenge is to avoid either extreme. Spirit without Torah is devastating. Torah without Spirit is death.

---

[8] James 1:23

HEBREWS 8

Truth #58: *The Torah is the law of the new covenant.*

After establishing that Yeshua is the mediator of a better covenant, the writer of Hebrews turns his attention to the new covenant.

> *"For if that first covenant had been faultless, then no place would have been sought for a second. Because finding fault with them, He says: 'Behold, the days are coming, says the Lord, when I will make a new covenant with the house of Israel and with the house of Judah-- not according to the covenant that I made with their fathers in the day when I took them by the hand to lead them out of the land of Egypt; because they did not continue in My covenant, and I disregarded them, says the Lord. For this is the covenant that I will make with the house of Israel after those days, says the Lord: I will put My laws in their mind and write them on their hearts; and I will be their God, and they shall be My people. None of them shall teach his neighbor, and none his brother, saying, 'Know the Lord,' for all shall know Me, from the least of them to the greatest of them. For I will be merciful to their unrighteousness, and their sins and their lawless deeds I will remember no more.'"* - Hebrews 8:7-12

Let's unpack this paragraph verse by verse.

> *"For if that first covenant had been faultless, then no place would have been sought for a second."* – Hebrews 8:7

It is not entirely settled that the writer is talking about a first and second covenant here. The word *covenant* is italicized in this verse in the King James version, because it has been inserted for contextual purposes. Typically translators introduce a transitional preposition, pronoun or linking verb for readability. Here an assumption seems to have been made.

Because *covenant* does not appear in the original manuscripts, given the context, the writer may not be referencing the first and second covenant at all. He is more likely referring to the first and second *priesthood*, since this has been the subject matter up to this point. Because the verse prior outlines the ministry, covenant and promises of our Mediator, he may be contrasting the ministry and promises of the Levitical priesthood against the ministry and promises of Yeshua as our High Priest.

This is further evidenced by the use of the word "first." Nowhere is the Mosaic covenant referred to elsewhere as the *first* covenant. We do not find that phrase anywhere in the Greek or throughout the Bible. Furthermore, the covenant at Sinai is not the first or even the second covenant found in Scripture. It is more reasonable to conclude that the author is contrasting the first and second priesthoods.

It is likely, though, that the writer means to at least include in the discussion the topic of covenant since he breaches the subject of the new covenant later in chapter 9. If indeed it is the first covenant that is referenced here, there is little doubt that it is the covenant made at Sinai. While not actually the first covenant found in the Bible, it was the first covenant that instituted priesthood.

Even though the Mosaic covenant is not the first, the writer cannot be referencing the covenants made with Noah, Abraham or David. It can only be the covenant made at Sinai, since it was the only covenant established with priestly services and the only covenant that was in need of repair. Because Israel had violated the terms of the first covenant, the covenant needed to be re-worked in order for its blessings to be appropriated. Perhaps this is one reason why there was a need for a new covenant.

Flawless is not Lawless

"Because finding fault with them, He says: 'Behold, the days are coming, says the Lord, when I will make a new covenant with the house of Israel and with the house of Judah.'" – Hebrews 8:8

Note that fault is found not with the promises, the Torah, and even so much with the covenant itself. Fault is found with the people of the covenant. This includes Israel, the Levites and sinful humanity. He writes, "For he finds fault <u>with them</u>" (8:8). When it comes to the need for a new priesthood, the imperfection lies with imperfect people, including imperfect priests. The covenant failed in part because the Levites charged with administering the covenant were proven to be human.

Fault is also found with those with whom the covenant was made - Israel. We cannot blame the Torah or a covenant-keeping God for the fault of the covenant. It was the people of the covenant and those who administered the covenant that were imperfect.

We know that the Levites fell short, but so did the children of Israel. When cutting the covenant, it reads that Moses,

> *"Took the Book of the Covenant and read it in the hearing of the people. And they said, <u>'All that the Lord has said we will do, and be obedient.'</u> And Moses took the blood, sprinkled it on the people, and said, 'This is the blood of the covenant which the Lord has made with you according to all these words.'" - Exodus 24:7-8*

The terms and conditions of this covenant were as such: God promised to Israel blessing (Ex. 19:1-6, 23:26), healing (Ex. 15:26, 23:25), provision (Ex. 16:4, 17:6), protection (Ex. 23:20-23) and an inheritance (Ex. 23:27-31). He swore, "If you will indeed obey My voice and keep My covenant, then you shall be a special treasure to Me above all people...you shall be to Me a kingdom of priests and a holy nation" (Ex. 19:5-6). In return, the people vowed to obey all that had been spoken and all that was required of them (Ex. 19:8, 24:7).

Notice that the covenant was not the Torah, because Torah and the old covenant are not synonymous. The covenant was Israel's <u>obligation to obey</u> all that was written in the Torah. That is a significant distinction. Inevitably, Israel could not honor the terms of the covenant. They were found to be rebellious, and when they disobeyed, the covenant was in turn broken. God is a covenant-keeping God. He upheld His end of the bargain, but Israel did not.

It didn't take long for the people to rebel. They were in the middle of worshipping the golden calves when Moses descended the mountain. This incident was the first in a series of countless violations of the covenant. It would continue to be broken over and over again. However, in His forbearance, God baked into the law a remedy. The Torah presumes that we are going to sin, so it provided a means for temporal restoration.

God instituted a system of priestly sacrifices that could atone for the sins of the people. Daily, weekly and yearly the priests were essentially in the business of covenant maintenance so that Israel's relationship with God would never be in jeopardy. Those who believed and lived by faith continued in covenant relationship with God through the covenant made with Abraham. The sacrifices allowed for them to receive the blessings promised in the covenant made at Sinai and approach God in worship in the tabernacle.

But the offerings of the priests did more – they pointed to the ultimate Remedy. Unlike Israel, Yeshua obeyed all that was written in the Torah. He did what Israel and its priests couldn't. He did what you and I couldn't. Because He was sinless, He instituted a better covenant for us. Now His blessing, His healing, His provision, His protection and His inheritance become ours when we place our faith in Him.

The New Covenant

In the longest citation of the Hebrew Scriptures in the Apostolic Scriptures, Hebrews 8:8-12 quotes Jeremiah 31.

> *"Behold, the days are coming, says the Lord, when I will make a new covenant with the house of Israel and with the house of Judah--not according to the covenant that I made with their fathers in the day when I took them by the hand to lead them out of the land of Egypt; because they did not continue in My covenant, and I disregarded them, says the Lord. For this is the covenant that I will make with the*

> *house of Israel after those days, says the Lord: I will put My laws in their mind and write them on their hearts; and I will be their God, and they shall be My people. None of them shall teach his neighbor, and none his brother, saying, 'Know the Lord,' for all shall know Me, from the least of them to the greatest of them. For I will be merciful to their unrighteousness, and their sins and their lawless deeds I will remember no more."* - Hebrews 8:8-12 quoting Jeremiah 31:31-34

The word covenant (*diatheke*) is found more times in the book of Hebrews than in any other book of the New Testament.[1] It appears 17 times in the epistle to the Hebrews and 33 times total in the Apostolic Scriptures. The new covenant is called "new" three times in this letter and is said to be "better" than the former covenant.

Most people are unaware, however, that the passage introducing us to the concept of a new covenant is surprisingly not found first in the New Testament. It comes from the Hebrew Scriptures. The promises of a new covenant are first outlined in Jeremiah chapter 31.

Here are some things we can glean from it:

1. *The new covenant is made with the house of Israel and Judah.*

God has no established covenant with Gentile nations or with Christians. The new covenant is between the house of Israel and the God of Israel. Outside of Christ, Gentiles have no covenant relationship with the Covenant-Maker. Paul supports this when he writes: "You were without Christ, being aliens from the commonwealth of Israel and strangers from the covenants of promise, having no hope and without God in the world. But now in Christ Jesus you who once were far off have been brought near by the blood of Christ" (Eph. 2:12-13), and "You, being a wild olive tree, were grafted in among them, and with them became a partaker of the root" (Rom. 11:17).

---

[1] *Strong's* #G1242 διαθήκη

Gentiles are outside of the covenants of promise and must become grafted into Israel in order to enjoy covenant relationship with God. Any benefit Gentiles gain from the new covenant is on account of their faith in Jesus Christ. Through the work of Yeshua, Jews and Gentiles alike can become partakers of this covenant and enjoy all of its benefits.

2. *The new covenant is not like the covenant made at Sinai.*

The new covenant is unique to the Mosaic covenant in several ways. (1) God puts his laws in our minds and writes them on our hearts (v.10). (2) None need to be taught (v.11). (3) From the least to the greatest, all of Israel will know the Lord (v.11). (4) It remains intact even when we fail to obey all that is written in the Torah (v.12).

Whereas God "disregarded" Moses' generation because "they did not continue in My covenant" (v.9), the new covenant is not predicated on the contingency of perfect obedience. It is predicated on the perfect priesthood and sacrifice of Yeshua. This means that the new covenant remains intact, because Jesus took it upon Himself to remain faithful to all that is written in the Torah.

3. *The Torah is actively instrumental in the new covenant.*

There is no change to the Torah in the new covenant. The change is to where it is written and what type of tablet it is written upon. God's laws are no longer etched only on tablets of stone and parchment. They are being written on the tablets of our hearts.

Verse 8 states that the covenant is made with the house of Israel and with the house of Judah. Yet, verse 10 says, "This is the covenant I will make with the house of Israel after those days." What days and what happened to the house of Judah? This is likely a future, national promise for Israel. It is still yet to be realized. There is coming a day when the house of Israel and Judah will be united under Israel and all the promises of the new covenant will be fulfilled.

Torah of the New Covenant

It is careless to assume that the new covenant was given because the Torah was proven to be too rigid. The old covenant failed not because of the impossibilities of the law. It failed because the participants were still in Adam.

A new set of laws does not come prepackaged with the new covenant. It is the same directives given to Moses that are being written on new hearts and renewed minds. There is no abolishing of the Torah in the new covenant. What changes is the heart of the Torah keeper, not the heart of the Torah.

You could make a case that the Torah is even more relevant under the new covenant than under the Mosaic covenant, since the new covenant broadens and deepens the requirements to the Law of Moses. Under the covenant of Moses, the Torah was external. Under the new covenant, however, it is more than something we just look to or read. It is something we take in and become. It is written upon our souls. It is now a part of our being, guiding our thoughts, motives and convictions from within.

God wants his laws within us, not just among us. How genius! Having the Torah internalized is much better than having it set in ink and paper where it could be misplaced, mishandled or destroyed.

By placing the Torah in our hearts, it fulfills the promise that says, "These words that I command you today shall be in your heart" (Deut. 6:6). Everyone under the new covenant has the Torah in mind. If those under the old covenant were expected to obey Torah, how much more under the new covenant now that it is branded upon our being?

Since God's law is being written on our hearts, we come to the question of, "Which laws are within us?" The answer can only be all of them. Does the Holy Spirit write some laws on our hearts to the neglect of others? Does He convict us of some sins but not others? Does He convince us of one truth leaving out another?

Just as the Spirit of Truth is faithful to confirm all of God's truth collectively to us, we are obligated to acknowledge all of God's word and to obey it as He enables. We cannot simply reduce the Bible to only ten suggestions or pick random commandments we prefer. If God's laws are being written on our hearts, then it must be all of them, including those we've traditionally neglected as irrelevant or Jewish.

> *"In that He says, 'A new covenant,' He has made the first obsolete. Now what is becoming obsolete and growing old is ready to vanish away." - Hebrews 8:13*

Some scholars make the mistake of equating the Torah with the Mosaic covenant or with the first priesthood. This is an oversight. Again, the terms are not synonymous. The Torah is not equivalent to the old covenant, and they are not the same thing.

Actually, the word *covenant* is not found in this verse either, just as it was absent from Hebrews 8:7. Translators have added it for context. When he writes that the first is becoming obsolete, he is <u>not</u> implying that the Torah is becoming obsolete. What was growing obsolete was the first priestly order. This order was put in place, because God needed to work within the constructs of sinful man and imperfect priests. This was the best that could be offered until a heavenly Priest came forth and an eternal priesthood could be established. It was these provisions written into the Torah that were becoming obsolete.

In saying that it was "ready to vanish away", this could be a clue that the book of Hebrews was written before the destruction of the temple. Perhaps sacrifices were still being offered in the temple at the time these words were penned. On the other hand, it could also be that the temple had already been destroyed, as there is some evidence that temple worship had continued even after the temple had been destroyed in 70 A.D.[2]

---

[2] Kenneth Clark, *Worship in the Jerusalem Temple After 70 A.D.*, found in *New Testament Studies,* Vol. 6 (UK: Cambridge Studies Press, 1959), 269-280; Louis

As stated, the Torah plays a significant (maybe even more significant) role in the new covenant than in the former. The chief difference to the law in the old and new covenants is to where it is written. Jeremiah does not announce a new Torah for the new covenant. The Covenant-Maker did not give a new Torah with the new covenant and an old Torah with the old covenant. Clearly, the Torah of the new covenant is the Torah of the old covenant. This is evidenced by the fact that God says, "They did not continue in My covenant," (Heb. 8:9) not "They did not continue in My Torah."

There is one Torah. Jeremiah announces that a more effective way for keeping it was in the works. Whether one was under the old covenant or is under the new, the word of God has always been a lamp unto our feet and our light unto our path.

Some teach that the new covenant has yet to be initiated; others contend that it has already been fulfilled. It does appear, however, that the new covenant was instituted the night Yeshua shared the Passover meal with his disciples. This event had all the elements of a covenant.

There was *a ceremony* (Passover communion), *a promise* ("The remission of sins" – Matt. 26:28), *a vow* ("I will not drink of the fruit of this vine from now on until that day when I drink it anew with you in My Father's kingdom" – Matt. 26:29), *a shared meal* (Passover Seder), and *a sign* (The resurrection – Matt. 12:38-40, John 2:18-19).

Moses made his covenant before the twelve tribes of Israel in Exodus 24:8, saying, "This is the blood of the covenant". In similar fashion, sitting with the Eleven, Yeshua echoed these words by saying, "This is My blood of the covenant" (Matt. 26:28). Jesus did not introduce the new covenant to a bunch of Gentiles. He bestowed it upon His Jewish disciples, who represented Israel and would one day sit on thrones judging the twelve tribes of Israel.

Feldman, *Josephus and Modern Scholarship* (New York: Walter De Gruyter & Co., 1984), 458

Though initiated by Yeshua, however, this covenant is still yet to be consummated. It is incomplete. This is evidenced by the fact that not all of the promises of Jeremiah 31 have been fully realized. Israel is still divided, and all do not yet "know the Lord." We still need teachers. Like the kingdom of heaven, the new covenant has arrived but is still arriving. What Jesus set in motion is still being accomplished.

It should comfort us to know that the writing of God's laws upon our hearts and minds is a promise and a process. We are still a work in progress, and the promises of the new covenant are still being achieved. We are the first fruits of the new covenant. The Torah is being stamped on our hearts. We are being awakened to it. This process is an important part of our sanctification and discipleship unto Yeshua.

Conclusion

The primary difference between the old and the new covenants, as it relates to the Torah, is where the Torah is written. Under the old covenant, the law is written on stone tablets. Under the new covenant, it is written on hearts and minds. In both cases, we find no change to the Torah itself. The change is to where it is written and to how it governs the life of the believer. As it turns out, the law holds a prominent place in both the old *and* new covenants.

When it comes to the Torah, Hebrews chapter 9 clarifies that what changes is not the heart of the law but the heart of the person. If the commandments of God have passed away, then what is written on our hearts? If the Torah is nailed to the cross, then God has written something crucified upon our minds. He has written something abolished upon our hearts.

It is no coincidence that the book of Hebrews, written around the time of the destruction of the second temple, quotes Jeremiah in teaching about the new covenant. Jeremiah himself prophesied a new covenant just prior to the destruction of the first temple. In both cases, the new covenant saw beyond the destruction of the earthly temple and offered hope of a brighter future. All of the promises of the new covenant will be fully realized in the millennial age, but until that time, we have the privilege to press into the reality of the kingdom that is already but not yet.

Section VII

Book of Hebrews

INTRODUCTION TO HEBREWS

Truth #59: *Hebrews was written to prepare us for a post-Temple era.*

Twenty years after the Jerusalem council and forty years after the Resurrection, Roman forces laid siege to the city of Jerusalem. Within six months the Roman army had breached the walls, overtaken Jewish resistors and burned the temple. Over one million Jews died in the conflict. Those remaining were either slaughtered or carted off as slaves. An estimated tens of millions of dollars in gold and silver was removed and pilfered from the temple.[1] It was another catastrophic page in Jewish history that is commonly referred to as the fall of Jerusalem and the destruction of the second temple.

Sacking Jerusalem was the triumphant result of a four-year military campaign leveled against the region of Judea. During the reign of Nero, Judea rebelled against Rome. This angered the emperor. In 66 A.D., he dispatched his army under General Vespasian to restore order. It was actually Vespasian's son Titus, who, four years later, marched into Jerusalem and razed the temple.

For almost two thousand years the temple lay in ruins. It remains dysfunctional to this day. Jerusalem has been "trampled by the Gentiles" (Luke 21:24) as Jesus foretold. Ever wonder why God has not allowed the temple to be rebuilt? The answer is found in the book of Hebrews.

Who, What, When, Where and Why

The book of Hebrews is believed to have been written anywhere between 64 A.D. and 85 A.D. Jerusalem fell in 70 A.D., which means that Hebrews was written around the time of the destruction

---

[1] Feldman, *Biblical Archaeology Review*, Vol. 27, July/August, No. 4

of the temple. This is a critical piece of information when considering the book of Hebrews. Whether it was before or after the fall, the future of the city and the holy temple no doubt weighed heavy on the minds of Jews at the time. This small fact will go a long way in analyzing this book.

Another observation to consider is that the writer of Hebrews does not identify himself. The author remains anonymous. This makes determining when and why the book was written a bit more challenging.

Traditionally, scholars have attributed the letter to Paul, Barnabas, Apollos, Luke, Priscilla, Clement of Rome or to some unknown author.[2] No doubt whoever penned Hebrews was a devoted follower of Christ and most likely a Jew who possessed a thorough understanding of temple procedures.

A comprehensive analysis laying out the arguments for or against a precise author and date is beyond the scope of this book. While important, our main focus remains on why the book was written and how that relates to the Torah.

The date and author have a significant bearing on the purpose and destination of the book; however, I do believe it is possible to draw some solid conclusions even without this data. In an attempt to correctly interpret any historical document, it is paramount to understand its purpose.

Unfortunately, the missing information opens the door for a wide-range of differing opinions among scholars about the purpose of the book of Hebrews. Here are some of those speculations:

- To communicate the excellencies of the gospel compared to the law

---

[2] Augustine affirmed Paul's authorship. Clement of Alexandria and Eusebius believed Paul wrote Hebrews and Luke translated it into Greek. Origen attributed the words to Paul but its literary form to someone else. Tertullian regarded Barnabas as the author. Hippolytus credited Hebrews to Clement of Rome.

INTRODUCTION TO HEBREWS

- To announce the character of Christ to Gentile audiences

- To counteract Gnostic heresy

- A warning to Jewish Christians against apostasy to Judaism

- A challenge to a restricted messianic audience to embrace world missions

- A dissertation on how Judaism is inferior to Christianity

- A letter of encouragement to a small community of converted Jewish priests

And this is just a partial sampling.

With so many opinions, I feel liberated to throw my hat into the discussion. I do believe we can ascertain a sound interpretation based on what is written and what we know of Israel at the time of its writing.

With any interpretation, these conclusions remain fluid, but I do want to offer a few of my insights. My goal is to first lay a foundation of what I believe is the main purpose of Hebrews; then go chapter by chapter through the book, specifically addressing those areas that pertain to the Torah.

In my opinion, the purpose of the book of Hebrews is:

A revelation of the priesthood of Yeshua, and an exhortation that prepares the reader for a post-temple era.

Here is my reasoning:

1. *A revelation of the priesthood of Yeshua.*

The author himself identifies the central scope of the letter in chapter 8, writing: "Now this is the main point of the things we are saying:

We have such a High Priest..." (Heb. 8:1) The doctrine of the priesthood of Christ is introduced to us in chapter 2 and continues throughout the book. This is a major thrust of the book of Hebrews.

I find it intriguing that this is the first and only clear exposition of Yeshua being a priest in the entire Apostolic Scriptures. Nowhere else is Jesus directly portrayed as a priest, let alone the Great High Priest. There are hints elsewhere, but this revelation is unique to this particular author. We are indeed indebted to Hebrews for revealing this prodigious truth. With beautiful insight, he profoundly expounds upon this revelation for the entirety of the book.

2. *An exhortation.*

The word "exhort" or some variant is found five times in Hebrews. Sprinkled throughout the book, as well, we find continual encouragement to resist falling away and hold fast to the faith. "Therefore we must give more earnest heed to the things we have heard, lest we drift away" (2:1), "Hold fast the confidence" (3:6). "Beware, brethren, lest there be in any of you an evil heart of unbelief in departing from the living God...lest any of you be hardened through the deceitfulness of sin...we have become partakers of the Christ if we hold the beginning of our confidence steadfast to the end" (3:12-14). "Let us fear lest any of you seem to have come short of it...lest anyone fall according to the same example of disobedience...let us hold fast our confession" (4:1,11,14). "Those who were once enlightened...if they fall away" (6:4-6). "Therefore do not cast away your confidence" (10:35). "If he shrinks back, my soul has no pleasure in him" (10:38). "Do no grow weary or fainthearted...lest anyone fall short of the grace of God...if we turn away from Him who speaks from heaven" (12:3,15,25).

Furthermore, the writer himself declares the epistle to be an exhortation. "I appeal to you, brethren, bear with the word of exhortation, for I have written to you in few words" (13:22).

It should be noted here that a good many scholars feel that chapter 13 was an addendum written by Paul and attached to the book of

Hebrews. It is suggested that the body of the book (chapters 1-12) is not Pauline but written by one of Paul's colleagues, perhaps in conjunction with Paul. I tend to lean toward this notion, which would explain why chapter 13 sounds very much like Paul and why the rest of the book does not. It also makes sense as to why in one of the longer books of the Apostolic Scriptures, he writes, "I have written to you in few words" (13:22).

3. *Prepares the reader for a post-temple era.*

Scholars are unsure of the exact date of when Hebrews was written. But whether before or after the fall of Jerusalem, what is evident is that Hebrews was penned at or around the time of the destruction of the temple. If before, Hebrews would have helped prepare messianic Jews for what was prophesied – the destruction of the temple and the "setting aside" (7:18) of the sacrificial system. If after, it could offer an explanation as to why the temple was destroyed, providing much-needed encouragement for those grappling for a post-temple expression of their faith.

Hebrews answers questions such as: Why would God allow the temple to be destroyed? How could a person follow Yeshua and worship the God of Israel without a temple and a priest? No doubt these hung as huge questions for the apostolic church. Though the answers to these questions may seem basic to us now, at the time, they weren't. This was new territory for followers of Yeshua, and the book of Hebrews helped provide some much-needed exhortation.

It is curious that the author references the tabernacle on numerous occasions but never the temple. This could be because (1) he was writing after the fall of Jerusalem, and the temple was non-operational at the time of its writing. It also could be that (2) he wanted to steer his readers away from temple centricity and toward something more eternal, knowing that the earthly temple was temporal. It could also be because (3) some Jewish groups during that time felt that the temple establishment had become corrupt. Maybe (4) the author was of that opinion or (5) was just being sensitive to an audience that held that regard.

It is said that the temple was never the same after an earthquake tore the veil and rocked Jerusalem during the time of the crucifixion. The death of Yeshua began a forty-year window of prophetic warnings and calls for repentance within the city. In addition to the words of Christ, Jewish historian Josephus outlines a series of signs that pointed to the imminent destruction of the temple. Various supernatural events occurred and accelerated in the years just prior to the destruction of the temple. These unique warnings did not go unnoticed by scribes or by the people.[3]

One argument for a pre-destruction date is that Hebrews 8:4 seems to suggest the temple was still operational. It reads, "For if He were on earth, He would not be a priest, since there are priests who offer the gifts according to the law" (Heb. 8:4). The author uses the present tense when describing temple activities. When describing past events, however, he consistently uses the past tense. It could be that Hebrews was written sometime just prior to the fall of Jerusalem and sought to brace the reader for the forthcoming destruction of the temple.

As far as authorship is concerned, a strong case can be made for Barnabas. Not only was he an apostle and close companion of Paul, he also was an encourager. Hebrews 2:3 seems to imply that the author was not an eyewitness of Jesus Himself, which fits with what we know about Barnabas. Being a Levite, Barnabas certainly would have been familiar with ecclesiastical matters, making him uniquely qualified to address this subject.

---

[3] Whiston, *The Life And Works Of Flavius Josephus*, 824-825; Josephus, *Wars Of The Jews,* Book VI, Chapter 5, Paragraph 3

HEBREWS 1-6

Truth #60: *Jesus is the living Torah.*

> *"God, who at various times and in various ways spoke in time past to the fathers by the prophets, has in these last days spoken to us by His Son, whom He has appointed heir of all things, through whom also He made the worlds." - Hebrews 1:1-2*

In the opening verse the author reminds us that God has spoken in various ways in times past through numerous people. Abraham, Moses, David, Isaiah, Jeremiah, Ezekiel, Daniel, Joel, Zechariah. The list continues. All were instrumental in proclaiming the word of the Lord.

The Messiah, however, *is* the word of God. Jesus Christ is the living Torah, God's perfect prophetic Word. He is the Father's ultimate and crowning Word, the one whom the prophets anticipated and foretold. He is the Seed of Abraham and the Son of David. He is Daniel's Prince and Isaiah's suffering Servant.

Just as God spoke through the Prophets and delivered the Torah through Moses, he sent his Son as an extension and completion of his voice. The coming of the Son of Man was not in contradiction to the voice of the Law and Prophets, but in continuation. Those who seek to honor the Law and the Prophets cannot do so without honoring and accepting the words of Yeshua. We must see him as none other than the Torah made flesh.

> *"Having become so much better than the angels, as He has by inheritance obtained a more excellent name than they. For to which of the angels did He ever say: "You are My Son, today I have begotten You"? And again: "I will be to Him a Father, and He shall be to Me a Son"? But to which of the angels has He ever said: "Sit at*

> *My right hand, till I make Your enemies Your footstool"? – Hebrews 1:4-5, 13*

As the firstborn Son, Yeshua obtained an "inheritance", "a more excellent name" and the right to "sit at the right hand" of the Father. The author addresses the supremacy of Christ over the angels perhaps for several reasons:

a) To contest the heretical angel worship of the Gnostics,
b) To address a possible rise of angelology within the Jewish community, and/or
c) To argue that Christ has authority to interpret the Torah.

Jewish tradition holds that angels were significant in the giving of the Torah to Moses. This is evidenced in chapter 2 where it reads,

> *"For if <u>the word spoken through angels</u> proved steadfast, and every transgression and disobedience received a just reward, how shall we escape if we neglect so great a salvation, which at the first began to be spoken by the Lord, and was confirmed to us by those who heard Him." – Hebrews 2:2-3*

Stephen said something similar. Rebuking the council of elders, he calls them stiff-necked, resisters of the Holy Spirit, murderers and betrayers. He adds that they had "received the Torah by the direction of angels and have not kept it." (Acts 7:53). In addition to identifying Torah neglect as the work of religious hypocrites, he supported the tradition that the Torah was received at the direction of angels.

The author's point here is that if the Torah was indeed given through the ministry of angels, then much more should we obey the One who is greater than the angels and came in the image of the Almighty. Yeshua is better than the angels, because He is "the express image" of the Father, the exact copy of His personhood. If disobedience to God's commands brings judgment, then judgment also awaits those who neglect the salvation of God through Jesus Christ.

> *"Therefore, in all things He had to be made like His brethren, that He might be <u>a merciful and faithful High Priest</u> in things pertaining to God, to make propitiation for the sins of the people. For in that He Himself has suffered, being tempted, He is able to aid those who are tempted"* – Hebrews 2:17-18

Yeshua is given the title of a priest well over 25 times the book of Hebrews. This is the first mention of it. Whereas chapter 1 establishes Jesus' place above the angels, chapter 2 demonstrates how He became a little lower than the angels for a time by taking on flesh and blood. This lays the foundation for the author's main thesis – that Yeshua is our Great High Priest. As the Son of God, He is greater than angels. As the Son of man, He qualifies as our High Priest.

Building upon Moses

Chapters 3 and 4 (as well as 5 and 6) build upon these things, comparing Moses to a house and Christ to its builder. Just as the builder is greater than the house, so Christ is greater than Moses and is deserving of much more honor. Moses was a servant, but Jesus is the heir. Moses was faithful in God's house, but Jesus is the Son in charge of the house. Christ built the house, and the builder always receives more glory than the house itself.

Unlike Moses and Aaron, however, our Priest is not subject to the Levitical lineage requirements prescribed in Scripture to claim His priesthood. He is the High Priest of this home. If we remain in Him, we become part of the house He is building.

Hebrews 7:1-11

Truth #61: *Jesus perfects the Torah.*

"For this Melchizedek, king of Salem, priest of the Most High God, who met Abraham returning from the slaughter of the kings and blessed him, to whom also Abraham gave a tenth part of all, first being translated 'king of righteousness,' and then also king of Salem, meaning 'king of peace,' without father, without mother, without genealogy, having neither beginning of days nor end of life, but made like the Son of God, remains a priest continually. Now consider how great this man was, to whom even the patriarch Abraham gave a tenth of the spoils. And indeed those who are of the sons of Levi, who receive the priesthood, have a commandment to receive tithes from the people according to the law, that is, from their brethren, though they have come from the loins of Abraham; but he whose genealogy is not derived from them received tithes from Abraham and blessed him who had the promises. Now beyond all contradiction the lesser is blessed by the better. Here mortal men receive tithes, but there he receives them, of whom it is witnessed that he lives. Even Levi, who receives tithes, paid tithes through Abraham, so to speak, for he was still in the loins of his father when Melchizedek met him." – Hebrews 7:1-10

Melchizedek is likened to Yeshua. Melchizedek was a priest. So is Christ. Melchizedek was the king of peace and righteousness. So is Christ. The beginning and end of Melchizedek's days are unknown. So are Christ's. Melchizedek ruled the city of Jerusalem. So does Christ.

Like Yeshua, Melchizedek was a priest separate from God's dealings with Abraham and independent of the Aaronic priesthood. Because his birth, death and genealogy are unknown to us, Melchizedek's office did not pass on to an ancestor. Thus, he remained a priest continually even after his death.

In the same way, Yeshua is Priest and King continually and eternally before the throne of God. We read that Abraham, the great grandfather of Levi, gave a tenth of the spoils to Melchizedek. Melchizedek in turn blessed the patriarch. Because he received a tithe and blessed Abraham, Melchizedek was proven to be greater than Abraham.

Likewise, like Melchizedek, the Messiah is greater than Abraham. Figuratively speaking, Abraham (with Aaron and the entire Levitical priesthood still in his loins) tithed to Christ and was blessed by Him. This demonstrates Yeshua's superiority to them.

The writer's point is that Jesus Christ is the Great High Priest forever. He came not from the line of Aaron but in the order of Melchizedek. Melchizedek's priesthood is proven to be greater than the priesthood of Levi, which makes Yeshua's priestly authority separate from and superior to Levi's. Unlike the Aaronic priesthood, Christ's priesthood is eternal, continual and not dependent on an earthly temple. His is a heavenly priesthood.

This is important, because the Levitical priesthood and daily sacrifices ceased altogether with the destruction of the temple. The messianic Jews who participated in temple activities during the first century would naturally be distressed at any threat or harm to the temple, so the writer is preparing them for a post-temple era. He wants to turn their attention away from temple operations and toward the work of the Messiah. No longer did they need an earthly priest to serve as their intercessor. They had a Great High Priest who forever lives to make intercession for us.[1]

The forgiveness of their sins was not secured in bringing a sacrifice to the temple but in the sacrifice of their Messiah. Neither was their redemption dependent upon an earthly temple or Levite. An available place of worship was irrelevant to their justification.

The destruction of the temple did not take the followers of Christ by surprise, for they had been forewarned. Jesus prophesied its ruin

---

[1] Heb. 7:25

forty years prior.[2] With the temple no longer standing today, our ability to see Yeshua standing at the right hand of the Father as our Great High Priest comes into better focus.

Perfect Priesthood

> *"Therefore, if perfection were through the Levitical priesthood (for under it the people received the law), what further need was there that another priest should rise according to the order of Melchizedek, and not be called according to the order of Aaron?" – Hebrews 7:11*

The fact that Yeshua did not come from the tribe of Levi proves that a priesthood outside the Levitical order exists and is superior. As it turns out, the Levitical priesthood with its sacrificial system was not the final order of things. When operational, the earthly temple was a shadow of a heavenly one. Another priesthood and a heavenly tabernacle still existed, which might explain why the author only refers to a tabernacle and not a temple in his letter to the Hebrews.

Compared to the temple, the tabernacle was provisional. Compared to Yeshua, so was the Levitical order. Jesus is the High Priest that all other priesthoods point to, for they could not do what Christ did – perfect us.

Perfection is a strong theme of Hebrews woven throughout the epistle. The word "perfection" or "perfect" is found several places throughout this exhortation. Here are some:

> *"For it was fitting for Him, for whom are all things and by whom are all things, in bringing many sons to glory, to make the captain of their salvation <u>perfect</u> through sufferings." – Hebrews 2:10*

> *"Having been <u>perfected</u>, He became the author of eternal salvation to all who obey Him." – Hebrews 5:9*

> *"Therefore, leaving the discussion of the elementary principles of Christ, let us go on to <u>perfection</u>, not laying again the foundation of*

---

[2] Matt. 24:1-2, 23:37-38

repentance from dead works and of faith toward God." – Hebrews 6:1

"For the law made nothing perfect."- Hebrews 7:19

"For the law appoints as high priests men who have weakness, but the word of the oath, which came after the law, appoints the Son who has been perfected forever." – Hebrews 7:28

"It was symbolic for the present time in which both gifts and sacrifices are offered which cannot make him who performed the service perfect in regard to the conscience." – Hebrews 9:9

"But Christ came as High Priest of the good things to come, with the greater and more perfect tabernacle not made with hands." – Hebrews 9:11

"For the law, having a shadow of the good things to come, and not the very image of the things, can never with these same sacrifices, which they offer continually year by year, make those who approach perfect." – Hebrews 10:1

"For by one offering He has perfected forever those who are being sanctified." – Hebrews 10:14

"God having provided something better for us, that they should not be made perfect apart from us." – Hebrews 11:40

"To the general assembly and church of the firstborn who are registered in heaven, to God the Judge of all, to the spirits of just men made perfect." – Hebrews 12:23

The words used for perfect are also translated *finish, fulfilled, completed* or *consecrated*. Each of these words accurately describes the work of Yeshua as our High Priest. He is the Perfect One. He is the completion of the Torah, and the fulfillment of God's priesthood. He finished all that was prophesied and written about Him. He accomplished what the Levitical order could not – the perfection of our souls. In Christ, our conscience has been cleansed and our spirit has been perfected.

Conclusion

The Aaronic priesthood was instituted to make provision for sinful man to approach a perfect God. It dealt with earthly things and fleshly matters. It was imperfect, because it was administered through imperfect priests and an imperfect sacrifice. It represents the offerings of man, which are limited and inadequate.

But the priesthood of Christ was able to bring about perfection in us, because it was administered through a perfect offering. Where the Aaronic priesthood was insufficient in perfecting us, Christ was more than sufficient. We can now approach God through a faultless sacrifice.

Likewise, the Torah is perfect, even if it could not cure the flaw of sin. This is why God gave us a Savior. Only Christ can redeem our souls and render us righteous. Trying to obey God's commands without Christ is like trying to play a guitar without strings. It's frustrating and futile. But while the law administered through man is imperfect, the law administered through Christ is flawless.

Hebrews 7:12-28

Truth #62: *A change in the priesthood was necessary to institute the new covenant.*

> *"For the priesthood being changed, of necessity there is also a change of the law." – Hebrews 7:12*

What is this change of the law that the writer speaks of? Taking into account the subject matter of the chapter, the change here is not regarding all aspects of the Torah but those specific aspects of the Torah dealing with the priesthood, sacrifices and temple activities. Priests, offerings, washings, sacrifices and tithes all find their purpose only when the Levitical system is functional.

With the coming of a newly Anointed Priest and the destruction of the temple, the requirements that accompany the Levitical temple are inapplicable and their services are no longer required. This includes the Aaronic priesthood along with its offerings and sacrifices. With no temple and no Levites to serve in the temple, the intercessions of priests cannot be performed. Without a temple, the priesthood of Aaron has no remaining context.

For example, suppose a person performed sacrifices in their backyard, because no altar or temple was readily available. They might think they are pleasing the Lord, but they would be grossly mistaken. God would not accept their sacrifice. According to Leviticus 17, sacrifices were to be made at a God-ordained place (like the tabernacle or temple) on a consecrated altar administered by a ceremonially clean Levitical priest. To do so in any other place and under any other circumstance would result in that person being cut off from Israel. It would be a sin on par with Jeroboam, who erected his own altars, priests and festivals in Bethel. We know how that ended.

In the same manner, laws pertaining to priests, Levites, washings and sacrifices need a fully functioning tabernacle before they can be rightly applied. Without a temple, these laws simply have no context and cannot be fully implemented.

Think of it this way. Most cities have laws governing pet ownership. Animal control laws prohibit people from owning endangered species and breeding certain animals. Pet owners must abide by local nuisance laws and regulations regarding commercial breeding and hoarding.

A dog owner, for example, is typically responsible for registering his dog, keeping it on a leash and cleaning up after it in public. These laws are specific to animal caretakers and to pet owners.

Animal control laws are written for the public's protection. To those who don't own pets, the same attention need not be given to these laws. It's not that the laws are taken off the books for non-pet owners. The law still pertains to all and protects all. It's just that these statutes are specifically written for animal caretakers, pet owners and to those who interact with them. While the laws are written for all, not all of them apply the same way to everyone.

In the same way, the laws regarding the temple are applicable only to those who interact and participate in temple activities. Offerings, sacrifices, washings and priestly requirements find meaning for those who worshipped at the temple and operated under the Levitical priesthood, but they do not find an application for those who live in distant lands or where there is no temple to frequent. These laws simply have no context without a temple. It's not that God has taken them off the books. It's just that these laws are specific to priests and temple goers.

As it was, Levitical priests were found to be insufficient as ministers of the new covenant. They were mortal, earthly sinners like you and me, unable to cleanse the conscience of man and unable to write the Torah on our hearts. In order for the new covenant to be instituted, there had to be a change in the priesthood. This is the change to the law that the book of Hebrews speaks of.

Perhaps God has allowed the temple to be destroyed to direct our attention to Yeshua. We now have a perfect Priest that has offered a perfect sacrifice on the heavenly altar. He is a heavenly priest in a heavenly temple. For the time being, the earthly version of the temple does not have a current application.

Annulment of the Priesthood

"For on the one hand there is an annulling of the former commandment because of its weakness and unprofitableness, for the law made nothing perfect; on the other hand, there is the bringing in of a better hope, through which we draw near to God." – Hebrews 7:18-19

What commandment does he speak of annulling? In staying true to the context, it can only be the commandments of offerings made through Levitical priests. The sin offering could not redeem the soul. It was powerless to break the law of sin and suspended at the coronation of a new High Priest. When he writes that the former commandment is annulled because it was weak and useless, he is identifying the former commandment regarding the sacrifices of the priests that was unable to make us perfect in cleansing our sins.

The Aaronic priesthood was based on a rule of physical descent from Aaron and Levi. In order to remain successful, it required a perpetual successor, something the sons of Levi could not accomplish.

Unlike the Levitical order, the priesthood of Yeshua set aside the need for a system that passes along the priesthood from generation to generation. Jesus is alive forever, so He does not need a replacement. His position is permanent, so He does not need to pass it on to someone else.

Coming from the tribe of Judah, Yeshua offers a better hope and a heavenly priesthood. It is not tied to an earthly temple or passing through the loins of Levi. Because His priesthood was given by oath, we now have a better promise of drawing near to God through Christ.

Imagine if a catastrophic event had taken place in ancient Israel that completely destroyed the temple and the entire line of Levites. How could Israel's priests then atone for sin? They couldn't. For this reason, the Most High watched over the temple of Jerusalem to ensure that this did not happen until the appointed time.

This is essentially what happened with the destruction of the temple in 70 A.D. This historic event was not only the consequence for Israel's sin but on account of their rejection of God's Messiah.

God has now provided for us a permanent solution for lawbreakers outside the physical temple. Because the blood of bulls and goats had to be renewed annually, the former provision for those who had broken the law was temporary. But God's Torah and God's provision through Yeshua are eternal.

In God's sovereignty, He allowed the temple to be destroyed. He has not seen a need for it to be rebuilt. Even if it were still standing today, the forgiveness of our sins wouldn't be dependent upon temple activities. This is why the author calls the former commandment "weak and unprofitable." It could not accomplish what the sacrifice of Yeshua could.

The priests had to offer sacrifices daily for their own sins before standing in a place of intercession for the people. But since Yeshua was blameless and without sin, He could offer Himself as one sacrifice for sin, once and for all. This is the change to the law that he refers to.

A Better Covenant

"Jesus has become a surety of a better covenant." – Hebrews 7:22

Hebrews calls Yeshua "better than angels" (1:4), "better than Moses" (3:1-6) and "better than Abraham" (7:1-10). His priesthood is altogether stronger, more useful, more serviceable and more advantageous. He is the guarantor of a "better covenant" that "speaks better things than that of Abel" (12:24). It is founded on a "better hope" (7:19), "better promises" (8:6), "better sacrifices"

(9:23) securing a "better possession" (10:34) in a "better heavenly country" (11:16) with a "better resurrection" (11:35).

Yeshua is a better priest of a better covenant for these reasons and so much more.

1. *He is a heavenly priest.* "Seeing then that we have a great High Priest who has passed through the heavens, Jesus the Son of God, let us hold fast *our* confession." - Hebrews 4:14

2. *He is compassionate.* "For we do not have a High Priest who cannot sympathize with our weaknesses, but was in all *points* tempted as *we are, yet* without sin. Let us therefore come boldly to the throne of grace, that we may obtain mercy and find grace to help in time of need." – Hebrews 4:15-16

3. *He is appointed by God through an oath.* "*He was* not *made priest* without an oath for they have become priests without an oath, but He with an oath by Him who said to Him: *'The Lord has sworn and will not relent, You are a priest forever according to the order of Melchizedek'*, by so much more Jesus has become a surety of a better covenant." – Hebrews 7:20-22

4. *He is indestructible, so His intercession is everlasting.* "Who has come, not according to the law of a fleshly commandment, but according to the power of an endless life. For He testifies: *'You are a priest forever according to the order of Melchizedek'*…Also there were many priests, because they were prevented by death from continuing. But He, because He continues forever, has an unchangeable priesthood. Therefore He is also able to save to the uttermost those who come to God through Him, since He always lives to make intercession for them." – Hebrews 7:16-17, 23-25

5. *He is sinless.* "For such a High Priest was fitting for us, *who is* holy, harmless, undefiled, separate from sinners, and has become higher than the heavens." – Hebrews 7:26

6. *His sacrifice is eternal.* "Who does not need daily, as those high priests, to offer up sacrifices, first for His own sins and then for the

people's, for this He did once for all when He offered up Himself. For the law appoints as high priests men who have weakness, but the word of the oath, which came after the law, *appoints* the Son who has been perfected forever." – Hebrews 7:27-28

7. *He serves in the heavenly temple, not the earthly temple which is a shadow of the heavenly temple.* "Now *this is* the main point of the things we are saying: We have such a High Priest, who is seated at the right hand of the throne of the Majesty in the heavens, a Minister of the sanctuary and of the true tabernacle which the Lord erected, and not man. For every high priest is appointed to offer both gifts and sacrifices. Therefore *it is* necessary that this One also have something to offer. For if He were on earth, He would not be a priest, since there are priests who offer the gifts according to the law; who serve the copy and shadow of the heavenly things, as Moses was divinely instructed when he was about to make the tabernacle. For He said, *'See that you make all things according to the pattern shown you on the mountain.'* But now He has obtained a more excellent ministry, inasmuch as He is also Mediator of a better covenant, which was established on better promises." – Hebrews 8:1-6

We have been given a better covenant with better promises through a better sacrifice. However, the writer of Hebrews does not say we have been given a better law. Why? It is because there is no change to the law. The Torah of Moses is the law of the new covenant.

Law Enforcement

The entire Torah, including the book of Leviticus, is useful and relevant, but there are certain instructions that are not applicable to everyone. God has given specific directives to husbands, wives, women and priests that only apply to those who meet the criteria.

Laws governing priests, for example, are only applicable to Levites. Likewise, commandments concerning offerings and temple activities are not applicable to those living in a foreign land or when the temple is non-operational.

Even though we are far removed from ancient Israel and the tabernacle, animal sacrifices and purification requirements have not "dissolved of themselves," as one scholar contends.[1] The temple was destroyed. The laws that govern priestly activity do not have a current application. Without a Levite and a temple, temple guidelines are not applicable. To lump all commandments in with the laws governing the temple is dubious.

The same cannot be said for instructions concerning circumcision, Sabbath, tassels and meat distinctions. These have not dissolved by the will of God. They have been ignored at the neglect of man.

Conclusion

Yeshua certainly is the Lamb of God who takes away the sin of the world. He is our Great High Priest in the order of Melchizedek. His sacrifice is sufficient for our sin. The revelation of Christ is found in all the offerings of Leviticus, for they foreshadow the atoning work of the Messiah.

Those who say that the certain laws of the Torah have dissolved have miscalculated. We simply do not meet the criteria for putting them into practice. With the arrival of a heavenly Priest and with no physical temple in operation, they cannot be observed as they once were.

Even Yeshua did not obey every precept written in the Torah. He was neither a biological husband nor a menstruating woman. He was not a priest from the tribe of Levi. He could not adhere to the commandments specifically related to women, husbands and Levites. Yet, He fulfilled all of the Torah and was not guilty of any transgression. He remained sinless, because He did not break one commandment that was applicable to Him.

In the same way, there are certain portions of the Torah that may not be currently applicable for you and me. Just because certain parts of the Torah are not specific for us or for our time does not imply they

---

[1] Spence and Exell, *Pulpit Commentary*, Book 33, St. Matthew, Vol. 1, 214

are destroyed. Neither does it mean we are at liberty to transgress them. We may not be able to take them all up in their entirety as written, but we can certainly seek to take up all that we are able to and that is applicable.

HEBREWS 9:1-12

Truth #63: *The Torah is consistent.*

Hebrews chapter 8 is included in the New Covenant section, so we turn out attention to Hebrews 9.

> *"Then indeed, even the first covenant had ordinances of divine service and the earthly sanctuary...The priests always went into the first part of the tabernacle, performing the services. But into the second part the high priest went alone once a year, not without blood, which he offered for himself and for the people's sins committed in ignorance; the Holy Spirit indicating this, that the way into the Holiest of All was not yet made manifest while the first tabernacle was still standing. It was symbolic for the present time in which both gifts and sacrifices are offered which cannot make him who performed the service perfect in regard to the conscience--concerned only with foods and drinks, various washings, and fleshly ordinances imposed until the time of reformation." - Hebrews 9:1,6b-10*

Food, drink, washings, ordinances - is he implying that the laws of the Torah have no bearing on us now that we are under a new covenant? Most scholars would give a resounding yes. Let's test this theory.

First off, the word *covenant* does not appear in the Greek manuscripts of verse 1, which is why King James places it in italics. Just like in Hebrews 8:7, 8:13 and later in 9:18, it is again added for context. This is disappointing, because the author's goal, it seems, is not to compare covenants. It is to contrast priesthoods. It might just as easily be translated:

> *"Then indeed, even the first priesthood had ordinances of divine service and the earthly sanctuary." – Hebrews 9:1*

Old vs. New

This is notable, because it contributes in part to our misreading of Hebrews and our general misunderstanding of the Bible. Too often we reduce the Bible to *new* versus *old*. We draw battle lines between the old covenant and the new covenant, between the Old Testament and the New. We see anything old as outdated, anything new as relevant.

Old is Torah, temple, Jewish, religion and judgment. *New* is Jesus, church, Christian, Spirit and grace. These kinds of old/new classifications are the seeds that germinate dispensationalism and replacement theology.

This author and the Scriptures as a whole do not make such stark contrasts. Hebrews neither vilifies something just because it is old, nor seeks to drive a wedge between the Hebrew and Apostolic Scriptures. What it does do effectively is decipher between the things that are of heaven and the things that are of earth.

We would be wise to refrain from calling anything old "bad" and everything new "good". From our vantage, everything we believe is quite old, actually. Since the New Testament is almost 2,000 years old, one could argue that there really is no *New* Testament. We have the Old Testament and the *Older* Testament.

It might be better to simply judge something by its measure of truth than its age. Just because something is old does not mean it is worthless, and just because something is new does not make it automatically better. When we do this we discredit our own message, which is well aged. When we do this we also become susceptible to giving undue audience to every new and passing doctrinal fad that blows our way.

We have to delineate between *man's* new and *God's* new. *Man's* new is often new for the sake of being different. It's a new fashion, new philosophy or a new resolution. Sometimes it's an improvement - a fresher look, an enhanced process, a higher quality. Other times it is new with an agenda - to sell a product or to push a program. When it comes to concepts and worldviews, many times it's nothing new at all. It's usually just refurbished, repackaged and rearranged ideas placed under a new heading. In his wisdom, King Solomon concluded that there is really nothing new under the sun.

God's new, however, is from beyond the sun. It really is new! When God does something new on earth, it is not because He's bored with the old or wants a different look. It's because the new has something wonderfully better for you and me. What is more, when God does something new, it does not negate His previously established revelation. On the contrary, it enhances it.

> *"Therefore also indeed, the first had regulations of worship and an earthly sanctuary...consisting only in foods and drinks and various washings – ordinances of the flesh being imposed until the time of reformation." - Hebrews 9:1,10 Berean Literal Bible*

If we seek to remain true to the context, it is clear that the author is not referencing Sabbath, feasts, dietary laws, tassels, adultery, murder, stealing or any such commandment of the law. The author's "ordinances of flesh" are those in connection with the tabernacle, such as food and drink offerings, *mikvahs* and ritual cleanliness. These are things pertaining to the physical body – fleshly ordinances.

These *foods, drinks* and *washings* are those precepts directly associated with the first tabernacle. They are called fleshly, because they could physically cleanse the body but not the soul. There is no mention of pork or shellfish or Biblical holidays here. These are foreign to the discussion, because they are things not directly connected to the tabernacle.

We forget that food and drink were a big part of temple operations. There were burnt offerings, grain offerings, peace offerings, guilt offerings, drink offerings, and morning and evening sacrifices. The inner court housed a table of showbread, where the priests baked twelve loaves of bread each week using fine flour for the holy table. Each Sabbath the priests were to remove the bread, eat it in the Holy

Place and replace it with freshly baked bread. Because the bread was consecrated to the Lord, it could only be eaten in the Holy Place.

Tithes were instituted primarily to provide food for the Levite and his family. These offerings of the people were given to the Lord. In turn, they were given to the priests and their families. Not only were the priests given instructions on what they could and could not consume, they were given specific instructions on how to prepare and eat it. These are the foods he is referring to here.

As for washings, a worshipper could not enter the tabernacle without first being ritually clean. In the Torah, God outlines detailed instructions for governing cleanliness relating to mold, mildew, dry rot, carcasses, festering wounds, bodily discharges, leprosy and contagious diseases. These clean and unclean laws are directly related to temple life. We can certainly glean from these guidelines, but their purpose was beyond health. These regulations consecrated the worshipper before presenting themselves before God in the sanctuary.

They have instructional value for us, but without a temple they are without a consecrating context. These are the *various washings* and *fleshly ordinances* spoken of here.

> *"But Christ came as High Priest of the good things to come, with the greater and more perfect tabernacle not made with hands, that is, not of this creation. Not with the blood of goats and calves, but with His own blood He entered the Most Holy Place once for all, having obtained eternal redemption."* – Hebrews 9:11-12

Here is a truth worth meditating on: There is a man who sits upon the throne of the Most High, a glorious High Priest who offered Himself as the perfect sacrifice for our sins by sprinkling His own blood on heaven's mercy seat. Because He is a priest forever, there is no need for a replacement. Because He made a way for us to enter the Holy Place in the heavenlies, an earthly temple is not needed to house His glory and atone for sin.

It is not accurate to say that priests and sacrifices had no worth. They had much value indeed, but they have no value when it comes to taking us out of Adam and into Christ. While they dealt with sin, they could not liberate us from our sin nature. They could not give us right standing before God or cleanse our conscience.

Conclusion

For the saints of old, the tabernacle was the representation of God's glory on earth. Only in this holy place could one could find atonement for transgressions and approach the Holy One.

In Christ, however, we are temples of the Living God. We do not have to rely on a building, a location or a sacrifice to encounter His presence. While a prayer room, a synagogue or a chapel may help to draw us closer to Him, the building is not the carrier of God's presence. We are.

The writer of Hebrews is not depreciating the value of the Levitical priests, the temple or its sacrifices. He is merely exalting the priesthood of Christ, the heavenly temple and His great sacrifice. When compared to Christ, the Levitical system was shown to be imperfect, because it was administered through imperfect ministers.

The tabernacle with all its activity served as a prophetic foreshadowing of the work of the Messiah. Studying how God established the priesthood of the tabernacle helps us grow in our appreciation of the priesthood of Christ. Perhaps this is why the writer of Hebrews felt compelled to write about such things.

There is much to gain in knowing and understanding the first tabernacle. In praising the new covenant, however, we should not assume that the former covenant had nothing glorious to offer.

Hebrews 9:13-28

Truth #64: *Dead works are the sinful works of the flesh.*

> *"For if the blood of bulls and goats and the ashes of a heifer, sprinkling the unclean, sanctifies for the purifying of the flesh, how much more shall the blood of Christ, who through the eternal Spirit offered Himself without spot to God, cleanse your conscience from <u>dead works</u> to serve the living God?"* – Hebrews 9:13-14

Innocent blood is a powerful agent in the spirit. The devil knows this well, which is why he seeks to gain earthly power and human influence through shedding innocent blood. When placed on a holy altar sanctioned by God, the spilled blood of a spotless bull had the ability to atone for sin. It could literally purify the flesh of unholy man and permit him to approach a holy God. Amazing!

But there is a power greater. While an animal sacrifice could cover our sins, it was powerless in taking them away, as the author of Hebrews writes,

> *"For it is not possible that the blood of bulls and goats could take away sin."* - Hebrews 10:4

There is something even more effective than the blood of bulls and goats. It's the innocent blood of God's own Son. It has the most power of efficacy. It is the ultimate life-bringing agent. Only the blood of the perfect Lamb of God has the ability to completely remove our sin and cleanse our conscience from dead works. Praise be to our God!

The term "dead works" is found twice in Hebrews and is used exclusively in this epistle.

> *"Therefore, leaving the discussion of the elementary principles of Christ, let us go on to perfection, not laying again the foundation of repentance from <u>dead works</u> and of faith toward God." – Hebrews 6:1*

> *"How much more shall the blood of Christ, who through the eternal Spirit, offered Himself without spot to God, cleanse your conscience from <u>dead works</u> to serve the living God?" – Hebrews 9:14*

What are Dead Works?

We have been led to believe that dead works are the works of the Torah. Many will define dead works as the legalistic attempt to earn salvation through obeying the law and attempting to be a good person. From their perspective, Jews, Catholics, Jehovah's Witnesses, Buddhists, Pharisees and some Christians fit the bill. According to this definition, the works of the Torah are no longer vital. Anyone trusting in these dead works destines a person for damnation; therefore, they are called dead works.

Often this position renders the Torah a book of dead works that must be shed and Judaism as something that needs to be rejected. It heralds the book of Hebrews, Galatians and Romans as a warning to Christians to avoid slipping back into legalism and Torah obedience.

I find this definition of dead works off base. We need not complicate the term *dead works*. The word used for dead is *nekros*.[1] It means *dead*.[2] The word used for works is *ergon*.[3] It means deeds.[4] It's pretty straightforward. Dead works are not good deeds with a twisted motive. Neither are they striving for moral behavior. Dead works are sinful deeds of the flesh. They are actions that lead to death. From an apostolic and linguistic perspective, dead works is

---

[1] *Strong's* G3498 νεκρός
[2] BGAD, *A Greek-English Lexicon of the New Testament, nekros*
[3] *Strong's* G2041 ἔργον
[4] Louw, *Greek-English Lexicon, ergon;* Brown, *The New International Dictionary of New Testament Theology,* Vol. 3, 1147

simply a synonym for fleshly behavior that results in death and destruction.

If dead works implies doing good deeds in an effort to merit salvation, as some define them, the writer of Hebrews should not be calling for repentance from good deeds. He should be championing a turning away from the false motives behind the good deeds. This he does not do.

Think about it. When a new convert comes to Christ, do we encourage them to repent of the good and moral choices they made in their past, even if it were for the wrong reasons or the purpose of earning God's favor? Of course not. God expects them to repent of their wicked behavior, not their righteous behavior. Regardless of motive, we should applaud unbelievers when they refuse to get an abortion, openly honor their parents or stay faithful to their spouse.

Sure, our motivation does need to be sanctified. But whether our motivation for something is pure or not, it is our behavior that defines our heart. We do not need to repent of good works or righteous deeds. It is from sin and disobedience to God's commands that our conscience needs to be cleansed of. This is what is meant by *dead works*.

> *"And for this reason He is the Mediator of the new covenant, by means of death, for the redemption of the transgressions under the first covenant, that those who are called may receive the promise of the eternal inheritance." - Hebrews 9:15*

The stated purpose of the new covenant is for "the redemption of the *transgressions* under the first covenant" not "the redemption from the *Torah* of the first covenant." This cannot be overstated. We are liberated from our sins, not from that which reveals our sinfulness.

Under the former covenant, Israel vowed to obey all that was written. Under the new covenant, however, there is no condemnation for those who are in Christ Jesus. We are no longer under judgment for our transgressions, for we have received the promise of our eternal inheritance through a better Mediator.

Jesus is identified as the Mediator of this new covenant. His role is to guide us, assist us and bring us into covenant relationship with His Father. Contrary to what some teach, the new covenant is not a contract made between God the Father and God the Son. There is no earthly covenant among the godhead. That concept is foreign to Scripture.

According to Jeremiah, the new covenant is clearly made between the house of Israel and the God of Israel. As our Mediator, Jesus Christ mediates the terms of peace so that our relationship with our Heavenly Father can be restored.

> *"For where there is a testament (diatheke), there must also of necessity be the death of the testator. For a testament (diatheke) is in force after men are dead, since it has no power at all while the testator lives. Therefore not even the first covenant was dedicated without blood. For when Moses had spoken every precept to all the people according to the law, he took the blood of calves and goats, with water, scarlet wool, and hyssop, and sprinkled both the book itself and all the people, saying, 'This is the blood of the covenant (diatheke) which God has commanded you.' Then likewise he sprinkled with blood both the tabernacle and all the vessels of the ministry. And according to the law almost all things are purified with blood, and without shedding of blood there is no remission."* - Hebrews 9:16-22

It is unfortunate that some translators translate *diatheke* as 'testament' in verse 15. Everywhere else it is translated covenant, except here. This translation gives the impression that the first covenant is likened to a last will and testament. This is a mischaracterization.

The death spoken here is not death to the law or to God's standard of righteousness. It is the death of our High Priest, who redeemed us from the sins committed against God's standard of righteousness. He is the Testator whose death opens wide the will of God.

Conclusion

Yeshua did not die to fulfill a sacrifice that is no longer required. He died to free us from our sins. Daily and yearly sacrifices are no longer needed, because the transgressions that those sacrifices atoned for have already been washed away. Oh, how precious is His sacrifice to us!

HEBREWS 10-11

Truth #65: *Setting aside the Torah leads to sin and death.*

The concept of perfection continues on into chapter 10. Perfection is the reason why the blood of Yeshua is greater than the blood of bulls and goats.

The sacrifice of Yeshua is perfect. The ministry of Yeshua is perfect. The priesthood of Yeshua is perfect. The intercession of Yeshua is perfect. While the sacrifices of the tabernacle "sanctify for the purification of the flesh" (9:13), only the blood of Christ perfects and "purifies our conscience from dead works to serve the living God" (9:14).

> *"For the law, having a shadow of the good things to come, and not the very image of the things, can never with these same sacrifices, which they offer continually year by year, make those who approach perfect. For then would they not have ceased to be offered? For the worshipers, once purified, would have had no more consciousness of sins. But in those sacrifices there is a reminder of sins every year."* - Hebrews 10:1-3

It might appear as though the writer is disparaging the Torah by calling the law "a shadow of the good things to come, and not the very image of the things." Some translations insert *but* or *only* or *merely* into the text, just as we encounter in Colossians 2:17. This gives the impression that the Torah is unimportant and irrelevant. But this is not how it should be construed.

It should read, "The law, having a shadow of the good things to come." In other words, within the law there is a shadow that is prophetic and points to something substantial and real. The entire Torah, including the Law of Moses, the Writings, the Prophets and the Apostolic Scriptures is not a shadow, but within them are shadows of things to come, prophetic glimpses of a future age. The fact that there is a shadow demonstrates there is something real within them.

In this case, the shadow is the Levitical sacrifices, and the reality is the priesthood of Jesus Christ. He is the substance of the law upon which the shadow is cast. He is the good thing to come. In Him everything comes into sharper focus.

The sacrifices are not the means of our forgiveness, but they point to the method by which God forgives sin. It is through the substitutionary death of our Lamb that we are redeemed. The nature of the laws concerning sacrifices and offerings gives evidence that a greater Priest and a greater sacrifice would be forthcoming.

> *"For it is not possible that the blood of bulls and goats could take away sins." - Hebrews 10:4*

This verse sheds a lot of light on the purpose of the sacrificial system. It is typically assumed that those who lived before the time of Christ could have their sins eradicated through offering a sacrifice at the temple. This is inaccurate. If animal sacrifices could eternally remove sins from the sinner, then there would have been no need to keep bringing offerings. If they were capable of spiritually washing us from sin, then there would be no reason for Christ to die.

The view that the tabernacle, priests and sacrifices temporarily did what Jesus permanently did is not quite accurate, either. It is only through the blood of Yeshua that sin can be taken away and removed, something that the sacrifices could not accomplish.

So, what was the purpose of bringing an offering to the temple? The purpose of a sin sacrifice was to cover the transgression so that a sinner could safely approach God's presence and worship as He prescribes. Sinful man needs an intercessor and innocent blood in order to stand before the Almighty. The priestly sacrifices provided such, not so much to gain salvation but to offer worship.

In this way, sacrifices were less about justification and more about purity. Bringing an offering to the Lord was an act of confession and humble obedience, not an act of conversion. Ultimately, the many different offerings were given to draw the sinner nearer to God and point them to God's ultimate sacrificial Lamb.

It cannot be over-emphasized that there are not two ways to be saved - one before Christ and one after. Salvation for Old Testament saints came through the same way in which we receive it – by grace through faith. Salvation has always been by grace through faith, never by religious works, rituals or ceremonies.

When bringing a sacrifice to the tabernacle, the sinner was not to look to the sacrifice as their saving grace. They were to look to the God of the sacrifice. They were to bring an offering believing that God would accept their worship and atone for their sin through their obedient act of faith. The sacrifices were neither received as a full payment for their sins, nor the promise for the remission of their sins. They were promised grace until One came who could save them out of their sin.

Faith Hall of Fame

This is the main point he is making in Hebrews chapter 11. Abel, Enoch, Noah, Abraham, Sarah, Isaac, Jacob, Joseph, Moses, Joshua, Rahab – they all trusted in the promise of the Promise-Keeper.

> *"Faith is the substance of things hoped for, the evidence of things not seen." - Hebrews 11:1*

Our spiritual forefathers possessed a faith that was forward looking. God warned Noah, and he "prepared an ark" (v.7). Abraham set out for "the land of promise" and "waited for the city which has foundations, whose builder and maker *is* God" (v.9,10). Sarah "judged Him faithful who had promised her." (v.11) Moses esteemed "the reproach of Christ greater riches than the treasures of Egypt; for he looked to the reward" (v.26). Rahab hid the spies and "did not perish with those who did not believe" (v.31). They all sought "a homeland" and "a heavenly country. Therefore, God is not ashamed to be called their God, for He has prepared a city for them" (v.14,16).

Of these champions, he writes:

> *"These all died in faith, not having received the promises, but having seen them afar off were assured of them." - Hebrews 11:13*

And,

> *"And all these, having obtained a good testimony through faith, did not receive the promise. God having provided something better for us, that they should not be made perfect apart from us." – Hebrews 11:39,40*

Yeshua is the Promise of God. Because our spiritual forefathers had faith in God and trusted in His promises, they possessed faith in Christ, even before the Messiah was manifest. When they looked at an animal sacrifice, God wanted them to see a prophetic picture of the coming Lamb of God. When they looked at the tabernacle, God wanted them to see the One who would someday tabernacle with us.

What they looked forward to, we look back on. They saw a coming Messiah. We see a Messiah who has already come. Their faith anticipated a God who would rescue them. Our faith appreciates a God who has and will continue to rescue us.

Possessing faith in something yet to come should not seem far out there to us. Within our own faith there remains an element that is both reflective and prophetic. We look back on the things that God has done, but we also look forward to the things that He has promised He will do. Our King has come but is still yet coming. In this way, our faith is both past looking and future expecting.

We see this demonstrated in the Passover communion. Reflecting on the broken body and shed blood of Jesus, we partake it in remembrance of Him.[1] Yet we are reminded that while Christ has

---

[1] Luke 22:19

come, He is still yet coming again. We will one day sit down with all the saints and enjoy a feast together in the kingdom of heaven. We are grateful for the salvation of our past, but eagerly await the salvation that lies before us. We remember what He has done and look forward with eager anticipation to what He said He will do.

It was no different for the saints of old. They had promises that they looked back on and forward to, just as we do. They put their faith in God's promised Messiah, just as we do.

Better than Sacrifice

> *"Therefore, when He came into the world, He said,*
> *'Sacrifice and offering You did not desire,*
> *But a body You have prepared for Me.*
> *In burnt offerings and sacrifices for sin You had no pleasure.*
> *Then I said, "Behold, I have come-*
> *In the volume of the book it is written of Me–*
> *To do Your will, O God.""* – Hebrews 10:5-7

Hebrews 10:5-7 quotes Psalm 40:6-8 prophetically as if Christ is the speaker. Here, Yeshua is the body that God prepared. He has come to fulfill all that is written of Him and is the One who takes delight in doing God's will.

> *"Sacrifice and offering You did not desire...In burnt offerings and sacrifices for sin You had no pleasure."* - Hebrews 10:5-6

This is not the only place we find the God of Israel expressing His displeasure at their offerings. Speaking through Jeremiah,

> *"Your burnt offerings are not acceptable, nor your sacrifices sweet to me."* - Jeremiah 6:20

Isaiah writes,

> *"'To what purpose is the multitude of your sacrifices to Me?,' says the Lord. 'I have had enough of burnt offerings and rams and the fat*

> *of fed cattle. I do not delight in the blood of bulls or of lambs or of goats...Bring me no more futile sacrifices.'"* - Isaiah 1:11, 13a

Hosea adds,

> *"For I desire mercy and not sacrifice and the knowledge of God more than burnt offerings."* - Hosea 6:6

As well David echoes,

> *"For You do not desire sacrifice, or else I would give it; You do not delight in burnt offering."* - Psalms 51:6

And Solomon,

> *"To do righteousness and justice is more acceptable to the Lord than sacrifice."* - Proverbs 21:3

How is it that God takes "no pleasure" in the very burnt offerings and sacrifices that He instituted and prescribed? Was the commandment faulty? If sacrifices and offerings were for the purpose of forgiveness, would God deny our spiritual forefathers the only means toward accomplishing that goal?

These verses give further proof that the sacrificial system under the Levitical priesthood was never instituted for the purpose of salvation. Why reject an offering if the offering is an act of repentance? This does not match the nature of God, nor does it match the nature of the offering. God's plea was that they would be restored to obedience and relationship with Him.

By expressing displeasure in their sacrifices, God is reminding us that salvation does not come through the deeds of the Torah. It is as though He was already preparing His people for a time when burnt offerings would no longer be necessary and of no effect. Fault is found with the ministers of the commandment and their need to repeat the offerings. Through the body of Christ, a better sacrifice would be offered - one that is perfect and would not need to be repeated.

Micah writes,

> *"What does the Lord require of you but to do justly, to love mercy, and to walk humbly with your God." - Micah 6:8*

It can only be that burnt offerings were never designed to take away sin, just as the writer of Hebrews indicates. The sacrifices of the Levites were for a different purpose than the sacrifice of Jesus. Whereas the sacrifice of Yeshua was heavenly and secured our salvation, the sacrifices at the tabernacle were for the purpose of earthly worship.

God was not rejecting their repentance in these verses. He was rejecting their unrepentant worship. God did not want a disobedient and rebellious people to draw near to Him, so He despised their efforts to bless their sinful ways. What He wanted was their obedience, not their sacrifice. Samuel conveys this same sentiment to Saul, "Has the Lord as great delight in burnt offerings and sacrifices, as in obeying the voice of the Lord? Behold, to obey is better than sacrifice, and to heed than the fat of rams" (1 Sam. 15:22).

First & Second

> *"He takes away the first that He may establish the second." - Hebrews 10:9b*

It cannot be overemphasized that "the first" here is not the Torah. Neither is it a reference to the old covenant. That which was vanishing is the sacrificial system of the Levitical priests. The first priesthood has been "taken away" so that the sacrifice of Christ (the second) could be firmly established.

> *"And every priest stands ministering daily and offering repeatedly the same sacrifices, which can never take away sins. But this Man, after He had offered one sacrifice for sins forever, sat down at the right hand of God, from that time waiting till His enemies are made His footstool. For by one offering He has perfected forever those who are being sanctified. But the Holy Spirit also witnesses to us; for after He*

> *had said before, 'This is the covenant that I will make with them after those days, says the Lord: I will put My laws into their hearts, and in their minds I will write them,' then He adds, 'Their sins and their lawless deeds I will remember no more.' Now where there is remission of these, there is no longer an offering for sin."* - Hebrews 10:11-18

The sacrifices made under the Aaronic priesthood had to be offered daily and yearly, which is the clearest evidence that they were impotent in putting an end to sin. If they could, why would they need to be repeated? It shows that the sin-guilt was still internally present within the person bringing the offering even after the sacrifice had been complete. If the sin had been removed, then there would have been no sin consciousness to remind them of their need of a sacrifice.[2]

While the blood of bulls and goats could cover sin, it could never completely remove it. It was ineffective in cleansing the heart.

Christ's sacrifice, however, was once and for all. It completely cleanses our guilty conscience and eliminates any other needed sacrifice for sin. Because our sins have been taken away, there is "no longer an offering for sin" (v.18) necessary.

Is the author saying that since Christ has offered Himself as our eternal sacrifice, there is no longer any use for animal sacrifices? Not so much. What he is saying is that Christ does not need to be crucified all over again to make payment for sins. The offense has been removed. No longer does the relationship need to be repaired. Another sacrifice is unnecessary.

> *"Their sins and their lawless deeds I will remember no more."* - Hebrews 10:17 quoting Jeremiah 31:34

---

[2] Some sacrifices were required due to no fault of the person. A person coming into contact with a dead body or a woman after childbirth were to bring a sacrifice to the tabernacle for the purpose of ritual cleansing. Once the offering had been made, there was no need to bring another.

What a glorious truth. Our sin and lawlessness has been forgiven, forgotten, forever! We are eternally grateful for our redemption and ever reminded that it was on account of our lawless deeds (*anomia*) that God sent His Son for us. This lawlessness includes all the commandments listed in the Torah. He has forgiven every one of them, whether our rebellion was intentional and not.

This is why I cannot embrace antinomianism. How can it be acceptable to continue in the behavior and willingly break the very laws that Jesus suffered on the cross for? Could it be that what caused the judgment of God in one generation is now the will of God for another? This is unacceptable to me. Any doctrine that teaches that what led to our falling away is now what God gives us license to do, in my opinion, is seriously misguided. And I am not alone in this sentiment.

> *"For if we sin willfully after we have received the knowledge of the truth, there no longer remains a sacrifice for sins, but a certain fearful expectation of judgment, and fiery indignation which will devour our adversaries. Anyone who has rejected Moses' law dies without mercy on the testimony of two or three witnesses. Of how much worse punishment, do you suppose, will he be thought worthy who has trampled the Son of God underfoot, counted the blood of the covenant by which he was sanctified a common thing, and insulted the Spirit of Grace? For we know Him who said, 'Vengeance is Mine, I will repay,' says the Lord. And again, 'The Lord will judge His people.' It is a fearful thing to fall into the hands of the living God." - Hebrews 10:26-31*

It is possible to willfully sin as a believer. But what is sin? What is a sin if the Torah has been removed? What are transgressions if the law has been annulled? The Torah is our dictionary.

If we remove the foundation upon which a house is built, that house will surely fall. If we remove that which is the standard of our righteousness and the foundation of Scripture, we are left with no knowledge of whether our lives are pleasing to God or not. God does not want to leave us ignorant of His ways. If sin is so strong that it could eternally separate us from God and require the cruel death of

His innocent Son, there must be a way of knowing what sin is or isn't.

Conclusion

When we set aside the Law of Moses, it leads to sin and death. How much worse if we spurn the Son of God and violate the spirit of grace through deliberate sin?

HEBREWS 12-13

Truth #66: *New covenant believers can be Torah honoring.*

"For you have not come to the mountain that may be touched and that burned with fire, and to blackness and darkness and tempest, and the sound of a trumpet and the voice of words, so that those who heard it begged that the word should not be spoken to them anymore. (For they could not endure what was commanded: "And if so much as a beast touches the mountain, it shall be stoned or shot with an arrow." And so terrifying was the sight that Moses said, "I am exceedingly afraid and trembling.") But you have come to Mount Zion and to the city of the living God, the heavenly Jerusalem, to an innumerable company of angels, to the general assembly and church of the firstborn who are registered in heaven, to God the Judge of all, to the spirits of just men made perfect, to Jesus the Mediator of the new covenant, and to the blood of sprinkling that speaks better things than that of Abel." - Hebrews 12:18-24

The author is not belittling what took place at Sinai. He is, rather, emphasizing how much more glorious our Mediator is. He is highlighting how much more effective His blood is and how much more secure the heavenly City is. Our hope is not dependent on the events surrounding Israel, Jerusalem or the temple. That is as true today as it was then.

The writer of Hebrews wants all God's children to know that we are a spiritual race that has come to a heavenly place. Our faith is not weighed down by earth. It is tethered to heaven. Any tension found in the book of Hebrews is not between the old and the new. It is between what is of heaven and what is of earth.

The Levitical priests with their sacrificial system are an earthly order, but the priesthood of Yeshua is a heavenly one. Since Christ serves in heaven, it is not necessary to think of His priesthood as superseding the Aaronic priesthood. Both priesthoods serve a purpose. One serves heaven. The other served earth. For an external cleansing, earthly sacrifices suffice, but for a spiritual cleansing a heavenly sacrifice is required.

> *"See that you do not refuse Him who speaks. For if they did not escape who refused Him who spoke on earth, much more shall we not escape if we turn away from Him who speaks from heaven, whose voice then shook the earth; but now He has promised, saying, 'Yet once more I shake not only the earth, but also heaven.' Now this, 'Yet once more,' indicates the removal of those things that are being shaken, as of things that are made, that the things which cannot be shaken may remain. Therefore, since we are receiving a kingdom which cannot be shaken, let us have grace, by which we may serve God acceptably with reverence and godly fear. For our God is a consuming fire."* - Hebrews 12:25-29

You will find commentaries that try to identify the Law of Moses as that which is removed and "being shaken" (v.27). Given the context, it simply cannot be. The previous verses regarding a heavenly kingdom reveal that that which is being shaken is the earth, the heavens and things that are made. He continues:

> *"Yet once more I shake not only the earth, but also heaven."* - Hebrews 12:26 quoting Haggai 2:6

And,

> *"The removal of those things that are being shaken, as of things that are made."* - Hebrews 12:27

The author is not contrasting the Torah with the new covenant. Neither is he denigrating the Hebrew Scriptures. He is comparing the voice of heaven with the voice of earth. He is contrasting those things that are heavenly with those things that are earthly. And when the shaking comes, only that which is of heaven will remain, including our faith.

Strange Doctrines

The author's voice changes in this final chapter of Hebrews, as many suspect that Paul picks up his pen to add a postscript to the teaching. He begins by addressing a few topics in shotgun style – brotherly love, strangers, prisoners, marriage, covetousness and spiritual rulers. He then writes,

> *"Do not be carried about with various and strange doctrines. For it is good that the heart be established by grace, not with foods which have not profited those who have been occupied with them."* - Hebrews 13:9

It has been presumed that Paul is attacking the "strange" doctrines of Torah's dietary guidelines and warns that those who follow them are being led away from grace. But which doctrine is strange here? Let's consider.

First, "strange" and "diverse" are not accurate descriptors of the dietary guidelines outlining animals unfit for consumption, especially considering that the author and the audience were both profoundly Jewish. God has the right to make some animals unfit for human consumption. This is not wacky or weird.

Never do we find Paul calling the Hebrew Scriptures or one of the commandments diverse or strange. Nor do we read of him steering people away from the word of God. In order for something to be strange, it would have to be new or foreign to the ears of the audience, something the dietary laws certainly were not.

Second, the doctrines that he speaks of here were an obligatory diet, not a restrictive one. In other words, the people pushing this strange doctrine insisted that eating certain foods could enhance one's spirituality. Paul was discouraging the believers from being preoccupied with these teachings and warned them to not to be carried away into believing that special or specified foods needed to be eaten in order to gain spiritual strength. Paul calls these doctrines diverse, strange and unprofitable to those occupied with them.

On the contrary, God's dietary standard is not obligatory but restrictive. It does not commend one type of food over another, as if grain is better than vegetables or meat is preferred to cheese. Neither do they demand the consumption of specific foods in order to increase spiritual power or gain favor with God. They simply outline those animals that are not to be consumed.

In contrast to the Biblical diet, the man-given doctrines of this strange doctrine make certain foods mandatory and hailed some foods as more spiritually beneficial than others. Now this qualifies as strange! This belief is more in line with first-century Gnosticism than with Biblical doctrine. Most likely Paul is addressing Gnostic doctrine here.

Therefore

"Therefore by Him let us continually offer the sacrifice of praise to God, that is, the fruit of our lips, giving thanks to His name." - Hebrews 13:15

Embedded in this verse is the last in a series of *therefores* found in the book of Hebrews. All in all, there are 28 *therefores* in this letter. Put together, they provide a nice overall summary of the book.

"You have loved righteousness and hated lawlessness; Therefore God, Your God, has anointed You with the oil of gladness more than Your companions." (1:9)

"Therefore we must give the more earnest heed to the things we have heard, lest we drift away." (2:1)

"Therefore, in all things He had to be made like His brethren, that He might be a merciful and faithful High Priest in things pertaining to God, to make propitiation for the sins of the people." (2:17)

"Therefore, holy brethren, partakers of the heavenly calling, consider the Apostle and High Priest of our confession, Christ Jesus." (3:1)

"Therefore, as the Holy Spirit says: "Today, if you will hear His voice, do not harden your hearts." (3:7-8a)

"Therefore I was angry with that generation, And said, 'They always go astray in their heart, And they have not known My ways.'" (3:10)

"Therefore, since a promise remains of entering His rest, let us fear lest any of you seem to have come short of it." (4:1)

"Since therefore it remains that some must enter it, and those to whom it was first preached did not enter because of disobedience." (4:6)

"There remains therefore a rest for the people of God." (4:9)

"Let us therefore be diligent to enter that rest, lest anyone fall according to the same example of disobedience." (4:11)

"Let us therefore come boldly to the throne of grace, that we may obtain mercy and find grace to help in time of need." (4:16)

"Therefore, leaving the discussion of the elementary principles of Christ, let us go on to perfection, not laying again the foundation of repentance from dead works and of faith toward God." (6:1)

"Therefore, if perfection were through the Levitical priesthood (for under it the people received the law), what further need was there that another priest should rise according to the order of Melchizedek, and not be called according to the order of Aaron?" (7:11)

"Therefore He is also able to save to the uttermost those who come to God through Him, since He always lives to make intercession for them." (7:25)

"For every high priest is appointed to offer both gifts and sacrifices. Therefore it is necessary that this One also have something to offer." (8:3)

"<u>Therefore</u> not even the first covenant was dedicated without blood." (9:18)

"<u>Therefore</u> it was necessary that the copies of the things in the heavens should be purified with these, but the heavenly things themselves with better sacrifices than these." (9:23)

"<u>Therefore</u>, when He came into the world, He said: "Sacrifice and offering You did not desire, But a body You have prepared for Me." (10:5)

"<u>Therefore</u>, brethren, having boldness to enter the Holiest by the blood of Jesus, by a new and living way which He consecrated for us, through the veil, that is, His flesh." (10:19-20)

"<u>Therefore</u> do not cast away your confidence, which has great reward." (10:35)

"<u>Therefore</u> from one man, and him as good as dead, were born as many as the stars of the sky in multitude-- innumerable as the sand which is by the seashore." (11:12)

"<u>Therefore</u> God is not ashamed to be called their God, for He has prepared a city for them." (11:16)

"<u>Therefore</u> we also, since we are surrounded by so great a cloud of witnesses, let us lay aside every weight, and the sin which so easily ensnares us, and let us run with endurance the race that is set before us." (12:1)

"<u>Therefore</u> strengthen the hands which hang down, and the feeble knees." (12:12)

"<u>Therefore</u>, since we are receiving a kingdom which cannot be shaken, let us have grace, by which we may serve God acceptably with reverence and godly fear." (12:28)

"<u>Therefore</u> Jesus also, that He might sanctify the people with His own blood, suffered outside the gate." (13:12)

"Therefore let us go forth to Him, outside the camp, bearing His reproach." (13:13)

"Therefore by Him let us continually offer the sacrifice of praise to God, that is, the fruit of our lips, giving thanks to His name." (13:15)

Conclusion

For forty years after the Resurrection, the temple continued to operate. Early Jewish Christians did not cease to participate in temple life, including the original apostles, the first-century church and Paul. These messianic believers did not look to a priest or a sacrifice for the forgiveness of their sins. They knew there was only One who could take away their sins. Just as we partake of communion as a commemoration of the finished work of Christ, so any offerings they would have brought would have served in a like manner.

Today, the daily sacrifices have ceased. The priests no longer minister and the temple no longer stands. This is of God's doing. With the destruction of the temple, daily and yearly sacrifices can no longer be offered and covenant maintenance no longer needs to be performed by a Levite. The destruction of the temple accelerated what had already been set in motion. A new priesthood has arrived.

The earthly priesthood was imperfect. It relied on imperfect priests offering imperfect sacrifices, but our heavenly Priest has provided for us a perfect priesthood established with His own perfect blood. What the blood of bulls and goats could not do, Christ did. While animal sacrifices could temporarily atone for sin, only the perfect sacrifice of Jesus could take them away completely and remove them once and for all.

Through this letter we discover that our life in Christ can be Torah honoring even within the context of the new covenant. The purpose of its writing was not to compare the gospel to the law or to warn against the apostasy of Judaism. It is an exhortation that prepares the new covenant reader for a post-temple expression through the revelation of the priesthood of Yeshua.

Upon examination, Hebrews is clearly less about the Torah and more about worship. Unlike the sacrifices offered under the Levitical priesthood, the perfect Lamb of God offered the perfect sacrifice through His own perfect blood to perfect our souls. It is Christ, not the law, that God gave to perfect us.

The book of Hebrews is Torah friendly. By my count, Hebrews quotes the law a total of 36 times, which is self-contradictory if one believes that the epistle is trying to prove that the Torah is no longer relevant. You don't cite the Torah authoritatively to disprove the Torah.

The Torah is not obsolete. What has grown obsolete are the earthly, man-involved provisions for approaching God.

> *"I saw no temple in it, for the Lord God Almighty and the Lamb are its temple." - Revelation 21:22*

Together with all the saints, we look forward to a day when our Mediator and Priest will return. On that day, there will be no more sorrow, no more pain and no need for a temple. He will be our temple in the New Jerusalem.

Section VIII

Book of James

JAMES 1

Truth #67: *James calls the Torah a law of liberty.*

The book of James has long been one of my favorites. As a young man it challenged me in ways that I needed to be challenged, and it still challenges me to this day. I find the language simple and the logic straightforward. Blunt at times, pastoral in tone, it is smooth and rich. Scholars tend to agree, as James' command of the Greek is excellent.

The author identifies himself in the first verse as James.[1] This is not James the son of Zebedee, the brother of John. James the apostle, one of the original Twelve, died much too early to have written this letter. King Herod had him put to the sword in Acts 12.

This is James, the son of Joseph and Mary, the half-brother of Yeshua and leader of the church of Jerusalem. Known as James the Just, he presided over the Jerusalem council and was well respected among the apostles.

This James, along with the elders in Jerusalem, advised Paul to fulfill his Nazarite vow and pay for the temple purification of four men as evidence that Paul was not teaching the Jews to forsake the Torah. Some scholars believe that James took a lifelong Nazirite vow. Quoting Hegesippus, Eusebius writes,

> "James drank no wine or intoxicating liquor, and ate no animal food; no razor came near his head."[2]

---

[1] Jacob or *Yakov* in Hebrew
[2] Eusebius, *Ecclesiastical History*, Book II, 23:4 [Online]. Available: http://www.documentacatholicaomnia.eu/03d/0265-0339,_Eusebius_Caesariensis,_Church_History_EN.pdf

Church history follows that around A.D. 62, James the Just was thrown down the pinnacle of the temple in Jerusalem and executed by stoning.[3]

I love how James opens his letter.

> *"James, a bondservant of God and of the Lord Jesus Christ, to the twelve tribes which scattered abroad. Greetings." - James 1:1*

James doesn't flash his credential badge as the brother of Jesus, the son of Mary or as having grown up in the same household with the King of the earth. He doesn't appeal to his status among the apostles or his leadership position in Jerusalem. Rather, he identifies himself as a bondservant of God and of Jesus Christ. He sees himself first as a servant of the Most High, just like any other disciple, just like you and me.

Humility must run in the family, because James' younger brother, Jude, begins his letter similarly.

> *"Jude, a bondservant of Jesus Christ and brother of James." - Jude 1*

While they both regarded themselves as servants of Christ, their view of their older brother was much higher than that. James refers to Him as the *Lord Jesus Christ*. Scripture does not elaborate on how James received this revelation or how he came to make this declaration. We do know that James, along with Jude and his brothers, did not initially believe in Yeshua's messianic identity, as it reads, "Even His brothers did not believe in Him" (John 7:5).

We learn from Scripture that Joseph and Mary had more children after the birth of Yeshua, and Yeshua's family had some level of interaction with Him throughout His ministry.[4] Yeshua's mother, brothers and disciples traveled together with Him from Cana to Capernaum after the famous wedding miracle.[5] On another occasion,

---

[3] Ibid, 23:1-25
[4] Matt. 13:55
[5] John 2:1-12

Mary and her sons came to inquire of Him but were unable to get through the crowds. When told that His mother and brothers were standing outside, Yeshua retorted, "My mother and brothers are those who hear the word of God and do it" (Luke 8:21).

In Acts we read that Mary and her sons were with the disciples in the upper room at Pentecost. They, too, had joined the fellowship of believers and experienced the baptism of the Holy Spirit. What changed between John 7 and Acts 1? The death and resurrection of Christ.

Mary and her sons undoubtedly were among the five hundred eyewitnesses of the Risen Lord. They must have viewed the empty tomb themselves and personally examined His nail-pierced hands. It is interesting to note that there was no more skepticism coming from those who were the closest to Him and saw Him grow up. Yeshua was indeed alive!

To James and the rest of his brothers, Jesus was no longer just their older brother born of a virgin. He was indeed the Son of God. Convinced of this, James calls Him the *Lord Jesus Christ*, perhaps the most profound and complete title given of Yeshua. It was for this confession that James would eventually surrender his life.

James' letter is addressed to "the twelve tribes which are scattered abroad" (v.1), giving little doubt as to the destination and audience of the book. James is speaking to Jewish believers who had been disbursed among the nations. These messianic Jews were most likely dispersed among the nations due to persecution.

Deception of Lawlessness

James' first reference to the Torah is found in chapter 1.

> *"Be doers of the word, and not just hearers only deceiving yourselves. For if anyone is a hearer of the word and not a doer, he is like a man observing his natural face in the mirror; for he observes himself, goes away, and immediately forgets what kind of man he was. But he who looks into the perfect law of liberty and continues in*

it, and is not a forgetful hearer but a doer of the work, this one will be blessed in what he does." - James 1:22-25

Nomos is the word used here for law. The first question we must answer is, "Given the context, is he referring to the Torah?" Without a doubt, yes. The topic centers on remaining faithful to God's word. The apostle is instructing them to not just hear God's word but to also put it into practice.

You will see that a warning and a promise are offered in these verses. The promise is: <u>Those who look into the perfect law, continue in it and are doers of good works, will be blessed in what they do.</u> James wants us to know that there is a blessing to be gained in keeping the Torah.

As disciples of Christ, we don't just read God's word. It reads us. Like a mirror, when we look into the Torah, we should not walk away and forget what it says. It is now a part of our identity and helps to shape the way we live.

James' warning is: <u>Those who only hear God's Word deceive themselves</u>. This is the error of hypocrites. They hear the word but do not put it into practice.

Proverbs 28:4 reads,

> *"Those who abandon Torah praise the wicked, but those who keep Torah fight them." (CJB)*

One way to be assured that you are not deceived is to keep the Torah. Now, how's that for a twist! We're so used to hearing the opposite. This verse ruffles the feathers of antinomians who purport the exact opposite.

According to James, the people aiming to practice the Torah are not the ones who are deceived. The deceived are those who hear God's word but do not act upon it.

Liberated from Lawlessness

In this verse and later in chapter 2, James refers to the Torah as "the perfect law of liberty." This is an interesting description, one that throws a wrench into the mischaracterization that the law is restrictive and burdensome. We've seen where the Bible calls the Torah perfect, but in what way is it liberating?

In my estimation, this liberation is the freedom to obey. Yeshua changed us and changed how we relate to the Torah. Outside of Christ, the law condemns us as sinners and cannot free us from our sins. In Christ, however, we are liberated from our sins and empowered to walk in obedience to God's commands. This is an emancipation like no other. It is the freedom to do good.

In Christ, we have been taken out of fallen man and restored to the original state of our created being. The Torah no longer renders us guilty sinners. We can now see it as the perfect Torah of liberty.

There is value in knowing what is right and what is wrong in God's eyes. It simplifies life and sets clear parameters for our conduct and conscience. We don't have to guess at what is expected of us. It leaves little room for relative truth. In a culture that is confusing evil with good and good with evil, we can find comfort in turning to God's word as our moral compass.

But the greatest value is in being free to choose good over evil, life over death, and what is right over what is wrong. When we know what is wicked, what is righteous and what is required of us, by God's grace we are empowered to please the Lord and walk in his will.

Some have argued that this requirement to obey the Torah applies only to Jews and to the nation of Israel. Since James is writing to a Jewish audience, it has been taught that any obligation to the Torah spoken here is intended only for Jewish believers. Gentile believers are under no compulsion to it.

That's cute.

Let's not forget that almost all of the books of the New Testament were intended for a Hebrew audience and written by an Israelite. Do we ignore them simply because they were addressed to Jews? Most of Jesus' ministry and parables were spoken to Jews. Should we disregard them as well? We have come to know the God of Abraham, Isaac and Jacob through a Jewish Messiah as revealed in the Hebrew Scriptures. Do we disregard the God of Israel and the King of the Jews as well?

These kinds of convenient interpretations reveal a couple of alarming doctrinal trends that plague us today. The first is that some segments of Christian academia are still stuck in identity theology. Jews, Gentiles, pagans, two houses, lost tribes of Israel – are we still trying to find an identity along these lines? No matter who we are ancestrally, it has no bearing on our faith in Jesus Christ and our commitment to Him. Our earthly lineage does not dictate our spiritual heritage. We should not allow ourselves to be divided by ethnicity or culture.

We are followers of Jesus Christ. We are one body in Yeshua. This is our identity, and this mentality should spill over into our approach to Scripture.

Heaven is not segregated. There will not be two lines leading into the New Jerusalem – one for the Jew and one for the Gentile. There are not isolated Jewish quarters in the Heavenly city with designated drinking fountains and segregated streets of gold. Nor does God have two separate standards of behavior for Jews and Gentiles in Christ.

We are one bride, one body, baptized into one Messiah. There is one law and one judgment for us all. It is our spiritual duty to resist anyone, including our own theologians, who insist on distinguishing and dividing us further along Jew and Gentile lines.

The second alarming trend is that we are still allowing replacement theology to dictate and distort our interpretation of Scripture. Replacement theology, which teaches that the Christian church replaces Israel, denies Israel her place in God's end-time plan.[6] Replacement theology insists that God the Father has rejected the Jewish people, because they have rejected God the Son. It teaches that the God of Israel has abolished His covenant with Israel and transferred the promises of Israel to the Gentile church, who are now true spiritual Israel. This theology has helped foment Christian anti-Semitism and is responsible for many of the evils done to the Jews at the hands of Christians.

When we see Scripture through this lens, it forces us to distance ourselves from anything Jewish and replace it with a spiritualized, Gentile-leaning form of Christianity. According to this doctrine, the church can claim any promise given to Israel. Consequently, any curse must fall right back on the heads of the Jewish people.

So, Gentile Christians get all the blessings and Jews get all the curses. That's convenient.

Paul states in no uncertain terms that Gentile Christians become grafted into Israel, not the other way around.[7] Christians don't replace Israel. They enlarge Israel. God doesn't ask the Jew to conform to Gentile morality. Rather, it is the Gentile who is to take on the Hebrew God, Hebrew Scriptures and Hebrew Messiah.

Before crying foul, realize this is a win for us Gentiles. Gentile believers get to have covenantal access to God through Christ. We are free to enjoy any blessing that God has given to His chosen people.

Conclusion

Sabbath, Feasts, tassels and kosher laws have traditionally defined Hebrew culture and served as Jewish identity markers. The Torah is also customarily used to distinguish Jews from Gentiles. This is a misstep, in my opinion.

---

[6] Dan. 9, Rev. 6-22
[7] Rom. 9-11

I do not view the commandments as markers of Jewish identity. God gave the Torah *through* the Jews, not exclusively *to* the Jews. The Bible never refers to God's commands as Jewish laws. God is the God of both Jews and Gentiles. So is the Torah.

The Bible's stance against cross-dressing, rape and kidnapping is not just applicable to Jews. Lying, stealing and murder are prohibitive actions for all. Refusing pork, honoring the Sabbath and celebrating the feasts are instructions given to every child of God regardless of gender or ethnicity. All of God's ways are for all of God's people. In them we are set apart.

That is not to say that there is no distinction between Jew and Gentile. There should be markers of Jewish identity. We should not deny any culture that privilege. But when we assume that certain laws outlined in Scripture are only for Jews and Jewish distinction, believing Gentiles lose the benefits of that moral blessing.

I do not believe that Jews becoming Gentiles and Gentiles becoming Jews is constructive. The goal is not to become more Jewish looking or embrace something more Jewish leaning. Just because something is Jewish or Christian does not make it better or more Biblical. Our goal is to become more like Christ.

JAMES 2-4

Truth #68: *Faith without the Torah is dead.*

> *"If you really fulfill the royal law according to Scripture, 'You shall love your neighbor as yourself,' you do well; but if you show partiality, you commit sin and are convicted by the law as transgressors." - James 2:8-9*

I referenced these two verses earlier in the book, but it bears revisiting. James is quoting Leviticus to convey the idea that loving our neighbor fulfills the law. Why would he cite the Torah authoritatively if the Torah is, as some teach, obsolete? And why would he encourage the law to be fulfilled if the law was already fulfilled in Christ and no longer relevant? There would be no law left to fulfill!

It can only be that fulfilling the law doesn't mean to bring it to an end. It means to carry out what it says. James is encouraging his readers to fulfill the Torah as Jesus did. This squares with the whole of the Bible and with how this phrase is used elsewhere in the Apostolic Scriptures.

Loving our neighbor as ourselves is not a new commandment, as it originates directly from the Torah. When we love our neighbor we fulfill the Torah, and in fulfilling the Torah we will love our neighbor. To do otherwise, according to James, is a violation of the royal Torah.

In this we can ascertain a part the Torah plays in our transformation – the conviction of sin. God's law through the Holy Spirit is still designed to convict us of transgressions. James appeals to the Torah in an effort to steer his audience away from sin, in this case, discriminatory behavior. This kind of partiality grieves the heart of God and violates what he calls the royal Torah.

> *"For whoever shall keep the whole law and yet stumble in one point, he is guilty of all. For He who said, 'Do not commit adultery,' also said, 'Do not murder.' Now if you do not commit adultery, but you do murder, you have become a transgressor of the law. So speak and do as those who will be judged by the law of liberty." - James 2:10-12*

Yet again, we can ascertain another role the Torah plays in the life of the believer – judgment. Those who remain in Christ will not be judged as the world is. Our judgment will be a judgment of works, not a judgment unto condemnation. We'll be held accountable for every idle word spoken, and we'll be rewarded for how we conduct ourselves in Christ. But praise God, our fate is not tied to that of the unbeliever. The godless will stand before the judgment seat condemned and without a plea.

We are all guilty of breaking the law, every one of us. We have all stumbled. We all need a Savior. It is our sinfulness that led us to Christ, and this is James' point.

Just as we once were under the judgment of God, so we should live as though we do not want to come under it again. We have escaped the wrath of God for our sins. What business do we have in entangling ourselves again with sin?

Peter agrees with James, writing,

> *"As obedient children, not conforming yourselves to the former lusts, as in your ignorance, but as He who called you is holy, you also be holy in all your conduct, because it is written, 'Be holy, for I am holy.' And if you call on the Father, who without partiality judges according to each one's work, conduct yourselves throughout the time of your stay here in fear." - 1 Peter 1:14-17*

James & Paul

> *"What does it profit, my brethren, if someone says he has faith but does not have works? Can faith save him? If a brother or sister is naked and destitute of daily food, and one of you says to them, 'Depart in peace, be warmed and filled,' but you do not give them the*

things which are needed for the body, what does it profit? Thus also faith by itself, if it does not have works, is dead. But someone will say, 'You have faith, and I have works.' Show me your faith without your works, and I will show you my faith by my works. You believe that there is one God. You do well. Even the demons believe—and tremble! But do you want to know, O foolish man, that faith without works is dead Was not Abraham our father justified by works when he offered Isaac his son on the altar? Do you see that faith was working together with his works, and by works faith was made perfect? And the Scripture was fulfilled which says, 'Abraham believed God, and it was accounted to him for righteousness.' And he was called the friend of God. You see then that a man is justified by works, and not by faith only. Likewise, was not Rahab the harlot also justified by works when she received the messengers and sent them out another way? For as the body without the spirit is dead, so faith without works is dead also." - James 2:14-26

It's hard not to notice the similarities between this portion of James and what Paul writes in Galatians 3, Ephesians 2 and Romans 4. James speaks of faith and works. So does Paul. James uses the life of Abraham to support his teaching. So does Paul. Yet it appears they arrive at two opposing and conflicting conclusions.

Paul writes,

> *"A man is not justified by the works of the law but by faith in Jesus Christ - Gal. 2:16."*

James writes,

> *"A man is justified by works, and not by faith only. For as the body without the spirit is dead, so faith without works is dead also." - James 2:24,26*

A more thorough study of the texts shows that there is no contradiction in scope or in content. Any contradiction between Paul and James is perceived but not actual.

In these passages, Paul is addressing a mostly Gentile audience that was grappling with pressure from certain Jewish groups to certify their newfound faith through circumcision and Jewish ceremonies. As the apostle to the Gentiles, Paul took it upon himself to tackle this false doctrine and clarify his position regarding the doctrine of grace. In so doing Paul dedicates much of his letters to the topics of faith and salvation.

When Paul speaks of justification, it is in terms of conversion. When he speaks of righteousness, it is often in reference to right standing with God, not righteous living. When he speaks of works, it is the works of Jewish rituals and ceremonies – the works of the law. Paul is not anti-Torah. He merely makes a point of saying that Torah adherence of any kind does not factor into our justification.

James, on the other hand, is a pastor who is writing to a more mature Jewish audience that is not grappling with salvation related issues. His letter focuses mainly on sanctification, discipleship and Christian conduct.

When James speaks of justification, it is justification evidenced by a holy lifestyle. When he speaks of righteousness, it is righteousness in terms of right living, not imputed righteousness. When he speaks of works, it is in reference to doing good deeds in Christ. James is no more Torah-friendly than Paul. He is merely addressing matters having less to do with redemption and having more to do with how we conduct ourselves as the redeemed.

So, here is where we find the reconciliation between the two. Paul is predominately writing to new Gentile converts wrestling with what it means to be saved. James is writing to grounded Jewish believers who are in need of wisdom and discipleship. One writes in the tone of an evangelist, the other with the heart of a pastor. One is addressing the doctrine of grace, the other our obligation to that grace. Any perceived contradiction is not attributed to the ethnicity of their audiences but to their individual needs.

Using the conventional definition of *works of law*, the two clearly contradict one another. But if *ergon nomos* is defined as Jewish regulations for entering and staying in the covenant, the doctrinal dilemma is alleviated. James is saying that a man's faith must be evidenced by his actions, while Paul means that salvation comes by faith and not by adherence to any law of man. Paul's use of *works of the law* is used very differently than James' use of *works*.

Being that Paul's writings were widely misunderstood in his time, you have to wonder if James felt compelled to use language similar, yet not in contrast, to combat any misinterpretation or misapplication of Paul's doctrine. It is only the definition of *ergon nomos* presented by the new perspective of Paul that successfully reconciles Paul's theology with James.

> *"Do not speak evil of one another, brethren. He who speaks evil of a brother and judges his brother, speaks evil of the law and judges the law. But if you judge the law, you are not a doer of the law but a judge. There is one Lawgiver, who is able to save and to destroy. Who are you to judge another?"* - James 4:11-12

It is curious to me that in his appeal to not speak evil of a brother, James warns against judging the Torah, as if judging and speaking evil of the Torah is more destructive than judging your brother. Who reasons like this? Apparently the Holy Spirit in James. This must have resonated with the ones reading this letter, as well. It can only be that they revered the Torah and held it in such high regard for this warning to be motivational and effective.

We all would agree that speaking evil of another believer is unloving and ungodly. But would we say that judging and speaking evil of the Torah is far more consequential? James does. He expects that his audience would never judge or speak evil of God's holy word. He uses this expectation to encourage them to treat their fellow believers in the same manner.

The Lawgiver

In wrapping up this book, we should take note that James refers to the Lord as the *Lawgiver* (4:12). Though not the most popular title for God, it is not a title we should overlook. We call the Torah the

Law of Moses, but in truth it is the Law of God. It is God's Torah. Moses was the faithful servant through which it was codified.

When it comes to how we scrutinize the Torah, we should keep this in mind. Would God give us a flawed gift? Would God say something evil? The law is like the Lawgiver - good and perfect. In the words of James himself,

> *"Every good and every perfect gift is from above, and comes down from the Father of lights, with whom there is no variation or shadow of turning." - James 1:17*

Conclusion

James 4 happens to be the last use of the word *nomos* found in the Apostolic Scriptures. The word does not appear in the books of Peter, the letters of John, Jude or Revelation. This should not surprise us. The relevancy of the Torah is a hotly debated topic currently, but it was not for the apostolic church. It was a given that Christ's followers would seek to keep the Torah and obey God's commands. Why would they not?

This expectation was not something that was seriously challenged, either in practice or in doctrine, because it was not in question. The apostles did not see a need to devote large portions of their writings to the topic of Torah's authority or to its rightful place in the life of Christ's disciples.

With that said, John the apostle still found a few more things to say about the Torah.

Section IX

Writings of John

LETTERS OF JOHN

Truth #69: *Keeping God's commandments pleases Him.*

It would be irresponsible to isolate Paul, Hebrews and the Gospels exclusively and independently from the rest of the Apostolic Scriptures. Any perceived negative depiction of the Torah dug up must be carefully weighed against the whole counsel of Scripture. Together, the entire Bible paints a complete mosaic of truth. This includes the writings of John.

John has much to say about the law in his letters, even though he withholds from specifically using the word *nomos*. He prefers the phrase "keeping His commandments" when referencing the Torah. According to Dr. David Friedman, the word used for commandments (*entolas*) is often used as the Greek cognate word for *mitzvah*, the Hebrew word for God's commandments.[1] If this is the case, John did have a lot to say about the Torah.

> *"Now by this we know that we know Him, if we keep His commandments. He who says, 'I know Him' and does not keep His commandments, is a liar, and the truth is not in him. But whoever keeps His word, truly the love of God is perfected in him. By this we know that we are in Him." - 1 John 2:3-5*

John states that the litmus test for determining if a person knows God is found in keeping his commandments. In John's eyes, a person truly knows God when they actively uphold and obey his commands. The Christian who professes to know God but shuns his word is only deceiving himself.

---

[1] Friedman, *They Loved The Torah*, 123

When we use the term "know God", we should seek to appreciate what it really means. By John's definition, to know God is to obey him, and to obey him is to know him.

This means that I could prophesy to the moon and raise the dead. I could pray until the earth stands still and impress the kings of the world with my eloquent words, but if I do not follow God's commands, I do not know the One I speak of. I am a truthless deceiver. We all could benefit from being reminded from time to time that the knowledge of God runs deeper than just a statement of faith or mental assent.

If I really want to know God and confess that I do, I've got to back up my declaration with my deeds. I must demonstrate that I know God by carrying out his commandments. To say that I know God requires evidence displayed in humble action. God is seemingly more than willing to reveal himself to those who commit themselves to his ways, but to those with a heart bent on disobedience, he will not allow himself to be known.

Leaving my Lawlessness

> *"Whoever commits sin also commits lawlessness, and sin is lawlessness." - 1 John 3:4*

Even though John doesn't use the word *nomos* in this letter, he does use its antonym *anomia*.[2] *Anomia* means a violation of the law. What kind of violation is John referring to? Given the context, it can only be Torahlessness. Breaking the law of the land or being civically lawless may indeed be a transgression, but it does not warrant such a statement as we read here. It can only be that John means to say that sin is Torahlessness, and Torahlessness is sin.

> *"And whatever we ask we receive from Him, because we keep His commandments and do those things that are pleasing in His sight. And this is His commandment, that we should believe on the name of*

---

[2] *Strong's* #G458 ἀνομία

> *His Son Jesus Christ and love one another, as He gave us commandment. Now he who keeps His commandments abides in Him and He in him. And by this we know that He abides in us, by the Spirit whom He had given us." - 1 John 3:22-24*

An oft-overlooked key to answered prayer is buried here in verse 22. According to John, we can know God by keeping his commands. In keeping his commands we make ourselves pleasing in God's sight. It is this pleasure that draws his favor. When believers live this way and ask for something in prayer, he is more than willing to answer. This is because we abide in him, and he abides in us. On the contrary, a heart bent on rebellion repeals God, as Proverbs 28:9 says, "God detests the prayers of a person who ignores the law." (NLT)

> *"By this we know that we love the children of God, when we love God and keep His commandments. For this is the love of God, that we keep His commandments. And His commandments are not burdensome." - 1 John 5:2-3*

Keeping God's commandments is the most practical way we can demonstrate our love for God and our love for others. When we keep his commands, we learn how to love more perfectly through God's word. We will invariably love our families better than we could have otherwise. We will be kinder to our boss. We will have more patience for those who rankle us, even to the point of loving our enemies.

> *"For this is the love of God, that we keep His commandments" (v.3).*

John is teaching us that love for God and love for God's word are inseparable. When we seek to grow in our devotion to God's word, we will always grow in our expression of God's love to the world around us.

If you have been led to believe that the Torah is too harsh, confusing and unbearable to take on, let this verse put your heart at ease. When John says that God's commandments are "not too burdensome," he may have had in mind Deuteronomy 30:11 which says, "Now what I am commanding you today is not too difficult for you or beyond your reach" (NIV).

If keeping the Torah was not too difficult for those under the old covenant, then how much more for those under the new? If it was not beyond their reach, then how much more is it within our grasp now that God's word is being branded upon our hearts?

Some estimate that there are over 5,000 U.S. criminal laws at the federal level. This does not include the 10,000-300,000 regulations that can be enforced criminally. This also doesn't take into account fraud, immigration, bankruptcy, civil rights and copyright laws, as well as the many state, local and traffic laws on the books. Because there are so many laws in our land, some estimate that the average citizen unknowingly breaks over three laws a day.

Seeking to obey the laws of the land is being a responsible citizen and is encouraged in Scripture.[3] How is it that some maintain we must keep civic laws but are free to break divine laws? In doing so, they admit that Christ didn't die to free us from the authority of the law.

While keeping every law of the land might be an impossible task, not so with God's laws. His expectations are not too numerous, too burdensome or too complicated for us to take on. God doesn't keep adding new laws everyday like our lawmakers; nor does he make them so confusing that they cannot be understood.

Be encouraged to know that walking blamelessly before God is not an impossible task. It is a goal worth pursuing.

> *"This is love, that we walk according to His commandments. This is the commandment, that as you have heard from the beginning, you should walk in it." - 2 John 6*

---

[3] Rom. 13:1-7, 1 Peter 2:13-25

This verse perfectly encapsulates John's opinion of the Torah – love. Loving God is keeping his commandments, and in keeping his commandments, we love God.

Book of Revelation

> *"The dragon was enraged with the woman, and he went to make war with the rest of her offspring, who keep the commandments of God and have the testimony of Jesus Christ...Here is the patience of the saints; here are those who keep the commandments of God and the faith of Jesus." - Revelation 12:17, 14:12*

In the last days we read that there will be those who maintain the testimony of Jesus Christ and keep the commandments of God. In fact, one of the hallmark characteristics of end-time believers is their radical commitment to God's commandments. This can only happen if we are convinced that the Torah is relevant and worthy to be kept.

John is writing about a future event, which means that Torah keeping is not going away. As you seek to make the Torah relevant in your life, you are contributing to a last-days generation who will stand up to the dragon.

Perhaps we can see now why John felt the way he did about God's commands? If we were to see what he saw and know what he knew, we might come to the same conclusions.

> *"Blessed are those who do His commandments, that they may have the right to the tree of life, and may enter through the gates into the city." - Revelation 22:14*

Happy are those who keep the Torah, for there is a two-fold blessing promised to those who do his commandments. (1) They will be given the right to eat from the eternal tree of life, and (2) they will be given passageway into the Heavenly city.

Conclusion

In a culture drunk on arguing the correct way in which the Torah should be followed, John refuses to serve up drinks. Instead of weighing in with his opinion, he simply emphasizes love.

Compiling all of John's statements together, we can ascertain his doctrine regarding the Torah and gain a richer understanding of what he means by keeping God's commands. Paraphrasing John:

- We know God if we keep his commandments. (1 John 2:3)

- The love of God is perfected in us when we keep his word. (1 John 2:5)

- We know we are in him when we keep his word (1 John 2:5).

- Sin is Torahlessness, and Torahlessness is sin (1 John 3:4).

- Those who keep his commandments receive whatever they ask of him (1 John 3:22).

- Keeping his commandments is pleasing in his sight (1 John 3:22).

- If we keep his commandments, we abide in him and he in us (1 John 3:24).

- Loving God and keeping his commandments is loving God's people (1 John 5:2).

- The love of God is keeping his commandments (1 John 5:3).

- God's commandments are not burdensome (1 John 5:3).

- Love is walking according to God's commandments (2 John 6).

- Keeping God's commandments is the commandment we received from the beginning and should walk in (2 John 6).

- The dragon makes war with those who keep the commandments of God and have the testimony of Jesus Christ (Rev. 12:17).

- The saints are those who keep the commandments of God and have the faith of Yeshua (Rev. 14:12).

- Happy are those who obey his commands (Rev. 22:14).

- Those who do his commandments will have the right to the tree of life and may enter through the gates of the city of God (Rev. 22:14).

Conclusion

Truth #70: *The Holy Spirit is restoring the ancient paths of truth.*

In 2 Kings 22, the scribe Shaphan is sent to the temple with orders to conduct business for the king. He and Hilkiah, the high priest, were to instruct the temple overseers to compensate and provide building supplies to those doing repairs to the house of God.

During his visit, Hilkiah stumbles upon a lost treasure in the temple. He tells Shaphan, "I have found the Book of the Law in the house of the Lord." Shaphan reads it and in turn delivers it to King Josiah.

Upon hearing the words of the book, King Josiah rends his garments. Scripture records that Josiah, being in great anguish, wept bitterly and was deeply troubled by how far the nation had fallen away from the Lord. He consults Huldah the prophetess who confirms that calamity was indeed coming upon Judah due their sin. But because Josiah humbled himself and responded tenderly before the Lord, the king would not see the destruction in his lifetime.

What happens next is nothing short of revolutionary.

Josiah gathers all the people of Jerusalem, both small and great, and has every word of the Book of the Law read to them. He orders all pagan articles removed from the temple and burned in the Kidron Valley. He tears down the high places, cuts down the sacred pillars, destroys the shrines built to false gods and desecrates every detestable altar. He strips the idolatrous priests of their posts. He then executes the sorcerers of the high places, grinds their bones to powder and spreads their ashes over the graves.

There the king made a covenant before heaven to keep all of God's commandments and wholeheartedly follow everything written in the book of the Law. Then King Josiah publicly proclaimed that everyone must, "Keep the Passover to the Lord your God, as it is written in this Book of the Covenant" (2 Kings 23:21).

Josiah stewarded a revelation that provoked a revolution. It was the first and perhaps greatest revival recorded in all of Scripture. Of King Josiah it is written,

> *"No king before or after repented before the LORD as he did, with his whole heart, soul, and being in accordance with the whole law of Moses." - 2 Kings 23:25, NET*

This story accurately depicts the waters in which the western church now navigates. We've erected pillars and idols and shrines. We've built large edifices and mega-ministries only to uproot the very spiritual foundations upon which they lie. Our culture has reduced pastors to businessmen, ministers to salesmen and preachers to hired hands. The affairs of the church have cluttered our image and damaged the house of God, leaving it fragmented and in need of repair.

It is this same Book of the Law that has been carelessly ignored and tragically misunderstood. The Torah of God, the very words of the Almighty God, given so gloriously and miraculously on that mountain, personally and intentionally spoken from heaven and in unprecedented fashion, has once again been misplaced, neglected and relegated to a broom closet in the basement of our theology. Like ancient Judah, we too are in need of a rediscovery of God's word. Like Elisha, it's time we are reunited with our lost axe head.

Our neglect of God's word has taken a toll on what we seek to build, and in the process we've lost touch with the ways of God. We are once again in need of revival.

I believe the Holy Spirit is arming scribes with fresh revelation willing to write the vision down, make it plain, run with obedience and present it as an offering before our King. His call goes out to those who are willing to search the courts of God, rediscover what has been lost and bring forth treasures both new and old. May God grant to us Josiahs in our time. Ones who will arise, rend their garments, steward a revelation, awaken a revolution and call a nation back to God.

> *"Repent and be converted, that your sins may be blotted out, so that time of refreshing may come from the presence of the Lord, and that He may send Jesus Christ, who was preached to you before, whom heaven must receive until the <u>times of restoration of all things</u>, which God has spoken by the mouth of all His holy prophets since the world began." – Acts 3:19-21*

Restoring the Torah to a more prominent place in the body of Christ is an integral part of the restoration of all things. What was prophesied two centuries ago is unfolding before our eyes.

We are living in unparalleled times of accelerated reformation. The Spirit of God is restoring to us the integrity and purity of the King's message to the world. He is exposing the lies we've inherited. He is reuniting us with the wisdom of our true spiritual fathers and returning us to the ways of our Heavenly Father.

For many, reformation in this manner is too dissentious, too precarious, too severe. This, however, is the stuff revivals are made of. All reformations have radical origins. New wine must have a new wineskin.

> *"No one puts new wine into old wineskins; or else the new wine will burst the wineskins and be spilled, and the wineskins will be ruined. But new wine must be put into new wineskins, and both are preserved. And no one, having drunk old wine, immediately desires new; for he says, 'The old is better.'" – Luke 5:37-39*

Torah pursuance is the new wineskin, and God's Torah is the aged wine. All who drink of this ancient archive of wisdom will not go unsatisfied.

WHAT NOW?

Where do we go from here? Here are five practical ways we can S-H-I-F-T the culture and S.H.I.F.T. our mindset.

1) *Stay balanced*

Some make the mistake of aimlessly taking up Hebrew culture and customs in their pursuit of the Torah. They readily embrace Orthodox Judaism, follow the Mishnah, take up the 613 commandments or even reject Yeshua as the Messiah. In coming out of Christian error, they flirt with falling back into a similar system of spiritless religion. Essentially, they exchange one set of man-made traditions for another.

God's truth is a narrow path of life. When we veer off to one side of the road, we must be careful not to overcorrect and tumble off the other. In pulling ourselves out of this ditch of lawlessness, do not make the mistake of plunging into an equally dangerous precipice on the other side of the road. Just because something is Jewish doesn't automatically make it spiritually superior.

My family and I recently attended a *bar mitzvah* at a local synagogue. During the ceremony, the Torah scroll was proudly and solemnly removed from the golden ark where it was housed under lock and key center stage behind the lectern. A mini processional formed as the scroll was presented and paraded around the room. People sang, danced and even kissed the Torah scroll as it passed by.

I was delighted that God's word was honored in such a grandiose way. At the same time, I was also grieved knowing this was a reformed synagogue that openly endorsed queer and homosexual lifestyles. How ironic that those idolizing the Torah blatantly undermined it. They honored God's word with their lips but desecrated it with their life.

Do not assume that because this book concentrates singularly on Torah matters that I wish to elevate the Torah beyond its rightful place. In our pursuit of a Christ-centered Torah, we cannot allow ourselves to make an idol out of the Torah or mindlessly embrace all things Jewish. Torah-worship and Torah-defiance are both deplorable.

Stay balanced. Refuse to allow modern Jewish culture or even Torah culture to supplant the Torah-Giver in your heart.

2) *Holy lifestyle worship*

Worship is often thought of as a Christian gathering that involves singing. No doubt this type of expression is meaningful and indispensable to the life of a believer. Some of the most powerful moments of my life have taken place in corporate worship settings.

True worship, however, is what happens when we leave the meeting. Worshipping God in the beauty of holiness is the God-honoring lifestyle we practice outside the doors of the church.

> *"Therefore, I urge you, brothers and sisters, in view of God's mercy, to offer your bodies as a living sacrifice, holy and pleasing to God-- this is your <u>true and proper worship</u>."* – Romans 12:1 NIV

True and proper worship is more action based than event oriented. Too often believers condemn themselves for not praying enough or going to church more often. I have come to the realization that my devotion to God is not limited to my prayer life or church attendance record. These matter, of course, but how we live our lives every day in holiness before God is truly how we worship Him.

This means that honoring the Sabbath can be a spiritual undertaking. Refraining from eating pork is holy behavior. Celebrating a Biblical festival or wearing *tzitzit* is a loving act of worship. Helping the homeless, feeding the hungry, discipling your children, guarding your eyes, honoring your parents, serving your spouse – all comprise a life of worship before God and all take place mostly outside church walls.

3) *Intentional community*

It may not be realistic to recreate the church of the first century in the modern era. We can, however, create communities of like-minded believers that gather together on God's appointed days.

> *"Not forsaking the <u>assembling together</u> of ourselves as is the custom with some, but encouraging one another, and so much more as you see the Day drawing near." - Hebrews 10:25 Berean Literal Bible*

Even though the earliest manuscripts are written in Greek, no doubt the writer of Hebrews originally wrote his letter in Hebrew. *Assembling together* in Hebrew implies more than synagogue or church attendance. It denotes the gathering together of God's people.[1]

When the saints are gathered together in the last days, it is a prophetic foreshadowing of when we will meet Him in the air. What cannot be lost is the connection this monumental event has to Sabbath and the feasts. As we see "the Day drawing near," assembling together during God's appointed times prepares us for the second coming of Christ.

The community Meljoné and I are blessed to serve is intentional about gathering together for every Biblical feast. My encouragement is that you find a community of like-minded believers pursuing the whole counsel of Scripture. Honest, loving community is vital to our discipleship in Christ. There is something richly prophetic about gathering together on God's appointed times.

4) *Fervent study*

> *"Study to show yourself approved unto God, a workman that needs not to be ashamed, rightly dividing the <u>word of truth</u>." – 2 Timothy 2:15, King James 2000 Bible*

---

[1] 2 Thess. 2:1, 2 Mac. 2:5

This word of truth that Paul instructs Timothy to study is the Torah. God's word, especially what is called the Old Testament, is not too lofty for you. It is not too deep, too holy or too complicated. It is simple and practical in application. It addresses every important aspect of life – relationships, marriage, parenting, prayer, worship, temptation, money, sex, food, work, sleep, health, rest, death, eternity and so much more.

I have found that as I sharpen my spirit on God's revelation, I sharpen my mindset. When I do, what pleases and displeases Him comes into sharper focus.

Because we have historically under-emphasized the Torah, it might take some time (1) revisiting, (2) reinvestigating and (3) reinvesting in the Hebrew Scriptures. My encouragement is that you be purposeful in reading and studying the entire Bible. Consider taking up the weekly Torah portion reading schedule for a year. Meditate on five Psalms and one Proverb a day. Take a deep dive into the Prophets with your study group. Search out those Hebrew passages quoted in the New Testament. With a little digging, Christ can be found on every page of the Bible, including the Torah.

5) *Torah-honoring theology*

It's becoming clearer to me every day that the most urgent problem besetting the church is not sin but our acceptance of sin. This is why theology matters. How we view God and what we believe about Him has a direct influence on how we live our lives.

I once watched a daytime talk show featuring swingers. Swingers are married couples that openly, mutually and consensually engage in adulterous relationships with other married couples. The four couples on stage boasted of their wild escapades and swinger parties, waxing long about how wonderful it was to be liberated from hiding their secret infidelities from their partner.

When the host turned to the studio audience, a woman stood up with a question for the panel. She asked, "Morally speaking, how do you feel about your lifestyle? Does God approve of your behavior?"

One of the guests was quick to interject. She eagerly retorted, "Oh, well, I'm Baptist. I believe once saved, always saved. So, it doesn't really matter what I do. I'll be alright with God."

False doctrine is far more dangerous than we might realize. Bad theology is responsible for more evil among us than bad leadership. We cannot be like Christ when our theology is anti-Christ. A doctrine that is lawless produces lawless behavior.

Modern Christianity doesn't accept that all Scripture is inerrant. Reformed theology believes new revelation can trump established truths. Antinomianism maintains that there is no law by which a believer must submit to. Dispensationalism teaches that truth is temporary and that God periodically changes how He deals with humanity.

Our theology needs emancipation from lawless indoctrination. You and I should not be comfortable with a doctrine that cuts whole chapters and verses out of the Bible. We must commit to roundly rejecting any theology that permits a believer to openly and willingly break God's commandments.

Large-scale theological reform doesn't happen overnight. Like seeing a chiropractor, it may require small adjustments in order to realign the backbone of our doctrine. We've endured centuries of traditional and theological misconceptions regarding the Torah, and it may take another century to undo them. But if we are serious about being more prophetically accurate, we must insist on being more theologically accurate as well.

Literature Consulted

Abegg, Martin. "Paul, Works of the Law and MMT." *Biblical Archaeology Review*, Nov-Dec 1994.

Achtemier, Paul J. *Harper's Bible Dictionary*. San Francisco: Harper and Row, 1985.

Aland, Kurt and Barbara. *The Greek New Testament*, 3rd edition. United Kingdom: United Bible Society, 1983.

Allen, John, Translator. *Institutes of the Christian Religion* by John Calvin, 2 Volumes. Philadelphia, PA: Presbyterian Board of Publication and Sabbath-School Work, 1921.

Aquinas, Thomas. *Summa Theologiae,* Vol. 1. Cincinnati: Benzinger Bros, 1947.

Augustine. *On The Spirit And The Letter.* 412 A.D., URL = https://www.newadvent.org/fathers/1502.htm.

Augustine. *Contra Faustum,* 400 A.D., URL = www.documenta catholicaomnia.eu/03d/0354-0430,_Augustinus,_Contra_Faustum_Manichaeum_%5BSchaff%5D,_EN.pdf.

Bamberger, Bernard J. *Proselytes in the Talmudic Period*. New York: KTAV Publishing House, 1939.

Barclay, William. *New Testament Words.* Philadelphia, PA: The Westminster Press, 1974.

Barclay, William. *The Letter To The Romans: The Daily Study Bible.* Edinburgh, Scotland: The Saint Andrew Press, 1955.

Barnard, L.W. *Justin Martyr, His Life and Thought.* UK: Cambridge University Press, 2008.

Barnes, Albert and James Murphy. *Barnes Notes on the Old and New Testaments.* Glasgow, Scotland: Blackie & Son, 1884-1885.

Barrett, C.K. *The First Epistle to the Corinthians.* Peabody, MA: Henrickson Publishers, 1968.

Bauer, Gingrich, Arndt & Danker. *A Greek-English Lexicon of the New Testament.* Chicago, IL: The University of Chicago Press, 1979.

Bayes, Jonathan. "The Threefold Division of the Law." *Reformation Today*, Issue 177.

Beecher, H.W. *The Biblical Illustrator.* Electronic Database, Biblesoft, 2002.

Belgic Confession, 156 C.E. Translation approved by Synod 2011 of the Christian Reformed Church in North America and by General Synod 2011 of the Reformed Church in America: Faith Alive Christian Resources, 2011.

Bell, H. Idris. *Jews and Christians in Egypt.* San Francisco, CA: Greenwood Press, 1972.

Ben Mordechai, Avi. *Galatians: A Torah-Based Commentary in First-Century Hebraic Context.* Israel: Millennium 7000 Communications, 2005.

Ben-Lyman HaNaviy, Ariel. *Acts 10: Peter's Vision of the Sheet.* www.graftedin.com.

Ben-Lyman HaNaviy, Ariel, *Exegeting Galatians.* 2018. www.servantofmessiah.org.

Benson, Joseph. *Commentary on the Old and New Testaments.* www.Biblehub.com.

Bertram, Martin H., Translator. *Luther's Works*, Volume 47 *On The Jews and Their Lies.* Philadelphia, PA: Fortress Press, 1971.

Literature Consulted

Bibliowicz, A.M. *Jews and Gentiles in the Early Jesus Movement.* London: Palgrave Macmillan, 2013.

Bivin, David. *New Light On The Difficult Word Of Jesus: Insights From His Jewish Context.* En Gedi: Lois Tverberg and Bruce Okkema, 2005.

Bostock, John and H.T. Riley, Translators. Pliny the Elder. *The Natural History of Pliny.* London: Henry G. Bohn, 1855.

Boyarin, Daniel. *The Jewish Gospels: The Story of the Jewish Christ.* New York: The New Press, 2012.

Brandt, Walter. *Luther's Works*, Volumes 1-55, English Version. Minneapolis, MN: Fortress Press, 1957.

Brecht, Martin. *Martin Luther*, Volumes 1-3. Minneapolis, MN: Fortress Press, 1985–1993.

Brown, Colin. *The New International Dictionary of New Testament Theology,* Vol. 1-4. Grand Rapids, MI: Regency Reference Library, 1967.

Browning, W.R.F. "Emperor worship," *A Dictionary of the Bible, Oxford Biblical Studies Online.* URL = www.oxfordbiblicalstudies.com.

Bruce, F.F. *New International Commentary of the New Testament: The Book Of The Acts.* Grand Rapids, MI: Eerdmans Publishing Company, 1988.

Bruce, F.F. *The Spreading Flame,* Grand Rapids, MI: WM. B. Eerdmans Publishing Company, 1954.

Bruce, F.F. *Tyndale New Testament Commentaries: Romans.* Grand Rapids, MI: Eerdmans Publishing Company, 1985.

Calvin, John. *Institutes of the Christian Religion.* Philadelphia: Presbyterian Board of Publication, 1813.

Chadwick, Henry, Translator. Origen: *Contra Celsum*. UK: Cambridge University Press, 1980.

Christianity Today. "Origen" article, August 2008.

Clark, Kenneth W. *Worship in the Jerusalem Temple After 70 A.D.*, found in *New Testament Studies,* Volume 6. United Kingdom: Cambridge Studies Press, 1959.

Cole, R. Alan. *The Epistle of Paul to the Galatians: An Introductory and Commentary.* Grand Rapids, MI: Eerdmans Publishing Company, 1965.

Cole, R. Alan. *Tyndale New Testament Commentaries: Mark.* Grand Rapids, MI: William B. Eerdmans Publishing Company, 1989.

Comfort, Ray. *The Evidence Bible.* Gainesville, FL: Bridge Logos Publishers, 2001.

Conybeare, William. *The Life and Epistle of St. Paul.* Grand Rapids, MI: Eerdmans Company, 1978.

Cranfield, C.E.B. *A Critical and Exegetical Commentary on The Epistle to the Romans,* Volumes 1-2. Edinburgh: T & T Clark, 1975.

Dacy, Marianne. "Anti- Judaism in the New Testament and Christian Theology," International Council of Christians and Jews, June 26, 2013. Web. March 4, 2014.

Dake, Finis Jennings. *Dake's Annotated Reference Bible.* Lawrenceville, GA: Dake Bible Sales, Inc., 1961.

Davies. W.D. *Paul and Rabbinic Judaism.* New York: Harper Torchbooks, 1948.

Deferrari, Roy J., Translator. *Ecclesiastic History* by Eusebius Pamphili, Books 6-10. Washington, D.C.: The Catholic University of America Press, 1955.

Didache. www.thedidache.com.

Dockery, David S. *Holman Bible Handbook.* Nashville, TN: Holman Bible Publishers, 1992.

Douglas, J.D. *New Bible Dictionary.* Leicester, England: Inter-Varsity Press, 1962.

Dryden, Jeff. "4QMMT," 2011, URL = http://www.tyndale.cam.ac.uk/Tyndale/staff/Head/4QMMT.htm.

Dummelow, J.R. *A Commentary on the Holy Bible.* New York: MacMillan Publishing Company, 1908.

Dunn, James D. G. *The New Perspective on Paul.* Grand Rapids, MI: William B. Eerdmans Publishing Company, 2008.

Edwards, Mark J. "Origen", *The Stanford Encyclopedia of Philosophy* (Summer 2018 Edition), Edward N. Zalta (ed.). URL = https://plato.stanford.edu/archives/sum2018/entries/origen/.

Einspahr, Bruce. *Index to Brown, Driver & Briggs Hebrew Lexicon.* Chicago, IL: Moody Publishers, 1976.

Eisenberg, Ronald L. *What the Rabbis Said: 250 Topics from the Talmud.* Pittsburgh, PA: Praeger, 2010.

Ellicott, Charles J. *Ellicott's Bible Commentary for English Readers.* Harrington, DE: Delmarva Publications, Inc., 2015.

Encyclopedia Britannica. "Great Dionysia: Greek Festival." www.brittanica.com.

Eusebius, *Ecclesiastical History*, URL = http://www.documenta catholicaomnia.eu/03d/0265-0339,_Eusebius_Caesariensis,_Church _History,_EN.pdf.

Falk, Gerhard. *The Jew in Christian Theology.* Jefferson, NC: McFarland and Company, Inc., 1931.

Fee, Gordon D. *Corinthians: A Study Guide.* Irving, TX: ICI University Press, 1979.

Feldman, Louis H. Biblical Archaeology Review, Vol. 27. 2001, July/August, No. 4.

Feldman, Louis H. *Josephus and Modern Scholarship.* New York: Walter De Gruyter & Co., 1984.

First Fruits Of Zion. *HaYesod: The Land, the People and the Scriptures of Israel.* Marshfield, MO: First Fruits of Zion, Inc., 2010.

Foulkes, Francis. *Tyndale New Testament Commentaries: Ephesians.* Grand Rapids, MI: William B. Eerdmans Publishing Company, 1989.

France, R.T. *Tyndale New Testament Commentaries: Matthew.* Grand Rapids, MI: William B. Eerdmans Publishing Company, 1989.

Friedman, David. *The Loved The Torah: What Yeshua's First Followers Really Thought about the Law.* Clarksville, MD: Lederer Books, 2001.

Garcia Martinez, Florentino, and Albert J.C. Tigchelaar. *The Dead Sea Scrolls Study Edition.* Leidon: Brill, 1998.

Gasque, W. Ward and Ralph P. Martin. *Apostolic History and the Gospels.* London: Paternoster Press, 1970.

George, A.C. *Hebrews: A Study Guide.* Irving, TX: ICI University Press, 1979.

Gephart, Rodger F. *C. Suetonii Tranquilli Vita Domitiani Suetonius's Life of Domitian.* London: Forgotten Books, 2018.

Gill, John. *Gill's Exposition of the Entire Bible.* Kindle Edition, 2012.

Literature Consulted

Golb, Norman. *Who Wrote the Dead Sea Scrolls?: The Search for the Secret of Qumran.* New York: Touchstone: Simon and Schuster, 1995.

Goodrick, Edward W. and John R. Kohlenberger III. *The NIV Exhaustive Concordance.* Grand Rapids, MI: Zondervan Publishing House, 1990.

Gordon, S.D. *Quiet Talks on Prayer.* Shippensburg, PA: Destiny Image Publishers, 2003.

Gould, Ezra. *A Critical and Exegetical Commentary on the Gospel according to St. Mark.* Edinburgh: T&T Clark, 1896.

Green, Jay P. *The Interlinear Bible: Hebrew, Greek, English.* Peabody, MA: Hendrickson Publishers, 1976.

Green, Michael. *Tyndale New Testament Commentaries: 2 Peter and Jude.* Grand Rapids, MI: William B. Eerdmans Publishing Company, 1989.

Grudem, Wayne. *Tyndale New Testament Commentaries: 1 Peter.* Grand Rapids, MI: William B. Eerdmans Publishing Company, 1989.

Guthrie, Donald. *New Testament Introduction.* Downers Grove, IL: InterVarsity Press, 1990.

Guthrie, Donald. *Tyndale New Testament Commentaries: Hebrews.* Grand Rapids, MI: William B. Eerdmans Publishing Company, 1989.

Guthrie, Donald. *Tyndale New Testament Commentaries: The Pastoral Epistles.* Grand Rapids, MI: William B. Eerdmans Publishing Company, 1989.

HaQoton, Chaim. "Becoming A Jew." Blog entry 6/1/06, URL = www.rchaimqoton.blogspot.com/2006/06/becoming-jew.html.

Harris, R. Laird, Gleason L. Archer and Bruce K. Walke. *Theological Wordbook of the Old Testament,* Volumes I-II. Chicago, IL: Moody Press, 1980.

Hastings, James. *Great Texts of the Bible,* Online version. www.Biblehub.com.

Hatch, Edwin and Henry A. Redpath. *A Concordance to the Septuagint and the Other Greek Versions of the Old Testament.* Grand Rapids, MI: Baker Academic, 1998.

Hay, Malcolm. *The Roots of Christian Anti-Semitism.* John Chrysostom, 344-407 A.D. San Francisco, CA: Anti Defamation League of B'nai, 1984.

HaYesod, Student Workbook. Littleton, CO: First Fruits Of Zion, 2010.

Hegg, Tim. *Acts 15 and the Jerusalem Council.* Tacoma, WA: TorahResource, 2008.

Hegg, Tim. *Commentary on the Gospel of Matthew,* Volumes I-V. Tacoma, WA: TorahResource, 2007.

Hegg, Tim. *Paul's Epistle to the Galatians: Notes and Commentary.* Tacoma, WA: TorahResource, 2005.

Hegg, Tim. *Paul's Epistle to the Romans Volumes 1-2: Notes and Commentary.* Tacoma, WA: TorahResource, 2007.

Hegg, Tim. *Ten Persistent Questions.* Tacoma, WA: TorahResource, 2009.

Hegg, Tim. *The Letter Writer: Paul's Background and Torah Perspective.* Littleton, CO: First Fruits of Zion, 2002.

Heine, Ronald E., Translator. *The Commentary of Origen on the Gospel of St. Matthew,* 2 Volumes. London: Oxford University Press, 2018.

LITERATURE CONSULTED

Henry, Matthew. *Commentary of the Whole Bible*. Grand Rapids, MI: Zondervan Publishing House, 1960.

Henry, Matthew. *Concise Commentary on the Whole Bible*. Nashville, TN: Thomas Nelson, 2003.

Hewitt, Thomas. *Hebrews: An Introduction And Commentary*. Grand Rapids, MI: Eerdmans, 1970.

Hillerbrand, Hans J. *The Protestant Reformation*. New York: Harper Torchbooks, 1968.

Horton, T.C. and Charles E. Hurlburt. *Names of Christ*. Chicago, IL: Moody Press, 1994.

Howard, Bernard N. "Luther's Jewish Problem." *The Gospel Coalition,* October 19, 2017, URL = https://www.thegospelcoalition.org/article/luthers-jewish-problem.

Howard, George. *Hebrew Gospel of Matthew*. Macon, GA: Mercer University Press, 1995.

Huch, Larry. *The Torah Blessing*. New Kensington: Whitaker House, 2009.

Humphreys, A. E. *Cambridge Bible for Schools and Colleges*. UK: Cambridge University Press, 1895.

Hutchings, W.A., Translator. *The Confessions of St. Augustine,* Ten Books. London: Longmans Green & Co., 1890.

Intrader, Asher. *Who Ate Lunch With Abraham*. Frederick, MD: Revive Israel Media, 2011.

Jamieson, Robert, A.R. Fausset and David Brown. *A Commentary, Critical, Practical and Explanatory on the Old and New Testaments*. Electronic version, Biblehub.com. Original copyright 1882.

Jewish Virtual Library. URL = https://www.jewishvirtuallibrary.org/shabbetai-zvi.

John of La Rochelle. *Tractatus de Divisione Potentiarum Animae,* 1233.

Johnson, B.W. *The People's New Testament.* www.biblestudytools.com.

Juster, Daniel. *Jewish Roots.* Shippensburg, PA: Destiny Image Publishers, 2013.

Kampen, John and Moshe J. Bernstein. *Reading 4QMMT: New Perspectives on Qumran Law and History.* Atlanta: Scholars Press, 1996.

Keil, C.F. and F. Delitzsch. *Commentary on the Old Testament in Ten Volumes.* Grand Rapids, MI: Williams B. Eerdmans Publishing Co, 1980.

Kelley, Ronda L. *The Aeneid by Virgil,* Translated by John Dryden. URL = http://faculty.sgc.edu/rkelley/The%20Aeneid.pdf.

Kemp, W. *The Biblical Illustrator.* Electronic Database by Biblesoft, 2002.

Kohler, Kaufmann and Broydé, Isaac. *Jewish Encyclopedia.* URL = http://www.jewishencyclopedia.com/articles/11382-nations-and-languages-the-seventy.

Kruse, Colin. *Tyndale New Testament Commentaries: 2 Corinthians.* Grand Rapids, MI: William B. Eerdmans Publishing Company, 1989.

Kuzmič, Peter. *The Gospel of John: A Study Guide.* Irving, TX: ICI University Press, 1974.

Lancaster, D. Thomas. *King Of The Jews: Resurrecting the Jewish Jesus.* Littleton, CO: First Fruits Of Zion, 2006.

Lancaster, D. Thomas. *Restoration*. Littleton, CO: First Fruits Of Zion, 2005.

Lancaster, D. Thomas. *The Holy Epistle to the Galatians*. Littleton, CO: First Fruits Of Zion, 2011.

Lancaster, D. Thomas. *The Torah Club: Messianic Commentary on the Weekly Portions.* Marshfield, MO: First Fruits of Zion, 2006.

Lancaster, D. Thomas. "The Weekly eDrash," First Fruits of Zion, August, 29, 2013.

Lancaster, D. Thomas. *What About The New Covenant?* Marshfield, MO: First Fruits of Zion, 2015.

Lebreton, Jules. "St. Justin Martyr," *The Catholic Encyclopedia*, Vol. 8. New York: Robert Appleton Company, 1910.

Lightfoot, J.B., translator. *The Epistle of Barnabas.* Online version. URL = http://www.earlychristianwritings.com/text/barnabas-lightfoot.html.

Lim, Timothy H. and John J. Collins. *The Oxford Handbook of the Dead Sea Scrolls*. England: Oxford University Press, 2010.

London Baptist Confession. Association of Reformed Baptist Churches of America, 1689. URL = https://www.arbca.com/1689-confession.

Louw, Johannes P. *Greek-English Lexicon of the New Testament: Based on Semantic Domains*. Minneapolis, MN: Fortress Press, 1988.

Luther, Martin. "Against the Sabbatarians: Letter to a Good Friend." 1538. In *Luther's Works.* Volume 47: *Christian in Society IV.* Edited by Franklin Sherman. Philadelphia: Fortress Press, 1971.

Luther, Martin. *Of The Unknowable Name and The Generations of Christ,* 1543. URL = https://www.scribd.com/document/374422693/RARE-Of-the-Unknowable-Name-and-the-Generations-of-Christ-1543-Martin-Luther-pdf.

Luther, Martin. "That Jesus Christ was born a Jew." 1523. *Primary Texts on History of Relations.* Council of Centers on Jewish-Christian Relations, 2008. URL = https://www.ccjr.us/dialogika-resources/primary-texts-from-the-history-of-the-relationship/luther-1523.

Luther, Martin. "Warning Against the Jews." 1546. In *Luther's Works.* Volume 47: *Christian in Society IV.* Edited by Franklin Sherman. Philadelphia: Fortress Press, 1971.

Mackintosh, C.H. *Genesis to Deuteronomy: Notes on the Pentateuch.* Neptune, NJ: Loizeaux Brothers, 1972.

Malina, Bruce J. *The New Testament World: Insights from cultural anthropology.* Atlanta, GA: John Knox Press, 1981.

Manson, T.W. *The Sayings of Jesus as Recorded in the Gospels according to St. Matthew and St. Luke,* Grand Rapids, MI: William B. Eerdmans Publishing Company 1979.

Marshall, Alfred. *The Interlinear Greek – English New Testament: The Nestle Greek Text with a Literal English Translation.* London: Samuel Bagster And Sons Limited, 1958.

Marshall, J. Howard. *Tyndale New Testament Commentaries: Acts.* Grand Rapids, MI: William B. Eerdmans Publishing Company, 1989.

Martin, Ralph P. *Tyndale New Testament Commentaries: Philippians.* Grand Rapids, MI: William B. Eerdmans Publishing Company, 1989.

Martinez, Florentino Garcia and Eibert J. C. Tigchelaar. *The Dead Sea Scrolls Study Edition.* Leiden: Brill, 1998.

Martyr, Justin. *Dialogue with Trypho*, 155-170 A.D. Public Domain. URL = https://d2y1pz2y630308.cloudfront.net/15471/documents/2016/10/St.%20Justin%20Martyr-Dialogue%20with%20Trypho.pdf.

Mason, Steve. *Flavius Josephus on the Pharisees: A Composition-Critical Study*. Boston: Brill Academic Publishers, Inc., 2001.

Mays, James L. *Harper's Bible Commentary*. San Francisco, CA: Harper Collins Publishers, 1988.

McGee, J. Vernon. *Thru The Bible,* Radio commentary.

McLaughlin, Thomas, S.T.D. *The Summa Theologica* by St. Thomas Aquinas. London: Burns, Oates & Washbourne, LTD, 1924.

Metcalfe, John. *Deliverance From The Law: The Westminster Confession Exploded*. Buckinghamshire, UK: John Metcalfe Publishing Trust, 1992.

Meyer, Heinrich August Wilhelm. *Meyer's Commentary on the New Testament*, Volumes 1-11. New York: Funk & Wagnalls, 1886.

Newman, Barclay M. *Greek-English Dictionary of the New Testament.* German Bible Society, 2010.

Mishnah Makkot. www.sefaria.org.

Montefiore, Claude Goldsmid. *Judaism and St. Paul*. New York: Arno Press, 1973.

Moo, Douglas J. *Tyndale New Testament Commentaries: James.* Grand Rapids, MI: William B. Eerdmans Publishing Co., 1989.

Moon, Jesse K. *New Testament Survey: A Study Guide.* Irving, TX: ICI University Press, 1975.

Moore, G.F. *Judaism in the First Century of the Christian Era: The Age of the Tannaim*, Vol. I-II. Cambridge, MA: Schocken Books, 1927.

Morris, Leon. *Tyndale New Testament Commentaries: 1 and 2 Thessalonians.* Grand Rapids, MI: William B. Eerdmans Publishing Company, 1989.

Morris, Leon. *Tyndale New Testament Commentaries: 1 Corinthians.* Grand Rapids, MI: William B. Eerdmans Publishing Company, 1989.

Morris, Leon. *Tyndale New Testament Commentaries: Luke.* Grand Rapids, MI: William B. Eerdmans Publishing Company, 1989.

Morris, Leon. *Tyndale New Testament Commentaries: Revelation.* Grand Rapids, MI: William B. Eerdmans Publishing Company, 1989.

Nanos, Mark. *The Irony of Galatians.* Minneapolis, MN: Fortress Press, 2009.

Nee, Watchman. *The Normal Christian Life.* Wheaton, IL: Tyndale House Publishers, 1977.

Norton, Thomas, Translator. *Institutes of the Christian Religion* by John Calvin: The Four Books - Complete and Unabridged. Createspace Independent Publishing Platform, 2017.

O'Brien, Peter T. *Word Biblical Commentary.* Vol. 44, Colossian-Philemon. Nashville, TN: Thomas Nelson, Inc., 1982.

O'Donovan, O.M.T. *Towards An Interpretation Of Biblical Ethics.* Tyndale Bulletin 27, 1976.

Online Etymology Dictionary. URL = https://www.etymonline.com/. Parkes, James. *Judaism And Christianity.* Londan: Gollancz, 1948.

Patrick, John. *Origen's Commentary on the Gospel of Matthew.* URL = http://www.documentacatholicaomnia.eu/03d/0185-0254,_Origenes,_Commentarium_in_evangelium_Matthaei_[Schaff],_EN.pdf.

Pelikan, Jaroslav. *The Vindication of Tradition: 1983 Jefferson Lecture in the Humanities*. New Haven, CT: Yale University Press, 1984.

Philo. *Concerning the Contemplative Life.* F.C. Conybeare. *The Jewish Quarterly Review*. Volume 7. No. 4. Pennsylvania, PA: University of Pennsylvania Press, 1895.

Philo. *Hypothetica.* URL = http://ccat.sas.upenn.edu/rak/courses/999/hypothet.htm.

Pierce, Larry. *The Outline of Biblical Usage.* www.blueletterbible.org.

Poliakov, Léon. "Anti-Semitism and Early Christianity." *The History of Anti-Semitism*. Pennsylvania, PA: University of Pennsylvania Press, 2003.

Qimon, Elisha and John Strugnell. "An Unpublished Halakhic Letter from Qumran." *Israel Museum Journal*, 1985.

Qimon, Elisha and John Strugnell. *Qumran Cave 4: V, Miqsat Ma'Ase Ha-Torah,* Vol. 10, *Discoveries in the Judean Desert.* Oxford: Clarendon Press, 1994.

Ratner, Ber. *Sefer Seder Olam Rabbah,* Hebrew Edition, Originally published in 1757.

Ringgren, H. *Theological Dictionary of the Old Testament*. Editors G. Johannes Botterweck, Helmer Ringgren and Heinz-Josef Fabry, translated by David E. Green. Grand Rapids: Eerdmans, 2001.

Ritchey, Charles J. "Luther and Paul: Their Experiences and Doctrines of Salvation." *The Journal of Religion*, vol. 50, No. 4. 1917, *JSTOR.* URL = www.jstor.org/stable/3135831.

Robertson, Archibald Thomas. *Word Pictures in the New Testament*, Vol. I-VI. Grand Rapids, MI: Baker Book House, 1930.

Ross, Philip S. *From the Finger of God: The Biblical and Theological Basis for the Threefold Division of the Law*. Geanies House, Scotland, Christian Focus Publications, 2010.

Sanders, E.P. *Paul and Palestinian Judaism: A Comparison of Patterns of Religion*. Minneapolis, MN: Fortress Press, 1977.

Sanders, E.P. *Paul, the Law, and the Jewish People*. Minneapolis, MN: Fortress Press, 1983.

Santala, Risto. *Paul – The Man and the Teacher in the Light of Jewish Sources*. Finland: Bible and Gospel Service, 1995.

Santala, Risto. *The Messiah in the New Testament In Light Of Rabbinical Writings*. Jerusalem: Karen Ahvah Meshihit, 1992.

Schiffman, Lawrence H. *Who Was A Jew? – Rabbinic and Halakhic Perspectives on the Jewish Christian Schism*. Hoboken, New Jersey: Ktav Publishing House, 1985.

Schoenberg, Shira. *Jewish Virtual Library*: Ancient Jewish History: The Sanhedrin. URL = https://www.jewishvirtuallibrary.org/the-sanhedrin.

Scott, Bradford. *A Concordance of Law in the New Covenant Scriptures: A Commentary on Every Occurrence of TORAH in the NCS*. Vernal, UT: The WildBranch Ministry, 2019.

Scott, Bradford. *Galatians 4:8-10*. URL = https://www.wildbranch.org/teachings/lessons.

Scott, Bradford. URL = https://www.wildbranch.org/teachings/lessons/lesson64.html.

Seekins, Frank T. *Hebrew Word Pictures*. Phoenix, AZ: Living Word Pictures, Inc., 1994.

Shanks, Hershel. *Understanding the Dead Sea Scrolls*. Reno, NV: Random House, 1992.

Shirer, William L. *The Rise And Fall of the Third Reich.* New York: Simon & Schuster, 1990.

Shotwell, W.A. *The Biblical Exegesis of Justin Martyr.* London: SPCK, 1965.

Smith, James. *Handfuls on Purpose.* Series 1-9, Fifth edition. London: Pickering & Inglis, early 1900s.

Spence, H.D.M. and Joseph Exell. *The Pulpit Commentary,* Books 1-52. New York: Funk & Wagnalls Company, 1945.

Stern, David. *Jewish New Testament.* Clarksville, MD: Jewish New Testament Publications, Inc., 1979.

Stern, David. *Jewish New Testament Commentary.* Clarksville, MD: Jewish New Testament Publications, Inc., 1992.

Stothert, Richard, Translator. *Reply to Faustus the Manichaean* by St. Augustine, Book VI. Bombay. URL = https://www.document acatholicaomnia.eu/03d/03540430,_Augustinus,_Contra_Faustum_ Manichaeum_%5bSchaff%5d,_EN.pdf.

Stott, John R.W. *Tyndale New Testament Commentaries: The Letters of John.* Grand Rapids, MI: William B. Eerdmans Publishing Company, 1989.

Strong, James. *Strong's Exhaustive Concordance of the Bible.* Peabody, MA: Hendrickson Publishers, 2009.

Tasker, R.V.G. *Tyndale New Testament Commentaries: John.* Grand Rapids, MI: William B. Eerdmans Publishing Company, 1989.

Tasker, R.V.G. *Tyndale New Testament Commentaries: The Epistle to the Hebrews.* Grand Rapids, MI: William B. Eerdmans Publishing Company, 1960.

Tenney, Merrill C. *John: The Gospel of Belief: An Analytic Study of the Text.* Grand Rapids, MI: William B. Eerdmans Publishing Company, 1976.

Tenney, Merrill C. *New Testament Survey.* Grand Rapids, MI: William B. Eerdmans Publishing Company, 1985.

Tenney, Merrill C. *The Zondervan Pictorial Encyclopedia of the Bible*, Vol. 1-5. Grand Rapids, MI: The Zondervan Corporation, 1975.

Thayer, Joseph. *Thayer's Greek-English Lexicon of the New Testament.* Peabody, MA: Hendrickson Publishers, 1996.

The Church Of England. *The Thirty-Nine Articles,* 1563 C.E. URL = https://www.churchofengland.org/prayer-and-worship/worship-texts-and-resources/book-common-prayer/articles-religion.

The Delitzsch Hebrew Gospels: A Hebrew-English Translation, USA: Vine of David, 2011.

The Jerusalem Bible. USA: Darton, Longman & Todd Ltd. And Doubleday & Co Inc., 1966.

The NIV Study Bible. Grand Rapids, MI: Zondervan Bible Publishers, 1985.

Tregelles, Samuel Prideaux. *Gesenius's Hebrew and Chaldee Lexicon.* London: Samuel Bagster & Sons, 1857.

Tucker, Dr. Spencer C. *The Encyclopedia of the Arab-Israeli Conflict*, Vol. I. Santa Barbara, CA: ABC-CLIO, 2010.

Turretin, Francis. *Institutes of Elenctic Theology.* Phillipsburg, NJ: P&R Publishing, 1997.

Unger, Merrill F. *The New Unger's Bible Dictionary,* Chicago, IL: Moody Press, 1961.

Vanderkam, James. "The People of the Dead Sea Scrolls: Essenes or Sadducees?" *Bible Review*, April 1991

Vaughan, Curtis. *James: A Study Guide*. Grand Rapids, MI: Zondervan Publishing House, 1969.

Vincent, Martin. *Vincent's Word Studies*, Volumes 1-4. Peabody, MA: Hendrickson Publishers, 1985.

Vine, W.E. *Vine's Expository Dictionary of the New Testament Words*. Nashville, TN: Thomas Nelson, 1996.

Von Gerlach, Otto, quoted by Johann Peter Lange. *Lange's Commentary on the Holy Scripture*. Vol. 6: Matthew to John. Grand Rapids: Zondervan, 1960.

Wesley, John. *Wesley's Notes on the Bible*. www.biblestudytools.com.

Westminster Confession of Faith, 1646 C.E. Administrative Committee PCA. URL = https://www.pcaac.org/bco/westminster-confession/.

Whiston, William, A.M., Translator. *The Life And Works Of Flavius Josephus*. Philadelphia, PA: The John C. Winston Company, 1957.

Wigram, George V. *The Englishman's Greek Concordance of the New Testament*. Peabody, MA: Hendrickson's Publishers, 1996.

Wood, George O. *Acts: A Study Guide*. Irving, TX: ICI University Press, 1980.

Woodhouse, S.C. *English-Greek Dictionary: A Vocabulary of the Attic Language*. London: Routledge & Kegan Paul, 1972.

Wright, Christopher J. H. *Walking in the Ways of the Lord: The Ethical Authority of the Old Testament*. Downers Grove, Ill.: InterVarsity Press, 1995.

Wright, N.T. *Justification: God's Plan and Paul's Vision*. Downers Grove, Ill.: IVP Academic, 2016.

Wright, N.T. *Paul: In Fresh Perspective*. Minneapolis, MN: Fortress Press, 2009.

Wright, N.T. *The Climax of the Covenant: Christ and the Law in Pauline Theology*. Minneapolis, MN: Fortress Press, 1993.

Wright, N.T. *Tyndale New Testament Commentaries: Colossians and Philemon*. Grand Rapids, MI: William B. Eerdmans Publishing Company, 1989.

Yoder, John Howard. *The Politics of Jesus*. Grand Rapids, MI: Eerdmans, 1994.

Young, Brad. *The Parables: Jewish Tradition and Christian Interpretation*. Peabody, MA: Hendrickson Publishers, LLC, 1998.

Wuest, Kenneth S. *Word Studies In The Greek New Testament*, Volume I. Grand Rapids, MI: Eerdmans Publishing, 1973.

Zodhiates, Spiros. *The Complete Word Study New Testament with Parallel Greek*. Chattanooga, TN: AMG Publishing, 1992.

ABOUT THE AUTHOR

Jeff Rostocil began as a campus missionary in 1994 at Chico State University. He and his wife started SoleQuest International in 2002. Together, they travel nationally and internationally communicating God's word and demonstrating the kingdom of God. The have ministered and led outreach teams in China, Hong Kong, Thailand, India, Switzerland, Germany, Austria, Morocco, Gambia, Mexico, Argentina, Nicaragua and the Middle East. They have three beautiful children and reside in Northern California.

Jeff has authored four books: *Unshakable, Bulletproof, Hand On The Line* with Steve Wisniewski and *Lies Of Our Fathers*.

Learn more about Jeff at: https://www.amazon.com/Jeff-Rostocil/e/B00AR1BFCE%3Fref=dbs_a_mng_rwt_scns_share

Learn more about SoleQuest International at: http://www.sqint.org

www.ingramcontent.com/pod-product-compliance
Lightning Source LLC
Chambersburg PA
CBHW071800080526
44589CB00012B/624